CANALOU

People
Culture
Bootheel Town

Dan Whittle

The views expressed in this document do not necessarily reflect the opinions of the Center for Regional History or Southeast Missouri State University and are solely those of the authors who took part in this publication's creation.

Copyright © 2013 by the Center for Regional History, Southeast Missouri State University. All rights reserved. No part of this book may be reproduced or transmitted in any form or by any means, electronic or mechanical, including photocopying, recording, or by any information storage and retrieval system, without permission in writing from the Publisher.

Southeast Missouri State University
Center for Regional History
One University Plaza
Cape Girardeau, MO 63701

Printed in the United States

ISBN: 978-1-890551-08-7

Table of Contents

Forewords

Mike Shain i

Garry Lewis iv

John Launius vii

Prologue

Dan Whittle x

Swamp Pioneer Era

The First Settlers Remembered 2

The Last Frontier Town 9

Mother and Teacher 14

Canalou poem 20

Little River Drainage District
Transformed Swamp 27

Floy Mae Remembers 34

Deaths of Engrams 39

Cooking and Hunting in the Swamp 45

Fugitive to Lawman 52

Blankenships Arrive 56

Legendary Uncle Harry 62

Above the Waters 67

Canalou's Funeral 74

Oran Timber 77

Westerfield Murder Trial 84

Canalou's Soft Side 87

Political Powers 91

Life of Michael Parkes 97

Farm Political Art Culture

Michael Parkes, the Artist 107

Few Missourians 113

Shy Pilot and Lawyer 116

A Blend Of Cultures 124

Hoppers On The Land 129

Whittle Visitors 134

Canalou Farmers 140

Sharecroppers Extraordinaire 144

Born in a Tent 151

Owning *Hitler* *156*

Daddy's Death 160

Daddy's Last Christmas 165

When Mamma Cries 169

Cadillac Shack Out Back 175

A. J. Neel 178

McCann 'Can Do' 182

Road Code 186

Ann Rice 192

Sister Was a Ho'er 198

Cow Milking 202

Time to Cut Hogs 204

Wandering Livestock 207

Hog-Killing Day 211

June Carter Cash's Bonnet 216

Frances Bishop 222

No Ordinary Cotton-Pickin' Day 227

Cotton Bloom Debate 232

Canalou Cash Registers 236

Crow cussin' 248

Uncle Harlan 251

Center of Commerce 256

Ginned Legend 259

Bill Newman 262

Granny Missed the Pot 267

Feelin' Froggy 272

Farm Talk 275

Daddy's Whippings 281

Mule Suicide 285

Loss of Floodway Bridge 288

Norman Harrison 293

The Buck Doesn't Stop Here 297

Whiskey Flowed 300

The Blue Woods 305

River Drama 308

Farm vs. Town 313

Watermelon Country 321

Tractor Accidents 325

Handshake Stockton 330

REA 334

Momma's Sharp Tongue 338

Musial Homers 343

Race, Soldiers, School, Church, and Careers

Canalou Heroes 348

Second Grade 'War Zone' 354

Bell Ringer 359

Morehouse Tigers 362

Grayridge School 369

Sinking Sand 374

Brother Rhodes 378

Brother, A Hero 382

Last Day of Sports Glory 387

Crawdad, Nicknames 392

'Egg caper' 396

School Bus Drivers 399

From Cotton Field 401

Race Relations 408

Major Hooper Penuel Pens Memories with Whittle 417

Forewords

The southern border of Missouri runs a straight line across the top of Arkansas until it bumps into the St. Francois River. It follows the flow forty-five miles and then takes another straight line to the Mississippi River.

The area protruding into Arkansas is shaped like the heel of a boot. It's called the Missouri "Bootheel."

This book is about the region's people. They live in six counties that were part of the Louisiana Purchase. Explorer Lewis noted in his annals that his now famous expedition made its first camp in what is now Scott County, where I was born.

Americans had not started settling the area during the period it was ruled by Spain. Note the town and county of New Madrid. More people came after the great Louisiana Purchase, but most fled when earthquakes devastated the region.

Witnesses say the ground rocked, rolled in waves, uprooting great trees, geysers of sand erupted and even the Mighty Mississippi flowed backward. The quakes ranged far and wide and are considered the largest series of quakes in U.S. history. They were of a magnitude so great that church bells in

Eastern cities rang, and the quakes continued for more than two months.

New Madrid, being the only settlement in 1811-12, gave its name to the disaster and to this day, the area is known as the New Madrid Fault and Seismic Zone.

The quakes left much of the Bootheel a "Great Swamp," and it remained so until around 1900 when demand for timber brought logging. The hardwood forests provided many of the crossties used by rapidly expanding American railroads. Once the timber was cut, companies had to continue paying taxes on the swamp land.

One of the greatest engineering projects in the nation's history began in 1904 to drain the swamps and convert the land to agriculture. One thousand miles of drainage canals were dug, and 300 miles of levees were constructed.

Sawmill towns were founded to process the timber. The names include Buffington, Morehouse, Gideon, Deering, and Canalou (pronounced kuh NAL ou), the focus of this book. The people who came to cut and mill the timber were hard working, and some were hard drinking. In its economic heyday, Canalou had up to seven saloons compared to three churches.

Once the Little River Drainage District did its work and big machines pulled stumps, the land was ready for the plow. Land was sold for pennies. The six counties of the Bootheel produce all of the rice and cotton grown in Missouri, and they lead the state in corn and soybean yields and volume. And the watermelons and peaches are the best anywhere.

The region is mostly Scots-Irish with a dash of Germans and a few old French names. Pride has long been the "first bale of cotton," the "biggest watermelon," the "top steer" and sometimes tempers flared. At times, it was almost like a good hotly-competitive basketball game when tempers would flare. These people are the salt of the earth, but they have pride and you're advised not to bruise it.

I came from this, and I am proud of it. I'll discuss what's wrong with others who have roots here. But outsider criticism isn't welcome, unless offered in a polite manner.

We have our problems. They go back to the old days when only an eighth grade education was needed to make it in farm labor. Educational levels in the region are as depressed as the economy is in some areas. Pemiscot County is one of the poorest places in the state and nation.

Southeast Missouri State University now has campuses in Sikeston, Malden, and Kennett, bringing higher education closer to many and perhaps lifting the learning bar.

The Bootheel has survived great earthquakes, murderous guerrillas during the Civil War, the mechanization of agriculture that eliminated farm labor, and the demise of shoe and clothing manufacturing that employed thousands.

Times are sometimes bad, but we have our pride and best of all, our sense of humor.

Canalou native Dan Whittle is a retired newspaperman, a reporter who always had the knack for listening for more than just the bare facts. His book of Bootheel stories is both funny and touching.

–Mike Shain

Dan Whittle's KFVS 12 interview with Mike Shain.

Grit and grime from Bootheel cotton fields do not wear off.

He describes a rugged way of life that no longer exists on modern America's landscape.

Having known "Danny" Whittle since venerable old Grayridge High School days in the 1960s, I can testify that he knows the back-breaking pain of picking cotton under the boiling hot sun of the Bootheel's tortuous dog days of summer.

Make no mistake, those who survived and benefitted by spending our youth in this unique area of the world, are proud of our heritage. . . and culture.

It taught us an honest work ethic and not to be instantly trustful of those outside our culture. Dan has captured the spirit of those brave forefathers who initially battled the swamp and wilderness to carve a sustainable life for those of us to follow.

As poor rent-crop-share folks, we knew how to survive, in what's termed poverty today. Then, we didn't know that word. Certainly, I remember my father, William M. "Dub" Lewis (born in Lilbourn) losing crops repeatedly due to floods, but we had each other.

My earliest Bootheel memories are the water. Water everywhere, up even to the high Floodway Bridge, covering all the fields and roads. Flood water from that swampy region covered most of Lilbourn, I recall from my earliest days.

Lilbourn is where my family's roots go deep, but from there, our family tentacles branch out to places such as Charter Oak, Hill's Store, Hunterville Road, and Grayridge.

In my earlier life as a Navy fighter pilot, we knew God. Actually came close to seeing Him a couple of times, when I lost an aircraft tail and had the engines blow apart more than once.

Same was true back in the days of our laboring in the seemingly endless rows of cotton. I can't recollect ever encountering a nonbeliever in a cotton patch. We might be Pentecostal, Baptist, Catholic, etc., but we believed. God is a huge part of Bootheel strength.

Faith and education were key to escaping what we later learned was actual poverty. When I moved to Grayridge School, Superintendent Robert L. Rasche was a bigger-than-life figure. Teachers such as Omar Brooks and Mr. Lawrence, Mrs. Norman, and math teacher Mr. Kellum, plus Mrs. Parks greatly impacted my life, and the life of author Danny Whittle.

I was a very shy student, while Danny had a more outgoing personality at our little rural school where we first became friends. In his book the author rightfully pays tribute to the great Bootheel educators who helped prepare us for adulthood, plus going out into the vast world beyond the fields of cotton, soybeans, and corn.

Math teacher Mr. Kellum, I recall, advised Dad: "Help your son toward more education. Garry can do algebra problems in three minutes that I have to write the algebra book publishers to get explanations for." I was blessed in mathematics, and eventually got a scholarship at the University of Missouri in Columbia. I also got a write up in the St. Louis newspaper about my high school art creations.

I recall my Aunt Margie attending the two-room school at

Charter Oak, where my mother, a Crawley, was born. A legend in our family is the day that Grandpaw Crawley, who never got any formal schooling, went to that two-room school in Charter Oak, threatening the teacher to quit scaring the girls. He drove his Model A car right up to the school house front door. The teacher promised Grandpaw he would do better. And he did.

The Lewis' hailed from Princeton County, Kentucky, before moving to the banks of the Mighty Mississippi River at New Madrid. Great-Grandparents Henry Lee and Melissa May Lewis had eleven boys rearing them for years on the river bank in and around New Madrid, on a houseboat skiff they used to float up and down the Mississippi and Ohio Rivers.

Great-Grandmother Melissa ultimately died of a heat stroke in the cotton fields between New Madrid and Lilbourn. It was anything but an easy life for those first brave souls who settled in the former swamp land of the Bootheel.

And, as I noted earlier, the Bootheel grit and dirt from the cotton patches does not wear off.

–Garry Lewis

On a recent excursion down one of the many gravel arteries that connect the patchwork of cotton, soybean, milo, rice and cornfields comprising this region, I noticed an all-too-familiar scene. An abandoned, weather worn, dilapidated, two-story farm house. Glass long gone from the windows, a shingle here and there. Even the trees standing guard had a tired, weary look.

And I could not help but ponder the history of this structure. It was someone's home-place, the focus of dear memories. Christmases come and gone. Laughter, births, games of tag, hide n' seek, mother-may-I, the pitching of washers, iced tea in the shade, talk of crops, hunting, and war. Without doubt there were also tears, sickness and the shadow of death. These are the things that, when looked at as a whole, constitute life. They reveal who and what we are.

This same analogy holds true for towns. Small towns. Towns in southeast Missouri like Canalou, Morehouse, Matthews. Towns that have "seen better days" and, while they no longer thrive, they continue to live. Denizens of these small clusters like to proudly reminisce about their glory days. Sometimes, they even fudge a little.

One thing that towns (like people), do not want is to be forgotten. With that in mind, it is necessary to have an enabler. Someone interested enough to help the town reminisce and do so with dignity, grace, and an occasional dash of accuracy. Meet Dan Whittle. . .

His childhood summers found him with blue jean cuffs rolled up and working on the family farm just north of Canalou, sometimes slipping off barefoot to explore the mysteries of Little River. He tells me that three of the happiest years of his life were spent in the 8th grade there at Canalou, but I get the idea he's "just joshin'."

And therein lies the nature of Dan Whittle. Easy-going, down-to-earth, doesn't take himself too seriously, the kinda guy you like to sit and talk with. That, my friends, is his calling.

This book is much more than a collection of stories, it is an opportunity to hop on H.G. Wells' time machine. It is the next best thing to being there. It is first person accounts from those who lived through the times. The struggles, the hardships, and, yes, the humor.

If you're looking for a historical edifice from which you can quote facts, amaze (and anesthetize) your friends, you may be in the wrong aisle. But, if you want to "know what it was like" to have survived the Bootheel Frontier, and to peer into the hearts and souls of those who chiseled this swamp into one of the worlds most productive farmlands, you're in for a treat. . .

–John Launius

Prologue

Dan Whittle in High School

Farm neighbor A. J. Neel proved to be a "prophet," and he never attended church that I know of.

He didn't need to go actually, for he was one of the kindest, smartest men I've ever known, who loved me dearly, so much that he offered to "adopt me" from my blood family when he and his beloved wife and elderly mother pulled up Canalou-area farming roots and moved down below Hornersville, in the deepest bowels of former swamp Bootheel country.

A. J. was miscast as a farmer, being a highly–read gent. Living a short one–half mile from our farm home, A. J. recognized early that I too had a love for words.

On one of our monthly treks to check out new books arriving from New Madrid to Grace Hewitt's tiny little Canalou Library, that doubled as the city calaboose, A. J. looked over from behind the steering wheel of his faded orange–colored truck, and observed: "Danny boy, words will take you around the world one day."

I've recalled the late A. J. Neel's prophetic words many times, especially when I was a foreign war correspondent, covering the Bosnian War in Europe, and on another assignment, covering the plight of orphans in Romania. . . and I was paid to go.

Hitler and A. J. Neel were my first two best friends of boyhood back on the farm.

Not the German tyrant name Hitler, he doesn't deserve to be compared to a good farm dog. Good farm guard dogs were "family" in our farming region. Like A. J., *Hitler* was very loyal to this former little farm boy.

Since farming was the biggest economic trigger of my youth in the rich fertile, ancestral Mississippi and Ohio Rivers' bottom lands today known as the "Bootheel" of Southeast Missouri, good farmers were my earliest role models. They included innovative farmers such as Bert Latham, Jay Hopper, Dick Bryant, Nelson Lumsden, Buck Croom, Judge X. Caverno, Ott Barnett, V. E. Hammock, Melton Bixler, Dale Geske, Lyman Whitten, and Harry Chaney. Their wives deserve to be listed here too.

Naturally, I'm partial to my own farming father, the late Hubert Alexander Whittle, who perished in a grinding car crash in 1950 when I was age six. Upon his death, Momma (Ruby Lee Stockton) Whittle shouldered the huge emotional load of rearing three children and became a prosperous farmer in her own right.

Although armed with little formal education, both parents practiced soil erosion control and crop rotation before they knew of such from college textbooks. Farmers Geske, Latham, Bixler, Lunsden, and Whitten were among first Canalou – area farmers to practice land leveling in order to slope and better drain their cotton, corn, wheat, and soybean–producing fields. . . a huge economic progressive step in the geographically low former swamp land.

Just how good were these early Bootheel farmers and how fertile was the soil formerly covered by a massive swamp? So good, that the six counties considered present-day Bootheel's farming region, produce a whopping thirty percent of Missouri's annual agricultural products. It's a Southeast Missouri State University documented fact.

To a young fatherless farm boy, farmers A. J. Neel and L. A. McCann and their families, helped instill the value of being good neighbors along with neighbors John and Versi Ling and John "Bunce" Scott who married the Lings' beautiful daughter, Marcella, plus neighbors "Big Red" and Nellie Bryant, along with their children, Bruce Gene, Harold David and Yvoin, plus the Knuckles, Bixler, Bishop, Bridwell, and Abernathy families.

Land owners can't do it alone.

Neighbors Vincent and Guy Nichols are legendary hired farm management hands who never owned a great deal of acreage. These men, both of whom still reside in the Canalou – Matthews communities as of early 2010, along with other area hired farm professionals, also helped instill a strong, prideful work ethic in the coming generation that benefitted from more formal educations.

Former Canalou farm boy, Donald Hammock, at age eighty-nine, shared that his parents, V. E. and Aimee Hammock made the dramatic move in 1937 from the Burdett (Arkansas) Plantation to farm 650 acres (Section ten near Third Ditch) between Canalou and Matthews, a huge farming challenge in that era of mostly mule powered farming.

They witnessed significant Bootheel farming history during the move.

"As we moved north into Missouri, although young, my twin brother, Douglas and I observed the farm workers' strike of the 1930s in the lower Missouri Bootheel," Mr. Hammock recalled. "They were lining the highway, walking, and picketing. . ."

Donald Hammock became a successful farmer in his own right prior to buying Bert McWaters' grocery store in downtown Canalou in the 1960s. He later achieved a successful banking career with banks in Morehouse and Matthews.

As fate would have it, the Hammocks and Whittles shared the same Burdette Plantation farming roots prior to moving up to the Bootheel. The Whittles followed in 1938 when Daddy and Momma Whittle literally had "one thin nickel" in their cash reserve.

"We were also school mates at Blytheville, Arkansas to the son of the engineer credited with devising the vision of draining the massive swamp that led to farming," Mr. Hammock shared in an interview March 1, 2010 at Sikeston's historic Kirby's Sandwich Shop that dates back to 1907.

The engineer is whom I credit most with formation of plans to develop the massive series of drainage canals that transformed the Bootheel into a world-class farming region following the removal of swamp-laden timber. It was a project opposed politically by powerful, rich lumber industrialists in Cape Girardeau, such as railroad man Louis Houck.

That vision led to the formation of the history transforming Little River Drainage District ultimately responsible for the twenty year largest dredging mission and land transformation project in world history, including being larger than the famous Panama Canal project. This has been documented at the university in Cape Girardeau, where present-day Little River Drainage District is located.

This led to the farming culture I was privileged to grow up in, although my family and others experienced some severely tough economic times with uncertain crop growing conditions, especially during flood years from the overflowing banks of the nearby Little and Castor Rivers.

Farming can be dangerous work, as evidenced in the loss of two cousins, Benny Prichard and Leroy Stockton, who perished on big, powerful farm equipment, along with farm neighbors John Mitchell and Joann Scott in separate accidents.

But perhaps the toughest souls with swamp era roots were those who braved the swamp elements in 1902 to form a village ultimately incorporated, platted, and named "Canalou."

Remarkable Florence Robinson Poe, granted interviews about surviving the Bootheel's former "rough and woolly swamp culture." Her soul stirring reflections helped set the platform chapter of this book. She's one of Missouri's rare individuals whose life has spanned parts of three centuries. I was honored to be invited to her 110 and 112 birthday celebrations before her death in 2010.

Her family floated into Morehouse, Big Ridge, and Canalou communities shortly after crossing the frozen Mississippi in a covered wagon. She confirmed that's when the Castor and Little River flooded thirteen times in 1903. She recalls her family and livestock literally "swimming for our lives" to escape rising and churning flood waters when a levee broke north of Morehouse.

She describes a big black panther coming perilously close to killing her younger brother, Harry Robinson, who later became a legendary hunter and trapper.

Farmer Harry Chaney, before his death at age ninety-five in 2009, also shared about a panther threatening the lives of him and his loyal farm dog of youth. Mr. Chaney had the distinction of being born in raw swamp elements of a logging tent in the Big Ridge community.

We're talking true brave hard working "frontier" families here, such as the Newmans, Landers, Engrams, Westerfields, Garners, Lumdens, Cavernos, Scotts, Greers, Greenlees, Arbuckles, and Tauls.

Being established in 1902, I pridefully consider Canalou one of the last true frontier towns in the great Show Me State.

My secondary wave of personal role models came in the form of great Bootheel educators, including Canalou sisters Earlyne Smith Barnes and Deloris Smith McWaters along with school superintendents Robert Rasche of Grayridge and Owen J. Taul of Lilbourn and Canalou.

Mr. Taul and his sister, Apalone, were among the first founding educators when Canalou High School was established in 1928. Canalou native James Coppage became a legendary teacher at nearby Morehouse High School, also now closed due to so-called progress labeled "consolidation."

Early Bootheel educator Agatha "Sissy" Weaks Parks memoirs on file at New Madrid County Library accurately chronicle the "brave challenge" those first regional teachers went through to help educate the coming generations.

Her personal history is "storybook" in quality, having to be read and documented to be believed, starting with a "frontier swamp style debutante childhood" as the daughter of prosperous timber baron H. E. Weaks to becoming homeless when her father left the Bootheel following the death of her mother. Her prosperous timber industrialist father entered the swamp in 1906. Agatha recalls having lunch on one of the large dredging boats on what is not known locally as the Floodway Channel.

Her subsequent marriage to an East Prairie farmer produced a son, Michael Parkes in 1944, whose artistic talent is known globally today from his home and studio located within view the Rock of Gibraltar near the coast of Spain. Michael and his wife, Marie, added the "E" to Parkes for artistic marketing purposes.

Michael matriculated with yours truly in grades one and two at rural Canalou School. . . the school we farm children pupils proclaimed as: "the Canalou School of advanced thinking and higher ciphering."

In this book, sixty-seven-year-old artist Parkes, full of pride, talks about his enjoyable small town formative years in

Canalou where a boy could play away from home all day without parents being worried about safety. He laughingly credits the unique heavy Bootheel gumbo mud with being part of his world class sculpturing techniques of today.

Not only did our culture produce a world famous artist, little Canalou School produced more than forty professional educators in its brief thirty year history from 1928 to 1958. That's a remarkable historical fact, and most of them matriculated at nearby Southeast Missouri State University.

Like some other swamp sawmill towns that attracted a tough and strong set of frontier men and women brought in to tame the swamp, Canalou had a dark side.

Back in the 1970s, a southeast Missouri newspaper publisher, Lloyd Erwin, described Canalou as "wild and wooly [sic]" in a headline. This description has merit.

For most of its brief history, Canalou's three churches were greatly outnumbered by wide open saloons and mostly hidden gaming rooms.

Two of the gaming rooms were in a side room of Moore's Mercantile and Grocery, Canalou's largest store enterprise in history, and in the back room of former Town Marshal Nathaniel G. Hewitt's barber shop.

A good friend to the Whittles, law man Hewitt had a multiple faceted, yes, colorful career of owning a liquor store and allowing a gaming room before he came in charge of enforcing town laws. I personally know about the gaming rooms because I'd sit on my Daddy's knee as he gambled.

During those early years, frequent life and death gun and knife fights were triggered out of the saloons and gaming venues.

Canalou High School graduate Bill Newman, now in his eighties, recalls growing up in Canalou's rough and woolly era when men chose to settle their personal character differences with knives and guns instead of mere fisticuffs.

The Engrams, a prominent early Canalou family, lost a beloved male family member when a fellow Sikeston Railroad Depot worker had a shootout in a dispute over which one got to transport luggage on and off trains. Both men died in the old wild-west-style shootout in the early 1900s.

At its economic zenith, Canalou's regional farming economy supported eight small groceries, a hardware, two cotton gins, a bank, a hotel, and several blacksmith shops. Later three service stations, a grade school, and a high school would be constructed.

With the early 1940s construction of the Canalou Theater by Boots Conn and the thriving groceries where families restocked their dietary staple needs, Canalou became a popular Saturday night recreational destination point. It became so popular that native folks knew to line up on Main Street early in the day in order to get a parking spot on Canalou's short mile long main street.

"So popular that you couldn't walk the town's one and only side walk. So many people flocked to Canalou on Saturday nights," confirmed Canalou native Norman Ernest Harrison, who operated the projector at the town's theater as a high school boy. "I would look out the theater's second story window and see mules and wagons, farm trucks, and tractors lined up all the way out of the city limits to Kasinger's Grocery at the north end of Main Street."

Canalou's unique, admittedly colorful history has spawned jokes that we natives have resented down through the decades.

Most early Canalou residents have heard the standing jokes voiced in the more metropolitan areas of Missouri: "If you gave Canalou and the Bootheel to Arkansas, it would raise the IQ of both states."

It's true; my native Canalou has a colorful past and a roguish heritage. But I'll put our small school educations up against modern day larger conglomerate schools. Car makers in St. Louis and Michigan evidenced this to some degree by being quick to hire Bootheel area folks known for their strong work ethic.

As Canalou native, Johnny Summers, who is retired from working for General Motors in St. Louis, put it succinctly one day on a visit back to his hometown roots: "Dummies can't build cars."

So why would this world travelled journalist have such fond memories of present day economic ghost town Canalou? And, commit to the effort over the years to create this journal?

I'll cite two classic examples. On the day of my father's funeral in 1950, all town stores closed their doors and a line was formed by Allen Davis Cotton Gin workers who covered their hearts with their caps as this man of the soil passed by in the Albritton Funeral Home hearse.

After Daddy's death, merchants of Canalou made allowances for me to bring my constant companion dog named *Hitler* into their premises. Only in a warm, small farm town culture would that happen.

I penned this book over several years with the motivational encouragement of my wife, Patricia, and notable Southeast Missouri State University historian, Frank Nickell.

As a former native Bootheel farm boy educated at Canalou and Grayridge schools, it will be interesting to me how book reading scholars will judge the finished product. To the author, it's more of a cultural-everyday-living-narrative than an officially captioned and more sophisticated historic journal.

I want the record clear of how much I admire the brave settlers, some of whom were on the run from Old John Law in surrounding states into the mostly uninhabitable swamp and the hard working cast of innovative farmers and merchants who instilled strong work ethics in my own generation.

However, it greatly saddens me to witness today's Canalou, an economic ghost town with little business, not even a pay telephone along Main Street.

Making the scene even more comatose in appearance are the fallen bricks along Main Street. The town's only theater building burned and fell last year into a smoldering mess. The theater building was a reminder of better times.

One last point, good manners were required learning from parents and educators. The fact that I answered Sikeston newspaper publishers, Charles Blanton Jr. and Charles Blanton III with "yes, sirs" and "no, sirs" didn't hinder the fact that they hired me as a sports writer instead of the janitor's job, a position I had gone to the newspaper office to originally apply for back in the 1960s. I was fresh out of Grayridge, now Richland, High School.

I also dedicate this book to our determined cast of great educators who not only taught us book learning but common sense that equipped Bootheel natives as we scattered out across the globe to find jobs when mechanization replaced manual labor jobs.

I hope you enjoy my journey back across time! It's been a labor of love, and I hope A. J. Neel would be proud.

–Dan Whittle

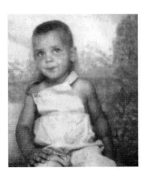

Swamp Pioneer Era

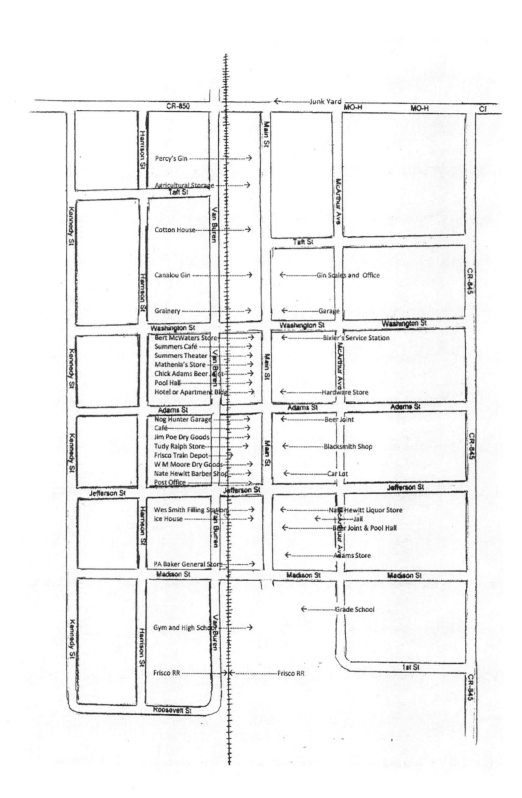

Leslie Allen: Whip Maker, standing in front of wood and lumber staves.

Early Canalou town standing on poles up out of swamp.

Chapter One
The First Settlers Remembered

CANALOU, MISSOURI:

Before there was an incorporated town, there was a mere settlement constructed on stilts.

Before that, there was swamp and wilderness, with sparse human habitation.

Now, the swamp has faded into the mist of time, and the unique village named Canalou is only a ghost of what it once was.

What the first white settlers found in one of mainland America's last frontiers from 1902 to 1905, were vast acres of uncharted swamp, cane breaks, and timber. This included the Mississippi River and its bottom land and cane breaks that stretched miles and miles further than eyes could see. Along with the Mississippi, two small streams, the Little River and Castor River, caused some big problems for folks of that era.

Because of the unique shape of this region of Southeast Missouri that sticks down like it could be a part of Arkansas, the region has been unofficially designated "The Bootheel."

Spawned out of those murky swamp waters was a harvesting village named "Canalou." The town later evolved into a thriving and bustling agrarian community through the 1950s.

The year 2009 marked the noncelebrated 100th birthday for the village that was not officially platted, incorporated, or chartered until 1909.

Today, Canalou is an economic ghost town with no commercial businesses operating on the now desolate Main Street.

In this undeveloped habitat, bears, panthers, wildcats, and wolves roamed. The waters were infested with huge swamp rats, venomous snakes, and disease-carrying mosquitoes.

This swamp setting was the scene of an early childhood experience for Florence "Aunt Flora" Robinson Poe, who granted her initial exclusive interview for this forum at the mere age of 105 in 2002.

She graced me with a second personal interview on her 110th birthday when present day hometown (Cape Girardeau) officials gathered to honor this remarkable "Bootheel frontier lady." She celebrated her 112th birthday on August 27, 2009.

She has the rare distinction of a life spanning across three centuries, from the horse and buggy era of the late 1800s, to man landing on the moon in the 1900s, to the present twenty-first century which is marked by depression-like economic times.

"There's not many folks who live in three different centuries," she claimed calmly and clearly as her mind slipped easily back across her century of life. "I suppose I'm one of the oldest Americans alive today."

It took a strong stock of people to tame the swamp and carve out a living in the wilderness.

"It was virgin timber that attracted my people, and most of the other hearty folks, with cane breaks so thick that those early settlers could only see a few feet in front of their faces," Mrs. Poe confirmed. "We floated into the foggy bottom swamp with all our possessions in a Jon boat with our farm animals wading slowly behind us. Although first settlers came in 1902, our family didn't arrive into the deepest swamp at Canalou until 1905."

Her father was motivated to enter the swamp by potential commerce, thinking his oxen would be very much in demand since mules, cattle, and horses could not snake the big logs through the murky water and deep winter mud that locals eventually labeled gumbo.

"My father Wid Robinson and mother Caroline Jones "Granny" Robinson, who was destined to serve as Canalou's first midwife, were true pioneers, very brave and adaptive people," she added.

However, flood waters nearly took their lives and all their resources before they arrived in the bowels of the deepest swamp.

"My family and I, before getting to the deep swamp, had to swim for our lives in 1902 during a particularly dangerous flooding period when a levee (near the Castor and Little Rivers) broke north of Morehouse," Mrs. Poe accounts.

"We knew there was serious trouble, however, before we knew the levee broke," she added. "There was rising water up to the bellies already on our two huge horses, as we tried to evacuate our temporary home located a couple miles south of Morehouse.

"With water rising so fast, Poppa put my sister, Carrie, on the back of the one of the horses and tried to tote me to safety at the same time. But Dad fell twice with me down into the water as he tried to walk us up to higher ground and safety. So he put me on back of Daisy, the plow horse, not knowing if she would let us ride double in that terrifying flood."

That left the family's milk cow, a vital nutrition source, exposed to the elements and the dangerous churning and rising water.

"We were worried about our cow named Annie, but we eventually believed her to be safely on higher ground when we finally heard her cow bell ringing in the distance. She, too, was swimming for her life as the water continued to rise," Mrs. Poe recalled.

Higher ground of the nearby Louis Houck Peavine Railroad spur leading from Morehouse to Canalou helped them escape the flood waters.

"We got to the safety of higher ground on the railroad tram line that was still being constructed to link Canalou and Morehouse. We spent the next several days in Morehouse. Little River flooded thirteen times in 1903, causing severe hardships for the people," she confirmed.

After surviving this life-threatening flood, the family moved down deeper in the swamp where Wid Robinson planned on marketing his oxen to haul out the timber.

"After Morehouse, we moved down to what was called Big Ridge, which is where my father should have stayed," Mrs. Poe recalled. "We prospered at Big Ridge with Poppa's oxen business, and lived easier while living up on dry land out of the swamp waters, but Poppa said we needed to move closer to the timber cutting. In 1905, we arrived at a swamp settlement that would ultimately be named Canalou.

"When we finally arrived, I remember catching fish out of my bedroom window, which was before they cut the drainage canals that eventually opened up the rich fertile land for farming," Mrs. Poe traced back in time. "I remember the day a big panther chased my brother Harry and a boyhood friend of his into our barn," she described. "They had to stay in the barn until Poppa came home and killed the big black cat."

Her nephew, sixty-seven year-old Willard Robinson, was the son of her brother Harry Robinson and resided in Canalou until his death in 2009.

Willard shared his father's description of the big cat during our last visit together in the spring of 2009.

"Harry told me that panther measured eleven feet in length, from head to the end of its long tail," Willard noted. "Panthers were not unusual, but my dad said bears were already becoming scarce in number in last century's first decade when the timber was being cut down. Dad knew the man down in Portageville who killed the last bear known to have roamed in New Madrid County.

"I recall Harry [his father] and Aunt Flora Poe sharing that folks were sometimes afraid to get off the train at Morehouse because of roaming bears and panthers," Willard shared.

Mrs. Poe recalls childhood chores and everyday life in the

swamp.

"Brother Harry would get out the family's Jon boat, the same one we floated into the settlement aboard, and paddle it around under the clothes line so me and my sister could hang clothes out to dry," Mrs. Poe accounted. "We must have lived a lot like the Cajuns down in the deepest bayou country of Louisiana.

"I also remember running and screaming to get back to the house when this other big panther came into the actual settlement and stepped up, big as you please, with no fear on our front porch," Mrs. Poe described. "I remember his blood-curdling yell and scream there on our front porch as clearly as if it happened yesterday. A panther's scream is terrifying.

"We ran on up to the safety of our family's second floor bedroom," she added. "I don't know why one of us simply didn't take the gun and shoot that screaming panther. It was terrifying to a little girl."

Mrs. Poe also described other survival techniques: "We fished and trapped as a means of survival in addition to the money Poppa made with his oxen," Mrs. Poe remembered. "Poppa's oxen were in demand, particularly during cold rainy winter months, when the heavy gumbo soil would turn into clinging mud that mules, horses and cattle could not pull wagons through, particularly wagons loaded with logs."

Illnesses common to swamp living of that era hit the Robinson family hard.

"One of the saddest times came when my brother Charley died of typhoid at age six," Mrs. Poe noted. "Typhoid was deadly. To battle for survival, town folks regularly waged organized snake and swamp rat hunts. But, there was no relief from the mosquitoes in the hot summer months."

But progress came as a few more settlers moved families and meager belongings into the swamp.

She was asked for the origin of the swamp's unlikely name: "Nigger Wool Swamp."

"I was told the swamp was named after a unique mushroom native to the swamp," Mrs. Poe accounted.

"After Canalou finally became a settlement with a post office, we thought we were uptown as we walked on board walks on stilt poles, to stay dry up out of the water," she traced back through time.

"A small ditch was dredged by hand to help channel some of the slow-flowing water around the settlement," she recalled. "But when we first floated into the area, two brothers named Utley had a cook shack and two tents set up," Mrs. Poe said. "Poppa and my brothers helped cut the right of way that led to the cutting of the first drainage ditch by hand that helped channel the water around the settlement, to give us more dry land on which to live. I recall the first road was made of rough-cut logs.

"Men folks of my family helped cut and lay the logs that resulted in the first road called the Corduroy Road to allow transportation from our settlement to a town five miles directly east called Matthews," she traced back in time. "Dad's oxen were used to drag logs for the Corduroy Road."

She described how Canalou received its name.

"The railroad man, Louis Houck, in Cape Girardeau, came up with the name in or around 1908," Mrs. Poe confirmed. "It's reportedly a foreign word, asking 'Where goes the channel?' which was appropriate at the time the region was still covered with snake-infested waters. During high rain periods, you certainly could not tell where Little River began or ended. The same was true to the big Mississippi River to the east of us when it flooded, too. Castor River, to the north of Morehouse, could be another big problem, sending its flood waters down south on us."

Upon maturity and eventually marriage, Mrs. Poe decided that it was time to leave the sawmill village that produced lumber shipped out on Louis Houck's railroad. Her remarkable sense of humor has survived the elements and multiple centuries of life.

"Leaving Canalou was as exciting and challenging as it was to have survived the elements of the swamp during my earliest childhood," Mrs. Poe noted. "I had married Butch Poe, and was pregnant with our third child when we finally packed up our wagon and mules to move to Virginia, where my husband was to continue a career in timber.

"Butch [now deceased] and I often recollected our days in Canalou, and we recalled witnessing the thousands of logs that were sawed, and moved out of the area on the trains we called 'dinkys' from the first Canalou Railroad Depot. We shared remembrances of the first little red building that became the first community store and then later, the post office.

"It was a big day when we got official post office designation," Mrs. Poe noted. "I recall floating up to the post office to get our mail, but it was time to move on, since we'd started our own family."

A lot of drama accompanied the family into the swamp, and drama accompanied Mrs. Poe out of the swamp.

"We prepared to leave as I was pregnant, but upon hitching the horses, the bridles were not done correctly," she described. "So when we started down the 'Corduroy Road' to leave town, those mules bolted, and ran five or six miles before my husband could get them choked down and under control. It must have been a comical sight, us leaving town in such a rush. My hair must have been flying straight backward as those mules bolted us out of Canalou."

Upon completion of timbering in Virginia, the Poe family first moved back to Charleston before moving to spend their "sunset years" in Cape Girardeau where the railroad was started that led to the formation of a swamp village uniquely named "Canalou."

Florence Robinson Poe died March 21, 2010, at the age of 112, and is recognized as the oldest citizen of Missouri at the time.

Mule and Loggers

Chapter Two

The Last Frontier Town

Most historians know of Missouri's more famous frontier towns such as Cape Girardeau, St. Louis, Sedalia, and Kansas City.

They are well-documented frontier towns as early European immigrants moved west, crossing the Mississippi River in significant numbers during the 1700s and 1800s.

But very few historians know that nestled down in the Bootheel region of southeast Missouri, in the huge former unseemly-named "Nigger Wool Swamp," is the remains of one of the very last true frontier towns in Missouri and on America's mainland for that matter.

Canalou, Missouri, is a historically unique Americana village that surfaced out of the swamp as recent as 1902 for the timber. There were various tribes of Native Americans located in the swamp down through the previous centuries. This swamp covered parts of six Bootheel counties.

Labeled a "rough and woolly no man's land," by early U. S. government surveyors in the 1800s, it took a tough visionary man named Dan Kreps to start the town.

"Uncle" Dan Kreps and Canadian Pete McLaurin are credited with being the timbering entrepreneurs brave enough to battle the snake-infested swamp waters, not to mention the dangers of influenza, diphtheria, and various wild animals, such as bears and panthers that threatened those early settlers.

The timber industrialists were after the thick timber, the cypress and oak hardwoods, growth the swamp had nurtured with centuries of water and silt loam buildup from the frequent flooding of the ancestral Mississippi and Ohio Rivers that formerly flowed through the heart of what is now called the Bootheel.

"Canalou has the distinction of being one of America's true last frontier towns," confirmed Canalou mayor, James Donald Taul. The highly decorated Vietnam War hero and well-read Bootheel historian explained, "Not many communities in America can rightfully claim to having its original settlers come in here as recently as 1902.

"It took tough resourceful frontier people to carve out a living in the earliest days before the swamp was drained," Taul described. "Canalou was not incorporated until 1909. Regretfully few Missourians know about Canalou's unique history."

Mayor Taul's ancestors were among the first settlers to move into the swamp.

"We came from Kentucky, along with the Westerfields, Arbuckles, Engrams, Greers, Scotts, and Landers," Taul confirmed.

The "Nigger Wool Swamp" name was used regionally for the area stretching down from Commerce, Missouri, on the Mississippi River, down to Arkansas. The Great Mingo Swamp to the northwest of Nigger Wool was also listed by U. S. government engineers in post Civil War surveys.

"The name, Nigger Wool, actually came from a large mushroom unique to the swamp," verified Mayor Taul. "When the mushroom matured, the plant was capped by grey-looking hairy-like filaments, similar to what hair looks like on a mature black man's head."

According to history annals, the Swamp was partially enhanced when the mighty Mississippi River, to the east, had ran backward during the massive New Madrid Earthquakes of 1811-12, forming Reelfoot Lake over on the Tennessee side of the big river. It expanded the existing swamp over in the Bootheel region of southeast Missouri.

"And when Little River to the west frequently flooded, we could not tell where the rivers began or ended," added the late Harry Robinson, who trapped and hunted in the swamp region all of his life.

Now deceased, Canalou area farmer Harry Chaney was born in 1913.

"Logging was the first industry, but as we cleared the timber, and then drained the swamp with a series of drainage canals by the Little River Drainage District, the farming industry blossomed," Mr. Chaney described. "But, yes, I was born in a logging tent. My dad recalled having to put up sheets and bed clothes, so my mother, Emma, a Cherokee lady, could give birth to me with some privacy. My daughter, Renda, is named after my Grandmother Renda.

"We had what we called stave mills, cutting the timber into small staves, that later could be used in the construction of whiskey barrels," Mr. Chaney accounted. "And it was Mr. Louis Houck's railroad spur lines that initially opened up the swamp region for the timbering industry."

The drainage ditches not only changed the landscape of Canalou, it changed the region's economy.

"In about 1900, a plan was made to dig a series of ditches that would channel the water away to the south and eventually into the Mississippi River," Les Landers accounted.

However, it would be 1910 before actual dredging started on the series of canals that eventually drained the often-flooded region.

"Draining the area also helped in harvesting the timber. And then, the land converted to farmland," added retired farmer Chaney. "The series of canals is to this day considered to be one of the greatest civil engineering feats in U. S. history."

Engineer Otto Kochtitsky is deservedly credited with being the catalyst to getting the swamp drained with the series of drainage canals, starting with the huge Diversion Channel up near Cape Girardeau.

Blacksmithing was one of the earliest crucially-needed industries.

"Grandfather Leslie Allen, who worked in the earliest sawmills, also had one of the last operating blacksmith shops in Canalou," Les Landers confirmed. "His shop was the last old-fashioned blacksmith operation and sat near the building that formerly housed the Bank of Canalou and then, the V. E. Hammock Hardware. He would take a bar of steel, and make a set of horse shoes and then, put them on the horses or mules needed to initially work in the sawmills, and later, the rich fertile farm land. Blacksmithing was crucial in both the sawmill and early farming eras.

"Both grandfathers, Leslie Allen and Abe Landers, were both born north of Canalou near Morehouse on what was then known as Landers' Ridge, which was up out of the swamp water, worked in the earliest sawmills as young boys," Landers confirmed.

Canalou was not an easy place to make a living with severe floods up into the 1940s.

"I was about six-years-old, in 1944, and there was this big flood when we lived out by Hale School, three miles west of Canalou, right next to the big Floodway Channel," describes Canalou native Arcile Haywood Boyes, daughter of Canalou farmer and inventor Herman "Fat" Haywood. "Dad took us to Canalou on the back of a tractor, the only vehicle high enough to keep us out of the floodwaters, because the nearby Little River was out of its banks. You couldn't tell where the river channel was, in fact.

"The water was also high in Canalou, came on up to Grandmother Aunt Sally Colston's house in Canalou, to the very edge of the porch," Arcile added. "That's the year that the last bridge over Floodway washed away, thus the east-west corridor was closed, making Canalou kind of at the end of civilization in that era, so to speak. My father always felt some local farmers on the Stoddard County side, for some reason, opposed rebuilding that bridge, and it's never been rebuilt, which could have helped Canalou's economy on down through the next decade or two."

It took innovation for those earliest farmers to have success.

"Dad, after World War II, bought a retired military warplane with no engine," Arcile accounted. "He wanted the plane's big wide ballooned tires, so he could work his combine in the wet marshy fields in times of rain and inclement weather. This was before the larger combines and big tires that are in use today to harvest the rice fields. Dad was a creative inventor, which came in handy for dealing with wet crop-growing conditions."

Chapter Three

Mother and Teacher

Agatha "Sissy" Weaks Parks fulfilled her life's ambition of being an educator at schools throughout the Bootheel and Lead Belt regions of southeast Missouri.

But today, that's not what she's most known for in world history annals.

The late Mrs. Parks is best remembered as mother of world-famous artist Michael Parkes.

In Mrs. Parks' memoirs, *The Bootheel and Me*, she details Bootheel swamp village life that ultimately produced one of the world's most famous artists. Her memoirs are available at the New Madrid Memorial Library.

Agatha knew wealth in her earliest years residing in the swamp that surrounded what became logging town Canalou after her parents moved to the Bootheel in 1905 from middle Tennessee.

Born in 1912, she was the daughter of timber baron L. E. Weaks, who moved into the swamp in 1906, four short years after the initial village surfaced out of the swamp waters. It would be another three years before Canalou was incorporated into an official town with platted building lots and laws.

In her memoirs written in 1994, she describes how quickly life's circumstances can change. For example, after her mother's death, young Agatha often became dependent on others for shelter and food.

"The house I was born in stood adjacent to the lumber mill houses, which were all built alike," the late Mrs. Parks accounts. "And the pioneer town grew fast as more families moved into the swamp to work in the timber harvest.

"Growth came fast as the Houck Peavine Railroad handled the transporting of wood staves out of the swamp and village," she detailed. "Mother wasn't healthy when I was born, having moved to Canalou in 1907 after marrying Father in 1906. She died of tuberculosis in 1919. I was seven."

She described how her life changed dramatically after her father remarried.

"There was an upset in my life at this time," Agatha said. "When my father's [second] marriage ended completely, he had been away for several months working, and my sister and I were at home with my step-mother and her children.

"She was very unhappy, and some of the problems took its toll on the home life of us all," Agatha traced her deteriorating life in the swamp. "She had two children when my father married her, and they had a little girl. Finally, the complete break came, and my step-mother moved out, taking all the things in the house that she could use."

Agatha and her sister moved in with some relatives prior to the break-up.

"This was around 1925," Agatha penned. "Our everyday lives became unbearable, so it was decided that my sister would go to live at my grandmothers' house, and I went to live with Uncle W. P. Press Weaks in Canalou."

Agatha returned to Canalou, after completing high school in 1929 in Alabama. "I returned home to Canalou and back to Uncle Press's house," she continued her early life's journey. "At that time, my father was established in business in Chicago. He sent for my sister and me for a visit. We had been there about a week when a telegram came that Uncle Press had died with appendicitis.

"That was one of the most traumatic things that had happened to me, for it was a complete upset of my life," Agatha added. "I not only lost the only home I had, I lost the people I loved more than anything."

As a small girl, she had seen the swamp and sawmill village transformed after the timber was harvested, and the Little River Drainage District began one of the nation's largest dredging and draining challenges in U. S. history.

Agatha Weaks Parks

"When the dredge boats came and started on the large Floodway Channel two miles west of Canalou, Father took me out there, and we had lunch on the dredge boat," Agatha added. "I didn't realize as a child, the significance of getting to have lunch on one of those big dredge boats that changed the face and culture of the Bootheel."

She recalled impassable roads during her earliest life.

"Plank roads were very necessary in order to be able to travel since the land was so low and wet in the Bootheel," Agatha recorded. "This road was first called the Plank Road and it went through New Madrid, Pemiscot, and Dunklin counties—all the way to the Arkansas line. This road was also used during the Civil War for troop movements.

"My father and grandfather were hunters and very familiar with Nigger Wool Swamp," Agatha reported. "Once, I can remember when my grandfather came home from several days' hunting. He had found a log cabin that had Jesse James, Frank James, and Bob Ford, the man who later shot Jesse James in the back, names carved in the logs of a cabin."

But the locally famous cabin was lost to time.

"I went to that cabin several times, and it was not destroyed until the late 1930s" recorded Agatha. "I felt a little sadness because to me it was a rather special landmark."

She recalled the swamp village's first on-site locomotive.

"Early in the 1900s, the stave mill added a steam engine and built a railway to our west across Little River," Agatha added. "Father would need to go out to look over the timber that was cut in the swamp water that sometimes measured up to ten feet in depth. The word he used for that was scale, for the timber had to be classified and brought to the mill.

"Sometimes, on weekends, he would take the engine and go to see what needed transported," Agatha recalls. "He would take my sister and me with him on these trips occasionally. I could never walk a log over the water. I was so clumsy. So usually Father would bring me back home soaking wet from falling in the water."

In that era, the swamp water level varied from a few feet to up to ten feet in depth. Some of the earliest businesses and homes in Canalou were built on stilts. Organized religion also snaked its way into the swamp.

"After my mother died, my sister and I were at home by ourselves a lot of the time while our father was at work. But we enjoyed and were comforted by church services," Agatha accounted. "The town's first Sunday School was organized in the spring of 1908. This was called the Union Sunday School. Meetings were in a vacant dwelling house. Later, in 1910, it was moved to meet in our town's first school building.

"F. D. Baughn was influential in the organization of the Canalou Baptist Church," she chronicled. "It was organized in the school building on November twenty-second 1912."

Agatha married Mississippi County farmer Albert Parks after starting her teaching career at Yellow Dog School. Although near river town East Prairie, Yellow Dog School sat in the remote northeast corner of New Madrid County.

The first time she references son, Michael David, was when her husband died in 1950. In her writings, Agatha addresses accusations of her time, both true and untrue. She appears to try to do it honestly. "In June 1931, after my first year teaching at Yellow Dog School, Albert and I were married," Agatha explained. "He was more than thirteen years older than me, and I know it was suggested that the reason I married was because I did not have a home.

"I don't think I'll ever really know whether the above was true," she added. "I do know I married the most wonderful and loving man in the world. For the twenty years we had, I was very happy. This was a happiness that was made without material things, as everybody was having a financial struggle during and after the Great Depression.

"When not teaching, I worked in the fields alongside my husband," Agatha added.

"While teaching at Yellow Dog School, I boarded with the Upton family and met my husband there. He was orphaned at an early age. His mother died when he was a baby, and he and his father lived with a family named England.

"He lived with this England family and worked on the farm with them until he enlisted at age eighteen in the Army in the First World War of 1917."

Although now married, times were tough and circumstances were not dependable.

"We moved thirteen times the first nine years we were married," Agatha confirmed. "The reason for this was we moved close to the school where I was teaching in the fall. And when the crocuses bloomed in early spring, it was time to load our box and barrel in a wagon and move back to the farm.

"All these moves and our work gave us the challenge we needed to keep us active and happy in our meager existence," she accounted. "I did not know we were poor. There was no class distinction; all of us were poor in that Depression era."

"I found another change was necessary during my years of teaching since the greatest tragedy of my life happened," she noted. "My husband died in 1950 and I was left without his support, and we had a little boy, Michael David, who was six-years-old at the time."

Chapter Four

Canalou poem
Penned in the 1950s By Agatha Sissy Weaks Parks

In new, New Madrid County to the west and north
You'll find Canalou's location
With all the changes from timber to farms
There's been little change in population.

Around 1900 as the century turned
Two young men met they say
At the last land run in Oklahoma we learned
From the east and up Canada way.

These two young fellows pooled their fate
And in the year 1902
They ended their trek at Canalou's gate
And started building this village for you.
Few are here now that knew these men
And the history they made in the town
For this country was only a wilderness then
The challenge they took without frown.

It was D. S. Kreps who came from the East
Whom later we called Uncle Dan
And P. L. McLaurin from Canada deep
Pete with a firm helping hand.

This wild, woolly country as I remember
Had resources in vast amounts
So a Boom Town grew from the Virgin timber
To bring abundance to many accounts.

The start was made as a sawmill town
In the year 1904
Then a stave mill and a lathe mill were found
And sawmills became many more.

The railroad and switch built by Louis Houck
Who gave our town its name?
To the Spanish he turned without any doubt
Canalou and "Where Goes The Channel?" mean the same.

The name was given in 1902
It was very appropriate then
For where the channel was one seldom knew
As drainage had never been.

D. S. Kreps and P. L. Pete McLaurin
Post Masters and in general merchandise
Later Kreps tried his hand on the farm
But Pete kept store til '45

Many other names can make up a list
Of merchants and good business men
Such as Bonner, Baughn, Hewitt, Poe, Weaks, Wilson, and Smith
W. M. Moore stands out now as well as back then.

In October 1909, a village was born
With J. R. Asa first Board President
Other members–B. D. Muffett, Pink Smith, and J. W. Baughn
And Wm. Pap Hartman time as first marshal spent.

Votes were cast in March 1920
By the voters qualified and legal
To make our village a fourth class city
Affirmative won by the seal of the Eagle.

On April 1st came the first city election
Grant Adams, Joe Mays, Wayne Wright, and Bill Dwight
For first offices the voters' selection
For Mayor, Aldermen, and Marshal to carry on the fight.

L. E. Weaks (my father) came here in 1906
With the Brown Stave Company mill
When the virgin timber was abundant and thick
And lasted more than twenty odd years.

With the better timber exhausted and gone
Sights were cast in other directions
So clearing and draining the land was begun
And the rich farms grew by the sections.

In 1909 the first school was erected
The first teacher was Artie Baughn Scott
The present school site then was selected
Each new school being placed on this lot.

From 1909 until the present time
Canalou's family of teachers were many
To be able to mention them all would be fine
But I feel limited to the first chartered twenty.

First were the Baughns - Artie, Alsie, and A. D.
Then the Tauls-Owen, Amel, and Appalone
And the Weaks '-R. Herman, Laraun, and Agatha B.
Each family had relatives to carry on.

Some other early teachers, who became a team
And were among the towns' citizenry too
Were Lumsden, Wilson, Werner, Hartman, Pratt, and Deem
Trained the young to carry on proceedings in lieu.

The first high school was approved in 1923
For two years operated third class
In 1925 second class it came to be
A year later a first class institution at last.

Bonds were sold for a building in 1924
It was ready to occupy in September
For some here tonight, it has memories galore
Until its death by fire we remember.

The last school construction is what we have now
But soon secondary students had a change
It was all well arranged by vote approval somehow
To receive all credits under a different school name.

Some influential board members I'd like you to know
That worked incessantly for the good of us all
Seth Nelson, John Engram, L. E. Weaks, J. H. Coppage, J. F. Sexton, and X. Caverno
Helped each of us to learn to stand tall.
A United Sunday School was organized first
To take care of the spiritual needs
Then in 1910 we had our first church
Organized by the Methodist Creeds.

The Baptist Church was organized next
In 1912 in the month of November
Rev. F. D. Baughn, most influential for its text
As many here can still remember.

First charter membership numbered thirteen
Barnhill, Baughn, Colson, Collins, Sexton, and Ford
Are family names which made up a team
And taught well in the memory of our Lord.

In 1913 in the fall
The Christian Church was chartered
But by 1914 by the consent of all
To the Church of Christ was altered.

To note and interesting surprise
This church's early members all
From Ohio County, Kentucky did arrive
Names–Arbuckle, Greer, Muffett, Nelson, Ralph, and Taul.

The Pentecostal doctrine was brought
By Walter Higgins and W. M. Childers
Then D. J. Carter donated a lot
And all became the builders.
In 1913 came the dedication and charter
And was called the Church of God

First deacons—Wm. Westbrooks, Thurman Drennon and D. J. Carter
Building site—the present sod.

In 1918 we had our first bank
President D. S. Kreps and cashier E. M. Ford
Stockholders and people came by the rank
Anxious for holdings to be stored.

In 1919 a brick building Canalou employed
Where Hammock's Hardware now stands
It housed our new bank and each member enjoyed
The town's pride made it seem quite grand.

The life of the bank was short, however
When one of Canalou's biggest tragedies struck
For in 1927 its doors were closed forever
For those dependent it brought sorrow and bad luck.

1924 brought our first cotton gin
Co-partners—Caverno, Hoover, Percy, Moore—and Grabenhurst
1933 brought the second and others followed when
The cotton fields began to swell and burst.

Other names connected with the growth of cotton
Are Cathey, Geske, Gruen, Davis, McCann, and Burnett
Sister states sent members not to be forgotten
But our own we mention lest we forget.

Three theaters were operated during the life of the town
The first one was W. M. Moore
For entertainment on week ends we were truly bound
And attended the show by the score.

The present theatre building opened in 1944
A record of its opening is known
The first picture gave some of history's lore
As the "Life of Jack London" was shown.

Three beauty parlors have been operated here
The first in 1938 by Emma Halloway
Others are Mrs. Hillis, Mrs. Drake, and Gladys Greer
And Virginia Bond is with us today.

The only drug store to relate
Was owned by L. D. Daugherty
From 1920 to 1928
Who came to us from Morley.

A formula for babies be made in a mixer
To save lives of infants in our city
He called this formula Baby Elixer
To have its ingredients die with him was a pity.

Canalou did not go untouched by the tragedy of war
Several sons gave their lives for the freedom we cherish
Clark, Cook, Newman, Thornburg, Bell, Chastain, and Gipson all left a scar
When we learned their fate was to perish.

Others took advantage of the G. I. Bill
Which helped them along to success
A variety of schools were chosen at will
Accomplishments in each were the best.

This agriculture town seems sleepy and lazy
During the long, hot months of the summer
But becomes alert in the fall as a pretty spring daisy
The noise of the harvest as familiar as a drummer.

There is one old familiar saying
In the Bootheel area around
To get your feet wet you'll be staying
Or to return often you'll be bound.

I was not only born in Canalou
But got my feet wet many times.
I'm always pleased to return to you
But this special visit is like musical chimes.

Thank you again for bringing us home
To join the fun with good friends,
With you I could never ever feel alone;
Bless each one till we meet again.

Chapter Five

Little River Drainage District Transformed Swamp

Today, only memories live along Canalou's vacant Main Street.

Most historians can tell you about St. Louis, Cape Girardeau, Sedalia, and Kansas City being well-known frontier towns in the great state of Missouri in the past.

Present-day Canalou is an economic ghost town; however, its history is also special and unique as one of Missouri's and mainland America's last frontier towns when the first permanent settlers moved into the former swamp as recent as 1902.

There were no roads, only swamp, timber, and vast cane breaks—not to mention panthers, bears, large rats, venomous snakes, and wild cats in that era.

It later became some of America's richest, most fertile farmland when the dredging effort by the Little River Drainage District (LRDD) drained the Nigger Wool Swamp into a region of world-class farmland. This is monumentally historic, in terms of impacting thousands of people and producing an equal high number of good jobs up through the present era.

Without that dredging, there'd be no Interstate 55, no Highways 25, 60, and 62, and no major manufacturers, such as Proctor & Gamble and Noranda, to name a few results of the impact, a director with the LRDD rightly described.

More earth was dug, for example, and moved in draining the estimated 500,000 acre swamp in the six county Bootheel region than was moved during the dredging of the world-famous Panama Canal.

"In 1976, the year of our nation's Bicentennial Celebration, the American Society of Civil Engineers designated Little River Drainage District's dredging and canal system, starting with the huge Diversion Channel and levee (near Cape Girardeau), as one of the top civil engineering feats in American history," accounted Dexter native Larry Dowdy, who has served as LRDD's chief engineer since 1975.

But the feat has never got the recognition compared to the more famous Panama Canal. To be historically correct, some of those brave souls who helped dig the Panama Canal returned to the states and helped dredge the miles and miles of canals that transformed the swamp into some of the world's most fertile farmland.

"We're not known nationally, for our work has been regional," Engineer Dowdy acknowledged.

To date, not many historians have come to the Bootheel to study the thirty percent of Missouri's agricultural products.

"I'd estimate maybe five to ten historians, including amateurs, come around each year," Dowdy added.

Formed in 1907, the Cape Girardeau-based LRDD transformed what was "Swampeast Missouri" into vast fertile flat farming acreage that can only be viewed in total scope today from a satellite in the sky.

In my growing-up era, 1940s-1950s, small family farms of 100 acres to 300 acres were the norm in New Madrid County.

Present-day Canalou/Matthews farmer Charles Hawkins, who has 2,600 acres in cultivation, is considered a small farmer.

Hawkins, who married 1956 Canalou High School graduate Margie Latham, the daughter of Irene and Bert Latham, one of the best farmers in the history of Canalou, describes the diversity and fertileness of the nutrient-packed soil that has exploded the Bootheel into a major agricultural force.

And with the advent of rice production in the Bootheel, the Canalou-area's heavy gumbo soil, is found to be ideal for retaining water needed for rice growth.

"With 2,600 acres, I'm a small farmer," Hawkins accounted. "Most guys around here farm 5,000 acres and up.

"The heavier tight gumbo land over around Canalou does not have the crop-growing diversity of the lighter mixed-loam prevalent over around Matthews, some of which is located up on Sikeston Ridge," Hawkins noted. "But Canalou's dirt is rich, plugs well, and is ideal for holding water and growing rice. You can grow corn there, although you have to know what you're doing to raise corn there. There's also a little cotton being grown again over around Canalou."

Asked about the historic impact of the engineering, draining and dredging work done by LRDD, Hawkins responded: "The Canalou area was always being flooded, but with the dredging of the huge Diversion Channel north up near Cape, and the series of drainage canals or ditches on down here in the Bootheel, it keeps the water from coming down on us from up in the hills.

"The constant flooding happened when all that hill-country water would come down on us through the Castor and Little Rivers," Hawkins described. "What they accomplished with those canals and levees is historic, both in terms of forming a strong agrarian economy here in the Bootheel, but also in terms of the dredging being one of America's largest land engineering accomplishments."

The largest canal near Canalou is the Floodway Channel located two miles west of what was downtown Canalou. First Ditch, Second Ditch and Third Ditch (between Matthews and Canalou) were dug to channel the water around Canalou.

During the swamp-timber era, it took a tough, strong breed of people to create livelihoods and rear families, decreed Canalou Mayor James Donald Taul, whose ancestors helped carve out a community from the dense wildnerness.

Former Canalou farm girl Patsy Hopper Bixler also recognizes the historic impact of LRDD's work.

"The land is historically important, as it was once a swamp with an abundance of virgin timber," present-day Cape Girardeau resident Mrs. Bixler describes. "The drainage of the swamps was the greatest reclamation of its time, starting in the 1914-era, with about 1,000 miles of ditches and 305 miles of levees. I cannot praise the accomplishments of the LRDD, and its chief engineer, Larry Dowdy, enough. What they did was transform worthless swamp land into some of the world's most fertile and versatile land anywhere to be found."

"After the virgin timber was harvested, the land was deemed worthless, and initially sold for a few cents per acre," she accounted. "Today, the land is worth thousands of dollars per acre. The soil, after the reclamation project by the LRDD, is now deemed some of the richest in the world. So rich, it's been compared to the Nile Valley."

"My father was a proud man of the soil, and had an appreciation for the diversity our ground had. It would grow virtually any crop," Patsy added. "Our farm was located about 5 miles out of Canalou, in the general proximity to what is called the Big Ridge area."

Today, the LRDD is responsible for operation of 957.8 miles of ditches and 304.43 miles of levees, as America's largest drainage entity. It serves an area ninety miles in length and varying from ten to twenty miles in width, from Cape Girardeau to the

Missouri/Arkansas state line. The 540,000-acre district serves parts of seven Missouri counties: New Madrid, Bollinger, Cape Girardeau, Dunklin, Pemiscot, Stoddard, and Scott.

The LRDD's own description of the former swamp is brief and to the point: "The swamp was a wild and dark region."

Canalou founder Dan Kreps carved a sawmill village out of the timber and swamp, starting a town in 1902 that was initially constructed on pole stilts for early settlers to walk above the water.

Cape Girardeau entrepreneur Louis Houck had constructed railroad spur lines down into the swamp down through Delta, Advance, Chaffee, and Morehouse that helped lead to the development of Canalou and the entire swamp area that covered parts of seven Bootheel counties. The spur line eventually snaked on through the swamp, on down through Charter Oak, Lavalle, Parma, Gideon, Malden, and Kennett to the Arkansas line.

Early swamp visionaries happened at the opportune time when President Teddy Roosevelt had the vision to dredge the Panama Canal after the French had tried and failed the previous two decades. It was an era when Americans were in the mood to accomplish the impossible in terms of engineering and taming Mother Nature.

In the meantime, over thousands of years, there was a vast 500,000 acre swamp with "nearly an impenetrable morass of trees, bogs and standing water with only a few roads and railroad crossings," according to history annals published by LRDD.

Historians around the globe know of the mighty Mississippi River.

Few know the vast impact of Little River, aptly named by early occupying French explorers. In non-flooding periods, Little River, approximately twenty-five miles to the west of the Mississippi, is a small stream that runs through Morehouse and one mile west of present-day Canalou. Today, it's only a trickle of its former formidable flooding self.

Although "little" in name and size, Little River's impact, before the dredging of multiple canals, was monumental in keeping mankind at bay and out of the swamp, which was intact for thousands of years, especially when it had Old Man River, plus the ancestral Ohio River, backing it up.

Florence Robinson's brother, Harry Robinson, fished and trapped along Little River his entire life. "When not cutting timber, we hunted, fished and trapped for survival," noted "Uncle" Harry (no relation to the writer) in his one and only newspaper interview. "Little River was a blessing and a curse. One day, it would flood and nearly wipe us all out. But later, when the flood waters subsided, it fed us."

Prior to 1850, the swamps were considered a "no man's land" with dangers lurking behind each beautiful Cypress and big thick Oak trees, including bears and panthers, not to mention quick sand that could swallow a man up never to be seen again.

In a publication celebrating LRDD's 100th-year anniversary is a partial description of what the region was still like in the earliest 1900's.

"A dragline operator, who worked in the lower district in the 1920s, recalled that, during his childhood, men from his hometown in Kentucky travelled to Morehouse, Missouri, to hunt bear and other game. They returned home with wild tales about the swamp wilderness.

"Later as a little boy, he recalled travelling by train through Morehouse to go to Poplar Bluff, and worried if the train stopped in Morehouse if bears would come out of the woods and board the train," the account included.

In doing extensive research for this forum, my respect and admiration has grown immensely for those men, women and children strong and smart enough to carve out a unique life for their families in one of mainland America's truly last Frontier Towns, Canalou, Missouri.

Great tribute should also go to Bootheel engineer Otto Kochtitzky who began working on a series of maps in 1902, detailing the unique characteristics of the swamp. It was Kochtitzky who had the vision that ultimately transformed the swamp region into some of the most fertile farmland in the world.

Before this series of canals and levees, the Bootheel was a natural basin to catch flood waters from the Castor and Little River streams.

There had been talk around 1900 about draining the land. Finally, in January 1905, a meeting was called in Cape Girardeau to discuss how the project could be completed. At this meeting, an elaborate network of proposed draining ditches, canals and levees was devised and eventually carried out. Before today's rich fertile farmland surfaced out of the swamp, less than ten percent of it was clear of water that varied from being a few feet to more than ten feet in depth.

Canalou, after the timber was harvested, became a bustling little farming hamlet.

Chapter Six
Floy Mae Remembers

Floy Mae Arbuckle Jones Gruen remembered the good times and bad times while being born, maturing, and ultimately dying with her heart deeply rooted in Canalou-swamp culture.

It didn't take long for the bad times to hit after she was born in 1913, the first child of L. L. and Coela Greer Arbuckle, two of the little town's earliest settlers who moved into the swamp from Kentucky.

The family arrived into what locals named: Nigger Wool Swamp.

"The year 1918 was devastating," she recalled. "I do remember the flu epidemic of 1918," she explained. "I lost an older half-brother to the influenza, and on the same day, I lost a cousin. We had a double-funeral for them, and buried them down at Big Ridge Cemetery that Canalou farmer Jim Wilkening keeps neat and trim to this day."

As of 2010 remnants of one of those two tombstones remain intact at the isolated remote rural little cemetery near the Dale Geske Farm.

"As a little girl, that was my first experience with death," Floy Mae confirmed.

"The name was appropriate, since the nearby Little River was constantly flooding out of its banks all the time in that era. We could never see the banks of the actual river because it was always flooded. Canalou was still in the middle of a great big swamp," Floy Mae added.

Canalou went its first few years in the swamp-era before there were any officially-formed churches along with no official town government.

"They'd been meeting in homes, until about 1910, and then in 1912, when three churches were formed: the Pentecostal, that became the Assembly of God, the Methodist, which sold its building to Canalou Baptist Church, and the Christian Church, which became the Church of Christ," Floy Mae traced religion back through the swamp era.

The Baptist and Assembly churches are still going as of 2010, although the business district of Canalou is now void of commerce. The town's Church of Christ merged in the 1990s decade with small country churches in Kewanee and Matthews.

"We had three well-known preachers, Catherine Barnham, Billy Butler, and Grady Evans, who came through our churches and schools," Floy Mae accounted.

Her own father, although not an ordained preacher, could marry people as a justice of the peace, and later as mayor of Canalou.

He was also a skilled maker of sorghum molasses.

Sometimes, making molasses and conducting marriages were intertwined.

The daughter talked about his sorghum that spawned an especially memorable marriage service.

"Folks for miles around loved my Dad's sorghum molasses," the daughter bragged. "I've never found any as good as his. You go in the store today and pick up a jar, and it has sugar listed as an additive. Daddy never used sugar, and it was THE BEST!

"One year, when he had his sorghum mill located out of Canalou two miles to the west (near the Floodway Channel that helped drain the swamp), this couple came to him to get married, out while he was working the mill," the daughter recalled. "Well, when he got home that night and talked to Mother Arbuckle, she reminded him the marriage was not legal, since his mill was located in Stoddard County, out of New Madrid County, and he was not licensed to marry anyone outside the county."

Family members were sworn to secrecy about this interesting turn of events in early Canalou history.

"Well, Dad rushed around and got the couple to come to our house that night, and he re-married them," Floy Mae noted. "And our parents swore all us children to secrecy, to never tell this outside our home, and I never have told it, until now, but since they were the only couple to get divorced that Dad married, well, I think it's okay to tell it now."

"Willis and two of my sisters played ball at Canalou High, but I was a bookworm, thinking I had to make the best grades in the whole school," Floy Mae described. "Willis, the one townfolks called Red, could have played professional baseball. He was that good, but four years in World War II changed his course in life and he never got back to playing sports."

"And we had some very successful farmers, including Lyman Whitten, Jim Wilkening, Charles McCann, Bert Latham, Roy Johnson, Conliff Blankenship, the Croom Brothers, Melton Bixler, Lonnie Lawson, Nelson Lumsden, Elmer Gruen, Fred Harris. . . . I can't list them all, but add L. A. McGann, Dale Geske, Roy Bixler, R. L. Abernathy, Abe Landers Jr. , Harry Chaney, and Jay Hopper to that list of successful farmers."

"Recreation in early Canalou was self-made," Floy Mae described. "As children, we'd have picnics down in town founder Dan Kreps Grove, and sometimes, we'd play games, you know hide-n-seek," she accounted. "And Judge X. Cavanaugh would hold fish fries every year there in Kreps Grove. I think members of the town's earliest churches cooked the fish."

And *love* blossomed in the former swamp too. "Oh, yes, we played romantic games too, you know, spin-the-plate and post office," Floy Mae added with a laugh.

In the late 1920s, the remarkable era of radio finally filtered its way into the swamp.

"Helen Drake got Canalou's first actual radio in 1928, so we all would gather over on her front porch, sit in the yard, you know, and listen to the Grand Ole Opry out of Nashville on Saturday nights," she recalled. "Later, V. E. Hammock got the first TV."

Early Christmases were sparse, in terms of gifts.

"We didn't decorate much, you know, we were poor. We hung stockings, and would get candy and fruit, and I was a pretty old girl before me and cousin stayed up late one night to see Santa, and well, we discovered there was no real Santa. We didn't tell the younger children," Floy Mae described.

When asked for her own most memorable Christmas gift Floy Mae answered: "I grew up, got married, and wanted a little girl, but our first two were boys," Floy Mae added. "Then we had a little girl, Alfreda Ellen, at Christmas one year, so yes, that was my very best Christmas present of life."

Orval and Floy Mae Jones had four children, Arlynn, Alva, Alfreda, and Reba, before they divorced. Mr. Jones, who had been born in 1912 in Canalou, died of a cerebral hemorrhage in 1958. Floy Mae died in January 2004.

Floy Mae Jone's Cousin

Fanny Ann Westerfield and George Allen Engram

Chapter Seven

Deaths of Engrams

Early Bootheel settler John Anderson Engram arrived by wagon train, along with his family in the late 1800s. Surviving winter weather elements while crossing the wide Mississippi River, with dangers from bears and big black panthers that still prowled the swampy Bootheel region, wasn't an easy journey.

He moved to Missouri from Dandridge, Tennessee. As a young man, he survived long, rigorous hunting expeditions while trapping throughout the massive Nigger Wool Swamp, survived the dangerous responsibilities of being a lawman in Sikeston and Blodgett, Missouri, and then, he got through the influenza outbreak of 1918-19.

He, along with other hunters of that era, reported the late-night *screams* from panthers "could make the hair stand up on your head and arms."

And as Mr. Engram was going through these ordeals, he amassed significant wealth for that era, between 1900 and 1925, although he lost a lot of it by the time the Great Depression hit the nation in 1929 that lasted through much of the 1930s.

After surviving all of the above, including the loss of his wife and daughter while living in Sikeston, in 1936 he died an unusually tragic death with a cow he was familiar with. Joy

Engram Whitten, a descendant, recalls the tragic death.

"Great-Grandfather Engram died two weeks after experiencing a broken neck when knocked down and injured at age seventy-six by a cow, usually a very gentle animal," verified Joy, the wife of present day prominent Bootheel farmer John Lyman Whitten. "He was leading the animal to the barn lot for milking, when it suddenly reared up, and its hooves struck him in the back and neck. He was carried into the family home at Canalou, and a few days later, taken to the hospital in Sikeston."

There were many hard times from that era! If you think John Engram had it tough, his brother, Nat Engram, was even more unlucky.

He was gunned down and killed at Sikeston's historic Train Depot. The local newspaper only made it worse by misspelling his name as "Nat Ingram." According to published newspaper accounts of that era, Nat Engram's demise came in a shoot out with James Golightly, who didn't take Mr. Engram's competition for hauling commerce lightly at all.

A Sikeston school teacher named Emerson gave the following account to the newspaper: "Mr. Engram and Mr. Golightly were engaged in transporting luggage to and from the Train Depot. However, Monday morning, they disputed as to who should deliver a certain trunk."

We're talking competition for livelihoods here! "When it was about time for the evening train to arrive, the two again met on the platform. Golightly had arrived with a load of salesmen trunks and in his hand, he held a leather check ring with brass checks thereon.

"The quarrel of the morning was renewed. Golightly struck Engram over the head with the check ring. Engram drew a pistol and began firing. The first shot struck Golightly on the forehead. The second shot took effect near the heart. In the meantime, Golightly drew his pistol, and it's presumed that the first shot struck Engram on the [lawman's badge], the second in the shoulder and the third through the heart," according to published reports.

Both combatants reportedly fell on the platform simultaneously with their feet entangled.

Engram died almost instantly, while Golightly lived until the next morning. The newspaper's reporter made the following editorial summation about the end of these men's lives: "Thus were two lives snuffed out in the mad rush for a chance to make a living. Both wanted work and quarreled over the privilege of doing what was within sight. This is called competition."

Like most families in this rugged frontier setting in the Missouri Bootheel, the Engrams had their share of tough times in the late 1800s and early 1900s.

And like many females throughout history, John Engrams' wife, the former Minnie Fulton, had a troubled birth during delivery of their son, George Allen Engram. From those complications at birth, physicians often prescribed morphine.

Descendant Joy Engram Whitten shares some details of this pioneer woman's life and gracious spirit.

"Grandmother Minnie had a very sad life," detailed Joy in an interview we did in November 2008. "After the very difficult birth of Allen, she became addicted to morphine. Physicians in that era gave it away very readily, I'm told.

"I think she became an embarrassment to her stepdaughters, from Grandfather John Engram's first marriage to Ora Wilbur, the mother of Ora Engram Summers and Mabel Engram Winters," Joy accounted. "I can only imagine being young girls of that era and having to live with the talk. My heart goes out to all concerned."

Despite reported drug addictions, Minnie Engram befriended many of her neighbors at Canalou, either by serving as a midwife or by inviting hungry children off the road as they were en-route to school often adding fruit and biscuits to hungry swamp children's lunch pails.

"My father, John Coleman Engram, loved Grandmother Minnie with all his heart, and he was adored by her," Joy added. "However, Grandfather John Anderson Engram threatened anyone with severe consequences if they aided Grandmother Minnie in getting her drugs.

"When families of the Great Depression era could not pay Grandmother Engram for being their mid-wife, they would pay with a chicken or vegetables grown in their garden," Joy noted. "My father often wondered, after her death at age fifty-one while visiting a relative in Murphysboro, Illinois, in 1939, if any of the people she befriended at Canalou remembered her good will and charitable nature."

The end to John Anderson Engram's life came while he was living in Canalou with daughter Ora Engram Summers. Mr. Engram had previously owned significant acres of farm land south of Canalou leading up to the Great Depression.

John and his birth family came from Tennessee in a wagon train that arrived at Sikeston, Missouri, in 1882, before moving down into the swamp surrounding Canalou to farm and to hunt and trap egrets for a St. Louis-based millinery company. On two occasions, he served as a marshal under Sikeston Chief-of-Police "Uncle" Joe Randall. For several years before retirement, Mr. Engram was chief-of-police in Blodgett, Missouri.

His funeral was held at Canalou Christian Church, which was filled beyond capacity with mourning friends and loved ones.

But, this was not the first time the Engram family suffered a tragic loss in unusual circumstances.

In August 1927, John Engram's son, George Allen Engram, also a Canalou farmer of that era, was struck by lightning along with one of his mules.

A front page account was carried in The Sikeston Herald newspaper on September 8, 1927.

"He had gone to the barn on his farm, four miles south of Canalou, to feed his livestock. While at the building, the electrical storm passed over that section late that afternoon, and struck the Engram farm. The unfortunate man had completed his work and had just stepped through the barn door when lightning struck the barn, killing the owner and one of the mules within the barn."

Unfortunately, his wife watched her husband fall dead to the ground in the barn's hallway.

One of the largest crowds in Canalou's early history gathered at the small white framed Canalou Baptist Church building where services were presided over by the Reverend T. F. Gray.

"School was dismissed and all businesses closed that all might attend the services," *The Herald* indicated. George Allen Engram, who married a daughter of earliest Canalou settlers, Ida and Isaac Coleman Westerfield, was born May 25, 1902, at Blodgett.

George Allen Engram's two sons, Joseph Allen Engram and John Coleman Engram, were among survivors. His wife was Fannie Westerfield Engram.

Descendant Joy Engram Whitten shared details from the tragic death-by-lightning scene.

"After witnessing Grandfather George Allen Engram falling after being struck by lightning, Grandmother Engram ran into the house to get my father, age five at the time, along with Uncle Joe, and took them out into the terrible storm. She said she was going to get help. As she was dragging Daddy along in the muddy road, he was saying 'Don't worry, Mama. I'll take care of you.' Later in life, she lived next to Dad [John Coleman Engram] at Vanduser, and my parents did faithfully help take care of her."

John Coleman Engram, who matured to become a successful Vanduser businessman and statewide known business and civic leader, died July 8, 2005, at age eighty-eight.

No doubt, George Allen Engram would have been proud of his oldest son, who after graduation from Canalou High School, became manager and board member of the Vanduser Gas Company, served as longtime board member of Sikeston's First National Bank, became manager of the Vanduser Gin Company plus serving as state board member of the Missouri Cotton Producers' Association.

Morehouse native Ronnie Carl Launius recalls working as a boy for John Engram.

"My uncle and I did carpenter work, putting brick siding on some buildings John Engram owned there in Vanduser," St. Louis-area resident Launius confirmed in 2009. "He was a nice man to work for, telling us that at the end of the workday, we could take a watermelon out of his field and eat it. It gave us something to look forward to after a hot hard day's work."

In 1941, John Coleman Engram wed Benton resident Olivia McDonald, who still resided on family farm acreage near Vanduser as of 2009.

This is a family whose roots go deep back into the wild and woolly swamp that spawned a village with the unique name of Canalou as one of mainland America's last frontier towns, founded as recently as 1902.

Chapter Eight

Cooking and Hunting in the Swamp

In 1907, Fannie Ann "Mammie" Westerfield, visited Canalou.

The girl's *visit* turned permanent. "I was thirteen when we moved into the swamp," Mammie chronicled in a recorded interview she granted at age ninety in 1986. "I reckon I didn't much like it there, didn't like the climate."

At this tender age, Mammie was thrust into harsh frontier conditions, primitive outdoor life in a wilderness so thick, an uncle "got lost for two days because he couldn't see the sun when out hunting for game."

Wild game included squirrels, raccoons, possums, fish, wildcats, panthers, and bears.

Heavy camp-cooking responsibilities were immediately put on the thirteen-year-old's shoulders.

"Sometimes I would cook [on open camp fires] for up to fifteen men who were working in the woods. I would cook from sunrise to sunset. We cooked just about anything we could get our hands on. It took a lot to feed hard-working, logging men," Mammie shared.

She described early timber-harvesting camp food fare by telling about an uncle's hunting expeditions out of the camp into the dense forest and deep swamp waters.

"After getting lost for two days, Uncle Aaron began carrying a compass because the timber growth was so dense, he couldn't see the sun to navigate by," she traced back in time. "One day, my Uncle Aaron said he was going to go out in the woods and get us a big mess of squirrels. Well, it wasn't long before he returned with squirrels hanging all over him.

"He returned with thirty-nine squirrels in a very short period of time," Mammie described. "We culled and selected the youngest and best squirrels for me to cook."

She cooked large servings in order to feed the hard-working, hungry men.

Mammie lived five years in Canalou before the Little River Drainage District was formed to begin draining the swamp that covered the six Bootheel counties. She didn't take to the primitive conditions in the swamp. Mosquitoes were described as "unbearable."

"I didn't like Missouri," she confirmed. "I missed my boyfriend back in Kentucky. They didn't have any good stuff to eat in Missouri. We had to tote dried fruit and canned stuff into the swamp."

Camp dogs were important components of early camp life, not only for hunting and companionship but for safety purposes against wildcats, wild hogs, panthers, and bears. Mammie had to keep them from being hungry.

"One time my uncle instructed me to take the possums and coons he had killed out in the woods and prepare some well-done dog bread for the dogs," Mammie accounted. "I was always cooking, including cooking corn bread for the dogs. I didn't know that dogs would eat without corn bread."

She had left her sweetheart back in Kentucky in a courtship that had begun at age twelve.

Those early camp settlers floated to Canalou's first post office on rafts and in Jon boats. That early postal service was crucial to Mammie's interstate courtship. Arriving mail helped divert attention from the drudgery and back-breaking hard work that came with morning-to-night logging and cooking duties.

"Heber [her beau] and I had got sweet on one another back

in our little rural Birch Valley, Kentucky, school," Mammie described. "He never came to Missouri, except one time when he came into the swamp to marry me. He liked the raisins I had prepared special for his arrival. We'd liked one another since age twelve.

"But for those five years, I got letters from him every week," Mammie shared. "Sometimes, my father wanted me to read and share his letters. But as I became friends with the postal man, well, he agreed not to give my letters to anyone. I'd go get my mail after attending school that was initially held in various Canalou make-shift homes."

Her cooking duties in the wilderness came to an end at age eighteen when sweetheart Heber O. Midkiff came into the swamp to wed and take his new bride back across the Mississippi to their beloved native Kentucky where they remained married for seventy-three years.

"I put on a big [cooking and preparation] effort when Hebert came out of Kentucky into the swamp to marry me," Mammie recalled.

Mammie died February 19, 1989.

Okie Wagoner was among the first camp cooks when Canalou became a logging camp in 1902. This was before the Nigger Wool Swamp was drained to make the county Bootheel region one of the most fertile farming regions in America.

"How could we not talk about my Great-Grandmother Okie Wagoner," shares Les Landers, a descendant to the legendary lady. "Cooks in our family seemed to make the most out of the least, which is an art form that we would do well to emulate in today's troubled economy."

We're talking going out in largely-uncharted swamps and bogs, using the sun as your compass, finding wild game, hitting the target with your rifle, skinning it, and dragging it back to camp.

"Granny Okie would get up in the morning, and cook breakfast for Canalou's earliest loggers, and when breakfast was over, she would take her rifle and go into the swamp and woods, and shoot something for supper," Les said. "And they ate whatever she shot, be it turkey, rabbit, squirrel, coon, or whatever came in her rifle sight, and she never missed. She liked a diversified menu."

Granny Okie Wagoner lived to be nearly a hundred years old.

Another early camp cook was the legendary Granny Robinson, who lived to be a hundred and three. She and her family floated into what became incorporated Canalou in 1905.

Granny's daughter, Florence Robinson Poe, recalls her mother going out into the woods and swamp waters.

"My favorite meal from Mother's table was breakfast," recalled Mrs. Poe, "The aroma of those camp-fire vittles woke us up, ravenously hungry, we were glad to get any food."

"Earliest meals in the initial sawmill camp in the 1902 to 1910 era were prepared over open fires in big black cooking kettles, or huge cast-iron skillets," described Uncle Harry Robinson, who arrived in the swamp waters as a boy in 1905.

Chicken was considered a delicacy when first settlers camped in the swamp for timber-harvesting beginning in 1902.

Families named Landers, Tauls, Robinsons, Westerfields, Arbuckles, Scotts, Engrams, and Newmans were among earliest permanent families to settle and rear families in what later became a town called Canalou.

"Some of them had chickens, but that was the exception when they first began moving into the settlement that officially became Canalou," acknowledged Les Landers. "A meal of chicken in the swamp-era of the Bootheel was a true delicacy, according to what my great-grandparents and grandparents shared with their children."

Robinson, who acquired his community-wide nickname "Uncle" by being a warm and friendly, and highly-colorful hunter, trapper and fisherman in his adult years, explained how they survived. "Us early settlers existed on the very basics, such as thickening gravy, if we couldn't kill a squirrel, rabbit, or coon. When we had managed to kill a varmint to go with that gravy, we were eating high on the hog, so to speak. We loved killing and eating those big swamp rabbits too.

But some early settlers often had "slim pickings." Slim

pickings meant tough survival conditions.

"On days of slim pickings, some of us had to eat possum, a varmint of the wild, but that was when we were desperately hungry," he shared. "You had to be mighty hungry to stomach a greasy ol' mess of possum.

"Truth be known, more than one family would cook and eat one of those big fat swamp rats in the cold winter time, but that was during extreme survival times.

"But most of the time, we could catch enough fish out of Little River and Castor River, or trap enough fresh meat to keep us going."

Bears were also a source of food in the swamps early days, "When someone would trap and kill a bear, bear meat could sustain a family for a number of days, according to my father and my grandmother, Granny Robinson, who was one of the earliest swamp camp cooks," Robinson verified. "But by the time the swamps began to be drained after 1912, very few bears had survived."

Current Canalou Mayor James Donald Taul is in possession of a huge bear trap used by the Robinson family in those earliest swamp camp days.

"Swine was considered some fine eating," verified the elder Robinson.

Hog-killing time was a big day in the community, when multiple families came together to butcher and cure meat that could sustain families through cold winters.

"But swamp-era community hog-killing days contrasted greatly from later hog-killing days when farming replaced the swamps and timber," Robinson related.

"The fresh pork tenderloin, which you had to eat the day of hog killing or it would spoil, was a meal fit for kings," Robinson confirmed. "Now don't think we just went out to the barn and killed a hog like they did in the later farm era.

This was *free range* country, which meant we had to go out in the woods, find the hogs with our ear-markings, and then kill them out in the wild," the aged trapper accounted. "This meant the hogs had to be transported as dead weight back into camp. We'd let them roam free to fatten up on the acorns out in the wild."

Robinson continued, "It was a tough task to haul those hogs in from the woods, maybe a mile or even more. I remember the day my dad [Wid Robinson] pulled his oxen off dragging the logs to construct the first Corduroy Road leading from Canalou to Matthews, to go to the woods and kill a hog because our family had run out of meat. We'd use Dad's oxen to drag the hogs through the tough gumbo and mud bog."

As a young reporter in 1968, I was fortunate to be the one to whom this historic Bootheel figure granted his only newspaper interview. Harry Robinson remained a hunter and trapper all of his life until he died in the late 1980s having learned to live by his wits off the land.

"Momma, [Granny Robinson] who became Canalou's first mid-wife, could fix a good breakfast when she had vittles to do it," Robinson shared. "She made great biscuits, and we had molasses; it became our candy as kids. We'd stick a spoon down into the thick molasses, spin it round and round, and we had us a sucker, especially when the syrup was thick on real cold winter mornings."

"One thing Canalou men enjoyed, especially in the winter, was to go rabbit hunting," Landers described. "They were after the bigger swamp rabbits, using red-bone and blue-tick hounds. Those swampers [rabbits] would be going really fast, with the dogs hot on their trail across those open soybean fields. And, you had to be a pretty good shot to bag a swamper.

"My Grandmother Allen made some of the best biscuits and gravy to go along with a fresh-killed swamp rabbit," Landers recalled.

There were hunting laws that were not observed in the swamp era.

"Since the Canalou of that early era had a rough and woolly reputation on some official documents, most game wardens didn't see fit to venture into the swamp," Les added. "If you know what I mean."

Later, when the culture changed following swamp drainage, farm-era cooks had to be resourceful and creative too.

Many farm wives and daughters would prepare a meal or two ahead of days spent in the fields.

When picking cotton in the fall, for example, we'd bring cold sandwiches to eat at noon in the shade of a cotton trailer. My parents wanted us to take a short lunch break in order to have more time going up and down those seemingly endless rows of cotton.

"If ya'll were picking cotton way back in the new ground behind Little River," Momma Whittle explained from her deathbed in 2003, "We didn't have time to come the half-mile to the house to eat dinner. So that's why it was important to take our meals there in the fields."

It was a huge treat when a farmer would surprise us with a cold soda pop from one of the seven small groceries that lined Canalou's short Main Street.

The men of one farm family would not allow anything but fried chicken and biscuits and gravy after a hard day of working on the farm.

"My husband, Norval, and son, Norman Ernest, never, ever wanted anything else, but my fried chicken and white milk gravy," I overheard Marguerite Gertrude Haywood Harrison sharing with my mother, Ruby Lee Whittle, one day in the 1970s. "I got so tired of fixing fried chicken, gravy and biscuits, but that's all that would satisfy the men of my family."

The Harrisons and Whittles go back as farm neighbors to the 1930s when they frequently shared mules and farm equipment. Two of the best country cooks in our families were Aunt Durette Reed on mother's side of the family, and Aunt Doris Whittle, on Daddy Hubert Whittle's family side.

Aunt Durette could take the simplest staples, such as white beans, and make them a delicacy meal. And her hog jowl breakfasts were to kill for.

My favorite off Aunt Doris' table was her steak and gravy, but her fried chicken came in a close second.

Chapter Nine

Fugitive to Lawman

The exact *when* Elisha Allen came across the Mississippi River to the Bootheel swamps is not known.

But the *why* is known. He was on the run from the law of Kentucky.

"Great-Grandfather Elisha Allen was from Casey County, Kentucky," noted Les Landers, a descendant to the man who crossed the Mississippi River to live in the swamps in 1902 or 1903. Landers has dedicated himself to the research of his ancestors and how they came to end up living in the swamp and sawmill village. "He was involved in an incident with a Kentucky lawman, which caused him to leave that state very quickly."

This brings us to the "why" he came to the swamp before it became an incorporated settlement known as "Canalou" in 1909.

"It seems there was a problem between one of his brothers and a deputy sheriff," Landers continued. "And Elisha came to his brother's defense. In the melee, he shot and wounded the deputy. Not knowing if he had killed him or not, Great-Grandfather Elisha first went to Tennessee, and then to Missouri, ending up in the swamp town that became Canalou."

Those of us growing up in post-swamp years in the 1940s

were told that this type of scenario often repeated itself; a high percentage of original settlers, who first opened up the swamp in 1902 and thereafter, were "on the lamb" from the law in surrounding states.

However, Elisha Allen was later cleared of any wrong doing.

"After moving into the swamp where they had started a sawmill community, Elisha sent for his family to join him there," added Landers, "There were warrants for his arrest in Kentucky, and they knew it. Yet, much later, Great-Grandfather Elisha received a full pardon from the Governor of Kentucky when it was decided he had acted in self-defense."

The swamp settler went from being *wanted* by the law to *The Law*.

"At one time, Elisha was Canalou's Town Marshall," the great grandson recorded. "We surmise the reason was that he had experience with firearms. . . ."

"We still don't know the precise 'when' date he arrived in Canalou, but we know the 'why'," added Elisha's descendant. "We know that his brother John linked up with him, and they made a living by working the sawmills, cutting timber, and dealing in livestock."

Elisha's son, Leslie Allen, the namesake of descendent Les Landers, later became well-known throughout the swamp region.

"Grandfather Leslie Allen went on to become a very good and accomplished blacksmith in Canalou," Les Landers confirmed. "Great-Grandfather Elisha became equally well-known for making 'Black Snake' whips for the folks who herded mules, horses, cattle, and oxen needed to do the snaking of logs out of the bog and swamp.

"He made the standard eight foot 'Bull' whips, and then there was the long and light, twenty foot 'Black Snake' whips that Great-Grandfather Allen made," Les accounted. "This was the same type of whip later made famous in the cowboy westerns featuring Lash Larue that we watched in the 1940s at Canalou's motion picture show house."

What eventually happened to Mr. Allen was not uncommon

in that wild and woolly era of swamp living. It was a tough existence.

"Later, great-grandfather Allen was overcome by alcohol, and he and my step-great-grandmother separated, and she moved out of the swamp to live with her daughter," Les says. "He later became one of Canalou's better-known town drunks."

There was "legal" whiskey and "illegal" whiskey being made in that era of swamp life. Both types of whiskey had their dangers.

"My other Great-Grandfather, Abraham Landers Senior, was a prominent land owner, with about two hundred acres between Morehouse and Canalou, a place was named for him called 'Landers Ridge' where only an old abandoned church now sits," Les Landers explained, "We have no idea when Great-Grandfather Abe moved to and founded Landers Ridge.

"But he was a legal distiller of whiskey, reputed to be the best around," Les Landers continued his journey back through his family's history. "He sold whiskey to the government, and at that time distilling whiskey in New Madrid County was a legal enterprise.

"Since this was before 1902 when Canalou was first opened, most of his customers must have been from Morehouse, Grayridge, Buffington, Salcedo and Sikeston," Les surmised.

But it was a dangerous occupation.

"His secret recipe for whiskey was the envy of other distillers in the area," descendant Landers added. "And one night, in an attempt to get the recipe, some men got my Great-Grandfather Landers drunk and poisoned him. They then told him what they had done, and he might as well go ahead and tell them the recipe, that he was going to die anyway.

"Being a strong-willed stout man, Great-Grandfather Abe Landers refused to give them the recipe, and made it home, advising his wife that he had been poisoned. He died taking his recipe to the grave with him," Les Landers recorded.

Abraham Landers Sr. was a man of means, judging by the inventoried possessions he left in his wake.

"We have a full inventory of everything he owned when he died, which included more than five hundred gallons of whiskey, ready to be sold and consumed," Les Landers records. "He also had several former slaves working for him."

Great-Grandson Les Landers was born in Canalou in 1940, to Willie and Norma Jean Landers, who moved from Canalou to Calvert City, Kentucky, in 1952.

Les' grandfather, the late Abe Landers Junior, was an early and highly-respected Canalou settler and worked in the early sawmills. He fathered sixteen children with multiple descendants living today in the Bootheel and several surrounding states.

Chapter Ten

Blankenships Arrive

What was the attraction for families to gather in and around Canalou, especially after the timber had been harvested and the swamp had been drained?

"My family came in the 1920s for the land. . . the farm land," confirmed Bonnie Blankenship Boutz. "For my family, it was the affordable land wanting to elevate themselves above sharecropper status," Canalou native Bonnie continued. "My parents, Conliff and Ruby Lucy Blankenship, were attracted to come to Canalou in 1925 by the cheap farm land made available after the swamp was drained. They'd heard about the farming opportunity while still living in Arkansas.

"They initially settled in the River Ridge community that once had a little country school one mile south of Canalou, between Charter Oak and Little River,"

Bonnie traced back over time: "Farming economy in the Bootheel, my parents told me, was better than down in Arkansas. Cotton was the King crop in the Bootheel and put spending money in people's pockets.

"During the fall, when everyone could have pocket change, we had Arkansas relatives who came up into the Bootheel and lived in tents in our front yard," Bonnie recalled. "They would cook their meals in our smokehouse, and at night they slept in tents after picking cotton all day. It was a tough life when our hands would bleed from the sharp cotton burrs and knees would get raw from crawling on the ground to continue picking cotton and stuffing it in your nine-foot-long sack."

She also recalled gifted cotton pickers. "If you can call picking cotton a gift?" She added with a wry smile. "Arkansawyer Ernest Weiland, who could pick up to four hundred pounds in a day, was one of those 'gifted' ones. However, I don't consider back-breaking hard work, such as picking cotton, a gift. For me, I could barely get a hundred and seventy pounds per day, and that was on my best days.

"Ernest and his family were one of those families who lived in tents in our front yard," she added. "You gotta remember, this was not long after the Great Depression, and money was hard to come by. Picking cotton was one way for a poor family to earn cash money."

She recalls families working together to survive in the 1940s.

"Hog-killing days were exciting, when neighbors came together," accounted Bonnie, who graduated from Canalou High School in 1954. "When we'd finish killing hogs on our place, we'd move to another family's farm place, and do it again.

"It was hard work, yes indeed, but it was something that had to be done, and we enjoyed the families working together and sharing our lives and tales of fun and survival. We had to do hog-killings in order to have something to eat during the winter months."

She laughingly recalled a special goat-killing day.

"Daddy [Conliff] one day just got plain fed up with all the goats hanging around our place," Bonnie described. "We had goats galore. Everywhere you looked, there was a goat. . . one was on top of the chicken house. . . one liked to stand up on our farm tractor. . . another liked looking down on us from atop Daddy's farm truck.

"Finally, Daddy said 'enough!' And we had us a goat-killing day," Bonnie confirmed. "And, yes, we ate the goat meat. Remember this was hard times, and meat and food was hard to come by. We didn't throw much of anything away."

This was in pre-electricity days before the Rural Electric

Administration (REA) ran poles, lines, and power out to farm homes surrounding Canalou.

"I was in the seventh grade before we got electricity," Bonnie noted. "Heck, it was after I graduated from Canalou High that we had indoor plumbing and toilets. Before that, we had the little building out back of the house. Electricity and indoor plumbing were big advancements in quality of life for the Blankenships. . . and for the rest of our farm neighbors."

Bonnie, who is living retirement years in Jefferson City, Missouri, recalls her large family coming to Canalou on Saturday nights to attend a moving picture show at the late L. A. McCann's little theater on the town's mile long Main Street.

"We'd all gather in the back of our big farm truck, just like other families of that era, and come to town," Bonnie described. "There'd be trucks, tractors and farm wagons lined up along Main Street and so many people you had trouble walking down the town's only sidewalk. Farm families shared the news of the community and stocked up on groceries and dry goods from little country stores such as that owned and operated by [the late] Jim and Stella Poe."

That was in the social and economic heyday-era of Canalou. . . now an economic ghost town.

Chapter Eleven

Corduroy Connection

So, how do you get *out* of Canalou?

Retired Bootheel sportswriter Alva "Alvie" Jones remembers a blogging debate about how many roads led into and out of his native Canalou.

"It's the only time this old Bootheel boy, who was born before computers, space travel, and mechanical cotton pickers, has ever blogged. But I felt like I had to defend the accuracy of my home town, where I was born the son of Orval and Floy Mae Arbuckle Jones in 1933.

"The blogger was of the opinion there was only one road leading to Canalou." Jones penned in assisting me research the material for this account of the culture in former Swamp-east Missouri.

"I think I proved my point, however, when this guy from Risco finally conceded that there was more than one road to exit and enter our tiny village that at one time was built up on stilts in order to get above the rat-infested swamp waters," Jones bragged about his birthplace.

Jones' ancestors go back to before there were roads.

"In those earliest days, in low-water periods, you were lucky to travel on a horse," Jones describes. "Otherwise, you traveled by Jon boat or log raft. I remember as recent as the 1940s, in the spring, floods from Little River and Floodway spilled over, and completely covered our farm for three consecutive years. This area lies below the level of the Mississippi River, thus the swamps went back several thousands of years."

"But it was roads we were debating recently over the Internet," Jones continued. "We blogged regarding the swampy bogs, but the more I researched my ancestors, the more I admired them, especially the ingenious way they came up with their first community-built road, a corduroy road."

Les Landers has the distinction of having both grandfathers, Abe Landers Jr. and Leslie Allen, who worked in the construction of the original Corduroy Road (sand covered tembers perpendicular to the center line of the road) that helped link Canalou to a town out of the swamp. Matthews had been established up on a higher elevation at the Sikeston Ridge.

According to legend, at least one Corduroy Road in New Madrid County caused a death, "Speaking of corduroy roads, there was an incident west of New Madrid where a man had built a plank road and charged a toll to use it," Landers accounted. "One customer thought the toll too high, and reportedly killed the man who constructed that corduroy toll road. That was before Canalou's Corduroy Road, however."

Although a corduroy road didn't appear in Canalou until after 1905, these roads had been in use in the Bootheel's swamp bottomland terrain since before and after the New Madrid Earthquake of 1811-1812. The original road leading from New Orleans to Cape Girardeau was reportedly a partial corduroy road, sometimes called a plank road.

"Typically, corduroy roads were just logs laid cross-wise, with plank runners, but the original El Camino Royale, or Kings Highway [that still runs through the Bootheel through Sikeston and Cape Girardeau] was a plank road," Landers confirmed. "This was logs running length-wise with sawed planks lying cross-wise to make a smoother road. Both roads were common in swamp areas, both before and after the earthquake of 1811 to 1812 that is until you reached New Madrid, which had an elevation called the Sikeston Ridge that was elevated ten feet or more above the swamps. They didn't require such roads up on the dry ridges."

Canalou resident Harry Robinson, who floated into what became Canalou in 1905, reconstructed his days as a youth spent working on Canalou's Corduroy Road.

"We used all types of lumber because it was plentiful, ranging from ash, to oak, to cypress, to cottonwood," "Uncle" Harry Robinson shared. "Such a road was needed not only for convenience but for economic reasons because the sturdier the road bottom, the heavier loads of timber the teams of mules, oxen, and horses could transport."

Uncle Harry noted the hard woods were preferred over the softer woods for durability purposes.

Wid Robinson, Uncle Harry's father, brought the first oxen to work in Canalou's initial timber mills.

"Those oxen were good for pulling heavier loads, and we used them on Canalou's Corduroy Road," Uncle Harry confirmed. "Like every job in that era, constructing the road was hard, tough work. We cut the slabs and planks at the nearby sawmills to be used in the road."

However, the need for such a road was short-lived in Canalou, because it wasn't long before the Little River Drainage District started the series of canals that led to draining the swamp. Once the swamp waters were drained, it freed up highly-fertile farm land that would grow a variety of crops. Permanent, dependable roads evolved throughout the Bootheel over the next few decades.

However, as recent as the 1940s and 1950s, tractors and mules were required to travel on Canalou-area dirt roads during heavy rain periods, especially during the winter months.

"When Little River would flood, our road turned into deep, heavy gumbo mud," assessed Jones. "And it took a tractor or mule to get to Canalou. That happened as late as 1952."

"I remember Grandfather Abe Landers having to haul us to town on a tractor when Little River would flood in the winter time," noted Les Landers. "Sometimes, we rode mules to get from his farm to Canalou."

Chapter Twelve
Legendary Uncle Harry

"Uncle" Harry Robinson was a hunting and trapping legend, a throw-back, a swamp hunter and trapper.

My first recollection of Uncle Harry, who literally floated into the swampy Bootheel region of southeast Missouri in a Jon boat in 1903, came when I was a mere tyke of a lad in the late 1940s.

Here was this legendary big and tall figure of a man I'd often heard my family and others talk about, walking down our hamlet's mile-long Main Street, greeting and being greeted as if he was a celebrated sports hero or prominent political figure.

He'd just stepped off the train at the Canalou Depot behind Moore's Mercantile and Grocery.

In reality, it was Uncle Harry's "welcome home" for having the distinction of being the last man of our community to go to prison for allegedly stealing chickens somewhere down in Arkansas.

Uncle Harry later told me about escaping from the infamous Tucker Prison Farm, reportedly one of Arkansas' toughest prisons from which to escape.

"I escaped by swimming the Arkansas River at night," Uncle

Harry clarified.

"I couldn't wait to get back home," understated Uncle Harry who, despite his lifestyle, was held in special Canalou community esteem, which is why most children of the community called him Uncle Harry.

He would share with children some of the early life before there was an incorporated village that was named "Canalou."

How swampy was it before 1910?

I remember paddling our family's Jon boat, so my sisters could hang clothes on the clothes line," Uncle Harry shared.

There was shared community-wide civic work too.

"And I helped work the oxen to transport the logs and lay the logs used to construct what we called the first Corduroy Road that linked Canalou to Matthews," Uncle Harry traced back over the decades. "When it rains, sometimes we can still see those logs. In that era, sometimes Corduroy Roads were the only transportable roads, especially during rainy winter seasons. That swamp land was so low and wet, and tough to deal with in the cold winter months."

Former Canalou farm boy, Donald Hammock, at age 89 in an early 2010 interview, recalled "once getting bogged down" on Canalou's Corduroy Road.

"We moved into the newly-drained former swampland to farm Section Ten by Third Ditch (between Canalou and Matthews), and we got bogged down with mules and wagon in the winter of 1937 on that Corduroy Road," Hammock described. "Travel and survival was tough in those times."

Him and his parents, V. E. and Aimee Hammock, and twin-brother Douglas, moved to the Bootheel up from Burdette, Arkansas to farm.

"We'd have organized snake and rat hunts," Uncle Harry related. "Although we had fun, killing those snakes and varmints, it was a serious survival thing. We mostly killed them on the high ground and where the railroad tracks ran. We tried not to kill King snakes, for they helped keep the number of rats and mice under control."

Uncle Harry's only son, Willard, who was one grade ahead of me at Canalou School, also described some of his late father's early life's adventures in the former swamp now known as Missouri's Bootheel region that sticks down like it ought to be a part of Arkansas.

"Dad remembered the time when his life was in jeopardy by a large panther that was ultimately killed by his father," Willard related. "My Grandfather Robinson killed that panther that was stalking my father, a boy at the time, out near their barn. When they laid the panther out, it measured more than eleven feet from head to the tip of its tail.

"There were a lot of panthers in the swamps and wilderness during that era and bears too," Willard added. "My Dad knew the last man, who was from down in Portageville, that killed the last bear to roam in this region. The last bear was killed in the 1920s."

Uncle Harry had a special way with animals too.

"It was nothing unusual to see a squirrel walk up my father's britches leg, and take a peanut out of his mouth as he sat out in his yard while living down by Little River," Willard accounted. "He seemed to have a way with animals out in the wild."

For years on up into his eighties, Uncle Harry fished and trapped the streams and channels throughout upper New Madrid County.

And although he never held what town folks would call "a regular job," Uncle Harry always seemed self-sufficient.

Uncle Harry was a great story-teller and had no hesitation at telling stories, even laughing at himself.

"The funniest story I ever heard Uncle Harry tell was one night when he and his best friend, Hubert Hill, a farmer, were out drinking the spirits," older brother H. Van Whittle shared. "He said that his buddy thought Uncle Harry had had too much to drink, and took over driving Uncle Harry's new automobile in the 1940s.

"Finally, as they were nearing Canalou, coming in from a night on the town over in Morehouse, Uncle Harry said he got displeased with how his buddy was driving the car. When stating to his buddy that he wasn't driving right, his drinking pal informed him curtly: 'I'm following the white line!' To which Uncle Harry said he responded thusly: 'White line, my ass! We're on a gravel road. There ain't no white lines!'"

Uncle Harry shared another tale with me, "Me and [farmer friend] Hubert Hill had run out of funds out late one night when we got fiercely hungry," Uncle Harry shared. "So we decided to go a neighbor farmer's house and 'borrow' a chicken or two.

"Since I was tallest and had the longest legs, it was decided that my friend would wait at the car as I crossed two fences to get to the unsuspecting farmer's chicken house," Uncle Harry whispered low, as if not wanting anyone to hear of his stealth and theft days. "Hubert's job was to keep a look out for the law back at the car, as I eased up to the chicken house in the dark of the night.

"You moved easy and quiet in order to not scare the chickens and start them to cackling," Uncle Harry added. "Well, I snatched two sleeping chickens, one under each arm, without the chickens making a sound, and as I was straddling that last fence making my way back to the road, my friend, who was supposed to be back at the car on lookout, leaned over my shoulder real close to my ear, and asked in the pitch dark night: **'How many chickens did you get?!'**

"Well, that scared me so bad, the chickens woke up and flew away when I threw my arms up in the air after being scared out of my wits," Uncle Harry recalled. "We lost our chickens, all because my buddy didn't stay back at the car as he was supposed to."

Former Canalou resident Larry Davidson verified in 2010 hearing the same tales directly from Uncle Harry.

"I was just a little boy, but Uncle Harry would take the time to talk to us, tell us those old swamp stories," Larry confirmed.

Uncle Harry came from strong stock, his father being an ox-driving man who snaked logs in and out of the swamp for northern, Yankee-owned timber companies. Uncle Harry's mother was Caroline "Granny" Robinson.

Uncle Harry also shared about one of the swamps earliest brutal multiple murders before we had any law. "I was seated, having a drink in one of our first saloons, when a gent named Bartell sat down next to me, and asked if I wanted to go hunt wolves," Uncle Harry noted. "Well, that wasn't unusual, since I was known to like to hunt, and since we still had wolves out in the dense-wooded swamps of that era, but I had something else planned and didn't take the man's invite. I didn't know him well, anyway.

"It was about a week later when news flashed around the camp town that the law had found this man having breakfast at the dinner table of this family named Wolf who lived south of town along the railroad tracks down around Charter Oak. He'd killed the entire family of people named Wolf. I never dreamed he meant to go kill people named Wolf."

The last time I saw the legendary Uncle Harry alive was in the mid-1980s, coming out of a saloon in Morehouse during a snow storm. Walking down the street with his long-legged strides, the now elderly Uncle Harry waved his arms skyward, and proclaimed mightily: "I'm a snow bird!"

Uncle Harry Robinson remains stitched strongly in the fabric of early swamp life of our former vibrant and colorful little timber and farming town called Canalou.

I was saddened to learn in 2009 that my lifelong friend Willard Robinson, died at age sixty-six. Shortly before his death, Willard helped me review and verify the above listed exploits of his legendary swamp-trapping father.

Sunshine Old Andy Boomtown!!

Chapter Thirteen
Above the Waters

What do communities Grayridge and Canalou have in common?

Both were founded as sawmill towns when Yankee timber industrialists determined there was money to be made in the swampy Bootheel virgin timber region of southeast Missouri.

Both towns were surrounded by swamp water from often-flooding Castor and Little Rivers.

And both communities today sit as sentinels to the past as economic ghost towns, having lost their schools, souls of their town, and the formerly vibrant, if small, retail business districts.

Unlike Canalou, Grayridge was founded upon a ridge of dry land. Canalou's earliest buildings were constructed from 1902 to 1905, up on pole stilts, to be out of the water. Initially, both villages were surrounded by swamp water and wild cane, plus, Gray's Ridge (original town name) was founded about forty years before first white settlers made their way to Canalou, which was located to the south and down deeper in the swamp.

"First known as Gray's Ridge, the town was located on a ridge of land jutting up from the swamp, approximately six and a half miles long and a half-mile wide," according to historian

Dan Whittle   67

and writer El Freda Cox in articles she penned for the Dexter, Missouri, *The Daily Statesman* newspaper.

The swamp's earliest communities of Gray's Ridge, Buffington, Salcedo, Morehouse, and Landers Ridge, were inter-connected by commerce and a shared desire of pioneering families to prosper in the swamp timber country, now a part the six-county-highly-productive-agrarian Bootheel region.

Cape Girardeau entrepreneur Louis Houck's Peavine Railroad was a major economic trigger that helped make it profitable for timber companies to enter Nigger Wool Swamp.

Grayridge 1922
Baptism of Celia Hartley
Photo Courtesy of Katherine Vanderbilt

William C. Gray and his family are credited with being the Ridge's first permanent white settlers back around 1860.

Today, on most government documents, Gray's Ridge is listed as one word, Grayridge.

Buffington, with no human habitation as of 2009, was once incorporated and bigger in population than Morehouse, Grayridge, and Canalou. At Buffington's peak, it had a bulging population of 700, comprised mostly of timber-related workers and businessmen in the late 1800s.

How important was Buffington between 1860 and 1900?

'Buffington, which was larger in population of both Grayridge and Canalou, was a primary market for my Great-Grandfather Abraham Landers Senior, a legal distiller of whiskey and spirits, and the namesake of Lander's Ridge, where he had a farm and made his whiskey," details descendant Les Landers.

Buffington was considered a *boom town* that surfaced out of the swamp where early settlers braved bears, panthers, snakes, and disease-bearing mosquitoes to harvest the virgin timber.

"Family records and stories passed down to our generation show that Great-Grandfather Landers considered Buffington an important market for his legally-made whiskey," Les Landers accounts.

Buffington's economic importance initially rivaled that of nearby Morehouse while both communities shared timber-industry-related roots from the Cape Girardeau-based Himmelberger timber family. The Himmelberger family reportedly set up a mill on the north side of the Castor River, which at that time ran and often flooded into existing swamplands to the south. That family's initial start in Bootheel timbering lasted until 2008 when Morehouse's former Himmelberger-Harrison lumber and furniture mill shut down the whirring sound of saw blades for the last time.

The mill was a substantial employment source throughout the past century for male workers from Morehouse, Canalou, Grayridge, and numerous other Bootheel towns, such as Matthews, Catron, Lilbourn and Kewanee.

However, Buffington preceded Grayridge and Canalou in official incorporation.

"Buffington was incorporated in 1884," historian Cox chronicled in a 1993 edition of Dexter, Missouri's *Daily Statesman* newspaper. "The area between Buffington and Grayridge was a quagmire as late as 1911, infested with snakes and mosquitoes."

Grayridge's Lin Hartly was born March 1, 1912, on the very day his family moved from Illinois to Missouri.

"My early memories of the place recall a lot of mud and water," Mr. Hartly penned in his "Memories of Grayridge" account.

"The principle way to get to Grayridge at that time [after 1900] was by train. The St. Louis, Iron Mountain, and Southern Railway operated four passenger trains and two local freight trains daily between Poplar Bluff and Bird's Point on the Mississippi River," Mr. Hartly recorded.

The train route ran through Grayridge, Buffington and Morehouse. "The passenger trains were called Sunshine and Old Andy," Mr. Hartly accounted. "The train Sunshine possibly received that name from the fact it operated mostly during the time the sun was shining. Old Andy, which carried the mail along with passengers, was named after her engineer, Andy Hill, who was known from one end of the line to the other after operating the train for several years."

"We rode [the train] to Morehouse to attend school," he confirmed. "One of the teachers, George P. Cole, lived at Dexter and travelled back and forth on the Sunshine train for several years."

Navigating the swamp was tough, not only for travelers, but also for families attempting to carve a living out of the heavily-wooded quagmire and swamp.

"There were two main wagon roads to Grayridge at that time," Mr. Hartly added. "One ran north along the east edge of the Ridge, which ended in the swamp. The north road you could go west to Bloomfield or go on north to Clines Island. There was a road, barely passable in good weather, from Clines Island across the swamp to Salcedo."

"My older brothers quite often guided travelers from Grayridge to Clines Island and headed them in the right direction across the swamp," Mr. Hartly detailed.

Morehouse-area native Jane Bryant Hicks traced her family's arrival in the Salcedo area around 1925.

"I remember Mom (the late Ollie Bryant) telling me about crossing the Mississippi River in their T-Model Ford," Jane journeyed back in time. "Mom was terrified because the river was frozen, and she was afraid they would fall through the ice."

After getting to the Missouri side of the river from Tennessee, the Bryants faced their toughest, most rugged part of their journey to the Bootheel. Brothers Dick and Dade Bryant had married sisters Ollie and Mattie Mae in Tennessee before their traumatic trek to Missouri's frontier-like Bootheel region.

"Dad [the late Dick Bryant] and Mom married on Dad's seventeenth birthday, and they came to Missouri shortly after that," Jane accounted. "After arrival on the Missouri side of the river, weather elements dictated use of mules and wagon.

"Dad's brother, Dade, and his uncle, Bob Bryant, and my mother, Ollie, and Dade's wife, Mattie Mae, were all in the same wagon," Jane added. "Their first house was west of Salcedo, and the dirt road was so covered with water and mud, it was all the poor mules could do to pull the wagon as they were up to their bellies in mud. Mother said she and Mattie Mae cried like babies at the sight. They were like babies themselves. Mom was only fifteen and Mattie Mae was barely sixteen.

"Once inside their first house, they could see water under the house through cracks in the wood floor," Jane noted. "You can understand their tears."

The Dade and Dick Bryant families ended up settling between Morehouse and Canalou. Dick Bryant was noted as one of the best farmers in that remote northwest corner of New Madrid County. His brother Dade worked at the Himmelberger/Harrison Lumber Mill.

After graduating from Morehouse High School and being crowned Sikeston's Cotton Carnival Queen, Jane Bryant married Grayridge High graduate Dee Wayne Hicks in the late 1950s.

Travel was difficult when the Hicks and Bryant families first settled in Stoddard and New Madrid counties.

"Due to the swamp, which was yet to be drained by the Little River Drainage District, there was no road to the east, directly out of Grayridge toward Morehouse and Sikeston," Mr. Hartly confirmed.

After the turn of the century "the principle industry at Grayridge was the manufacture of slack barrel staves," Mr. Hartly recorded. "The mill was owned and operated by J. W.

McColgan, who also established a store there in 1901. There was also a hoop mill at Grayridge around the turn of the century with a wooden tram railroad running south to furnish the logs from which the hoops were made."

"The Harlan brothers, Lee, Frank, and Ed, operated saw mills at different locations in the area," Hartly added. "They also ran the first, locally-owned, steam-powered thrashing machine in that part of the country."

Early Grayridge had two barbers, Barney Haley and Tote Miller. Barber Haley has descendants living in Morehouse and Sikeston as of 2009. Barber Haley's son, the late J. L. Haley, eventually became a prominent businessman and elected city government official in Morehouse.

Mr. Hartly experienced history as it was being made in what turned out to be America's largest earth-moving project in history, even larger in scope and dirt tonnage than the famous Panama Canal project.

"The swamps were being drained by 1912," Mr. Hartly heralded. "There were ditches running north and south every mile from Crowley's Ridge to within one mile of Grayridge. The big swamp to the east [which included Canalou to the south of Morehouse] was yet to be drained. Two floating dredges were assembled here. There was also a floating cook shack and bunk house for crews that accompanied each dredge."

"These were busy times," Mr. Hartly continued. "Several people from outside the area were working here and needed a place to stay. We had a large eight room house that had been built by the original Gray family in the 1880s, and my mother kept boarders for four dollars per week; plus, she served a noon meal for twenty-five cents.

"One of Mother's regular customers was large landowner J. W. McColgan, who also owned a mill and store. He owned a great deal of farm land and much livestock."

"Stoddard County [and New Madrid County] was open range country and most people just let their livestock run loose," Mr. Hartly shared. "The hogs were left in the woods to fatten on the acorns in the fall. Each farmer had a registered ear mark by which he could identify his stock. Our family mark was the swallow fork on the left ear and a half crop on the right ear."

Roads were tough to establish and maintain in the early swamp land prior to Cape Girardeau-based Little River Drainage District's massive dredging project. During rainy weather, particularly during cold winter months, the mud and swamp seemed bottomless and didn't lend its self to permanent solid-bedded roads.

Grayridge didn't become an official incorporated village until well past 1900.

"Grayridge was incorporated [only briefly] as a village in 1919 and a custom of the era was a poll tax," accounted Mr. Hartly. "Everyone had to pay or spend so much time working on the roads with designated teams. This was the way roads were maintained, if such could be called maintenance. You were credited with time worked. Most road work was done by mule teams and scrapers. The mud gave way to gravel in the 1920s and to concrete in the 1930s. U. S. Highway 60 eventually split the farm where I grew up."

And this account of recorded history provides us a road back into time, when our Bootheel forefathers (and mothers) braved the swampy elements and dangers to carve out a timber-related existence.

Obviously, they were brave, tough, and hard-working souls.

Chapter Fourteen
Canalou's Funeral

Norma Arbuckle Busby's funeral in early 2008 symbolized yet another passing of one of Canalou's bedrock families dating back to when the former sawmill village initially arose out of the swamp to become a vibrant agrarian-based farming community.

Her passing on December 29, 2007, brought the curtain down on former Canalou Mayor L. L. and Coela Greer Arbuckle's family that goes back to when first settlers came in boats and on log rafts to retrieve their mail and get supplies at town founder D. S. Kreps' first little red-building store and post office in 1903, one year after original settlers moved into the Nigger Wool Swamp to harvest the huge Cypress and Oak trees.

The symbolism of Mrs. Busby's death, the last of seven children born to Mr. and Mrs. Arbuckle, was not lost on present-day Canalou Baptist Church preacher, Reverend Dewayne Coleman, who attended Mrs. Busby's Church of Christ funeral service at Sikeston's Blanchard Funeral Home. Burial followed in Sikeston's Garden of Memories, the resting place of numerous early Canalou residents, including my father, Hubert Alexander Whittle.

"When I see an obituary in area newspapers for one of Canalou's early families, I try to come out of respect to the community where I pastor one of only three congregations to have served the spiritual needs of this historic, once vibrant little New Madrid County town," the Reverend Coleman noted. "The Church of Christ, Assembly of God and Canalou Baptist congregations go back to when they were founded in 1912. Sadly today, only the Assembly of God and Canalou Baptist congregations continue on. We came today out of respect for our Church of Christ brothers and sisters, especially those who blazed a trail and Christian lifestyle in that former rough and woolly swamp.

"It was no accident that when the town's only three churches were founded in 1912, that was the same year town residents voted to close saloons and outlaw the sale of liquor, which remained illegal until Prohibition was lifted in the 1930s," the Reverend Coleman accounted.

In addition to helping start the Church of Christ, the Arbuckles were leading forces in the fight against whiskey consumption in the swamp village that early historians accurately labeled as "rough and woolly" dating back to its inception as one of Missouri's last true frontier towns.

"As a grandson of L. L. Arbuckle, who died as mayor of Canalou during an actual town council meeting in the 1950s at tiny Canalou City Hall, I would have been horse-whipped if caught in one of Canalou's saloons or pool halls," confirms Canalou native Alva Jones, a nephew to Norma Ellen Busby, eighty-nine, whom he called Aunt Norm.

"I was groomed, as a boy, to become a preacher. We were devout Church of Christ folks dating back further than I can remember," noted Jones.

New Madrid Church of Christ Minister Ed Thomason, who also owns and publishes New Madrid's *Weekly Record* newspaper, conducted the funeral for Mrs. Busby.

"Her upbringing in a Christian family was evidenced by the way she lived her life, as a devoted child member of the early Church of Christ in Canalou. Later in adult life, she was a faithful wife of Church of Christ minister, the late Daryl Gene Busby," Brother Thomason accounted. "This family was on the front line of early Christianity in former swamp village Canalou that sits today in the northwest corner of New Madrid as an economic ghost town."

Canalou Mayor James Donald Taul touched on representation of Norma Ellen Arbuckle Busby's death.

"As the last living child of the historic Arbuckle family, Mrs. Busby's death is very symbolic of what's happened in the decline of Canalou from its economic and social heyday in the 1930s, 1940s, and first half of the 1950s. When there were, during those times, five hundred residents surrounded by seven grocery stores, the Bank of Canalou, and the Lampher Hotel," Mayor Taul notes. "With the advent of farm technology, and the loss of our school in 1958, Canalou started losing its businesses one by one, starting when Jim and Stella Poe moved their grocery store from Canalou to Morehouse in the mid-1950s."

Johnny Arbuckle, another nephew to Mrs. Busby, led the prayer at his Aunt Norm's funeral.

"Lord, we're thankful for having Aunt Norm as long as we did," Johnny noted "Our grandparents and parents made a good place for us to grow up in Canalou. My Grandfather Arbuckle not only led in formation of our Church of Christ in Canalou, he was a leader in terms of serving as mayor, and as a justice of the peace."

Chapter Fifteen

Oran Timber

Retired Navy career man Sherm Greenlee, born in 1936, loves the hustle and bustle of living in New York.

But he couldn't be prouder of ancestors who helped settle what is now known as southeast Missouri, often called the Bootheel by locals.

It was the military promise of no cotton picking that launched Greenlee out of cotton, soybean, and corn fields.

"I have never felt prouder of a group of people. Our forefathers were tough, rugged, and innovative to brave the elements to settle southeast Missouri," noted decorated Vietnam War veteran Greenlee. "It was a slower way of life in the Bootheel, but when the Navy promised me I would never, ever have to pick or chop cotton again, well, that was my way out."

His Bootheel ancestry trail began after his forefathers moved to the region from Kentucky in the 1880s. The family trail led from Oran, down to the inner-most bowels of the massive Nigger Wool Swamp.

"My mother [May Hilton, born in 1901] told stories about how she worked in the common kitchen while menfolks of the family worked in logging and timber-cutting camps in and around Oran," Greenlee traced back through time. "Although she was only six-years-old, all females were expected to work in the common kitchen as my Grandfather George Washington Hilton worked with the other men in logging. She worked alongside Grandmother Virginia Dismuke Hilton, a small frail woman who had a lot of stamina despite her diminutive size.

"My grandmother was the oldest of five children. She was a frail little woman who never agreed about anything with Grandpa," accounted Greenlee. "They disagreed so much. I don't know how they agreed to move to Canalou. And I don't know how they got together enough to have five children of their own.

"George Washington Hilton landed his initial Bootheel farm job. Cavanaugh Farm that comprised most of what was called Big Ridge," confirmed Greenlee. "But they had floated to their destination down into the bowels of the big swamp region.

"It was around 1918 when our grandparents moved south, further into the Bootheel," Sherm detailed. "They had to use a boat to navigate through the swamp to get to the dry ridge of acreage known as Big Ridge.

"Grandpa Hilton became a farm foreman for Judge Cavanaugh, and he rode herd over the farm operation atop a big Pinto steed," Greenlee shared. "Fellow farm laborers referred to him as Mister George. To friends and neighbors, he was affectionately known as Uncle George.

"Our family still refers to that large farm as The Cavanaugh Place. Grandpa Hilton was foreman for Mr. Cavanaugh for many years, overseeing the other farm workers who lived in cracker box houses along the farm-to-market road that led from Big Ridge to downtown Canalou. Those tenant houses were across the road from what is now the Big Ridge Church, and just down the road from the old Negro Big Ridge School."

Sherm Greenlee recalls going to church at Big Ridge General Baptist Church.

"Farm and church neighbors included Roy and Offie Johnson whose oldest son, Gay Johnson, was in the same class at Canalou School with my brother, Curtis," Sherm shared. "Gay's younger brother, Jerry, was my classmate. As fellow church members, the Johnsons were part of our life back in Canalou farming country that followed the vast timber-harvest era.

"Grandpa was a deacon at Big Ridge Church for as long as I can remember, and was well known for his amens voiced throughout the sermon," grandson Greenlee reported. "He'd often visit other churches, but found them too quiet, as in not enough amens."

"Mom and Pop (Carles Greenlee) produced twelve children, three of whom died in infancy," the youngest Greenlee son accounted. "Nine of us grew to adulthood, but Mom had several miscarriages that they simply didn't count. All of her children were delivered by mid-wife Bessie Turner except our youngest sister, who was called a show-off since she was born in the hospital at Cairo, Illinois.

"Pop was twenty-four years old when he and Mom tied the knot in 1917," the son noted. "They didn't talk much about their courtship. Mom, who was sixteen at the time, did acknowledge meeting him. I would meet him walking on the road, and I would walk way on the other side of the road, Mom told us. Well, at some point, that changed, for they walked down the aisle together in 1917."

"Pop was almost immediately 'drafted' into the Army, and his company, while stationed in Kansas, was preparing to ship out to Europe when the flu epidemic broke out. Pop became a flu victim, and received a medical discharge, a fact my father was happy to accept.

"I had three siblings die during this time. One died of diphtheria, another from whooping cough," Greenlee recalled. "There was just no way to treat childhood diseases and no prevention in the late 1930s and early 1940s.

"While living on the Wild's Farm, in the very early 1940s, a cousin of mine came down with double pneumonia, a deadly malady of that era," Greenlee noted. "In those days, we just waited for them to die, but Morehouse physician, Dr. Sam Sarno, came out to the farm and administered a new miracle drug called penicillin. My cousin was up and about in a day or two."

Young farm boy Sherm Greenlee remembers excitement born with a new cloud of dust on their remote unpaved farm lane in the 1940s.

"While working in the cotton fields, we hoped the approaching car or truck would turn off at our house, for Pop would have to stop picking or chopping cotton to talk to whomever it was," Sherm recalls. "This would give us a little break, time to goof off a little from the back-breaking hard work in those cotton fields.

"We particularly got excited when route men would come. Not only did ice delivery man Hubert Bond (of Canalou) bring us ice, he brought news from the outside world," Sherm detailed. "In the winter time, Mr. Bond delivered coal to heat our home. The traveling shoe-cobbler man was Price Baker, whose home and shop was located just across the street from Canalou School. His wife was a Durbin before they got married. The Durbins are some of our in-laws."

Sherm doesn't recall any atheists being found in a field of cotton.

"We all prayed. If you picked cotton, you were a praying person," Sherm added. "We'd look for clouds on the horizon and pray for rain. We were very disappointed when rain did not come.

"During this era, Granddad George Washington Hilton and our granny rented a house inside Canalou city limits, from Emmitt Greer, on streets now named Van Buren and Jefferson," Sherm traced his family legacy.

What did folks do for entertainment when not cutting timber or working in the cotton fields?

"Legend has it that Charter Oak, like Canalou, was known for having strong drinks and gambling opportunities," Greenlee accounted. "A man named Tucker, I believe, had a pool hall and beer joint along with a little side room for weekend gambling down at Charter Oak. I had a brother-in-law ([Byford Durbin] who frequently occupied one of those seats in the little gambling room to the side."

The Greenlees greatly impacted the culture of Canalou.

"Yes, my uncle Leonard Greenlee was quite the businessman with a skating rink in Canalou," Sherm described. "In the 1940s, Uncle Leonard moved the skating rink to Lilbourn, and eventually to Dexter where he sold it to Zurel Satterfield."

Leonard Greenlee also served as Canalou's town marshal in that period.

"Uncle Homer Greenlee also lived at Canalou and was initially a half-owner of the skating rink that was filled to capacity on Saturday nights with the likes of town girls Patsy Hopper and Maxine Harrison," Sherm noted.

Children from farms miles around would flock to Canalou on Saturday nights in that era. They would either go skating or attend a moving picture show at the new theater built in 1944 by Canalou entrepreneur Boots Conn.

"Uncle Homer, after operating a theater at Essex, later moved to Texas for a career in home building," Sherm recalled. "Uncle Kirby Greenlee went from the Wild's Farm to Sikeston, and then to Texas, for a career in carpentry. All were successful in life and enjoyed their retirement years."

Following life in a tenant house on the Cavanaugh Farm, Carles and May Greenlee moved their family to a farm in nearby Landers Ridge.

"Although we lived on the Witt Farm, in the first house on the left past Landers Ridge Church, we helped farm on the Trammell Farm just down the road between the two curves in the farm-to-market road between Canalou and Morehouse.

"One enjoyable aspect of life on the farm came as a surprise when some fast-moving truck or car would run over and kill a chicken," Sherm shared. "Nothing went to waste, so Mother usually fried that road-kill chicken. Sometimes, when our parents were not looking, we'd help the cause along, for we dearly loved Mom's fried chicken when fixed with a big bowl of milk thickening gravy. It was a meal fit for royalty.

"Sometimes we'd sneak a fryer-sized chicken from the chicken coop, and throw it off the chicken house roof to see if it could fly. Usually, they could not fly, and the fall would kill them. We would have fried chicken for supper, but we ate only after receiving some corporal punishment for sending those chickens to their premature, fowl deaths."

From Landers Ridge, the Greenlees resided in Stoddard County's unincorporated Clines Island community where Sherm and his three sisters attended elementary school.

"On Clines Island, my three younger sisters and I walked one and a half miles to the one-room school house, which still stands today and serves as a church," Sherm shared.

He recalls some "rough and tumble" skirmishes among schoolyard boys of that era.

"Being smaller and younger than some of the boys usually meant I got my butt kicked during elementary school years," Sherm remembers. "Being smaller, I sometimes felt picked on by the bigger boys."

Sometimes, it was the affection of a girlfriend that triggered those youthful fist fights.

"I always tried to save a seat for this one particularly cute and bright little girl, but Fat Roper and Pee Gink Wren would also try to sit beside her. I usually got my butt kicked.

"I recall one teacher at Clines Island School named Mrs. Muir, who would see me do something against the rules," Sherm noted from school days. "She would walk slowly around the room, taking her time and come up behind me, and then, strike me upside the head, knocking me all the way out of my seat. They'd call 911 today if a teacher did that to a student."

There was life after Bootheel farming for Sherm Greenlee and his parents.

"Pop eventually got a job as a night watchman at the old Brown Shoe Factory in Sikeston," Sherm noted. "Pop retired from the shoe factory at age sixty-five and became a gentleman farmer in Cedar Hill, Missouri, with one of my brothers. Pop died in 1976 at age eighty-four. Mom died at age ninety-seven in 1998. She kept count of all the grandchildren, and then the great- and great-great-grandchildren. At the time of her passing, there were more than ninety."

Sherm credits the Navy with greatly impacting his life away

from Bootheel farming country.

"Joining the Navy was the greatest thing I ever did. Not only was I honored to serve my nation for thirty years, but now they are caring for my wife and I in a great manner. When I joined the Navy, the recruiter in Sikeston held true to his word: I would never pick or chop cotton again. . ."

He had quit school in the eighth grade at Sikeston, and joined the Navy there.

"The Navy encourages continued education, so after my GED, I entered college and never looked back," Sherm accounted. "I now have two degrees from the university, one in medical technology and the other in management and communication."

From Bootheel cotton fields of boyhood to a distinguished military career served around the globe has been the real-life saga of Sherm Greenlee.

"Being a sharecropper's son and moving often was a hard life, but a good life," Sherm summed up. "It taught us strong loyalty among family, and a strong work ethic, as in doing an honest day's work for an honest day's pay."

Chapter Sixteen

Westerfield Murder Trial

After the arrival of the initial loggers in 1902, it wasn't long before improvised saloon tents popped up in the swamp village uniquely named Canalou by railroad man Louis Houck of Cape Girardeau, Missouri.

Activities in those first tent-covered "saloons" earned Canalou the reputation of being a wild and woolly place.

As Canalou evolved from swamp camp to incorporated town in 1909, more permanent buildings were constructed. Many were built on stilts to keep folks and commerce up out of the water of Nigger Wool Swamp.

The timber-working men would work hard all week out in primitive tent camps out in the swamp, "and then would drink, fight and land in jail on weekends," explained Joy Engram Whitten of Sikeston, in a 2009 interview.

Personal disputes often bubbled up during the swamp's tough and dangerous timber-harvest era.

"But in that swamp culture, it wasn't a fight merely to see which was the best man," accounted Alva Jones, now age seventy-seven. "They fought to kill, especially in the first thirty to forty years, according to legends handed down by my ancestors."

"In Canalou as I was growing up in the 1930s and 1940s, it was not mere fist fights each and every Saturday night," added Canalou native Bill Newman. "When the logging men were insulted, they meant to kill one another."

Through the mid-1950s, Canalou's saloons outnumbered churches. Several shootings and knife fights that began in the saloons or over strong drink resulted in multiple deaths in the community's first four decades.

One of those fierce feuds occured between Joy Whitten's Great-Grandfather Isaac Coleman Westerfield and Perry Arnold, another timber-working-era resident of Canalou. It resulted in the latter's death.

"But this time the quarrel was more personal," Joy accounted. "Mr. Arnold told Great-Granddad Westerfield he was coming to kill him. Granddad was waiting, but not before warning the man that he would kill him if he came on his property."

According to Westerfield family-preserved annals, only a few days passed before neighbors came to warn Mr. Westerfield, one of Canalou's earliest settlers, that "Perry Arnold is coming!"

True to his word, Mr. Westerfield did shoot and kill the approaching Mr. Arnold, a slaying that made instant sensational news headlines in Bloomfield, Missouri's *Standard-Tribune* and the *Dexter Statesman* newspapers, since the slaying took place on the eastern-most edge of Stoddard County near Canalou.

The shoot-out had occurred at the Tanner Logging Camp near Tanner School.

On November 23, 1926, the *Standard-Tribune* gave account of Mr. Westerfield's ultimate trial on a murder charge. His defense attorneys included Morehouse lawyer J. Val Baker, attorneys George Munger and Eugene Munger of Bloomfield, and O. L. Munger of Piedmont.

The newspaper's lead paragraph set the highly-publicized murder trial scene: "Coleman Westerfield, charged with the murder of Perry Arnold at a logging camp in the vicinity of Tanner school house, went to trial in circuit court here yesterday afternoon, (November 22, 1926)."

After being granted a change of venue, defendant Westerfield's trial was presided over by Judge E. P. Dorris of Alton, Missouri.

Newspaper files that also chronicled: "The state is being represented by Prosecuting Attorney C. A. Powell and Prosecuting Attorney-elect R. Kip Briney."

"The jury is composed of G. A. Asa, Authur Cooper, L. L. Smith, Levi Hoyt, Elmer Linge, Ed Badgley, K. W. Tarpley, W. T. Hayden, J. B. Siler, Wilson Frank, J. H. Bolin, and Walter Rankin."

It didn't take long for jurors to acquit Mr. Westerfield, as chronicled in the *Dexter Statesman* newspaper after hearing the evidence.

"Two days were consumed in hearing the evidence and argument of counsel. The case went to the jury at nine o'clock Tuesday night, after an evening session of the court to complete the argument," noted the *Dexter Statesman*. "The jury deliberated for about an hour and a half before bringing the *not guilty* verdict."

This was after "Westerfield satisfied the jury that he was acting in self-defense in slaying Arnold," according to files of the *Dexter Statesman* and *Standard-Tribune* newspapers.

Many Canalou residents sighed with relief with Mr. Westerfield's acquittal, for by the 1920s, the family had earned high community respect.

"I remember as a boy growing up in Canalou, we all, although not actual kinfolks, referred out of respect to them as Uncle Coleman and his wife as Aunt Ida," noted historian Les Landers. "It was a respect thing. I know, for we all attended the Canalou Church of Christ together."

Chapter Seventeen

Canalou's Soft Side

Although Canalou, particularly in its earliest days, was often described as "wild and woolly," the community had a soft side with a tender touch confirms native females Gladys Johns Drake, Frances Abernathy, and Sue *"Baby"* Bixler.

"I take great pride in being reared in Canalou," noted Gladys. "When a family needed help, help was there, whether it was transportation, food, quilts, clothing, or medical care."

"It was family, growing up in Canalou," Sue Baby recalls. "My memory of life in Canalou begins at about age four. We lived on a dirt road, about a mile north of town next to the Whittles. Beginning at a very early age, it became apparent the entire town was one huge family."

"Everyone lent a helping hand anytime a family needed help," verified lifelong resident Frances Bishop Abernathy.

Giving begins at home, and one of my personal earliest recollections of charity came the year that my sister Mary June and Momma Whittle had worked extra hours picking cotton to earn enough coins to purchase their dream coat, a bright red full-length coat as pictured in the latest Sears-Roebuck catalogue.

And finally, the day of high drama for the two females of our family arrived, when Post Master Don Kochel left a note in Box fifty-two, our family's long time numbered mail box. There was a package to be picked up at the window.

Sister June and Momma emitted girl-like giggles as they picked up the parcel. Instead of waiting to get it home, June ripped the big package open as Momma drove our dark blue 1951 Plymouth coupe to our home and farm located on old railroad maps at Tram Switch between Canalou and Morehouse.

"Oh, Mother, it's so pretty," June judged as she held the soft, bright red cloth to her cheek.

"It's prettier than it looked in the catalogue," Momma chimed in agreement.

And as good fortune would have it, the coat fit both Momma and her teenage daughter, which meant June could use it for important social events at school and church, and Momma could use it for important business meetings at the Production Credit Association in Sikeston and at funerals.

But as fate would have it, they never wore the coat publicly.

Tundra like conditions set in as fall ended and winter arrived with a vengeance in 1952 with sub-freezing temperatures causing problems, such as frozen pumps and pipes.

It was on one of the coldest mornings of the winter shortly thereafter that sister June did something that made a deep lasting impression on a little farm boy.

"Mother, look here comes [farm laborers *Little* Polly and *Tall* Lum] walking down the road," June assessed from our kitchen window looking north toward farm neighbors Bruce Gene, Harold David and Yvoin Bryant's farm house.

As the two walking neighbors got closer, Mother could see that Little Polly had no coat to cover her bare arms in the sub-freezing weather.

"She's shivering in the cold," Mother observed.

"She's freezing to death, with only a thin, short-sleeved shirt," added June.

As a boy of eight, it amazed me to observe what happened next.

When June looked at Momma, without one word being spoken June walked out the front door of our farm house and wrapped their new warm red coat around Little Polly's shivering shoulders as she and her tall husband walked on toward town.

"Mother, tears came to Little Polly's eyes as I put our new red wool coat around her cold shoulders," June shared upon reentering our warm farm house.

We always enjoyed watching Little Polly and Tall Lum walk up and down our dirt farm road, for the woman with the short legs had to skip and hop every second and third long-legged step that Tall Lum took toward their destination. They were known for being dependable good farm folks.

As a real small tyke, I remember the older women of our community, such as Louise Landers, Addie Bixler, Mommie Gowen, Edna Taul, Vera Kochel, Mrs. Moffett and Mrs. Hicks, Ailene Lasters, Mae Landers, Mrs. Metcalf and Mrs. Melton, Nell Neel, Helen Drake, and Momma Whittle would gather at Canalou Baptist Church for a quilting party. Don't let the word party throw you, though. The women were working their fingers nimbly and quickly to construct and sew quilts to be given to needy families before another cold winter arrived. Most often, this charitable work was done during rainy and cold non-crop working times.

Regular sewing circles were also held by ladies at nearby Landers' Ridge Baptist Church.

It was high drama to a little farm boy to witness these ladies, who had artist level talents with needles and thread, assemble their wooden quilting frames that hung from the ceiling, and then listen to the debate about which pattern they would use to design the next quilt.

It was also a great opportunity to catch up on town gossip, especially for the farm ladies who didn't get to town over once or twice a week.

Each winter, women of the community would quietly go about gathering extra britches, shirts, and jackets for children of the community whose parents could not afford for them to have nice warm clothing to wear to school and church.

Lifelong Canalou-area resident Frances Abernathy describes the neighborliness. "If a family needed transportation to the doctor, someone always stepped forward," added Mrs. Abernathy, at age seventy-six. "If another family was short on food due to illness, others would cook and bring food to them."

"And we had food at frequent community gatherings at the church and school cafeteria," recalls Sue Baby, a successful Enid, Oklahoma, businesswoman and one of the most financially successful people to have grown up in Canalou. "In growing up there, everyone gathered for everything. Food at the church was especially funny. Mom would cook a whole meal. But we were only allowed to eat what she took, for some folks were just not clean enough to satisfy our mother. But we fed everyone. I remember even the town drunks were our friends and we were taught, strongly instructed, to treat them with respect too. I have such fond memories of so many people there even the town drunks we counted as friends and treated with respect."

Such was the soft side of life in a former swamp village described as "rough and woolly."

Chapter Eighteen

Political Powers

How did "Bootheel" voters help change state, national and ultimately, world history?

More specifically, how did J. V. Conran and Roy W. Harper, both young relatively-unknown lawyers from New Madrid and Pemiscot counties respectively, get in position to play pivotal roles in the 1934 election of dark house, Kansas City-area politician Harry S. Truman to the U. S. Senate?

This ultimately led to the Show Me State's most famous political person to occupy the White House.

Primarily, research for this chapter about the political culture of the Bootheel in that era was done at the Truman Presidential Library in Independence, Missouri, former President Truman's home town.

And some information came through Poplar Bluff native Brenda Gayle Harper Lewis, a cousin to lawyer Harper, and wife of (retired) prominent Missouri and Louisiana attorney Garry Lewis, who graduated from Grayridge and Richland High School in Stoddard County in the 1960s.

"My wife Gayle's father, (Rodney Harper) who had a barber shop in Holcomb before moving the family to St. Louis, was a close 'first cousin' of Pemiscot County Prosecuting Attorney

Roy W. Harper," noted barrister Lewis. "We were blessed to be frequent guests in Judge Harper's St. Louis-area home prior to his death. He was always more than happy to help anyone who had roots down in his beloved boyhood Bootheel."

"They [Conran and Harper] helped get Harry Truman elected to the Senate [1934] by delivering the vote in the Bootheel," Gayle Harper Lewis accounted. "Subsequently, both were offered significant cabinet posts in Washington after Truman became U. S. President following the death of Franklin D. Roosevelt."

Although neither took Truman's offer to move into powerful national political slots in Washington, D. C., Truman did ultimately help Harper become senior federal judge in Missouri's Eastern District, based in St. Louis.

President Truman's Republican counter-parts in Washington had repeatedly blocked Bootheel lawyer Harper's judgeship appointment because of cited "cronyism" until President Truman threatened to kill some of their bills after quipping publicly: "Do you think I'm going to appoint someone I don't like?!"

In researching annals of history in the Truman Library, two early political threads led Harper and Conran to establish working relationships and close friendships to "Give 'em hell, Harry," as Truman came to be known out on the campaign trails across Missouri and America.

It was cotton, a major Bootheel crop, and Judge Harper's and Conran's help in establishing an effective statewide Young Democrats Club that helped cement their political influence with the man destined for the White House.

The late Judge Harper described in an oral history to Truman Library interviewer J. R. Fuchs, how "the Bootheel" gained influence with "The Man from Independence."

"I first met President Truman during the primary campaign (for U. S. Senate) in 1934, the first time of many times he campaigned at the Pemiscot County Fair," Judge Harper noted.

Judge Harper, who had moved as a boy to Steele from his 1905 birthplace of Gibson down in Dunklin County, the southern-most county geographically in Missouri, did not start out being for Mr. Truman in the primary.

"As a matter of fact, I [as chairman of Pemiscot Democrats] introduced him when he made a speech at Steele, although I was not one of his supporters," confirmed Harper, who had attended the University of Missouri for his law degree.

Harper did back Truman in the general election and all subsequent elections.

It was at college that young Mr. Harper became active in Young Democrat Club activities, thus building contacts throughout the Show Me State. Mr. Conran, after attending public schools in New Madrid, also got his law degree from the University of Missouri and was active in promoting the Young Democrat Club throughout the state.

New Madrid's historic newspaper, *The Weekly Record* that goes back to the 1860s, described Mr. Conran's impact on Missouri Young Democrats: "He, many years ago, was president of the Missouri Young Demcrats, an organization that enjoyed great growth under his leadership."

Mr. Conran was born in 1899, in rural Mt. Pleasant, a son of the late Susan Robbins Conran and James V. Conran, an attorney who committed suicide while young J. V. was about ten years old. J. V. lived his entire life in his beloved New Madrid County.

After failing twice at being elected New Madrid County's prosecuting attorney in the 1920s, J. V. Conran finally got elected prosecuting attorney in 1930, an office he held for more than three decades.

"I learned a lot about politics in 1926 and 1928 [when he lost races]," Mr. Conran was quoted in *The Weekly Record* newspaper that remains in publication today. "For one thing, I learned how to go after blocks of votes instead of individual votes. . . ."

"Later, political leaders would say that Mr. Conran headed the 'slickest rural machine in the state," and had the 'most desirable block of votes anywhere in Missouri," *The Weekly Record* recorded.

Mr. Conran quickly elevated to a position of strong political influence not only in his home county, but the entire Bootheel, as described by the late Durward W. Gilmore, a lawyer who came from an influential Mississippi County political family.

Lawyer Gilmore ended up serving as a state senator and as a circuit judge in the twenty-eighth Judicial Circuit. He also served as president of the Young Democrats of America from 1949-51.

When Truman Library interviewer Neil M. Johnson asked lawyer Gilmore about "what kind of Democrat was J. V. Conran?" the late Judge Gilmore minced no words.

"He (J. V.) didn't know there was any other party but the Democrat Party," Gilmore responded. "He was prosecuting attorney of New Madrid County for years and years. If you wanted to do any business in New Madrid County, you had better be getting along with J. V. Conran because he sent innocent men to the penitentiary and he let criminals go free, depending on where you stood with him. That was true.

"We called him [Conran] 'The Boss of the Bootheel'," Judge Gilmore described. "If J. V.'s for you, we're all for you."

Mr. Conran's hometown newspaper credited the man thusly: "He was said to have cleaned up gambling in New Madrid County, improved roads and schools, and put local government on a sound financial basis."

It was during and after the hotly-contested 1934 U. S. Senate race that Harper and Conran bonded closely with Truman. However, Truman had detractors in the Bootheel, stemming primarily from his controversial alliance with Kansas City political boss Tom Pendergast, who later went to prison.

Gilmore's father, Mississippi County Judge (known as commissioner today) Ernest G. Gilmore, helped deflect Bootheel opposition to Truman. Prior to 1934, Harry Truman and Ernest Gilmore served in similar political posts as "county judges" in opposite corners of the state.

"As county judge, he (Ernest) talked about (fellow county judge) Truman being an honest man, when people would bring up that Pendergast mess up in Kansas City," Durward Gilmore testified. "Dad would tell folks that he had witnessed Truman in action, that he was always for what's right."

Bootheel business and farm interests came together politically for the "good of the Bootheel economy" after Truman went to Washington. Judge Harper helps trace the political trail of impact from the Bootheel to Washington.

"I first became really well-acquainted with him [Truman] when I went with a Bootheel delegation consisting of Sikeston newspaper publisher and Polecat Columnist Charley Blanton Senior, Sikeston banker Ed Coleman and J. V. Conran to lobby for a cotton allotment bill, which gave the South states twenty acres of cotton to the forty [acres], but it only gave Bootheel of Missouri eight acres to the forty, which meant that our [Bootheel farming] section of Missouri was in real trouble if the original bill was enacted as law.

"I was leading the efforts to have the allotment raised for Bootheel cotton growers," Harper described. "My only interest in it was that if we were able to get a fair allotment, the area would do well, and I would indirectly profit."

When the final vote was taken in Congress, Bootheel cotton producer allotments were increased from eight to sixteen acres (of cotton) to the forty after Truman and the increasingly powerful Bootheel delegation had threatened to kill the entire bill.

"Senator Truman had promised his support," Judge Harper confirmed. "I drafted the proposed amendment that would change [the bill]."

Although cotton was primarily grown only in the six-county Bootheel region, it was the state's largest cash crop in that era.

"In other words, while cotton was the biggest cash crop in Missouri at the time, it was only raised in basically the six Bootheel counties," Judge Harper assessed. "The South (states) wanted all the acreage they could get…they did not look with favor upon southeast Missouri cotton growers…"

How Bootheel politics helped win Truman's 1934 senatorial election was explained by Harper.

"We reached an agreement with St. Louis political bosses,

where we [in the Bootheel] would give the big end of our vote for their candidate for governor, and they would deliver either eight or nine big St. Louis wards for Truman," Judge Harper described. "The campaign became a very bitter, hotly contested race, especially in the early part of the campaign.

"In late spring [1934] one of my dear friends and one of my close political friends, J. V. Conran, went with me to St. Louis," Harper confirmed. "J. V. and I worked together [politically] for a number of years."

Harper said he and other Bootheel political leaders felt Truman had done more for southeast Missouri interests, along with Sen. Bennett Clark, than other state politicians of that era.

Interviewer Fuchs asked Harper to describe Conran's political clout.

"He [Conran] pretty well determined who they [Bootheel electorate] supported for state races, congress and senate races, and so on," Harper assessed. "They could deliver eighty to eighty-five percent of the vote in the Bootheel. In Pemiscot County, we didn't operate the way that New Madrid did, although our [county] organization delivered seventy-five to eighty percent of the votes to the people we supported."

That's how J. V. Conran and Roy W. Harper, two young rural politically-savvy attorneys from the Bootheel, came to wield state and national political clout!!

President Truman paid a "personal visit" to Mr. Conran in 1962, after the Bootheel political power boss became seriously ill.

When Mr. Conran died in January 1970, prominent state and national public figures who attended his funeral included former Missouri Governor Warren E. Hearnes, U. S. Sen. Thomas Eagleton, Secretary of State James C. Kirkpatrick, State Auditor Haskell Holman plus multiple state senators and representatives from throughout the Show-Me State.

Chapter Nineteen
Life of Michael Parkes

Meet Mike Parks, Canalou Elementary School first grade pupil in 1950.

Meet Michael Parkes, 2012, world famous artist/sculptor who was born and nurtured through early years of life in the culture of a former Bootheel swamp village that his grandfather, timber baron L. E. Weaks, helped carve out of wilderness and cane breaks.

Michael is Canalou's most famous world-acclaimed celebrity/artist/sculptor, who has made his fame painting and sculpting from his home and studio overlooking Gibraltar in southern-most Spain.

After contacting him by Internet, the famous man made a special effort to make time for interviews to contribute to this book about the unique culture, time, and place he grew up in.

"It was as joyful a boyhood a boy could hope to have," Michael described.

Michael was born October 12, 1944, at a Sikeston, Missouri hospital, the parents were East Prairie farmer Albert Parks and Agatha "Sissy" Weaks Parks, a Canalou native girl born in Nigger Wool Swamp in 1912.

She dedicated her life to nurturing her husband and son and began a lifelong teaching career at small country schools in the Bootheel such as Yellow Dog and old Higgerson School, a museum today in New Madrid.

Hoping to help with marketing, Michael and his wife Maria added the "E" to the Parkes name in their early marriage-era, thinking it helped in marketing.

"We were young," Maria admitted.

Although Michael markets across the globe, he still talks like he's from Canalou.

During his numerous media interviews from around the world, Michael frequently refers to his unique hometown of Canalou in the Bootheel of southeast Missouri.

"When I discuss my boyhood experiences with friends here in Europe, they often think I'm talking about growing up back in the economically-depressed years of the 1920s and 1930s, and culturally speaking, it was like that in Canalou during the 1940s and 1950s." Michael described.

"There were no wealthy people, maybe the cotton gin man had money, but no one of great wealth resided in Canalou.

"But we didn't consider ourselves poor or in poverty, for we all were in similar circumstances. Canalou was a great little town to grow up in. Most merchants of the small groceries were not wealthy, making it from one Saturday to the next. I recall outdoor toilets and pot-bellied heating stoves, so it was some kind of poverty. But I never felt poor.

"I drive my wife and friends in England crazy when instead of saying refrigerator, I say ice box," added Michael with a smile. "Many artists are influenced by the masters, such as Van Gogh, but I was influenced by Canalou's little cinema, and Mother Nature in a special culture, plus parents and a special aunt whom I have grown to respect and admire more and more as I've matured.

"It took a special, strong stock of people, intelligent and strong-willed people, including my Grandfather L. E. Weaks, who came to the big swamp to harvest the timber," Michael noted. "The people before our generation did the hard part, carving a life and creating a culture that afforded me and others a very special, safe, and unique boyhood place to grow up."

The world-famous artist/sculptor remembers the culture but not a lot of individual people.

"I don't remember my earliest school teachers, for example, but I remember how I sculpted mud turtles in the unique mud that the Canalou-area was known for," the artist stroked back through time. "I would get a handful of mud, for example, and begin a process of sculpturing that I continue to use today."

Let the journey begin from remote Canalou's "culture" that helped nurture a talented native boy into a world-acclaimed artistic genius.

"How did your childhood influence your creative nature?"

"Many artists relate back to the masters, such as Rembrandt or Van Gogh, but I relate back to my Great Aunt Zula Ogle who came to live with us and helped Mother with daily domestic details after my father died in 1950. She wore a whale bone corset due to a hernia condition," Parkes shared. **"I was maybe three or four years old, when I asked about where whale bones came from. She replied initially that a whale was a giant fish, but then corrected it to say a whale was a big mammal that lived in something called an ocean.**

"I didn't know what an ocean was, but when I'd go fishing down in Little River, I'd wonder about the creatures swimming around down under the water," Parkes described. **"That answer about my great aunt's whale bone corset started an exploration and curiosity journey that continues today."**

"Explain about those childhood mud turtles influencing your world-acclaimed artistry."

"It's that simple, really. As a boy, I'd stop beside the sidewalk on Canalou's Main Street (the only sidewalk the town had) and get a handful of mud" Parkes detailed. **"I'd divide up the mud into sections, and let the process begin using the various stages of drying in the creation of my mud turtles. I'd let some of the mud dry in the sun, for example,**

and keep part of the mud wet while another part was in another phase of the drying out process; it's a process I implement today in my sculpting."

"Describe your typical boyhood day back in Canalou."

"It was nothing unusual for me to go get a cold biscuit and bacon left over from the day before and be off on adventures for the entire day. If I didn't show up again for the entire day no one would worry about me, for we were 'safe' in that era. It was an incredible time. We had lots of freedom to grow up in Canalou."

"How did your artistry begin?"

"Chicken livers, gizzards, and hearts were free for the asking from the butchers at the little grocery stores that lined Main Street in Canalou," Parkes shared. "It was mainly at Moore's Grocery Store I'd go for the free chicken parts, and I'd ask [store clerks John Smith and Biddy Moore] for extra wrapping paper. It was that brown wrapping paper that I'd use for my childhood drawing. Of course, the free chicken parts were fried for our supper when I'd get home from the store."

A present-day legend back in Canalou has you drawing and sculpting before you could read and write…

"I'd draw on that brown store wrapping paper, so yes, I was drawing before I began first grade in 1950 and learned reading and writing at Canalou School."

Do you remember the name of your teachers or the store clerks who let you have the free chicken parts and brown wrapping paper?

"I don't have the type of memory where I remember a lot of people and their names from that era. I do have great recall of things and circumstances out in nature, such as when I'd go fishing in Little River or go catch crawfish at a little drainage ditch that bordered the east side of town. While fishing, I'd imagine all sorts of things swimming and moving around under that water. I think that was where my creative nature was beginning to kick in."

Another legend back in present day Canalou is that you drew a picture at age four of a horse named "Reno" that belonged to theater owner John Summers. Do you remember that?

"I remember the horse, but I don't remember drawing the horse. Yet, it's probably true that I did. It sounds like something I'd do."

You mentioned Canalou's "little cinema" with influencing you as a boy...

"When you're three, four, and five years old, you didn't know what was real or not real at our town's little cinema. After the movie with my little childhood friend Ellen Campbell, we'd go home and sometimes we would play Tarzan, after what we saw on the movie screen. There was this big tree in our back yard, with huge extending roots on top of the ground. We'd jump from tree root to tree root, you know, to avoid the alligators, you see. Ellen was fine with playing Tarzan and Jane. But she couldn't relate to our playing 'Creature from The Black Lagoon,' a 1950-era horror movie."

The world-famous artist chuckled at this recollection.

One of his life's most distressing traumas occurred in 1950.

What was that trauma?

"I was only six, and my father, who was older than my mother, had been ill and was over in the [John J. Pershing] VA Hospital in Poplar Bluff. I thought that was where he was. So when they took me, the first I knew of his death was when they lifted me up to see him over the casket at the funeral home in Sikeston. I think that's when I blocked out a lot of memories of that era. Mother later on related to me that she felt bad in handling that the way she did. It was such a sudden shock, looking down at Father, realizing for the first time, that he'd actually died."

You mention your Aunt Zula a lot during interviews. What impact did she have on you, and how did she come to live with your family?

"My great-aunt Zula was a grand lady with a lot of style and grace like a Victorian woman who came to our family after Father died to help Mother with domestic duties and responsibilities. She helped raise me, especially during the months that Mom went back to school at Southeast Missouri State University to get her master's degree in library science.

Aunt Zula was a great influence, strict in her ways, strong in her ethics-sort of like having a second mother. A lot of how I feel today, my outlook on life, was greatly influenced by those two remarkable ladies Mother and Aunt Zula who introduced me and encouraged me to seek answers and new knowledge. They gave me a lot of freedom to explore things in my formative boyhood era."

When did you leave Canalou?

"That requires an explanation, for we kept a home in Canalou after Mother and I moved to the Lead Belt region where we lived with an uncle and aunt [the Baughn family] in order for Mother to teach school. But during non-school months, we'd go back to Canalou. Later on, we sold our house next door to the Campbell family and moved, along with Aunt Zula, to a house we bought on the other side of the railroad tracks in Canalou. Aunt Zula continued to reside in Canalou for a number of years. I guess you could say I left Canalou for real as a teenager when I began college in Lawrence, Kansas."

In December, you postponed our initial-scheduled interview? Was it something special that happened?

"Maria and I became grandparents. It was a long time in coming, our first grandchild. But he was worth the wait. We went to England where our daughter and son-in-law reside and welcomed our grandson into our lives and world. At age sixty-four, I'm proud to finally be a grandfather."

Maria and Michael's journey in life has paralleled his artistic development.

"We were married December 28, 1968," Maria Parkes shared. "When Michael and I met both of us were interested in everything, especially the mystery of life. We searched for it after we read some books about meditation. The first book, *Adventure in Consciousness* sort of summed what we wanted to do. So we took off for India after travelling for about four months in Europe. We stayed at an Indian ashram (center for spiritual studies) and in the beginning, hated it. We lived in a guest house and had all our meals cooked for us and our laundry was beaten daily on the rocks to be washed.

"After going through withdrawal of no TV, radio, or newspapers and not eating meat or salad and living very, very simple, well, we had more time to reflect and see clearly," Maria shared. "The town was very small and most everyone went around by bicycle. It changed our lives. And we never looked back.

"But we needed to make a living, so we returned to Spain, and started a leather business," Maria shared. "After I became pregnant, we decided that we would return to India. In 1974, our daughter was born there."

"Michael did the delivery with a doctor standing by in a country clinic with water buffaloes as our only visitors as they came to the window to check on us," Maria recalls. "Everything was fine except two months later I was very ill and had to go to the next city, Madras, for an emergency operation. The taxi drive took five hours, and I was operated on immediately."

Due to a food crisis and shortage of appropriate nutrients needed by the recovering Maria, they returned to the U. S. to stay with her parents and recuperate until they could return to Spain.

"We borrowed a small amount of money from Michael's mother, bless her, and we returned to Spain in 1974," added Maria.

Although Michael's world-acclaimed artistry and sculpturing has been reviewed and revered by internationally-known writers and critics, there's no one better prepared to judge Michael's creative genius than his wife, herself a music thanatologist.

"This means that I play the harp and sing, primarily Gregorian chant, at the bedside of the dying in homes, hospice, and hospitals," Maria shared. "I mention this because you may see an occasional harp in Michael's work."

"We frequently return to India," Maria added. "Karma Yoga is when one uses one's work as their direction towards union with God. Michael's works are most definitely his way of searching for the Divine. And while his roots began in Canalou, and were extremely important to him, I would say that his time in India studying is certainly the flowering of his direction."

"We both feel the painter and the viewer together create the painting," Maria continued her word picture of her husband's genius. "When one views art with a contemplative openness, one subconsciously or consciously vibrates with the same frequency of the art created.

"That is the power of good art," Maria detailed. "For years people have asked Michael what his paintings mean. And frankly, we both avoided the question. But times are a changin' and Michael has now begun speaking about his art. If his work can transform a space by creating a calm sense of wonderment and beauty, then the rest is up to the viewer."

Yet, home is home.

"We love adopted Spain and her people but will always love and be eternally grateful for what our country of birth gave us," Maria added. "We continue to live in Spain because Michael does his sculpture in Florence, Italy and his stone lithographs in Zurich, Switzerland. We're still American citizens.

"As most artists, we like being outsiders and that is what we can be here," Maria accounted. "We live a quiet life. Michael's paintings began to reflect what he was searching for. He paints from the heart and his work is authentic, not trying to be clever or tricky. That is the difference between him and many other magic realists. Cleverness and trickiness can just go so far. To tell you the truth, we were shocked to see so many people in America standing in line waiting to see him when we went to the first book signing. There were old, young, educated, uneducated, bikers, professors amazing. This is what we had hoped for. We did not want Michael's art to be elitist."

"From our balconies we see Gibraltar and the mountains of Morocco most days," Maria detailed. "We never cease to be amazed when we see the Gibraltar straits, especially at sunset. That was the end of the known world only five hundred plus years ago. And that sort of puts our lives in perspective in some way."

Farm
Political Art
Culture

Chapter Twenty
Michael Parkes, the Artist

In 1950, I had noticed how pretty the little girls in teacher Billie Margaret Greer's first grade class were, including one particular blond-headed girl with gorgeous, big blue eyes named Ellen Campbell.

The problem was, Ellen already had a "boyfriend."

And she made it clear, that she was smitten by this little boy named Michael Parks, who also had blond hair.

"Michael is my boyfriend," Ellen confirmed, much to the sadness of me and the other boys in our class.

And everywhere that Ellen went in downtown Canalou, whether it was to the post office or to a Saturday night ten-cent moving picture show at John Summers' Theater, most of the time Michael was there too. And sometimes, when they thought no one was looking, they'd hold hands.

Oh, how I and my first grade buddies Harold David Bryant and Kirky Durbin envied Michael Parks.

Few people outside the Bootheel know about the unique town named Canalou, but that former little school boy named Michael is known around the globe today as an artist whose work is sought after and collected in art shows throughout the

U. S. and Europe.

When the famous artist does media interviews around the globe, he never hesitates to mention his boyhood hometown: Canalou.

So who is this famous person from Canalou who has impacted the world?

Meet 67-year-old Michael Parkes, now a famous artist/sculptor in Spain, whose talent to produce "Magical Realism" art has made his work a highly-sought-after global commodity.

Few Missourians know that the globally-acclaimed artist's earliest roots go deep into the culture of Canalou and the Bootheel region.

"I knew Agatha "Sissy" Parks, his mom, as a strict educator and a good teacher," noted Canalou native Alice Jean Harrison VanNoy. "I didn't know she had a son, much less a world-famous son. I recall from my school days, and I'm now seventy-five, that we did not talk in Mrs. Parks classroom."

Born in a Sikeston hospital in 1944, Michael's earliest public education started in 1950 at Canalou Elementary School.

Michael was an easy boy to like, well-behaved and achieved high academic standards. I still owe him an apology for a practical joke that ended up not being funny. You see, I pulled a chair out from under Michael as he was taking a seat one day in second grade.

I recall Michael looked up from the floor where he had landed hard on his bottom, and he said quietly, but sternly: "That's not funny."

I remember feeling ashamed that I had done this dastardly deed to a boy I claimed as a "friend" in first and second grades. I think I realized I had lost some of the trust Michael had for me before I jerked that seat out from under him.

So, Micheal, fifty-nine years later, I profoundly apologize for my dastardly deed in second grade.

Although I considered Michael one of my "friends" in school, I lost track of him when his family moved away from our farming hamlet.

But the former little Ellen Campbell has vivid memories of their childhood friendship. She and Michael lived next door to one another in the late 1940s and early 1950s.

"Michael and I were both born in Canalou in 1944, and I remember I'm six months older than he is," recalls present-day Sikeston, Missouri, resident Ellen Campbell Polley, who married Paul Polley, one of my best high school friends I acquired at Grayridge High School in Stoddard County.

"Michael and I were special, little friends, and we lived next door to each other the first years of our lives," noted Ellen. "I remember that as little children, we'd sit on our front porches,

Mike Parkes   Ellen Campbell   Jeanie Campbell

and Mike would draw beautiful pictures of (the late) John Summers' horse named Reno. I'd try to draw too, but my little drawings were pitiful compared to Mike's. Michael could always draw so well, even before he learned how to read and write at school."

When I asked about their childhood friendship, Ellen, responded, "We'd hold hands sometimes walking to and from Canalou School on the town's one and only sidewalk in front of Jim Poe's Grocery Store."

"When one of us had a nickel or dime, sometimes we'd stop in Moore's Grocery and share an ice cream cone," she added. "Sometimes, Michael would ask for extra meat-wrapping paper to use for his art when he'd get home from school."

They often visited back and forth.

"Sometimes, I'd stay all night with him at their house next

door, and I'd sleep beside his Great Aunt Zula Ogle, who helped raise him after his Dad passed away at an early age," Ellen continued. "Michael would sleep at the foot of the bed, but we'd hold hands during the night.

"Sometimes, we'd sit on the bed at his house or my house, and just read comic books," Ellen shared.

She smiled at another recollection of their friendship that extended over a number of years into the late 1950s, after Michael and his school teacher mother moved away from Canalou to Flat River, Missouri.

"One summer, when our school in Canalou was out for cotton vacation, I went and spent two weeks with Mrs. Parks and Michael and visited school with him in Elvins, Missouri, where Mrs. Parks was teaching at the time," Ellen traced back through the decades. "I just went to Flat River that one time, to spend part of the summer with them. This was when Michael and I were age twelve. I thought it odd their school didn't let out for cotton picking in the fall. I realized later, they didn't grow cotton in the Lead Belt.

"At age thirteen, Michael and his mother invited me, and we drove all the way up to St. Louis to attend the St. Louis Opera," Ellen said. "It's the only opera performance I've ever seen.

"We may be the only people from little rural remote Canalou to ever attend the St. Louis Opera," she added with a smile.

She recalled other special times she and the famous-to-be artist shared in Canalou where its only high school was closed in 1958.

"Sometimes, we'd take tiny pieces of bacon, and walk down to the big drainage ditch that borders the east side of Canalou, and we'd fish for crawdads," Ellen said. "He'd bait my hook, I remember, if I asked him to. And he'd take the crawdads off my hook."

Ellen's father Lee Joe Campbell, who formerly drove a school bus at Canalou, also recalls Michael, his mother and aunt as next door neighbors.

"Super nice people, all of them, and Michael Parks was always real nice, well-mannered, and never spoke badly of anyone,"

Mr. Campbell recalled at age eighty-five in 2008. "We always had good neighbors in Canalou where I lived for sixty years before moving to Sikeston. And the Parks were among the nicest of them."

"Oh, yes, I remember that Michael and Ellen had a crush on each other, and they remained friends on up until their teenaged years before life took them on separate journeys," the father shared.

It's been decades since Ellen last saw her special childhood friend.

She still possesses a photograph showing her, Michael, and her older sister, Jeanie Campbell sitting in the grass in front of their Canalou homes.

"I also have a picture of him in his little Boy Scout uniform," Ellen shared.

Canalou native Renda Chaney Buck, who was a grade ahead of Ellen, Michael, and myself, also recalls Michael.

"Mike Parks was one of the nicest, well-behaved little boys in our school, particularly in your class, Danny Whittle," declared Renda. "He was a quiet, unassuming boy, who had a very nice mother, Sissy, a very good school teacher."

After marriage, Renda and husband John Buck moved into Canalou city limits where they purchased the last house owned there by the Parks family.

"We bought the old blue house, there on the corner just across the street from where the railroad was before they took up the tracks," John Buck accounted. "I never met any of the Parks, but they left very solid reputations in their wake after they moved away.

"One room in that old house was finished in cedar, in contrast to the rest of the house," John Buck shared. "We were told that room was built especially for Michael's visits in the hot summer time. Renda and I recently stopped and went back in the house, which is falling down except for that cedar-finished room. It's still intact."

Renda recalls purchasing the last Parks' home in Canalou from

Michael's great-aunt Zula Ogle.

"She was very much the classic Victorian-type lady, who was pleasant to do business with," added Renda. "A quiet dignified lady, actually."

How high has this former Canalou boy soared in the art world?

Art critics around the world write about his work, including *London Times'* newspaper Art Critic John Russell Taylor, who touched on Michael's humble, rural beginnings back in Canalou, Missouri.

"Other aspects of Parkes' childhood were not so advantageous, or not necessarily so," Taylor penned in his critique of the artist. "He was an only child, which often leads to children's being dreamy and introspective, especially if their family lives in a small community with not much social life going on all around. The town where Parks was raised, Canalou, Missouri, had fewer than 350 residents."

Michael, after moving away from Canalou, attended college in Lawrence, Kansas.

After getting his degree, he was hired as a lecturer in graphic arts. His early work was primarily in the "Abstract Expressionist" style. Michael also taught four years at Kent State in Ohio and at the University of Florida.

In 1970, he set off with his wife, Maria, and $800 in savings. They traveled widely in Europe, then flew to India, Nepal, and Pakistan. But this was no sightseeing trip. Michael was educating himself in the philosophy, mythology, and mystical imagery of many cultures developing a foundation for what would later become the vocabulary of his fantastical art style, sometimes labeled "Magical Realism."

Mike Parkes

As I write this in 2012, Michael Parkes is the most famous person to have matriculated at our little Canalou School of higher ciphering and advanced thinking.

Chapter Twenty-One
Few Missourians

Here-to-fore, New Madrid County, Missouri, has been primarily known globally for one event, the massive New Madrid Earthquake of 1811-12 that was so strong, it caused the mighty Mississippi River to run backwards and caused church bells to ring as far away as Boston, Massachusetts.

But now, a native from New Madrid County is giving the region another day in the sun of global attention.

If you're an art collector living in Romania, chances are you've heard of artist/sculptor Michael Parkes, who now resides in Spain where he originates his own personally-created Magical Reality art forms.

As a native son, he's the remote rural village's biggest claim to world fame.

Few Missourians know the famous artist/sculptor is from tiny southeast Missouri farm hamlet Canalou.

Even fewer southeast Missouri natives realize that Michael Parkes was born in a Sikeston, Missouri hospital in 1944, and spent his early formative years at Canalou.

"We polled our professors here at Southeast Missouri State University, and none knew that he was from Canalou," confirmed Southeast Missouri State University Historian and Professor Dr. Frank Nickell. "It didn't become widespread public knowledge that Michael Parkes is from Canalou until research was started for this book by author Danny Whittle, also a native of Canalou."

Michael escaped the doldrums of rural cotton picking farming country when his educator mother, Agatha "Sis" Weaks Parks, moved out of the "Bootheel" to teach in the Flat River region.

"Michael Parkes is our little town's biggest claim to world fame," credited Canalou Mayor James Donald Taul in 2008. "For example, he started school at Canalou Elementary in 1950 and was in teacher Billie Margaret Greer's first grade class. He was a very good, even shy little boy."

His art today is in such high demand, that multiple famous galleries around the globe seek to have his works on display.

"To view the creations of the acclaimed painter, sculptor and his rare stone lithographs is to enter a meditative state of heightened appreciation. . . a state of unmistakable marvel," is how one art critic/author in Europe described Michael's art.

© Michael Parkes
Image used with his permission.

After marriage and getting his degree in art from the University of Kansas at Lawrence, Michael initially followed in his educator mother's footsteps and began teaching.

But after marriage, Michael and his young wife, Maria, left teaching armed with only $800 and began travelling the globe, with stops all over Europe and India.

But he and his young wife were not your traditional young tourists. Michael and Maria were seeking the deepest meanings of spirituality known to mankind globally.

And that helped form the basis of his art.

But, the most basic embryonic foundation phase of Michael's now world-acclaimed artistry began back in the culture of southeast Missouri's "Bootheel" region, more specifically, his boyhood hometown of Canalou.

Chapter Twenty-Two

Shy Pilot and Lawyer

Garry Lewis was a shy friend who couldn't pay the price of two Cokes on his first big date as a former student at Grayridge High School (later called Richland High) in Stoddard County.

Now meet former Navy fighter pilot Garry Lewis, multi-millionaire, entrepreneurial investment attorney with former practices in Missouri and Louisiana. He and his wife, Poplar Bluff-born Gayle Harper Lewis, make their home in Baton Rouge, Louisiana, but also have extensive property holdings in Columbia, Missouri.

In the forty-seven-year lapse of contact in our friendship, Garry not only married and fathered six children, but the former shy school boy became a daring and brave Navy pilot. He retired from the Naval Reserve as captain, and is now retired from law practice.

"I've had a roller coaster life," Garry describes modestly. "Before college, a John Deere A model tractor was my biggest daily ride back there in Bootheel farming country."

My former shy friend sheepishly agreed to share about that big first date back in high school.

"Sweet Sue Mays agreed to go out with me to the War Drum Restaurant in the big city of Sikeston," Garry journeyed back across the decades. "She was so nice, and yes, all I had was the price of one Coke, so I bought her the soft drink, and tried to take up the time by teaching her to drive a 1962 straight-shift Plymouth. She seemed okay with that, thankfully.

"Dad [the Reverend William M. 'Dub' Lewis, a native of Lilbourn who farmed 120 acres near Risco] had so little money, and he thought I should be happy to have a car with gasoline to drive. I embarrassed both of us when I asked for some extra coins for the biggest date of my young life. I resolved in that era of life I would one day have money to live life to the fullest."

I first became friends with Garry and his cousins, Betty Jo and Ann Brower back, in the 1960s, while attending Grayridge High School. As Garry approached maturity, he had to get through severe youthful bashfulness, which I think you will agree he has accomplished.

"At age five, I started first grade at Grayridge, I had a crush on little Linda Long, now a successful realtor (Collier Realty) in Dexter," Garry recalled. "But, she never knew she was my girlfriend."

Shyness apparently caused some Grayridge educators to mistakenly presume Garry "was backward."

"Teachers whispered that I was self-conscience because I was smart, and it was true, I began hating being smart in classes such as algebra and art," Garry added.

How smart and shy was he?

First, the smart. "Mathematics teacher Mr. Kellum encouraged Dad to help me continue my education because he said I could solve algebra problems in three minutes that required the teacher to write the algebra book publishing company for answers," Garry accounted. "So, I was blessed to get a full scholarship at the University of Missouri, thanks to encouragement of so many good teachers at Grayridge."

He was so shy, it hurt Garry to answer questions in classes at the university level too.

"At college, on scholarship out of Richland High School, I was too bashful and self-conscious to answer any question asked of me by a professor," Garry detailed. "One reason for my silence was because I was sitting behind a girl [Brenda Gayle Harper], who I was secretly in love with."

Somehow, Mr. Shy finally garnered enough courage to make his feelings known to his female classmate.

"After two years of courting, we married at the end my junior year. She quit school and worked to get me through college," Garry added with a satisfied smile. "We had six children from our union, one of whom drowned in an accident."

By this time, Garry had overcome any serious lack of confidence.

"After college in 1968, I joined the Navy. They sent me to schools to become an officer and a fighter pilot," Garry shared.

How well did he fly? So well he became a recognized Centurian after making more than 100 landings on floating landing decks and living to tell about it.

"I flew several, very fast jet aircraft, among the nation's best, actually, off of floating airfields including such carriers as the USS America, Lexington, Intrepid, Kittyhawk, Ranger, and Enterprise on oceans around the globe," the former fighter pilot soared back across the seas and pages of military history. "I flew many hours and missions and made carrier landings in the McDonnell Douglas F-4 Phantom, and later, I flew the F-14 Tomcat that was featured in the movie Top Gun."

Garry's fighter squadron was VF-142, the Ghost Riders, and he was not the only successful retiree. One squadron mate, Jerry "Boomer" Smith, now runs his own winery at Scott City, Missouri. And another, Carmen Henry, became a senator's assistant in Arkansas.

"We seldom discuss our military experiences," Garry acknowledged. "Boomer and Carmen were radar operators and navigators in the back seat with no flight controls. They had to be crazier than the pilots to fly with us."

Apparently, a fighter pilot's psyche can be fragile.

"I never dreamed nor expected to live long, not even through the next flight," Garry confirmed. "I had lost lots of friends to a destructive death where sometimes, nothing remained to be buried.

"But, I was not fearful, just enjoyed every moment and thrill that it had to offer, which was an unusual mental condition, as I now look back on those years," Garry added during some serious reflection. "I often recall a close friend, fellow flight instructor Sherman Hindrum, who confided in me he had lost the edge, and he wanted to quit flying off carriers, and to go home and live with his young son, Sean.

"It was a secret that he had a son and an honor that he shared that innermost private aspect of his life with me," Garry noted. "The son lived with Sherman's parents after the girlfriend had given up custody. I felt honored to know about the privileged, most private part of my friend's life.

"Less than a week later, we were the two (VT-9) instructors assigned to lead eight student pilots to do carrier landings aboard carrier, the USS Lexington," Garry shared. "After being assigned with the flight number 913, Sherman was clearly distraught, and it being a Friday mission."

However, other carrier flight crew personnel didn't take the pilot's fear seriously.

"Sherman was kidded about being a superstitious Navy pilot," Garry detailed. "Just before takeoff from the Pensacola, Florida, air field, to stop the kidding, I agreed to give him my aircraft side number 929. He was immediately happy, and said, 'Garry, you would do that for me?' I simply said, 'Sure,' and was anxious to stop the embarrassment, for I understood his emotions from our prior private conversations."

There was a long pause at this deeply emotional juncture of the interview.

"After we safely landed aboard the USS Lexington for our training exercises, Sherman was instantly killed on his first catapult launch, nose diving at full power immediately in front of the ship," Garry noted. "His plane exploded; with only one wing emerging from the right side of the bow…I was sitting right behind him for my turn at a catapult launch in flight side number 913. We all continued operations, except the helicopter rescue crew, as if nothing ever happened. We never found Sherman, only a crushed helmet, a boot, and two gloves. That is the way it was!!"

Any Navy fighter pilot's career, including Garry's, is filled with constant dangers.

"I have landed on fire, one engine without power, and lost part of my aircraft when flying too low and too fast," Garry shared about his U. S. Naval fighter pilot flying days. "Although still young in years, I realized every day that life is a gift. I still live my life that way."

The crop-share renter's son had come a long way from his youthful days of driving a John Deere A model tractor as his main mode of transportation back in Bootheel farming country days. He flew Navy missions in the Pacific, Atlantic, and Mediterranean seas between 1968 and 1976.

Garry's roots go back to Lilbourn, where his parents, Mr. and Mrs. William "Dub" Lewis, began their family after their great-grandparents moved to the Bootheel from Kentucky and Tennessee respectively.

"I recall the water, the flooding, and Dad losing so many crops," Garry noted. "Our biggest enjoyment as children was going to church and attending the big Lilbourn Carnival held each year on the dirt Main Street. It was memorable for a little boy to float in a boat to get to and from our rural home near Lilbourn.

"New Madrid County was still swamp country, but nothing compared to the vast swamp, cane breaks and timber found by my great grandparents, Henry Lee and Melissa Kay Lewis. She later perished due to a heat stroke suffered in a cotton patch between Lilbourn and New Madrid," Garry traced his ancestors' arrival in the former swamp. "Initially, the Lewis' lived and survived on a houseboat skiff they used to journey up and down the Mississippi River.

"One time, Henry Lee got into a skirmish at the end of Main Street that ended at the river's edge in downtown New Madrid. Upon learning the circumstances, which included Great-Grandmother Melissa sitting on the family's meager supply of bacon while her husband went to a sinking riverboat, the sheriff sent word; finally, that Great-Grandfather Henry Lee Lewis could come home because the sheriff knew the man who was killed had started the fight."

Garry's father, now in his eighties, was one of eight children born to George and Bertha Lewis. He began his family in Lilbourn in the early 1940s. Due to repeated crop failures in the 1940s and 1950s, the family temporarily moved to St. Louis, which was not an enjoyable experience for Garry.

"Faith played a huge part of life in the Bootheel, as I recall Grandmother Bertha often prayed and shouted her hair down at the Lilbourn Methodist Church," Garry traces back across the cotton fields of youth. "God is a big part of strength to have survived the elements of being a rent-croppers' family. We all needed God, and I don't recall ever encountering any non-believers who worked in the painfully hot and sultry cotton fields to put food on the table and clothes on their backs."

After exiting the Navy, Garry returned to the classroom at the University of Missouri in Columbia where he achieved his law degree.

"After returning to native Missouri soil and family, I was licensed to practice law in both Missouri and Louisiana, doing mainly Maritime law and lots of product liability litigation until 1992 when I purposefully discontinued taking any new cases but have kept my law licenses active," Garry detailed.

He had some unusual cases, including one soft drink case that had international marketing impact.

"This involved a Jackson, Missouri, girl who lost an eye due to improperly-designed caps on a soft drink bottle," Garry recalled. "Our lawsuit, which we won, resulted in the change of the bottle thread design of all carbonated beverages."

Garry and former law school classmate, Paul M. Brown, doggedly pursued this case, taking depositions as far away as Florida, and portraying themselves as newspaper reporters while sneaking in bottling plants to uncover falsified records to uncover long-known bottling defects.

"Today, corrective vertical slots in the twist-off threads can be seen on every beverage bottle," the retired barrister confirmed. "That is a result of that milestone law suit back in the Bootheel."

The next case was even more personal to Garry and his family.

"Gayle's mother, Nancy, was killed in a Ford vehicle, park-to-reverse (false park) injury, and it was settled in St. Louis, receiving limited coverage in *St. Louis Post-Dispatch* as Ford's largest park-to-reverse settlement to date" the attorney with Bootheel roots accounted. "Both cases had amounts protected as privileged as part of the final payments made. The Ford Motor Co. did change their design, not just a warning posted on the dash as Ford had previously offered."

His mother-in-law was the 126th fatality due to the faulty park-to-reverse design.

Garry, when asked for a summation of his life, responded thusly: "At the request of my wife, I never entered politics, although both sides of our family have always had strong interests in the special brand of politics that the Bootheel is known for. A portion of my family worked tirelessly in behalf of candidates, for example, supported by the [late] J. V. Conran Democrat political machine in New Madrid County. My dad, who became a preacher back in his native Lilbourn after I left home, joked that he was only one of two Republicans in New Madrid County, and he didn't know the other one. Gayle's Democrat cousin, Roy Harper, was also a strong Bootheel Democrat political player back in the 1930s and 1940s who, along with J. V. Conran, played major roles in first electing Harry S. Truman a U. S. Senator and later, vice president and president of the United States.

"I have accumulated millions of dollars, not for the money, but for the enjoyment of getting to live life another day" Garry concluded. "I've always loved taking risks or a business gamble. I have that ability only because I'm still alive."

Garry still flies jet planes, but on a personal note, he ordinarily flies under the radar while not seeking credit or publicity. He was hesitant to grant this interview.

"I still fly my own aircraft ninety percent of the time, although I do have a pilot on full-time retainer when I want to just ride." Garry concluded the interview softly. He and a business partner purchased the old Kaiser Aluminum site in Baton Rouge in 2009 to reopen it as an ocean and river port.

Garry credits his life in the Bootheel with preparing him for a bountiful life.

"The Bootheel's grit and dirt of the cotton fields does not wear off," Garry noted. "Those of us privileged to grow up in this unique part of the world are proud of our Bootheel heritage."

Chapter Twenty-Three
A Blend Of Cultures

Like most of America, Canalou was a melting pot of talents, cultures, and breeds.

The Hoppers, one of the community's most respected farm families, had one of the most unique heritages. This fact was not widely known by a lot of Canalou people during the era my generation was growing up in the 1940s and 1950s.

The late James William "Jay" Hopper, born to a farming family in the Lilbourn area, married Mary Welsh, whose folks were Irish Travelers, a traveling clan of people with origins going back in Europe where they're sometimes called Gypsies and Tinkers.

"Mother was from what we would call a dysfunctional family today," noted Patsy Hopper Bixler, the couple's oldest daughter. "I was born in 1933 to a most unlikely combination. For my dad's folks, the Hoppers, were pioneer-type farm folks, tied to the soil as their way of life. They were fundamental Baptists.

"Mom was a second generation Irish Catholic, and as Travelers, they moved around a lot," offered the couple's oldest daughter (seventy-nine in 2010). "Mother's early life was spent with her family, who finally settled in Lilbourn where my Grandfather Welsh was a horse-trader."

It was not unusual for the Travelers, who do not have the best reputations with law enforcement on the different two continents, to be involved in the dealing and breeding of horses and mules. Dating back to the clan's ancestral days in Ireland, they were also known to be interested in breeding and dealing fine dogs. It was through Mr. Hopper's family dealing with Mr. Welsh for some horses that Jay Hopper and Mary Welsh met.

"Mother and her people spoke a secret language called Shelta, which was a combination of Galic and Romany," Patsy Bixler traced back through the decades when Canalou was evolving from a former swamp village into a thriving little farming hamlet. "Back when they were traveling, if any of the clan died, they were shipped to the Greenfield Mortuary in Memphis, and the clan would gather each April fifteenth, for wakes and to arrange future marriages."

Jay Hopper had graduated from high school at Lilbourn High School, uncommon in the 1920s. Mary Welsh had been placed in a Catholic boarding school as a child when Patsy's grandmother Rose, divorced Robert Welsh and ran off with a stockman.

"I think Mother felt badly because she didn't get much of a formal education [eighth grade]," the daughter describes. "Momma always told us that we must learn how to make a living, learn a trade, or get an education. During my growing up years, I never saw much of Grandmother Rose as Mother never quite forgave her for abandoning her family. I think that is why she tried to give us a stable, loving environment as a farmer's wife, that which she did not have in her own childhood."

"When Mother was small, the Welsh Clan traveled a lot," Patsy continued. "She told us stories of riding the Mississippi River on paddle-wheel steamers, marketing horses and mules up and down the river.

"She had some colorful relatives, who would come to our farm from time to time to visit us," Patsy added. "One of the most colorful was Henry Stanley, an English gypsy that one of Mom's cousins had married. He traveled the U. S. selling lightning rods and wore a gold earring in one ear, and that was in the 1940s."

"When they were in our area, they camped in a grove of trees [called Oak Grove] between Sikeston and Morehouse," Patsy traced back through time.

"Her sister, Margarette, settled down in Lawrenceburg, Tennessee. But Mother's brothers, James, John, and Charley, just wandered in and out, without writing. They just appeared."

Mary Welsh Hopper's older brother, Bill, died after being shot.

"Uncle Bill died after being shot by his mother-in-law in the 1940s when they lived in Lilbourn," Patsy accounted. "I remember the Sunday we came up to 'The Cape' to visit him at the old St. Francis Hospital where he was being treated. I had just made my first communion at the Catholic Church in Sikeston that Sunday.

"Grandma Hopper made my communion dress out of white silk, and Mom bought my veil," Patsy said. "We left the church and went to the hospital to visit. Uncle Bill died a few days later."

This resulted in a "wake" back at the Hopper farm in New Madrid County.

"We lived in a little four-room house, and relatives came for the wake and slept out on the lawn and in cars," Patsy noted. "Uncle Bill had two sons, Bobby and Jimmy, and we didn't see them after the shooting because there were hard feelings. However, when Mom was killed in a traffic accident in 1975, they came to the funeral."

Born during the Great Economic Depression that gripped America, Patsy heard "hard time" family stories dating back into the 1920s.

"Grandpa and Grandma Hopper saved enough money to ride a train to St. Louis, where they smuggled Aunt Nola and her husband Ray and brought them back to the Bootheel farm, where there was no money but plenty of food," Patsy accounted. "Aunt Nola and Uncle Ray were starving in the city, living in a one-room apartment, cooking on a hot plate, when they had anything to cook. Uncle Ray was so hungry that he ate so much watermelon and wet the bed when they got down home to our farm."

How poor were the Hoppers during that era?

"One year, they used a cotton stalk for a Christmas Tree," Patsy recorded. "Dad's sister, Aunt Fay Hopper Chaney, told me this."

Baseball was an enjoyable pastime, especially during the hard times of the Great Depression.

"My dad was a good baseball pitcher [who later was a star player on the Canalou Town Team]. And he was asked, as a young married man, to play semi-pro ball with the Southern Conference in Memphis," Patsy shared. "This was before I was born. Train tickets were provided for Mom and Dad to journey down to Memphis, a huge trip in that era of about 150 miles to the south."

"They were walking the railroad tracks from the farm into Lilbourn to catch the train, carrying their suitcases, when Dad said to Mom: 'My God, Mary, what have you packed in this suitcase? It weighs a ton.' Mom had packed a ham and all kinds of canned goods. They weren't going to be hungry. Well, that lasted only a few weeks as the Southern Conference fell victim to the Great Depression, and they returned to the farm."

Her Grandma Hopper never trusted banks.

"There was no money during the Depression; the banks had failed, taking any savings the people had," Patsy recorded. "Grandma Hopper never trusted banks after that. She'd cash her checks and hide the cash somewhere in her house. So many people of that generation felt the same way.

"Mom's sister, Aunt Margarette, who lived in Tennessee, sent Mom postage stamps so they could exchange letters," Patsy shared. "World War II ended the Depression, and money was more available. But having been raised partially in that era, it has made us conservative."

One of my favorite Hopper family stories involves the birth of Rosemary Hopper, Patsy's baby sister and one of my most-cherished lifelong friends who died in 2002.

"Mother had to go to the old Sikeston Hospital that later housed Welch's Funeral Home, to birth Rosemary, which brought the dreaded Aunt Margarette to babysit us on our farm," Patsy recalls. "Well, what a joke, for Aunt Margarette thought she looked like famous beautiful actress Vivian Leigh, so when she arrived at the Matthews Train Depot, she was dressed to the hilt wearing a big picture hat, high-heeled shoes and a black striped suit when it must have been one hundred degrees. We were ashamed to pick her up at the Matthews Train Depot, and bring her home. At her home in Lawrenceburg, Tennesse, she envisioned herself as a 'Southern Belle.' It was a horrible two weeks, but worth it when Mother finally brought Rosemary home for us all to finally look at. We were sure glad when Aunt Margarette finally had to go back to Tennessee."

This gives a "snap shot" glimpse of the blending of cultures at farm hamlet Canalou, one of mainland America's last frontier towns that was birthed in a swamp as recent as 1902.

Chapter Twenty-Four

Hoppers On The Land

After the timber and swamp-draining era, Canalou and the six county Bootheel region became a historically-prolific agriculture producing region to the point that today, the region grows thirty percent of Missouri's farm products.

The Jay and Mary Hopper family was among Canalou's earliest and most respected agrarian families after the swamps were drained.

Their oldest daughter, present-day (2012) Cape Girardeau resident Patsy Hopper Bixler, at age seventy-nine, has an appreciation and understanding of the special and, yes, difficult culture her parents and grandparents not only survived, but prospered in.

"The land is historically important, and the drainage of the swamps by the Little River Drainage District [based in Cape Girardeau] was the greatest U. S. reclamation project of its time, and was accomplished from 1914 to 1928 with about one thousand miles of canals and 305 miles of levees, starting with the huge Diversion Channel here just below Cape Girardeau," Patsy chronicles.

"Timber men first recognized the value and bought the land for the lumber," Patsy said in presenting a glimpse back in history. "Some of the oak trees were twenty-seven feet around and the

Cypress was ten to twelve feet around, my ancestors verified. After the timber was harvested, the land was initially deemed worthless, and sold for a few cents per acre. Today, the fertile land is worth thousands of dollars per acre."

How fertile is Bootheel soil?

"The soil is deemed some of the richest in the world. With its centuries of flooding, silt buildup and vegetation decay, it's been compared to the historic Nile Valley," Patsy noted.

And farm life was "ideal" for rearing children of that era, she described.

"Our farm was a wonderful place to grow up," Patsy described. "We were rather self-sufficient. We milked cows, made butter, and canned fruits and vegetables. And Grandma Hopper kept us warm with her homemade quilts. Not a shred of clothing, when too worn to wear, was wasted. Grandma Hopper made use of every scrap of cloth."

Everyone in the family had farm duties.

"Grandpa Hopper, although elderly, was responsible for planting the garden in spring," Patsy recalled.

"In the winter, we killed hogs, curing the bacon and hams and making sausage. We ate the fresh meat immediately, for we didn't have refrigeration, just ice boxes, made of wood and lined with aluminum," Patsy described. "The ice man [Hubert Bond, of Canalou] would deliver ice several times a week. The ice boxes were usually kept on the porch, so when we were working in the fields, the ice man could leave what ever size block of ice you wanted.

"Everyone had ice dial signs, with numbers that you turned, twenty-five, seventy-five, or a hundred pounds, and you turned to the dial to whatever size ice block you wanted," Patsy remembered. "The ice man also picked up any excess milk and cream we had."

"Most families left correct change for the ice man," Patsy added.

Farm neighbors helped farm neighbors during and after the Great Depression.

"We shared the hog-killing meat with other families and they shared with us," Patsy accounted. "Hog-killings were exciting times, with multiple families gathering in. I hated the part where the hogs were shot, but we accepted this as a way of life then. We'd prepare big black kettles of hot, boiling water when the weather got cold.

"We had a smoke-house in back of the house, and it had one larger room with windows," Patsy recalled. "It was specifically built for this purpose, and had big hooks to hang the bacon and hams."

A typical farm day began early.

After cows were milked by the Hopper men folk, it was time for the women to get busy.

"One of my favorite jobs was churning the butter," Patsy described. "We had a Daisy churn, and you could see the yellow butter particles rise to the top of the milk. When it was ready, Grandma Hopper or Mom would take the butter and press it into one-pound molds.

"The buttermilk was left to have when Grandma would fix cornbread or hoe cakes," Patsy shared. "We usually had most of the hog-killing meat ate by spring, and then, we ate fish and chicken during the summer."

By this time, Mary and Jay Hopper and his sister, Fay, who had married farmer Harry Chaney (born in a Canalou-area logging camp in 1913), had acquired adjacent farms near Canalou in the unincorporated Big Ridge community.

And raising chickens involved the outside world off the farm.

"We ordered our chickens from a hatchery, and they arrived by train at the little depot and post office in Canalou in late February or March, and were fed-out and ready to eat in May and June," Patsy traced back in time. "The post office was quite the lively place, especially when little chickens began arriving at the Canalou Train Depot ran by B. P. Melton. Post Master Don Kochel was an important and patient man as he helped deliver the mail and our little new chickens.

"We would usually order a hundred chicks, but some would be dead on arrival, so you had to order extra," Patsy added. "They were cute baby chicks. Chickens were a vital part of farm life.

"It was usually my job to gather the eggs every afternoon, a job I didn't like," Patsy detailed clearly. "For one thing, you had to be careful not to step in chicken shit. Two, sometimes the old hen would peck your hands when you reached under them to gather the eggs. That was painful."

This brings us to one of the most important, but not often talked about buildings on the farm, to wit, the "outhouse."

"Not a nice place," Patsy declared. "It had two holes and a sack of lime to keep the odor down. But our outhouse was nice for an outhouse, for it was built by WPA government workers, and had a concrete floor in it, the only concrete we had on the farm in that era. We had the Cadillac version of an outhouse."

And Grandpa Hopper was special.

"Grandpa Hopper raised watermelons, peanuts and popcorn, and the usual garden vegetables," Patsy noted. "It seemed like Grandpa knew everything. He showed us how to dig worms, how to fish, how to bait our hooks. . . a very patient man. We loved his roasted peanuts in the winter time."

Fall was an exciting time on the farm.

"It was fun riding a load of fluffy cotton, a real soft ride on top of that cotton, but on the return trip from the Percy Cotton Gin in Canalou, it was a rough, bumpy ride on the rough farm-to-market gravel roads," Patsy recalls. "I remember one time Dad didn't have the money for a hospital bill, so he borrowed, with a handshake, the money needed from Mr. Percy. My parents had a very good name in the business community.

"The old mules would pull the cotton wagon, and after initial weighing of the loaded cotton trailer, the mules would ease the wagon under the gin suck," Patsy recalled. "That big piece of tin gin equipment would literally suck the cotton out of the wagon into the mechanized ginning equipment, where there were lots of belts and pulleys. It was a very noisy place."

After cotton trailers were emptied of cotton, they were re-weighed on the huge scales in front of the main gin office. This determined the amount of cotton the farmer was paid for as the main cash crop of that era. In Canalou during the 1940s, it was not unusual for cotton trailers and mules to be lined up more than a mile waiting to be weighed and ginned.

"We farmed with mules until after WW II, when we got our first tractor, a 'B' model John Deere," the former farm girl accounted. "We were so proud of, that we all, including sisters Betty and Rosemary, and brother, Johnny, had our pictures made on that new tractor."

Fall time of year was exciting.

"Fall and Saturday nights were special, ranging from touring carnivals to Saturday night movie shows," Patsy recalled. "There was excitement in the air. Usually, a carnival or traveling show would sit up in the small towns for everyone had a little pocket money to spend. They usually set up on the school grounds back then. I recall winning a small gold basketball necklace at the carnival.

"We didn't have a movie theater in Canalou until 1944," Patsy remembers. "Before that theater was built and opened by Boots Conn, on Saturday nights, a projectionist from Morehouse's Dillon Theater, would come to Canalou and show a movie in the old Lampher Hotel, which was also called the 'White Building.'

"There were not many seats, just benches, and the building had formerly served as the town's hotel during the timber-harvesting era. It and our old high school, before it burned in 1950, were the only three-story buildings in Canalou. A pot-bellied stove was the heat source on movie nights."

Patsy recalls her first "queen dress."

"When I was in seventh grade, I was crowned queen," Patsy traced back in time. "I was very tall, but didn't have any figure yet. We didn't have the money to spend on a formal, so Mom borrowed one from Virginia Bond's sister. It fit perfectly, except I didn't have any boobs to fill it out. But I really felt dressed up. And Virginia Bond, the town's professional hair stylist, came out to the farm and gave me a Toni home permanent."

Yes indeed, Canalou farming country and culture were ideal for the wholesome nurturing of farm children.

Chapter Twenty-Five

Whittle Visitors

We counted cars, trucks, and tractors that came up and down our lightly-travelled, graveled farm road. We would count anything just to take our minds out of the boring doldrums of farm work.

A mere cloud of dust on the horizon was cause for excitement as we would try to guess who was coming, and whether they would stop. It was a *status* thing to be the first kid in the cotton patch to notice that a mystery vehicle was coming down our lane.

It was unadulterated glee when one of those vehicles was coming to make a delivery, such as Alva Jones of Best Way Cleaners. He came out of Lilbourn and Parma, and that meant at least one of us, generally my older sister June, got to lay down their cotton hoe and go greet the new arrival.

It generally also meant a break for all the field working Whittles when we'd get to the end of the latest row of cotton we'd been chopping to rid our fields of careless weeds, cockle burs, morning glories, and milk weed.

"It's the dry cleaning man!" my older brother H. Van would verify excitedly.

Since we could almost set our watch by when the delivery man would be working his route, Momma Whittle and June would generally have for Alva Jones, or his brother, Arlyn, a piece of pecan pie, fudge, and/or a fried apple pie waiting on the kitchen table, that is if we weren't behind in our farm work in the year 1955.

It also generally meant that we children got to not only take a break from field work, but we also got to partake of a tasty piece of pie. Now, looking back, it's no wonder we held Alva Jones and other route men in such high esteem.

And Alva's arrival was more than just to pick up or deliver our dry cleaning because men like him and our ice delivery man, Hubert Bond, brought us news from the outside world, since during crop-growing and harvest times, we didn't get to town very often except to go to school or church.

A huge block of ice would last about four days in our ice box, except in the hottest dog days of summer.

Canalou native Les Landers, now age sixty-seven, remembers other rural route men.

"I also recall Hubert Bond delivering ice, from his ice house located between the post office and what was a shoe cobbler's business across the street from the new high school in the early 1950s," Landers accounted.

Landers continued, "I also recall a man who would come by and repair a leaking cooking pot or sell different kinds of utensils. Then there was the Fuller Brush salesman, and a man who came by collecting scrap iron and junk of all types for the war effort in the 1940s. Living near the Church of Christ on the east side of town, we always had traveling salesmen coming through."

Jones, now age seventy-six and a resident of Freeburg, Illinois, was asked to recreate a typical day on his dry cleaning route in and around Canalou from the mid 1950s.

"I had a personal car, a 1938 Packard, but we drove a 1950 Ford on my dry cleaning route out Farm Market Road leading from Parma, to Hills Store, through Charter Oak to ultimately come to the end of my route and work day in Canalou," Jones recalled.

Being that he had grown up and still had relatives in Canalou, it was no accident the town was his last stop of the day.

He smilingly recalled always stopping in Charter Oak, small unincorporated New Madrid County community, regardless of whether he had a pickup or delivery of dry cleaning.

"Charter Oak presented me with several customers, but I always enjoyed my stop at the Garner family's house," Alva said in retracing his route. "Their young daughter, Pat, was the nicest and loveliest young lady I had ever seen. Even days I got no cleaning in Charter Oak, I enjoyed visiting, always made it a point to stop and chat a spell with the Garners. And gaze at lovely Pat."

From Charter Oak, it was approximately four more miles to downtown Canalou. One can begin sensing here that Jones' route was as much socializing as it was work."

"It being mid-morning, and a little too early for a cheeseburger at John Summers' Café, I would go to Grandmother Coela Arbuckle's house," Jones shared. "She was a terrific cook, except for her biscuits that she always put too much baking soda in. But Granddad [L. L. Arbuckle and former mayor of Canalou] and I loved them anyway. Granddad Arbuckle was famous locally for making molasses. So add some butter, despite Grandmother's bad biscuits, it was a meal fit for royalty."

After leaving Grandmother Arbuckle's house, Jones regularly stopped across the street at the Haywood and Harrison homes.

"Mrs. Haywood was one the smartest, nicest, and neatest ladies in Canalou," Jones recalled. "The Harrisons had a son, Norman, and two pretty daughters, Maxine and Alice Jean."

A short distance down Taft Street was the spot where Jones would stop and visit with his Great Uncle Emmit Greer, one of the most talented wood-working carpenters who ever lived in Canalou.

"Uncle Emmit was a great man of wisdom, I could hear talk for hours," Jones noted. "Uncle Emmitt, since he always wore carpenter overalls, never had any dry cleaning. He was just great to visit with."

Ed Scott and Charles Asa were respected carpenters in the town that had a whopping population of 420 folks, according to the

1950 census, not counting the estimated thirty or so lazy coon dogs that mostly slept lined up on the town's mile-long Main Street.

Since Jones had been born in Canalou in 1933, he was kin to just about everyone in the Landers, Scott, Greer, and Arbuckle families. "After Uncle Emmitt, I'd mosey on down the street, where I'd visit my Great Uncle Abe Landers and Aunt Mary Landers, a quiet lady by nature," Jones threaded back in time. "Aunt Mary was a sister to my Grandma Esta Scott Jones. Uncle Abe and Aunt Mary were so interesting to talk with, and they had so many children. I can't to this day list them all."

After paying his respects to family, it was time for Jones to get back in his Best Way Cleaners' vehicle.

"Now that I was updated on family matters, I needed to stop and visit my friends that I had grown up with before we moved out of Canalou in the 1940s," Jones remembered. "I was weaving in deliveries and pickups among the farm houses that dotted the streets and farm roads as I went about my route.

"Edna Taul, mother to my childhood buddies Richard, James Donald, Jerry Lee and Larry Dee, was one of those 'friends' whom I never failed to stop and visit with for a spell," Jones remembers. "Mrs. Taul and my mother [Floy Mae Arbuckle Jones-Gruen] were always so close in their friendship, dating back to the time I was born in 1933. Mother always credited Mrs. Taul being a big help in teaching her how to be a good mother."

And there were trappings at the Taul house, that documented the fact that only a few years earlier, before the massive series of drainage canals were dug by the Little River Drainage District that Canalou had been a sawmill town located in a massive swamp and woods inhabited by big wild animals.

"Although it had been years since anyone had last killed a bear, I remember this bear trap in the Taul's back yard," Jones said. "Hanging from a tree, that old bear trap was at least six feet long. Ernest Taul, Edna's husband, must have been a trapper, as were most menfolks of Canalou in that era of the swamp culture. I remember my older ancestors recounting days when bears and panthers roamed the woods and swamp in and around Canalou."

In the meantime, Jones had picked up clothes from the Bixler, Neel, Bishop, and Whittle families to be dry-cleaned and delivered three days later when Jones would rerun his route making certain to always stop in Charter Oak, whether he had any dry-cleaning business or not.

"But in Canalou, it's apparent that my run there was as much visiting as it was working," Jones admitted "I remember the pretty Bixler girls, little sister Sue Baby, plus Annette and Shirley, as teenagers and always interesting to talk with. They were younger sisters to my childhood friend, Charles Lee Bixler, who unfortunately we lost to a heart attack at his home in Cape Girardeau [in 2007]."

"Between Charter Oak and Canalou, I had one certain stop, which was at Roy and Offie Johnson's farm house, where I'd catch up on the latest from their oldest son, Gay, who later moved away from Missouri and settled down in Middle Tennessee, where I'm also sad to report, Gay died several years ago," Jones reported. "Gay was a classmate at good ol' Canalou School, before my family moved from Canalou to Lilbourn."

Arlyn Jones was Alva's older brother. In Canalou, they were known as Arlie and Alvie. "Arlie and I would always stop at Mrs. Ella Smith's home, since they lived on the edge of town near one of the big drainage canals that helped rid Canalou of its swamp water," Alva noted. "We'd stop in her backyard and smoke our last cigarette before we'd go back to our own home and family. Mrs. Smith was loyal, never once telling on us for smoking."

By this time, it was nearly sun down. "My day was almost over, but I had one last stop I always made, to visit Ed and Aileen Scott, to catch on our family's history," Alva noted. "I've always loved history, and Canalou has always had an interesting history.

"Ed, although not old enough to have known my namesake Grandfather John Alva Jones, he had a lot of good family stories passed down through the generations. I've always loved learning the history of my ancestors, who braved the elements of a wild woolly existence in those earliest days when Canalou was swamp and a sawmill town. The main sawmill, the last one that I knew about, was located on what is now the Chaney farm, about one mile south of downtown Canalou," Alva restructured.

But things did not always go smooth out on Jones' route.

"I can't count the number of flat tires, for rubber in that era was not durable, especially on those old rough gravel roads, leading in and out of Canalou before we had paved roads," Jones recalls. "Plus, we'd often hit a chicken that wandered out in the middle of the road, and we'd have to stop and apologize and deliver the dead chicken to the family it belonged too."

During that time, farm families ate their road-kill chickens, if they were not mangled too badly or been allowed to lay in the sun and road too long.

There was one more that one pretty girl that Jones admits to making certain he eyeballed on his route.

"Jo Ann Summers, who worked in her mom and dad's café, was very attractive to look at, although she was younger than me and my late brother, who died a few years ago of cancer," Jones confirmed. "I'd always order one of her fountain cherry Cokes Summers' Café was famous for, along with their great cheeseburgers and chili. I always timed my route where I'd go to Summers' Café around lunch time." Such was the way of life in that unique culture.

In addition to regular route salesmen, that included the Watkins Products man, there were a steady stream of hobos who stopped by the Whittle farm house for a meal.

As a small boy, I was enamored to sit and listen to hobo tales as they munched on the plate of food that Momma Whittle seemed to always have on hand. One hobo shared that there was a system he and other hobos used.

"There's a mark out on the railroad tracks in front of your house showing that your Mother is always willing to give us a plate of good home cooking," the hobo said.

As a curious little farm boy, I searched and searched for that mark left by the hobos, but I never found it.

Chapter Twenty-Six

Canalou Farmers

"If you wanna a good neighbor, be a good neighbor."

Those were among last words of wisdom passed down to my generation from Daddy Whittle.

Melton Bixler, one of Canalou's most successful agrarians, came down with back problems, so severe he could not plant his spring crops.

No problem, for his farm neighbors pitched in, as recalled by Melton Bixler's middle son, Cordell "Crawdad" Bixler, a resident of Springfield, Missouri. This was no small act of farming neighborliness, for at that time, Melton Bixler was farming more than 2,500 acres, no small farming operation during the 1950s.

"Dad came down with a ruptured disc in his back," Crawdad traced back across the fields of time. "Being unable to put in his crop, his neighbors pitched in to fully put the crops in, and later that year, they harvested Dad's crops for him. It's acts of kindness and neighborliness like this that we will always remember from living in Canalou."

Neighbors who brought their own tractors, plows, planters, and thrashing machines to the Bixler fields included farmers such as Gube Landers, Tom Morgan, Jewel Chaney, Phillip

Newman, Lois Newman, and Roy Bixler, a brother to Melton.

"Uncle Roy Bixler and the other farmers all pitched in and helped Dad, which was not unusual in that era and in our rural culture, for you had to have good neighbors in order to scratch out a living from that tough heavy gumbo dirt that surrounded Canalou after Nigger Wool Swamp was drained," Crawdad noted.

Daddy Whittle and Roy Bixler, who farmed 100 acres adjacent to our farm located north of Canalou at Louis Houck's railroad Tram Switch, often cooperated and exchanged farm labor, including helping round up livestock that escaped out of other farmers barn lots.

The Whittles also exchanged mules and equipment with neighboring Savage, Harrison, and Bramlett families, who farmed between Canalou and Morehouse in the 1930s and 1940s.

"My family initially came to Morehouse, Canalou during the Great Depression as sharecroppers with the prominent Rauch drug store family," accounted Donnie Savage, sixty-six, who resided in Louisiana as of 2010. "Grandfather Savage and my father initially farmed Honey Island south of Canalou. My older brother Hank, who played minor league ball for the old St. Louis Browns, and sister attended early school at Canalou."

Former Canalou farm neighbor R. L. Abernathy had a theory about how to judge the quality of a farm family.

"If a man keeps his fences in good shape and takes good care of his livestock, that generally means he's a good person and a good farmer," R. L. shared one day.

Melton Bixler, Nelson Lumsden, and Bert Latham, now deceased, were among Canalou's most progressive, innovative farmers in the 1940s and 1950s after Little River Drainage District had drained the Bootheel's six-county swamp region as part of America's largest dredging project in history.

How much dirt was moved in the dredging? More than had been moved in the historic Panama Canal that America finished when other countries had failed.

"They were on the cutting edge of irrigation," noted Memphis resident Berta Jean Latham Nance, youngest daughter of Bert Latham. "Dad had witnessed irrigation techniques while visiting an uncle down in Lonoke, Arkansas, and came back excited about trying it in order to increase our crop yields."

"Then, I think Daddy figured out how we could make cuts or grade the land, land-leveling, so that the water would flow from one end of the field to the other," Berta Jean added. "The better-drained fields were monumental in future increased crop production."

"In that era, farming techniques were changing so fast, it was hard for our farming dads to keep up," Crawdad added. "To be successful, it took more than just hard work; it required doing more with less, which brought on revolutionary land-leveling, irrigation, and drainage techniques. Plus, our fathers recognized the value of crop rotation long before it was an accepted popular practice.

"I think it was Canalou farmer Nelson Lumsden who actually was first to irrigate his fields, but my father (Melton Bixler) and Bert Latham also started that practice about the same time, which was in the early 1950s. This new technique was ahead of the curve of progress in that region of the Bootheel."

Courtships, and consequently families, were started in the post-swamp and timber era of Bootheel culture.

Crawdad's parents, for example, met and began a courtship in a cotton patch. Their trail of life was not an easy path that led to carving out a good life in the newly-drained swamp.

"We're talking poor here, in wake of the Great Depression when cash was scarce," echoed now retired Canalou farmer Harry Chaney. "All of us were poor."

The Bixler family was no exception to "hard times" and "poverty," Crawdad confirmed.

"While living on a farm at Matthews, Dad's father died of rabbit fever, leaving ten children," Crawdad recalled at the annual 2008 Canalou School Labor Day Reunion that has been held continuously since 1952. "Grandmother Bixler took the kids to Hattiesburg, Mississippi, where Dad and the older children did farm labor in order to have something to eat.

"The family later moved back to Missouri, and began farming with Uncle Paul Crouthers down around Lilbourn and Catron in lower New Madrid County," Crawdad noted. "After a while, Dad began farming for himself, and he also had a small country store. Around 1946, we moved to Canalou where Dad farmed until retiring in 1970."

"Dad and Mom met in a cotton patch, while picking cotton," Crawdad traced his family history back through the decades. "Mom is from Pope County, Arkansas, and like my father, they were a very poor family. After meeting in the cotton field and sharing some cotton rows, after two years, they married and had four children, the oldest being Harley, who still resides on the family home place at Canalou, Margie, our dear sister, and my brother Gary "Bixie" Bixler, the youngest at age sixty-two."

"After striking up a romance, our parents married in Atkins, Arkansas," Crawdad concluded. "The rest, as they say, is history, but it's a colorful history in the culture of Canalou, a unique and special place to grow up."

Chapter Twenty-Seven
Sharecroppers Extraordinaire

Meet Canalou resident Vincent Nichols, who stands tall in Bootheel farm culture as a highly respected professional farm hand.

Ironically, he's never owned a clod of farm dirt of his own in his seventy-three years of agrarian life in Southeast Missouri.

"It's men like Vincent and his hard-working brother, Guy, who have made farming here what it is today," credited successful Canalou and Matthews, Missouri, farmer Charles Hawkins. "They've been loyal, very dependable, and treat your land and equipment like their own. They mean a lot, not only to our family, but to the way of life in these parts."

"Vincent is a Canalou legend, not only as a great farm worker, but a great human being who has taught Sunday school for years at his church," echoed Canalou native farmer Lonnie Lawson. "His brother Guy is the same way, whether he was working for former Canalou merchant Bert McWaters in his caterpillar operation or as a professional field hand for Bert Latham."

"Vincent and Guy are consummate professional farm hands," credited Lawson, who farms about 1,700 acres between Canalou and Matthews. "They're like hired guns as professional farm hands. Everyone respects them."

It had been more than fifty years since personally sitting down and jawing a spell with Vincent, dating back to the time I was a neighbor farm boy who had the privilege of briefly working alongside Vincent and Guy Nichols in the heyday of their young manhood years. I left the farm in the 1960s for a career in journalism, but I knew Guy and Vincent Nichols and their work ethics well as a boy.

Our modern-day conversations quickly drifted to the grueling old days of picking cotton. "What's been the roughest job on the farm for you over the past sixty plus years?" I asked Vincent.

"Picking cotton. That was hardest, most drudgery job for me," Vincent recalled at age seventy-three in 2009. "My best day was two hundred and one pounds, the only time I snatched enough cotton boles to get over two hundred. It's the most back-breaking hard work I've ever done."

He then mentioned the cotton patch grab row.

It had been decades since I'd heard the term grab row. For unlearned present day city-fied types, a grab row was when two cotton pickers partnered up, as in former Bootheel cotton pickers Ruth Peridore of Matthews and Vincent Nichols, of Canalou.

"Ruth was a cotton-picking legend, a cotton-picking machine before there were mechanical cotton pickers," accounted Vincent on a warm summer morning when he had time to talk to me because his crops were laid by the phase of summer, which means they're safely planted, growing and headed toward maturity for the fall harvest.

Picking cotton was obviously not one of Vincent Nichols' favorite remembrances of a lifetime of farming.

"Ruth Peridore, who married my older brother, Guy, could pick anywhere from two hundred and fifty to three hundred pounds a day," Vincent recalled. "We'd pick three rows at a time, but Ruth, who was an accomplished cotton picker, would not only pick her row clean of the tufts of cotton, but she'd pick most all of the grab row, too, I did good to just stay up with her on my one row. "I've always loved working outside, working the soil, getting dirt under my finger nails, and smelling the soil and crops after a fresh spring rain," Vincent noted. "It has all been good."

"I guess making good neighbors is the other most enjoyable aspect of farm life," Vincent added. "For example, I've always admired the Peridore family. Ruth's father, Albert, taught all his children to work hard to do an honest-day's work for an honest-day's pay. I've known a lot of good, hard-working, down-to-earth folks like that here in the Bootheel."

My first cousin, Robert Terry Reed, recalls at age sixty-seven working alongside Guy and Vincent Nichols as a farm boy.

"I remember working with Guy and Vincent, driving a John Deere A model tractor, disking for farmer Bert Latham," present-day Texas resident Robert Terry plowed back through time. "We would go in, eat lunch, refuel, and grease the tractor and equipment.

"One of the Nichols' brothers would stand over me to 'get'er done' and not miss greasing that last grease fitting," Robert Terry remembered. "Bert would always stay back, letting us do our job and not say anything. He was a nice man to work for, but Guy and Vincent were always there, encouraging us young guys to 'get'er done' which is the work ethic we grew up with on the farm."

Vincent recalls his father working as a sharecropper for a wealthy Canalou land owner.

"My father, who came to Canalou in 1939 to work as a sharecrop farmer for the late E. H. Percy [prominent land and cotton gin owner] on his farm out near the Floodway Channel," added Vincent. "As little boys, Dad taught us to give an honest days work for an honest days pay.

"I've always worked for others with that creed," accounted Vincent, who presently is on year-round payroll of farmer Charles Hawkins, who although he grew up in Matthews had the good sense to marry Margie Latham, one of the prettiest farm gals over in nearby Canalou.

Having moved to Canalou at ages three and eight respectively from Morrilton, Arkansas, Vincent and Guy have experienced farming evolve from mules to modern-day mechanization, from days of praying for timely rain to dependable irrigation of crops, from pesky cotton bole weevils to present-day mosquitoes that plaque the Bootheel in waves each summer after the Purple Martin birds migrate away.

"Loyalty" is one of two of the brothers' shared traits.

"I've only worked for two farmers since I first hired out as a field worker for the late Bert Latham, who during the 1950s farmed more than six hundred acres, which was large acreage to tend to in that era," Vincent noted. "Bert was a fair man and the type man who rolled up his sleeves and worked out in the field alongside you. He was innovative and a very, very hard worker who died in 1992."

In the days of early Bootheel farming that didn't come until after the swamp was drained starting in 1910, some would have classified the Nichols boys as sharecroppers. "Our father, may the good Lord rest his tired old soul, was a sharecropper and proud to be a farmer, after hearing of the good farm land and moving up here from Morrilton, Arkansas," confirmed Guy, the oldest brother now retired at age seventy-eight. "Technically, Vincent and I are not scharecroppers. We're farm boys for hire. We've lived on salaries."

Like his brother, Guy admits to a weakness dating back to earliest days on the farm.

"I could never pick as much cotton as my brother, and I hated it," Guy added. "I could never pick cotton worth a nickel. Maybe on my best day, I could pick a hundred pounds, tops. So, yes, I guess you could say Vincent was the better cotton-picker. I've known men, and women for that matter, who regularly could snatch more than three hundred pounds of cotton a day. They were real COTTON PICKERS!"

So what was the greatest innovative step of progressive farming to hit the Bootheel, a region comprised of six counties where thirty percent of Missouri's farming products are grown annually?

"Mechanization. Specifically, mechanical cotton-picking machines," confirmed Guy from his Matthews nursing home bed. "Not only innovative, it changed the farming landscape because human cotton pickers had to leave the farm and find other sources of income. Plus, cotton picking machines allowed farmers to enlarge their acreage and crop production.

Also, both brothers are partial to green tractors with big yellow wheels.

"I'd also say tractors are among biggest changes when we were boys. We thought we were riding high when sitting on the lone hard steel seat on the old tractors with iron-spiked wheels. That was a heckuva step forward from those two teams of lop-eared, hard-headed Missouri mules we first learned to plow behind. But today's tractors not only are bigger and more powerful, but air-conditioned, and some even have radios, TVs, and refrigerators," Guy added.

Which brand of tractor holds highest ranking in Guys' eyes?

"John Deere is the most dependable, but the old Farmall-Internationals were also powerful before that company sold out," Guy added. "But overall, I'd take John Deere because of their durability and dependability."

"I agree, John Deeres are the best," echoed Vincent.

The interview with Guy took place in early-morning hours, for that's when farming folks are accustomed to waking up and getting their day started.

"Like most farm folks, I've always been an early riser, enjoyed the sunrise, have a solid breakfast and a cup of coffee and then, go check on the crops' overnight growth," confirmed soil guru Guy. "Mechanized farming changed the landscape of farming forever, especially from the days that our Daddy taught Vincent and I to plow with a stubborn team of strong and sturdy Missouri mules."

Younger brother Vincent still tills the soil and like his brother, is known as a legendary artisan of working the uniquely-fertile soil in the Bootheel.

Weeds are a never-ending battle for farmers. And Guy remembers the toughest to eradicate down through the decades.

"Johnson Grass was once a big problem," Guy recalled. "In the earliest days of chemical farming, the poison to kill Johnson Grass would kill ground from crop-growing for up to five years. Farmers couldn't afford to let land lay out for five years. So we dug a lot of Johnson Grass out by the roots. You had to kill the weed's roots to get rid of it."

What does Guy remember most about farm life in and around Canalou?

"I remember when there were more than twenty homes occupied by farm families on the two-mile stretch of road from Canalou to the Floodway Channel," Guy confirmed. "Now, there are no farm families living out that direction. No houses, period.

"I recall that Canalou had five saloons compared to three churches," he noted with a smile. "Our town's three blacksmiths were kept busy by us farm folks. Everyone was treated the same. We've come a long way from the days we walked behind mules in the fields and used little hand-held spreaders that cranked and twirled to spread seed and later, the fertilizer.

"Hog-killings were a big deal, when families of the community would all come together, not only to share in the work, but in fellowship and share in the meat," Guy accounted. "In that era, Canalou was a lively little town. Now, there ain't anything there."

Vincent and his wife, the former Janie Hill Nichols, still reside in Canalou in the old Haywood family home.

Vincent is known as a devout Christian man.

"We still go to the Church of Christ, which no longer meets in Canalou," added Vincent. "At one time, Canalou had two Churches of Christ. But as the years went by, so many folks moved away, we merged with the churches from Kewanee and Matthews.

"The Lord has been mighty good to me and Guy and has especially blessed my health, for I'm still able to do farm work now at age seventy-three," concluded Vincent. "I wouldn't change a thing, except I don't miss the cotton patch."

He was asked to compare the heavy gumbo soil that Canalou is known for.

"I wouldn't give you one acre of good fertile mixed sandy loam soil for five acres of the best gumbo ground," Vincent described. "You really have to know what you're doing to be successful at raising crops in that heavy, dark gumbo soil."

As of 2009, Vincent headed the work crew that helps farmer Hawkins till and grow corn and cotton.

"In the old days, we did good to produce sixty-five bushels of corn, but now, we're hoping to produce as much or more than two hundred bushels of corn per acre," Vincent noted. "With corn being so tall this spring, we've got a good shot at producing more than two hundred bushels per acre."

Vincent estimated he got a third grade education before he had to go to work full-time as a boy back during his father's sharecropping days on the old Percy Farm.

His present-day farm boss, Charles Hawkins, explains the business relationship with Vincent.

"Since I married Margie, the oldest daughter of Bert and Irene Latham, Vincent has remained working in the family continuously since 1947, a span of sixty-one years," farmer Hawkins accounted. "He remains with us on year-round payroll and has been one of the biggest assets a farmer could have. We value him as a friend and as a part of our family."

Vincent Nichlos

Chapter Twenty-eight

Born in a Tent

The late Harry Chaney knew the Bootheel when it was largely a swamp.

"Before it was labeled the Bootheel, locally, it was called Swampeast Missouri," the retired agrarian described with a spirited grin in our research interview conducted in 2008.

He should know for he was born September 19, 1912, in a logging camp tent in the unincorporated Big Ridge community located on higher ground above most of the surrounding water-covered, mosquito-infested, low-lying swamp of that era.

"It was a hard life for all of us, including my parents, John and Renda Chaney," Mr. Chaney credited. "Dad had boxed up some privacy in one of the logging tents and stretched out a tarpaulin for Mother to have shelter when she had me. The tent was located behind what became Ray Dowdy's house and farm.

"Mother was full-blooded Cherokee and my daughter Renda Chaney Buck is named for her," Mr. Chaney added. "Mother had real black eyes, as daughter Renda and son Harry Joe Chaney do today, with long black hair hanging down her back. We also have a tin-type photograph of Emma, my Renda's great-grandmother who was also Cherokee."

"Dad didn't talk much, as we all worked hard in cutting timber and hauling lumber to the stave mill behind nearby Canalou School," Mr. Chaney described. "I remember some of the most beautiful Cypress trees that grew up out of the swamp."

"But it was hard times, not much money, as we all worked from daylight to dark to clear-cut two hundred and forty acres that later become rich fertile farm land," he added. "In wet winters, the heavy gumbo dirt would become thick heavy mud so heavy that mere mules, horses, and cows could not pull the heavy-loaded timber wagons. Oxen owned by Wid Robinson were required."

At the tender age of nine, Mr. Chaney graduated to working behind a team of stubborn ol' Missouri mules as they began farming what they called the New Ground.

"The New Ground was created by our newly-cleared timber that we hauled to the stave mill in Canalou," Mr. Chaney described. "I remember flooding was a real problem, a frequent problem especially before they came in here and dug all the drainage canals that drained the flood waters that eventually made some of the most fertile farm land in America."

What little education Mr. Chaney received, he received from Hale School, a little one-room school on the other side of the newly-incorporated logging village of Canalou that had risen out of the swamp in 1902 due to logging and a railroad spur line that ran south from Cape Girardeau to the north.

"Dad didn't believe much in education," Mr. Chaney recalled. "I had to be a strong boy to work behind a team of plowing mules in that new ground."

His father's non-belief in schooling caused problems with the law of that era.

"Dad and the truant officer would almost fight as he kept us out of school most of the time. Truth is, he used me much like you would a slave. But I managed to get seven years of schooling. However, it was tough being raised like a slave."

Mr. Chaney's father had a second grade education.

"His saying was, 'If I can make it, that's good enough for you too,'" Mr. Chaney shared. "We'd go to school a few days to get the truant officer off of us, and then we'd be back out working in the timber cutting or farming behind of the team of mules."

There were dangers lurking in that foggy-bottom, marshy, wooded swamp land.

"You had to keep an eye out all the time for your safety," Mr. Chaney noted. "I remember out hunting rabbits one day when I looked up the trail, and there stood this big panther. It was big and black with a long tail. I jumped down on the ground to keep safely away from that big panther. I remember hearing the panthers and their eerie screams in the dark of the night. Finally, that panther jumped down out of its tree and went on down the trail. My huntin' dog and I got home safely."

But times and circumstances changed along with the disappearance of the swamps, timber, and panthers.

"When they dug those drainage canals, what evolved was some of the most fertile farm land in world history," clarified Mr. Chaney, who evolved into one of the region's most successful and respected farmers. "The rich soil, made up of rich loam and silt from centuries of being covered by flood waters, can grow anything from corn to cotton to soybeans. Today, there's a lot of rice grown in these parts; although, I retired before rice became popular."

And Canalou changed, too, from a logging camp town to a burgeoning, prosperous farming community. It's described to be at its economic zenith in the 1920s, 1930s, and 1940s when it had a bank, hotel, numerous black smith shops, two automobile service stations, seven grocery stores, and three churches that battled the evils of the town's notorious saloons and pool halls.

"After the swamps were drained, we no longer had to walk up on board walks in downtown Canalou, which by this time had all those grocery stores and two cotton gins: the Percy Gin and the Cathy Gin," Mr. Chaney recalled.

But cash got scarce in the late 1920s when the Great Economic Depression hit America. Mr. Chaney remembers the closing of Canalou's one and only bank.

"Dad had his money in the Bank of Canalou; but after talking to Abe Landers, another farmer, he went to the bank where the banker told him the bank was solid as a brick wall," Mr. Chaney recalled. "Dad had sold about four hundred dollars worth of hogs, and when he said he wanted to draw his money out, the banker asked him not to do that. Shortly after that, the bank failed along with thousands of others in 1929 when the Great Depression hit. But Dad got his money safely out of the bank, thanks to advice from Abe Landers."

"Saturday and Saturday nights saw Canalou's population double, even triple," Mr. Chaney recalls.

"People came to town by the hundreds to do their shopping and to get away from the hard toiling farm work for a few hours," he added. "It was exciting especially when a carnival would come to town. And we had L. A. McCann's moving picture show house to go to see the movies in the 1940s.

"On Saturday nights, you couldn't walk shoulder-to-shoulder down the town's Main Street because of all the people, most of whom were farm people and workers in that area," Mr. Chaney accounted. "We did our shopping for vittles we couldn't raise on the farm, such as sugar, salt, and coffee. A lot of times, we bartered fresh-laid chicken eggs for our vittles or maybe an old fat hen that had quit laying."

He remembers one particular man was very accurate with a .22-caliber rifle.

"Our town's black smithy was known far and wide for his shooting prowess with his little Stevens .22-caliber rifle," Mr. Chaney added.

How good was he?

"I remember him aiming up in the air, saying over and over, 'watch that bee', 'watch that bee', and he would, without fail, blow that tiny flying bee to smithereens," Mr. Chaney recalled.

There were dangerous times, including several shootings and knifings, in the 1930s era.

"I remember the town marshal had to chase a man down after he'd shot a man and had hid out in the woods out by Little River. The fugitive's wife would slip him food as he hid out," Mr. Chaney traced back in time.

"The law ultimately chased him down in a field out at Big Ridge, near Jay Hopper's farm, and shot him in the hand as he tried to escape. I remember them bringing him back to town and placing him in jail. His wounded hand was bleeding, and I saw that.

"There was also a knifing in one of the saloons, where this one man had his guts cut out, but he somehow survived," Mr. Chaney remembered. "There were some tough times and tough people."

Mr. Chaney remembers how important a man's good name was in that era.

"A man was no better than his good name," Mr. Chaney recalled. "That's what made me so mad at another farmer named Dude when he claimed that I had somehow misplaced a cotton trailer. After asking him to quit going around and saying that, I'm ashamed to report that one day I met him out in front of Moore's Mercantile and knocked him down there on Main Street. I don't recall that he ever said anything else against me and my family after that. I'm not real proud of this though."

Mr. Chaney, who died in late 2009, was one of the last men in Canalou to see my own father, Hubert Alexander Whittle, alive in 1950.

"Your Dad had been drinking and gambling and disturbing the peace all day, so the town law asked him to leave town," Mr. Chaney advised. "I remember he asked farmer Les Durbin, one of his favorite gambling buddies of that era, to go with him on up to Sikeston, Missouri, that night. Your Dad had a fast new car, a Hudson that would run with the wind. But Les turned him down. Your Dad was killed later that night in a head-on crash in front of KSIM Radio. That was in 1950."

Chapter Twenty-Nine

Owning *Hitler*

Hitler was a dog, a really good dog.

Not the *Hitler* of Germany infamy for he doesn't deserve to be compared to any dog, much less a good, steady-performing farm dog.

The late Reverend A. C. Sullivant, our farm region's old-timey Baptist preacher of the 1950s, preached a sermon in my youth indicating there will be good dogs in heaven. So, that's good enough for me.

Although the minister didn't hold a funeral for our old farm dog named *Hitler*, it was for that fiercely-brave dog that he made remarks about in the pulpit one day after our canine had died—a fact for which I am forever grateful. Because of this canine's intense loyalty, he was as much family as anyone among the Whittles.

Hitler was Daddy Whittle's dog, being extremely devoted to my father's well-being and presence.

Daddy showed his unusual brand of humor in naming this dog *Hitler* in the wake of World War II.

"This dog will have to be tough to get along in this world carrying the name of *Hitler*," Daddy Whittle proclaimed to his best farm neighbor buddies, Les Durbin, L. A. McCann, and A.

J. Neel, as they came to view our new farm dog that was half bulldog and half German shepherd. Needless to say, *Hitler* was a stocky, stout-built dog, with a shepherd-shaped head and a burly-bulldog torso.

How devoted to Daddy was this unusual-looking dog?

If Daddy was plowing our fields of cotton, *Hitler* took every step Daddy and our mule named Bert made. If Daddy slopped the hogs, *Hitler* was nearby.

But *Hitler*'s dedication to Daddy became regional folklore in 1947 when Daddy was taken down by an enraged, boar hog, out in our pasture's pig pen.

Hitler, who had been overlooking my well-being while I played in our nearby front yard, immediately bolted for the barn lot upon hearing Daddy's piercing screams for help as that mad hog tore into him with its dangerous, long tusks.

Although I was a mere three-years-old at the time, what happened next will remain burned into my soul forever. *Hitler* bolted for the barnyard with such speed that he cleared a fence that was head-high to a grown man. And he hit that enraged hog with such force that it knocked the animal off of the top of my father. Anyone who knows anything about pigs knows it's almost impossible to knock a mature hog off its feet.

When Daddy finally cleared out from under the enraged hog, he bolted for the house to get his rifle. But that left *Hitler* in the pen with the attacking hog.

Although *Hitler* was a fierce-fighting, strong dog in his own right, he was no match for the much larger and stronger male hog. By the time Daddy got back with his trusty .22-caliber rifle, the hog had tossed *Hitler*'s torso up in the air multiple times and ripped him to shreds. I can still recall the hog's foaming, bloody mouth.

Finally, Daddy was able to bring the hog down with a clear shot between the enraged animal's eyes.

This left *Hitler* lying over in the corner of the pen, appearing lifeless as blood gushed from multiple deep gashes and wounds.

Daddy quickly cradled *Hitler* in his arms and told me to follow him to our old black 1943 Ford truck.

My job, Daddy instructed, was to cradle *Hitler*'s bleeding head and body in my lap in back of the truck as we headed for the nearest veterinarians' office in Sikeston, Missouri, located about twelve miles from our remote farm in New Madrid County.

It was one of the longest journeys of my life despite the fact Daddy floor-boarded that old Ford farm truck.

Upon finally arriving at the vet's office, I overheard the doctor consulting with my father.

"Mr. Whittle, ordinarily I would put this animal out of his misery because of so many deep wounds that would have killed most dogs," the vet diagnosed. "But this dog is fighting harder to live than any animal I've ever witnessed. So, I tell you what I will do, if it's okay with you. Leave the dog with me, and I'll tend to him for the next twenty-four hours, to see if he can live. I'll not charge you for the round-the-clock care because of this dog's huge amount of courage and determination to live."

Since we didn't have telephones in our area, Daddy had to return to the vet's office personally each day.

Finally, on the third day, the vet came out front of his office, greeting us with a big grin on his face.

"*Hitler* has come out of his coma and is taking nourishment," the doctor decreed. "He's going to live to fight another day."

"He's the strongest-willed dog to live than any animal I've treated," the physician diagnosed.

Word of this dog's courageous act to save my father's life spread so quickly throughout our farm community to the point neighbors such as Jay Hopper, John Ling, Roy Bixler, and "Bunce" Scott came to pay their respect to this brave dog named *Hitler*.

But this dog had another tough trial to go through with our family the fateful night Daddy's life was snuffed out in a car crash at age thirty-nine.

Although we never brought Daddy's body back to the farm that winter in 1950, *Hitler* knew something had happened to his master and best friend.

I'll not soon forget that old dog's mournful howls during the cold and long winter nights as he laid mourning outside our bedroom windows for months and months following Daddy's death. *Hitler* had never howled before.

During each day's daylight hours, I would go out beneath our front yard's hickory nut tree and sit and peer into that dog's sad eyes. And finally, after several months, the odd-looking dog with the shepherd-shaped head and burly bulldog body, switched his allegiance to me. He became my protector too. When *Hitler* was around, none of the older bully boys of the community laid a hand on me.

"His dog will tear you up," judged neighbor farm boy Harold David Bryant.

Although I was deeply saddened when we lost *Hitler* at the ripe, old dog age of seventeen, I was proud when our preacher man paid his respect to our old farm dog from the pulpit. He said that he thought *Hitler* was already in heaven following in the steps of my farm father as they tilled heavenly soil for Daddy Whittle was truly a man of the earth.

Hitler was truly Daddy Whittle's dog while they jointly roamed the fields here on Mother Earth in fertile farmland that evolved from the former Nigger Wool Swamp.

Chapter Thirty

Daddy's Death

One of my earliest life-changing moments came early in life on October 24, 1950.

Our lives changed tragically when neighbor Norval Harrison came speeding down our farm lane in a cloud of dust bearing the news that my father, Hubert Alexander Whittle, had been in a car wreck.

How serious was it?

"It's bad," the bearer of bad news whispered softly back to my mother, Ruby Lee Stockton Whittle. "You need to get to the hospital in Sikeston, as soon as possible."

With those words my older brother Hubert Van, named after Daddy Whittle, bolted while screaming hysterically from our neighbor's farm house.

He ran so fast and so far that A. J. Neel had to use his new red Dodge truck to chase brother down as he was running emotionally out-of-control down the railroad tracks back toward our own farm house screaming at the top of his voice: "My Daddy ain't dead! Daddy ain't dead!"

As brother bolted into the night, Mother made arrangements for us children to be taken to the Murray Lane home of friends

Herber and Ivarene Bailey up in Sikeston, to be near the hospital.

We learned later that Daddy's car had hit head on with an automobile driven by a woman from Morehouse in front of Sikeston's KSIM Radio Station. The accident had occurred about 6 p.m. We got word of the wreck about 9 p. m.

It wasn't until doing research in 2008 for this book about this past century's culture in Canalou that I realized Norval Harrison and his family actually witnessed Daddy's car crash.

In fact, Norval's daughter, Alice Jean Harrison VanNoy, kept a diary of the incident. Reading the following sent chills down my spine.

"Oct. 24, 1950: *Went to Dexter early this morning. On the way home tonight, we came through Sikeston. We were behind Hubert Whittle when he had his wreck.*

"Oct. 25, 1950: *Mother stayed with Mrs. Whittle all day. Maxine* [sister] *and I stayed at* [grandmother] *Momo's. Went out to Whittles tonight. Mother stayed with Ruby Lee. Hubert Whittle died at 5:50 this morning.*"

"Oct. 26, 1950: Went to *Momo's to eat breakfast with the Bramletts. Went to Hubert Whittles' funeral this afternoon. Went out to Whittles for a little while tonight. Then we came home.*"

Alice Jean went on to share that Daddy Whittle was weaving back and forth across the center line of Highway 60 between Morehouse and Sikeston.

"You could tell your father been drinking," Alice Jean verified.

Waddell and Lavern "Tuta" Bramlett came in from Memphis for the funeral, where they had moved after being mule-sharing, best farm neighbors to Daddy and Momma Whittle in the 1930s. Sharing mules and farm equipment and labor was also how the Whittles became lifetime friends with the Harrisons and to the Savage family, all of whom had roots down in either Arkansas or Mississippi.

At about 5:45 a.m., on the morning of October 25th, family physician Sam Sarno of Morehouse, came out of surgery at

Sikeston's hospital to share with Momma that Daddy had died, mostly from severe head wounds. "But Hubert put up a hard fight to live," Mother credited the doctor with describing.

"He fought like a tiger, but there was too much damage for him to survive," Dr. Sarno diagnosed.

News of father's death didn't reach us children until about 6 a.m., as we were being fed breakfast at the Bailey home.

After breakfast we accompanied Larry and his father to the wrecker service building in downtown Sikeston to view the damage on Daddy's 1949 Hudson, a new vehicle that father took "great pride" in owning.

"It will run with the wind," I'd heard Daddy brag to other farm neighbor men.

At age thirty-nine, Daddy left Momma Whittle a young widow at age thirty with three children: Mary June, fifteen; H. Van; eleven; and me, the baby of the family, at age six.

Multiple dramatic changes for our family happened that fateful night back in 1950.

For example, our dog named *Hitler* started howling at night, which was something the fierce farm guard dog never did prior to Daddy's death. It's understandable since the canine was the devoted companion that accompanied my father to the fields. How *Hitler* knew Daddy was dead, I don't know, for it wasn't unusual in cold winter months for Father, who loved to gamble, to be away from the family for extended periods. He frequently took trips over to Cairo, Illinois, to gamble in the casinos and on the river boats.

Although Daddy's body was not brought back to the farm, *Hitler*, joined the rest of the family in mourning the death of our father.

One blessed aspect of growing up in a small farming community was when one family hurt, the entire community hurt alongside them.

That was evident by the huge turnout of mourners as Daddy's corpse was on display at Sikeston's Nunnelly-Albritton Funeral Home. Mother equated this turnout to the number of people who came to show their support and respect at the hospital the night of Daddy's death.

Do *you* believe in premonitions?

Daddy Whittle apparently did, as evidenced by farm neighbor Mildred Parks, who often sang duets at church services, funerals and weddings. "I remember looking down at you during your Dad's funeral, while we were singing 'Precious Memories'," noted Mildred, who could sing like a song bird. "When you looked up at the funeral with your big brown eyes and smiled at me, I nearly lost it. I tried to get through that song and the next song, 'Amazing Grace'."

"About three months before his car wreck, Hubert came up to me one night at Canalou Baptist Church following a special that Vera and I had sung during the service," Mildred accounted. "Your Father asked if I would sing at his funeral. I told him I would, although, since he was just a young man at the time, I told him that he would probably outlive me.

"To which Hubert replied: 'I know one night when I'm out on the highway, I'll probably wrap my car around some tree, especially since I love to drive fast.' As it turned out, your Daddy was prophetic in that he did perish in a grinding car crash, and it happened as darkness was setting in."

Although only a tyke, there are fond memories from Daddy's funeral that remain burned in my soul forever.

When someone died in our farming community, the town's entire business district shut down. That included the business doors of Moore's Mercantile, Tootie Ralph's Grocery and Whiskey Store, Kasinger's Grocery, Hammock's Hardware, Jim Poe's Grocery, Bert McWater's Grocery, Nog Hunter's Service Station, the Canalou Cotton Gin, Maw Mathenia's Grocery, and Hubert Bond's Ice House.

"Our farm town knew how to show respect, especially when someone died," recalls my sister June. "No commerce, not even the town's black smith shop, operated during Daddy's funeral."

A particularly touching moment came beside Daddy's casket. Although elderly, preacher man A. C. Sullivant, was able to lift me up in his arms and let me view my Daddy's body.

"I want you to look at your Daddy as long as you like," the gentle preacher man instructed softly.

It must have taken all of his strength to lift a little boy and hoist him for several minutes to permit my last viewing of Father. Another particularly touching moment came after the funeral, as the procession left the church house to slowly travel the town's short Main Street.

It came as cotton gin manager L. A. McCann, who was Daddy's best friend, had gin employees line up beside Main Street with their cotton lint-covered caps removed, holding them respectfully over their hearts as one of the community's farmers, a man of the soil, was being transported to his final resting place in his beloved Mother Earth.

Daddy is buried in Sikeston's Garden of Memories.

Chapter Thirty-One
Daddy's Last Christmas

Being a pet little boy on our farm road had its perks and privileges.

For example, I was the only kid on our gravel road who had two Christmases.

Two Christmases?

You read it right, one at farm neighbor A. J. Neel's house, where his mother Myrtle Delemma "Mommie" Gowen and wife Nell plus all their relatives, had numerous goodies and treats with Little Danny Whittle's name on them under their *special*, glowing Christmas tree.

Special Christmas tree?

You read it right. This was no ordinary Christmas tree, for Nell and Mommie went all out on tree decorations. Me and Tonto, A. J. Neel's loyal dog that could nearly talk, would sit and stare for hours on end at their beautiful Christmas tree.

A talking dog?

You read that right too because on a good day, with A. J.'s prompting, Tonto could warble out the word "hamburger" with sincere, doggone good clarity. And "talking dogs" were big in that early television time.

The Neel's tree was special because Mommie and Nell decorated their tree with "angel" hair. Their tree had a heavenly look, with that sweeping and flowing angel hair laced with ample, shining strands of silver icicles.

But the 1949 Christmas was special in many more ways and not just because I had multiple gifts with Little Danny Whittle's name on them at A. J. Neel's house.

I was five-years-old that Christmas when I took on some unexplained, "weird feelings". I noticed just how pretty A. J.'s niece, little Jackie Marion Gunter, was.

However, at age seven, she was too much of an older woman to officially be my girlfriend. But I could dream. She was a little princess beauty and is now a lifelong friend who lives in Kennett, Missouri.

It was later this Christmas Eve day that I remember a scene very clearly through my childhood lens. It's such a fond farm Christmas remembrance. This scene is so clearly etched in my soul; I feel I can reach back and touch the day it happened.

Daddy Whittle had picked me up at A. J. Neel's house in our family's brand new Hudson, his car that would "run with the wind" due to a new-fangled mechanical invention he called over-drive.

Never will I forget that fateful moment Daddy pulled up in front of our own farm house and instructed his three children to watch the chimney in hopes of seeing Santa come and go with our Christmas gifts.

A stick of dynamite could have not have got my eyes unglued from watching that chimney but a meddling and lying older brother did.

"There ain't no such thing as Santa," older brother whined after Daddy went in the house to assist Santa.

"Is too," I retorted.

"Ain't" brother re-retorted.

"Is too," I claimed emphatically.

"Ain't neither," brother countered.

With those words, I sailed over the back seat with fists flying.

Brother's claim that there is no Santa were fighting words to this believing little farm boy. And Santa knew exactly where I lived on our farm road at a place noted as Tram Switch on early railroad maps of the Bootheel region of southeast Missouri.

As I sailed over that car seat, I remember suddenly seeing stars, as I immediately landed the first punch, you know, by blooding my older brother's fist with my red, now-glowing, and profusely-bleeding nose.

Then I threw brother down, you know, right on top of me as he continued pounding on my defiant noggin.

After a few more whacks of brother's fist to my head, Daddy Whittle mercifully stepped back out the front door and announced that Santa had already come and gone.

"I told you there was a Santa," I remember whimpering to doubting older brother.

"Santa came by our house while we were all down at the Neel's house," Daddy explained satisfactorily to me. When Daddy Whittle said it, that settled the matter.

A gift handed to me by Daddy Whittle was my best boyhood Christmas present.

Inside a big box was, drum roll please, a two-holstered set of Roy Rogers' weapons. The holster was made out of sturdy, genuine leather. The guns, well, they were made out of "genuine plastic," my doubting older brother reported while still trying, unsuccessfully, to throw cold water on Christmas 1949.

As it turned out, Christmas 1949 was the last spent with Daddy Whittle before he perished the next October in a grinding car crash in Sikeston.

Needless to say, I cherished that Roy Rogers' gun and holster set. Okay, the durable leather holster set I kept for years, but the genuine plastic pistols didn't last long while I shot up the "bad guys" as I rode my imaginary "Trigger" horse, which was a designated bale of hay out by our barn.

Yes, Christmas 1949 was special for I knew I was a loved little farm boy by multiple families up and down our dirt farm road.

To this day, I still believe in Santa because my farm Daddy said so. It was one of his last decrees made clear to his youngest son before he died. And I make certain today to pass on Santa to my beloved grandchildren.

This way, Daddy's last Christmas lives on. . . .

Chapter Thirty-two

When Mamma Cries

There are benefits to living in a small town, and there are pluses to dying there, for Canalou folks knew how to be respectful during a funeral.

The whole town closed down, for example, for the funeral of my father, Hubert Alexander Whittle, who died in 1950.

Although farm life went on, it was never the same after Daddy perished in a car crash at age thirty-nine, leaving a young widow with three children ages fifteen, eleven, and six.

I only saw Momma Whittle cry three times in life. The first was the day Daddy was laid to rest and the reality of her plight must have started sinking in.

I had watched Momma closely during the days following Daddy's fatal wreck and noted how appreciative she was to every kind deed, including farm neighbor girl Mary Jane Bramlett driving us to the Albritton Funeral Home in Sikeston after noticing how much Momma's hands were trembling in trying to get dressed for the visitation.

It touched the entire family when every business, from Kasinger's Grocery on one end of town to W. M. Moore's Mercantile on the other end of town, closed business doors when the hearse pulled through town toward Canalou Baptist

Church. We counted each set of closed business doors appreciatively as we rolled slowly through town as a grieving family.

"Out of respect for your father, every business owner not only closed their stores and black smith shops, most of them came to the funeral preached by Brother A. C. Sullivant," explained neighbor farmer A. J. Neel, one of our family's closest friends.

Never will I forget the preacher as he took me, a little boy, up in his arms to let me view over the top of the casket to see my Daddy for the last time.

"You look at your Father as long as you like," the Reverend Sullivant instructed softly.

Nor will I ever forget the beautiful, mournful, heart-felt singing of "Amazing Grace" and "Precious Memories" by church vocalists Mildred Parks and Vera Kochel, who could sing like songbirds in the spring.

Following the tasteful country church funeral, Mother's shoulders shuddered a bit as the hearse left the church, and slowly motored back along Main Street.

As I got older and reflected back on the boyhood experience of losing Daddy, I was accurate in realizing that those closed businesses and acts of kindness were as much out of respect for Momma Whittle, maybe even more so, than they were for Daddy Whittle, a man noted for being a good farmer and paying his bills. But, Daddy was also noted for his gambling, drinking and partying in non-crop-growing times.

Suddenly, Mother was soul provider of food, clothes, and the emotional and spiritual care for three children. A heap of responsibility for a woman in 1950, which was long before something called women's liberation swept through American society.

In that era it was not unusual for men folks, especially in the farming culture, to exclude women from business dealings. For example, Momma Whittle had never used a telephone prior to Daddy's death.

But she courageously adapted, including teaching herself to drive the farm truck and new Plymouth coupe car we bought at the Goza-Harper Motor Co. up in Sikeston.

Gin manager L. A. "Pete" McCann had been named my godfather by my parents. So Mr. McCann became increasingly impactful in our family's future after Daddy died.

So it was at the cotton gin, ironically the last place we saw Daddy alive on October 24, 1950, that Momma learned how to use a telephone in making a long distance call to Sikeston.

"I had to take over the farm business, which Mr. McCann started me out by using the phone for the first time in my life, to call the Production Credit Association people up in Sikeston who handled some of our farming business," Momma described later in life. "I was so nervous that I couldn't dial the number. Mr. McCann kept encouraging me, and I was finally able to make that first phone call. He encouraged me a lot, especially in those first days without your father. Sikeston lawyer David Blanton was also a great encourager."

Big changes came for all of us, including my sister Mary June, who was fifteen when Father perished. Since Mother had to take over the farming business, big sister assumed many of the household chores, including cooking, washing, and mending clothes.

She also assisted Mother in helping tend to me, the baby of the family.

Brother Van, at the tender age of eleven, had to step up and take over as many man-type physical farm activities as possible, including the early-morning milking of the cows and slopping the hogs. These were no small tasks, especially in the dreadful painfully cold winter months when a chopping axe was required to break the ice in order for the farm animals to have drinking water.

Van and farm neighbor boy Bruce Gene Bryant became our family heroes that fall when they, at ages twelve and thirteen respectively, taught themselves to operate our farm's cantankerous old, orange-colored Minneapolis-Moline two-row, tractor-pulled combine in time to harvest the wheat and soybeans.

"The boys did a remarkable job learning to run that combine, for that brand was known to break down often in the field," judged farm neighbor Johnny 'Bunce' Scott, a neighbor who also stepped up to help our family in our time of need.

In the first crop year without Daddy, there was also high drama too.

The spring planting season of 1951 was unusually wet, meaning that it was difficult in not only getting our crops planted, but there was the added danger of flood waters washing away new-sprouted soybeans and cotton.

Spring planting was expensive, often requiring families to borrow money from banks or the Production Credit Association up in Sikeston to be paid off at harvest time later in the fall. So, anytime those crops were threatened, it was a time of nervousness among farm families.

It was raining cats and dogs one particularly dreary day when Momma Whittle came crashing into the house, madder than a hornet. How mad was she? So mad she didn't take off her muddy knee boots she'd worn to walk and inspect our flooding fields.

"Get the shotgun!" Momma instructed loudly

Normally, that meant there was a varmint in the corn crib or a snake in the chicken house.

"It's a snake, but one that walks on two legs," Momma Whittle instructed angrily as she loaded both barrels of the shotgun, and older siblings Van and June hurriedly placed heavy cinder blocks, shovels, hoes, and a chopping axe in the back our old farm truck.

"We gotta get back to the New Ground," Momma instructed as she floor-boarded our pickup.

As we turned the corner behind the flooded Little River that split through our farm, we saw the reason for the Mother's anguish.

A neighboring farmer had cut a ditch across a county road from his flooded soybean field in order to run his flood water out of his fields onto our fields, which meant that our fields of new-planted crops would "drown out."

"He'd never have cut this damn ditch if your Daddy was still alive," Momma Whittle declared between clinched teeth as she instructed sister Mary June and brother Van to start filling up the newly-dug ditch with concrete blocks and dirt.

My job was to hold the shotgun, since I was too small to help dam up that "damn ditch."

Drama really developed when the farmer, who had dug the ditch, pulled up to a stop in his own farm truck about a quarter of a mile away.

"That son-of-a-bitch knows better than to come any closer," Momma declared. "But Danny get that gun over here closer to me in case the SOB's crazy enough to pull on down here."

That farmer may have made a wrong decision in cutting the ditch, but he made the smart decision to not come any closer as we dammed his damn ditch. That was the one and only day I saw Momma Whittle mad enough that she would have shot the man dead in his tracks. It was the second time I saw her cry.

The fact that our farm was split by Little River, a stream that was prone to flood, could make my farm family's position a precarious one, especially in years it rained heavily.

When was the last time I saw Mother cry?

It was 1957, another unusually wet year, when the whole family had worked long hard hours getting crops planted during the brief times it was dry enough to work in the fields.

Finally, all of our soybeans and cotton were up through the ground, and all looked well each morning Momma drove her Plymouth car around our field roads to see crop and ground conditions.

But one night in late May, Mother grew increasingly alarmed when it was forecast over KSIM Radio up in Sikeston that more thunderstorms were on the way down toward the Bootheel.

"We can't stand much more rain," Mother judged as Sikeston radio announcer Dick Watkins forecast more incoming storms.

Announcer Watkins' forecast proved accurate, for about

midnight a severe wave of thunder bolts came out of the sky as more heavy torrential rains swept over area farms.

But, as it turned out, the rain was not the danger. The next morning was the last time I saw tears come to Mother's eyes, as she kneeled down on her knees to see where hail had stripped the little leaves off our newly-sprouted soybeans and cotton. We lost about half of our crop that year due to that hail.

Farm life could be hellishly cruel at times.

Momma Whittle and Aunt

Chapter Thirty-Three

Cadillac Shack Out Back

Our shacks out back, you know, the little houses at the end of the path could be status symbols in the era before we had plumbing and running water inside farm homes.

Although farm life often included seemingly endless days of hand-labor out in the fields, there were frolicsome moments.

Such was the case when Daddy Whittle, who worked in winter months tearing down houses in nearby Sikeston, Missouri, brought home something new to us farm children, items that he called commode lids. Since we children knew the family he was working for was Catholic, we assumed commode lids had something to do with Catholic religious customs. Being country Baptist children, you see, we were taught that Catholics were *different*, and Daddy, having the unusual sense of humor that he did, let us assume that commode lids and Catholics go together.

In fact, family stock in the community seemed to soar when we Whittle children went to town bragging that we had some slightly-used Catholic commode lids. Families from miles around started coming around to visit, some of them had not been to our farm in months, and before they'd get back in their farm trucks or farm wagons, they'd go sit on those fancy Catholic commode lids.

We could have charged admission. "Shucks, they're just here to view our Catholic commode lids," older brother, Hubert Van, explained to his little brother. "It ain't because they like us. They just want to sit their fannies on those fancy, smooth-sittin' commode lids."

A farm neighbor boy sized up our outdoor toilet's status.

"Your family has the Cadillac shack out back," judged Harold David Bryant, my best farm neighbor buddy of youth.

Neighboring farmers, the Hoppers, also had a Cadillac quality shack out back because theirs was made of concrete, and had been built by WPA workers to create jobs during the Great Depression.

Being anchored in concrete, the Hoppers never had to worry about someone turning over their toilet on Halloween nights.

But high drama could come out of those shacks out back.

Flying "waspers," for example, could make us run fast, like folks did on Saturday nights down at the Pentecost church when they'd get fired up by the Holy Ghost.

One day, my older sister Mary June came streaking and shrieking out of our Johnny after being stung on her backside by two wasps.

"Either the waspers got her, or she got religion," my older brother shared as we shared a few guffaws at sister's painful dilemma.

When I was age five, I was peacefully seated on one of those smooth-sittin' Catholic commode lids tending to business, when unbeknownst to me Ol' Red, our main and very mean barnyard rooster, snuck under the back side of our outdoor privy. While concentrating on my business, I hadn't paid attention to the commotion under our new Catholic commode lids, that is until Ol' Red must have spotted something he thought was a little worm dangling all exposed there for the taking.

WHOW! I'm talking some real, raw penetrating pain here!

With that assault, I screamed bloody murder and flew terrified into Momma Whittle's kitchen where I fell out on the floor, rolling around in blood-dripping pain.

Finally, after Momma got me under control, she managed to ask what had me as terrified as I bawling uncontrollably.

I told her, while pointing to my bloodied appendage: "That damned ol' rooster pecked my peck peck!"

Raw pain is what I'm talking about here as older brother and sister June were rolling around on the floor too.

But they were laughing uncontrollably, which mystified me while I displayed my wounded little appendage, seeking sympathy.

"That ol' rooster nearly made a girl out of you," older brother decreed with another guffaw.

It was the only time I remember Momma Whittle not thrashing me for cussin'. I guess she understood my anxiety when that rooster nearly made a girl out of me. Our shack out back was also a learning center, since I partially learned to read in pre-school days, mostly by looking at girly pictures. I associated words in old Sears-Roebuck catalogs that were considered upgraded outdoor toilet business-tending equipment when doing our business.

Getting a new Sears-Roebuck catalog was big, for that meant we could take the old Sears catalog to our outdoor two-holer. Why was this important?

Because those slick catalog pages were a lot more comfortable than old rough barnyard corn cobs we had to use when catalogs were not available. It was my job to gather up the cleaner cobs to use later in our privy.

For college-educated folks of today, who may not know the farm toilet formula for using corn cobs, it was the following: "First red, then white, and then red again, if needed."

Think about it.

Attaching those commode lids was one of the last things Daddy did on the farm before he perished in the grinding car crash in October 1950. It's just one of many fond memories this old country boy has of one of his father's more colorful deeds.

Chapter Thirty-Four

A. J. Neel

A. J. Neel was not a good farmer, but he was a great neighbor.

A. J. was known to take a drink of liquor at saloons in Canalou and the neighboring town of Morehouse and Nippy Jones Tavern up in Sikeston.

He was a good man who would give you the shirt off his back.

He wouldn't go to church with his wife Nell and mother, Myrtle Delemma "Mommie" Gowen, devout Canalou Baptist Church-going ladies.

A. J. lived by the Golden Rule, treating others like he wanted to be treated without the "hell fire" condemnation that many preachers were known for in our farming culture.

A. J. Neel was a paradox on our farm road; he disliked farming and "damn Republicans," but loved children, dogs, and book learning.

He could have been many things, including a scientist or a great school teacher. Eventually, after he ended up selling his farm on our farm lane, he was a successful country store merchant when he owned little rural State Line Grocery on the Arkansas/Missouri state line below Hornersville, one of the southern-most incorporated towns in southeast Missouri.

How much did I love and respect A. J. Neel? It was he, his wife, and mother who asked Momma Whittle to let them adopt me when they moved away in the mid-1950s from Canalou to go operate State Line Store.

These dear farm neighbors loved me, and I adored them. Plus, Mommie Gowen was regionally famous for her chicken and dumplings. She and Nell would cook anything that Little Danny Whittle wanted, and at anytime.

Their home was like a safe harbor when this former little farm boy would get in trouble down the road at the Whittle household.

Any time my family missed me from our farm, they didn't worry, for they knew I'd slipped off to walk with my faithful farm dog named *Hitler* down to A. J. Neel's house.

Understand this: Daddy Whittle was a stern disciplinarian who, when you needed a whipping, would apply the belt vigorously to our behinds.

I knew I was in a heap of trouble one particular morning when I disregarded Daddy's personal orders for me not to slip off back down to the Neel home. I remember getting a hankering for some of Mommie's white syrett and biscuits.

I recall many folks in Canalou making me speak because I couldn't talk plain in that young boyhood era of the 1940s.

After getting my white syrett and biscuit, I began to fret that Daddy Whittle was going to "blister my behind" because I had directly disobeyed him.

Well, Mommie Gowen had a soft way of dealing with folks, so she gave me a *special* formula to use on Daddy when he came in from working in the fields that day.

When Daddy came towering up over me, I sat my little tush down while playing with my little toy tractors between two big roots under our front yard hicker-nut tree.

When Daddy started in, Mommie had instructed me to look up at him with "your big brown eyes" and say thusly: "Daddy, if you just give me a good kalking [talking] to, I'll not do it again."

Well, lo and behold, Daddy, for some reason, could only turn around and walk away.

To which Momma Whittle explained later: "Your Daddy had to put his hand over his mouth to keep you from seeing him grin and laugh. It was one of the few times one of you youngen's ever talked your Daddy out of a whipping."

And I didn't slip off again to A. J. Neel's house. . . until a day or two later.

Mommie's beloved husband, Marion "Poppy" Gowen, was one of the sweetest, soft-spoken, pipe-smoking, country gentleman you'd ever hope to meet.

It was Mommie and Poppy who would keep Little Danny Whittle any time Mother or Daddy had to make an urgent trip to Sikeston or Canalou to replace a broken part on our farm equipment.

I was prone to have multiple severe "earaches" when I was little, especially between the ages of two and four.

Poppy Gowen would smoke his aromatic old pipe for hours and hours, patiently blowing that soothing warm smoke in my aching ears. Oh, how I loved that elderly gentle soul. My sister, June, who didn't smoke, was also very patient to "blow smoke" in my ears.

At age four, I did something one morning that I had never done before. As I was leaving our beloved neighbors' house to get my dog, *Hitler*, and walk back home, I leaned over and kissed Poppy on his forehead, while declaring: "I love you, Poppy Gowen!"

I don't remember why I did it, but as it turned out, it was a fateful moment for Poppy and me. I learned later that night that tears had come to Poppy's eyes there on the couch after I'd planted an affectionate kiss on his forehead. It was the only time I kissed this kind, gentle soul's forehead.

So I've always felt warm and snuggly feelings in knowing that Poppy knew how much I loved him before he died from a stroke later that night. It was my first experience with death being a part of life.

Poppy further endeared himself to me when he'd save his empty tobacco pouches for me to store my treasured marbles. Older brother, H. Van, was always jealous that I had those "fancy tobacco sacks" in which to store my marbles.

It was farm neighbor A. J. Neel, who initially took me to Grace Hewitt's Canalou Town Library, this helped prepare me for a forty-five-year journalism career that took me out of the cotton fields to covering race riots in Cairo, Illinois, to the White House, and to being a foreign war correspondent in covering the ethnic-cleansing civil war in Bosnia.

"You'll read books, and you'll travel the world," was A. J.'s prophecy when he'd check out books for me at our little farm hamlet's town library that tripled as Canalou Town Hall and town jail.

I loved to read, and with A. J.'s help I made fifty-nine book reports in sixth grade, only to be beat by classmate Vernon Shorter and his record sixty-seven book reports. Vernon was smarter than me, coming from a long line of school teachers including his aunt who taught us in third grade at Canalou School of Higher Ciphering and Advanced Thinking.

A. J. Neel and his family became really close and emotionally crucial to this former little farm boy, especially after Daddy Whittle's death in 1950. I cannot describe the affection I hold for this neighbor farm family who loved me dearly as a little impish farm boy.

May our good gracious Lord nestle and rest their sweet ol' souls where truly good farm neighbors go.

Chapter Thirty-Five
McCann 'Can Do'

Nicknames on the farm were popular. Because of my dark complexion, "Little Black Boy" was my first nickname that I recollect while growing up on the farm. The second of childhood was "Little Pete," my favorite. Why? One, it was my "go-to-town" nickname, where I was called "Pete," "Re-Pete," and/or "Little Pete" by the likes of Canalou Postmaster Don Kochel and theater owner John Summers when I went to town from the farm.

Two, the name was in honor of L. A. "Pete" McCann, the town's cotton gin man who kept records of everyone's crop yields and the amounts farm families owed the Allen-Davis Gin Co. until fall harvests were complete.

One cold winter day as Daddy Whittle and I were moseying toward town, having to walk up on the railroad tracks due to our farm road being flooded by nearby over-flowing Little River, I asked why it was that everyone in town seemed to call me "Pete," "Re-Pete," and "Little Pete"?

"Son, do you see the big stomach that hangs over Mr. Pete McCann's britches?" Daddy asked.

"Yes sir," I replied.

"Look at your own belly that hangs out due to you eating

at two homes all the time, our house and at farm neighbor Mommie Gowen's dinner table," Daddy described. "You both have big bellies."

I proudly recall pooching out my stomach even more there on the railroad tracks, for I loved being compared to Mr. McCann, one of farm town Canalou's most respected businessmen.

After that, I wore being called "Pete," "Re-Pete," and "Little Pete" like badges of honor.

Daddy died one night in a head-on car crash. After that, L. A. "Pete" McCann became really prominent in my life's ledger, for he and Daddy had struck an agreement that Mr. McCann would be the godfather to Daddy's children if anything bad ever happened. And when it did, Mr. McCann was the type of man who took the responsibility serious.

For instance, it was Mr. McCann who taught me the finer points of playing a competitive game of Canasta.

I guessed "Canasta" to be a sin of some sort at Canalou's Baptist, Church of Christ, and Pentecostal churches because we'd always pull the window curtains down before we'd get out the card table and double-deck of cards, which is required for Canasta.

One thing I learned from Mr. McCann, was to have fun with the game but play to win. That meant you concentrated hard to remember how many cards had been heaped on the mounting discard pile.

"The better you remember the cards, the better chance we have of winning," Mr. McCann instructed.

I loved getting to be his Canasta-playing partner.

I even got to loving church Sundays because instead of having to go to church, Momma would drop me off at Mr. McCann's house when he'd planned on barbecuing a heaping pile of chickens he'd bought down at Bert McWaters' Grocery that later became Hammock's Grocery.

Anything Mr. McCann did, he did it well. And it was that way with his barbecue routine.

"You gotta wait until the fire calms down, to cook the chicken good and slow, you know, to let that hickory smoke permeate throughout the meat," Mr. McCann instructed. Another detailed pain-staking step was preparation of his highly-secret recipe for his barbecue sauce.

Since I was sworn to secrecy by Mr. McCann, a man who placed a high value on "keeping your word," I've never shared the secret ingredients of his fantastic barbecue sauce.

I will tell you this much. It's a vinegar-lemon juice-based sauce jazzed up with multiple spices. . . One day when I was the ripe old age of seven, I confess to being so prideful that my overall galluses nearly burst with chest-swollen pride as Mr. McCann ordained: "Little Pete, it's time for you to have your own barbecue pit."

"You're the only child around who seems to really want to learn the finer art of good slow Southern barbecuing," Mr. McCann judged.

I was floating on cloud nine the day Mr. McCann got around to constructing my very own personal barbecue pit out at our farm located at Tram Switch, a mile north up the railroad tracks from downtown Canalou.

I knew Mr. McCann meant business when he opened his new Plymouth car trunk and extracted his brick-laying tools, complete with mortar. It was also the same time Mr. McCann taught me how to lay bricks for he was always good at instructing me how to do things.

Okay, it was only a one-foot by one-foot little pit, but to this little farm boy, it was a monument, a huge symbol of friendship to a man I highly respected.

Mr. McCann was probably the smartest man in Canalou; at least, he was in my eyes, particularly on the day he brought his "new-fangled fishing worm-hunting contraption" out to our farm. His new invention, he said, would mystically bring fishing worms to the top of the ground.

This happened after the REA (Rural Electric Administration) had turned "on the power" that lit up our light bulbs located in the center of the ceilings in each room of our farm house in

1951.

You had to see it, to believe it! What Mr. McCann had constructed was this set of two-wire prongs that he would stick down into the ground. And sure as shooting, when he plugged in the electrical wire he attached to those wire prongs, up *popped* a bunch of highly motivated and fast-wiggling worms out of that gumbo dirt.

It was like magic how those worms would pop up out of that moist ground out behind our chicken house, which meant that it would be only a matter of minutes before Mr. McCann and I would be getting the backside of our britches damp as we sat fishing on the ditch bank of nearby Little River.

This country-smart business man did some strong, positive steering in my life at a crucial time I needed positive adult male influence after the death of my own father.

Later in life, one of my saddest newspapering duties was writing L. A. Pete McCann's obituary report.

But I think Mr. McCann would have been proud, for I penned his obituary to the best of my ability, you know, the way this strong man of my youth taught me to do things.

Chapter Thirty-Six
Road Code

We're talking some serious inside farm culture information here, the type not normally shared with *outsiders*.

We had a "farm road wave code" as created by neighbor (the late) A. J. Neel, a farming man who was like a father to me after my own daddy died in 1950.

I still use remnants of the code today down in Tennessee, much to city-gal wife Pat's dismay, although it's been fifty years since I lived on a farm.

Basically, I just flip up my index finger off our vehicle's steering wheel to greet folks, few drivers today signal back to me when I'm cruising the boulevards of town living.

Some city folks fling a finger back at me, but not the same finger I hold up to them.

"You're no longer a farm boy," Pat chastises.

Being a cityfied female, we can't expect Pat to grasp "once a farm boy, always a farm boy."

It's a "roots thang" as in a Swampeast Missouri gumbo mud that gets between your toes "thang."

"It's a tied-to-the-soil loyalty thang," agrees Canalou native

Les Landers, whose family roots go back to our swamp village's first formative days in 1902.

"It's a pride thang," added Alva Jones, who was born in Canalou in 1933. "A good Bootheel farm boy doesn't get above his raisin'. How you greet folks from one vehicle to the next was kind of a prescribed courtesy thang."

Or as former farm neighbor girl Sue "Baby" Bixler states it succinctly: "If we didn't like your ass, we didn't wave atcha!!"

It was a cultural thang, as explained by one of our more educated folks from Canalou.

Canalou School and Higgerson School teacher (the late) Agatha "Sissy" Weaks Parks put it: "Once you get your feet wet in the damp former swampy soil of the Bootheel, you always come back. We're all neighbors and wave friendly to everyone who comes into our town. We never leave our Bootheel roots."

We'll take it slow here, step by step, so Pat and other non-farm types can maybe get a handle on A. J. Neel's "farm road wave code."

Step one, being farm folks, we're known for being "neighborly." It's almost universally known that rural folks are friendly.

Everyone, whether traveling our farm road by car, truck, farm tractor, or mules and wagon, got a "one finger wave" because farm folks are basically friendly. That's the least "wave" we can give them, though. It's just barely more than an old, impersonal nod-the-head acknowledgement.

"Even if we don't know folks, we give them the ol' trusty one [index] finger wave," instructed A. J. when he thought I was "old enough" (age four) to start getting a grasp on the code. "It's just the neighborly thing to do. . . if you know them fairly well, you might wiggle the finger off the steering wheel a time or two. Just a wiggle. . . "

"But we don't want to over do it," A. J. cautioned. "Just practice your basic one-finger wave initially."

But A. J. got real "firm," even emotional, at his next level of farm road wave instruction since it was an election year down in New Madrid County.

"We never, ever raise more than one finger when waving at a damn Republican," A. J. noted after the election year when Missourian Harry S. Truman defeated some Yankee with a sneaky-looking mustache named Dewey for U. S. President.

It would be after I left the Bootheel that I learned Republican was only one word.

Present-day Canalou and Matthews farmer Lonny Lawson recalls A. J.'s rule against being over-friendly to Republicans.

"He would barely wave, if at all, if he knew you voted Republican," confirmed farmer Lawson in an interview done in 2009 at the Harvest Café in downtown Matthews, Missouri, where farmers from the region gather for early morning coffee and to share the latest farm-related news.

"A. J. Neel definitely didn't like Republicans," farmer Lawson verified.

A. J. admitted he would have made a better school teacher than he was a farmer. I loved the man dearly for taking the time to teach me important stuff about life up and down our farm road. Thankfully, he and his family took me under wing after Daddy Whittle perished in a 1950 car wreck.

So each time I'd be riding in A. J. Neal's faithful, old, red-faded Dodge pickup, he'd have me practice the wave code. "Do we wave at men coming down the road on farm tractors?" I asked.

"Yes, you wave at everyone, especially professional farm tractor drivers such as Vincent Nichols and his brother Guy," A. J. instructed patiently. "The Nichols brothers are two of the most dedicated, hard-working professional farm workers in our country."

"What about the train engineer driving the passenger train [called The Moose] up and down our railroad tracks?" I remember asking.

"Yes, in fact, that's a good place to practice the one finger wave when we're not actually driving and meeting people on our farm road," A. J. instructed.

So, when I'd hear the trains' "clackety-clack" sound coming slowly down the tracks, I'd make a run for the railroad to flash the "one finger wave."

Sure enough, A. J. had been right, for when I flipped up my one finger wave in the train's general direction, the train engineers usually stuck their index fingers back at me.

I recall my overall galluses nearly bursting with pride as the train folks and I began exchanging our one-finger waves daily, except on weekends because the train didn't run on the Sabbath Day when farm folks went to town church to get right with God.

One special engineer and I became friends of a sort, for once in a while he'd give a special mighty loud "toot" of the train's whistle. I think my older brother and sister were jealous of me because the train engineer would give me a "personal wave and whistle toot" when he'd pass by us while we snatched white, fluffy, fully-matured, cotton bolls out in the fields near the tracks.

Now, that pretty well covered the basic "one finger wave" level of the code.

It was a big day when A. J. Neel judged me ready to advance to a higher level of the code. Slow and easy here, for when you understand the code, you understand a tad more about our unique farm-cultural up-bringing.

"Pay attention, Little Danny Whittle," A. J. began earnestly in his advanced level of farm road code waving instruction.

I knew to listen up and listen tight when A. J. referred to me by my full name. "Little Danny Whittle" was sort of a pet name most Canalou folks called me, especially after Daddy Whittle died.

"You're ready for advancement," A. J. continued. "We're to the two-finger wave level now."

"The two finger wave?!" I asked excitedly! I was pumped emotionally.

"The two finger wave is reserved for folks you really know well," A. J. instructed. "You know, for folks you know well, but not good enough that they come to eat Sunday dinner after church. It's an acknowledgement that you know them well, and it's a step up in greeting over the ol' trusty one finger wave."

So, for the next several weeks, when A. J. and I would ride in his faded red-colored pickup to get a Nehi orange belly-washer at Kasingers Grocery and Junk Yard that sat at the north end of Canalou's mile-long Main Street, he'd have me practice the new level of two finger farm road waving.

"You gotta use some judgment in this one," A. J. instructed. "The ol' two finger wave is reserved mostly for folks you really know well."

Sure enough, the next time we met farm neighbor (the late) Charles McCann speeding down the farm road in a huge cloud of dust, I threw up "two fingers."

And as usual, A. J. was right, for Charles McCann immediately replied with his own version of the two-finger wave off the steering wheel of his big grain-hauling farm truck that the farmer seemed to always run wide open and full throttle.

"But you have to be quick with fast drivers like Farmer McCann," A. J. instructed. "He tends to drive fast, like a bat out of hell."

Momma Whittle trusted me with A. J. Neel but threatened a whipping if I ever used that "bat out of hell" phrase again.

The next day it was time for another trial when farm neighbor Dick Bryant and his wife Ollie and their son Billy Gay, and b-e-a-u-t-i-f-u-l daughter Jane came motoring slowly down our farm road to get some groceries and conduct some cotton gin business down at Canalou.

Did I mention that this farmer's daughter was real pretty? How pretty? So pretty she won Sikeston's annual Cotton Carnival Beauty Pageant back in 1957.

When I flipped up my new two-finger wave, sure as tootin', up came Dick Bryant's two fingers off his old gray farm truck's steering wheel.

"You're getting a handle on it," A. J. acknowledged. His praise made my overall galluses swell with heartfelt "farm road wave code" pride.

Finally, it was time for the really big day of instruction. I'd noticed that A. J., when we'd meet someone on the farm road that he really, really liked, he'd take his whole hand off the steering wheel, and thrust it toward the farm road visitor in one, big, dramatic swoop.

"But you only do that to folks you really, really like," A. J. confirmed. "You know, family-type loved ones. . . and folks you trust. . . as in Preacherman A. C. Sullivant or cotton gin man L. A. 'Pete' McCann, or neighbor Roy Bixler, and good farm boy Robert Terry Reed."

And most of the time, those folks would thrust their whole hands back in our direction.

You see, A. J. Neel really knew his stuff.

So, it wasn't long before my whole family began practicing A. J. Neel's farm road wave code. In fact, everyone on our farm road ended up adopting A. J. Neel's farm road wave code. As I described, A. J. Neel was smart enough to have been a college professor. Cityfied folks today, especially those with college educations, might term our "farm road wave code" as unsophisticated farm social etiquette. "You know, we had a special culture, a special way of life in little Canalou, a town I was blessed to grow up in," concluded Alva Jones, the son of the late Orval and Floy Mae Arbuckle Jones Gruen. "And while I drove our dry-cleaning routes between Canalou, Lilbourn, and Risco, I frequently used the one finger wave of friendliness, which is all I could safely take off the steering wheel in that era before power steering."

So the next time you're in and around our beloved Canalou, just throw up a finger. And you'll find they'll wave "back atcha."

Chapter Thirty-Seven

Ann Rice

To the former Ann Rice and me, Robert L. Rasche was more than just a great educator.

He was a godsend.

I would not have finished high school, much less achieved a world-travelled journalism career, if not for this great man. The stern, but fair, educator was a "man's man" who had faith in me when I didn't deserve it.

Sharecropper's daughter Luanne Marie Ann Rice Simones of Murfreesboro was two years ahead of me in school.

I remember her well, not only for her beauty and bouncing pony tail, but she was one of the brightest students at good ol' Grayridge High, Missouri.

Ann's own words best describe the huge impact Superintendent Rasche had on her life.

"I got married at age fourteen and fell behind my class," Ann traced back across the pages of life. "When Mr. Rasche sought me out and encouraged me to do make-up summer studies, he took it upon himself, without pay, to guide and grade my work in order so that I could catch back up and graduate with my class of 1960.

"He was a giant of man in our young lives," she confirmed. "I thank God daily for having Mr. Rasche encourage me at a critical time of my youth. I didn't know it at the time, but Mr. Rasche came to our home to grade my papers while experiencing serious health ailments."

Ann's childhood poverty typifies a standard of life shared by thousands of families who qualified as sharecroppers. Their family's meager existence became even more precarious when large cotton picking machines took away manual cotton-picking jobs in the 1950s.

But most farm families, rich or poor, maintained a certain pride. "We were sharecroppers, but proud people, a loving family of eight siblings who have stayed close all these years," Ann added.

"Ours is simply a story of a poor farm family having little else but each other," shares Ann, who recalls being kicked off numerous Bootheel farms, mainly because of her father's mental illness.

"After farmer, Ed Clines, a nice man, died with cancer, Daddy [Loren Ray Rice] couldn't tolerate the man's son. Plus, Dad's new impudent young boss didn't want us there anyway," Ann accounted. "It felt like the end of the world as we finally drove away after living and working for eight years for the benevolent Mr. Clines, who made an effort to understand our father, his struggles, and special needs."

"We landed in a shot-gun house on Mr. Fowler's farm, and then, the next year we moved to boss Tom Baker's Trailback Plantation, and for the first time, we kids started hiring out as field hands," Ann traced. "Mr. Baker had quiet competent straw-bosses, including Beck Maddox, a nice man.

"We lived in a row of tenant houses, with mostly black neighbors, except for the white Dykes' family," Ann added.

The Dykes family included brothers Jimmy, and twins Roy and Troy, who attended Grayridge School with Ann and me.

From there, life deteriorated for the Rice family as they moved from farm shanty to farm shanty, not knowing if they had a next meal much less how they would get through the next winter. Her father's emotional issues continued.

"I recall the year Daddy and farm owner, Dan Frizzell, had a terrible fist-fight over the garden. We moved right away," Ann accounted. "It became a yearly routine: moving in, working a share-crop, Daddy fighting with the owner; moving out.

"Life became a morbid, crawling, groveling hell for us all," Ann noted with deep emotions. "We were all young kids whose only income-producing abilities consisted of hiring out in the cotton fields.

"We went hungry a lot of times. We were humiliated all the time. We often worked six-day weeks, ten-hour days, spring through fall and into the winter. We went to school when we could. This was the lowest time of my life."

While living on the Trailback Plantation, Ann recalls a major flood in the early 1950s, which was not uncommon in that former swamp, low-lying region of the agrarian Bootheel region.

"Water was everywhere, something like Biblical Noah's dove on the ark must have seen," Ann describes. "We [children] were anxious to investigate the swirling water now running through our fields. This was something worth investigating. Stumps were starting to come loose at the side of the road, with gnarled and twisted tree roots visible.

"The water was making strange gurgling sounds, like where Little River empties into the Mississippi River," Ann added. "Ohhh, it was high drama away from the painful toils of field work and the heart-aches of constant insecurity."

The children's curiosity proved dangerous.

"The boys had found a plank that floated down from somewhere and managed to plop it across one great big chasm, which looked like it had just been dug," Ann continued. "Its water bubbled like a witch's brew, complete with vapors rising when the warm rain met the cold earth and air. It was fascinating.

"We began dancing our way to spring, even daring one another to dance across that plank above the swirling water," Ann accounted.

But then, someone missed Judy, the youngest child. "Jimmy first let out a yelp, 'WHERE'S JUDY?!'"

"Larry began to stammer and point as Peggy started to cry," Ann recalled. "There she is! Her little brown head appeared, then instantly disappeared, covered by the debris in the swirling froth and foam. Judy had fallen into that deep bubbling cauldron and was bobbing up and down.

"I paced back and forth, scared to death because none of us could swim," Ann added. "But then I remembered something I'd heard, that a drowning person goes down three times before they are dead. Judy was still alive! I had to reach her. So I laid down real careful on my stomach, inching out on the plank to the point where I'd last seen her, and, sure enough, up she bobbed again where I'd last seen her hair floating in the swirling water.

"Well, that hair saved her, for I grabbed two big handfuls, tugging with all my young might, never mind that big tufts of hair came out in my hands," Ann detailed. "Then Jimmy ran around from the other side and grabbed on. And up she came!"

Ann, at the tender age of eight, had gathered her wits, her courage and strength to snatch her baby sister from certain death in the churning muddy flood waters.

"She was blue and black, red and beautiful, all covered with mud. Judy was gasping, choking, and groping, her little eyes trying to focus. Then she began crying, trembling from head to toe like I'd never seen before. So I took my big ragged old coat off and wrapped her in it, water, mud, and all. Oh, she was so precious. Oh, she was saved." Religion helped the family cope as their mother was a deeply spiritual sharecropping farm lady who not only cared for her family, but for others, which is taught in the Good Book of life.

"Mama [Jessie Kaneta Mitts Rice] didn't just get religion. She got the old-time shouting and crying, hand-clapping, singing and dancing and speaking-in-unknown-tongues religion," Ann shared. "Not only did it make her love her enemies, she'd go out and ask them to come to fellowship with us. She was quick to share her knowledge of the Bible.

"There were times when her prayers were beseeching: 'Lord, I just ask you to let me live long enough to raise my babies.' Let me assure you, Mama and her praying and tireless work was the glue that held this fragile woman and all her eight children together."

By this time in the family's life, Mr. Rice required shock treatments and frequent isolation at the state mental hospital in Farmington, Missouri.

Ann details the hard work and a spiritual miracle while working in a cotton patch between Morehouse and Grayridge.

"Five or six of us kids, along with Mama, were working in a cotton field a few miles out of Morehouse," Ann reported. "Two children from a family in Morehouse were so thin their limbs looked like little birds' feet. They had brought only bits and pieces of food for their lunches to the field. Momma finally was able to get the shy children to talk with her. She learned their father had left them, and their mother was home, gravely ill.

"Mama wanted so badly to help these children," Ann accounted. "She believed in Biblical tithing [paying one-tenth of what you earn to God]. We all collectively earned about seventy-five dollars a week by picking cotton. And she gave those two children seven fifty to take home to their sick mother, and I recall the little girl cried."

That's when a miracle born in a cotton field occurred.

"That very evening we traveled straight from the cotton field into Morehouse to Jim Poe's Dry Goods store, where all of us kids lined up to get fitted for new school shoes," shared Ann. "This really impressed the store clerk, all these feet at one time.

"As one by one, we children chose our new shoes, I remember thinking how badly Mama needed a pair. She had put so much white shoe polish on her worn-out Sunday shoes that they were cracked and they looked very run-over. But she only had enough money to pay for our shoes.

"As we started piling into the farm truck, all of a sudden the store clerk came running out, waving for us to stop," Ann added. "The clerk said: 'Mrs. Rice, we want you to come back in here a minute. We want to give you a new pair of shoes too.'"

"What they gave Mama was a new pair of white Sunday shoes. The price marked on them was $7.50, the same amount Mama had tithed to the poor hungry children out in the cotton field earlier that day. Mama went to praising the Lord, right there in downtown Morehouse."

"That kind of living will make you do right, whether you want to or not," Ann concluded.

Ann went on in life to become a successful business lady. While living her retirement years in Murfreesboro, she's organized a huge reunion of folks "blessed to have attended Grayridge High School where Superintendent Robert L. Rasche reigned supreme."

La Vergne businessman John Vest is a product of Superintendent Rasche's influence.

"All the Rice children have risen above our sharecropper youth days, economically speaking," Ann accounted. "We all owe a great deal of credit to Mr. Rasche, one of the great educators of rural Missouri and our faithful praying mother."

Mr. Rasche only lived one more year after I graduated in 1962. His huge legacy in life lives on.

Chapter Thirty-Eight

Sister Was a Ho'er

My older sister was a "cotton ho'er," but not the kind of "whore" you might be thinking.

My older sister, Mary June Whittle Cox, who retired in 2008 from being secretary for an important state senator in Missouri's capitol Jefferson City has never forgotten her farm roots. She proudly acknowledges being a "cotton ho'er" before working in the state capitol.

But make no mistake, June hated the cotton patch.

"Back in New Madrid County, we didn't like anyone who got above their rasin'." She shared.

I didn't like it either, but June really didn't like it when boys would tease the girls about being a cotton ho'er.

"That wasn't funny then, having to work so hard in those cotton fields back home" she said firmly from her present-day home in Jefferson City, Missouri. "Hoeing a field of cotton, ridding the crop of weeds was hard work, but that's what we were called. . . cotton ho'ers."

As a small tyke, I didn't understand the joke of a girl being called a cotton ho'er.

Sister June and I never had the desire to be known as effective cotton choppers. On the other hand, our older brother, H. Van Whittle, was considered a "good cotton chopper," but that title just brought more work to him. . . .

"Lead" cotton choppers were valuable to farmers.

"And a fast cotton chopper," added Momma Whittle. "We used Van as the lead cotton chopper to lead the field of other cotton choppers. They'd have to try to keep up with your brother, which meant that they got more rows of cotton chopped free of weeds and vines that particular day. We got more cotton cleaned of weeds for our money that way."

I finally ran across someone who hated cotton field work as much as June and I. Chopping cotton was serious business to the farmers, but it was painful to those who had to take hoes in their hands, which became blistered before the long day of chopping cotton was over. Eventually, the skin on your hands would toughen into calluses.

"I had never chopped cotton, but farm neighbor girl Fay Shorter talked me and my sister, Maxine, into helping her chop cotton one day," noted Alice Jean Harrison VanNoy, a native of Canalou and daughter of Norval and Marguerite Haywood Harrison. "Well, about noon farmer Lyman Whitten took us home to Mother, telling her in no uncertain terms: 'Keep those G** d*** girls out of my cotton field'."

Alice Jean, age seventy-four and living her retirement years in Overland, Missouri, said they noticed the farmer's anger and displeasure right off.

"'Those girls laughed and cut up so much, they interrupted the whole patch of cotton choppers,'" Alice Jean quoted Mr. Whitten, one of the best farmers in the Bootheel. "'And Mrs. Harrison, when you finally teach them how to chop cotton, don't bring them back to my field.' You know, I don't think he liked the way we chopped his cotton." Alice Jean noted with a sheepish grin.

Whoever coined the phrase "cotton vacation" would have been excellent at selling ice to Eskimos because picking cotton in the fall was NO "cotton vacation." The phrase goes back to when school officials *let out* school for six weeks in order for children to help in the fall harvest, the hardest part of which was cotton picking.

Alice Jean also recalled her first day of picking cotton.

"School was letting out for cotton vacation, so on the last day of school, Mother told us to ride [school bus] driver George Lefler's bus to the very end of the bus route to Dado [grandfather] Haywood's farm near the Morehouse Colony [Delmo Housing Project] on the farm-to-market road between Canalou and Morehouse.

"I thought Mother had lost her mind, but she insisted that it was time for her girls to learn how to pick cotton," Alice Jean added, "I tried to talk her out of it, but she would have nothing to do with that."

Alice Jean said they recognized that cotton picking season was at hand when people from Arkansas arrived to take part in the harvest each fall.

"I knew how grueling cotton picking could be by seeing how tired and worn out those poor folks from Arkansas were at the end of the day," Alice Jean continued, "They were so tired, they'd only partially wash their potatoes before cooking them, leaving dirt on the outside. I thought that was awful.

"That first day of my picking, I gathered enough to make a pillow, so I laid down there in the cotton patch, but after a while, the ground got so hard that it motivated me to pick enough to fill my sack, which made a mattress I could lay down on.

"I think I picked enough cotton to earn $3, which was enough to pay for my cotton sack we'd purchased at Jim Poe's Store back in Canalou," Alice Jean added. "Thankfully, we never had to pick cotton again. . . "

But there were some good times, such as when farm neighbor A. J. Neel would surprise us and bring ice cold Pepsi Colas out to the field. Add a big Baby Ruth candy bar to that cold drink, and we were good for another two or three rounds in the cotton field.

For unlearned city-fied types, a "round" was when one would chop one row up the field and one row back down the field.

Some of the good times came when Aunt Durette and Uncle R. T. Reed moved from Arkansas to a neighboring farm owned by prominent farmer Mr. Whitten.

I also lay claim to some local fame by being the only farm boy to ever have an aunt named Durette from Burdette, which is near Blytheville, Arkansas, where they held the National Cotton Picking Contest each year.

I remember making up a little ditty of a poem about "my Aunt Durette from Burdette," a jovial, joyful lady who could lighten the burden of chopping and picking cotton. She was also a wonderful cook with a specialty for white beans and fried hog jowl. Did I say she was mischievous too?

To lighten the doldrums of farm work, she would tip us kids off about when Uncle R. T. would be slipping out of the cotton field to go to the bathroom over nearby Little River's ditch bank.

It was high, dramatic entertainment when we used green cotton bolls and dirt clods as missiles for Uncle R. T. to dodge as he was trying to "do his business" on the other side of that ditch bank.

Sometimes, merely thinking of Aunt Durette's good country cooking helped take our minds off the hard back-breaking work of picking cotton back before they had machines to do those chores.

If cotton was "King of the South," it was a brutal king before the advent of modern-day farm mechanization that replaced us human cotton ho'ers and cotton pickers.

Aurora, Kentucky, resident Les Landers, born in Canalou in 1940, recalls trucks slowly rolling through Canalou during the fall to take town folks to area cotton fields.

"Picking cotton was back-breaking hard work," concluded Les, who, with his parents Willie and Norma Jean Landers, moved away from Canalou in 1952. "I never missed picking cotton after we moved away from Canalou."

Chapter Thirty-Nine
Cow Milking

As a small child, I was allergic to milk. If I drank too much milk, I'd break out in big painful water blisters all over my scrawny torso. When one of those big old water blisters would burst, raw burning pain consumed me.

It was late one night when I heard my parents talking future farm work duties for me and my older brother. "They're in there strategizing," my older brother whispered as we listened.

"Little Danny is old enough now, and strong enough in his hands, to take over the cow-milking duties, which would relieve Van to work more in the fields," we heard Momma Whittle declare.

Now, cow milking isn't that tough in the warm summertime. But goodness gracious, at 4 a.m. in the blue-blazing cold weather of bone-hurting wintertime mornings, it's a painful ordeal, both for the milker and the bovines about to give up their milk.

I remember one soothing trick we did to help the milk come down for the cows, was that we'd take their udders and massage them with warm water before we got down to some serious squeezing and tugging on those utters. The warm water also helped limber up our hands that were partially frozen after we'd taken a chopping axe and sledge hammer to break the ice on the livestock's drinking pond.

So when I learned of the precise morning they'd decided to make Little Danny the family's official designated cow-milking boy, I did some strategizing of my own.

Upon learning the D-day of cow-milking duties, I sneaked off to a farm neighbor's house and consumed at least a half-gallon of milk.

Come Monday morning, I was up bright and early, eager to get at those cows. I even acted joyful to brother about the task.

So I squeezed away on those cow teats to get that first day's cow milking out of the way.

But the next morning, I was broke out, you guessed it, in big ol' beautiful water blisters all over, and I do mean all over, including my wonderfully-pain-swollen buttocks covered with biggo blisters.

To which Momma Whittle declared once and for all: "Little Danny can't milk the cows, he's allergic to those cow teats."

Momma's *bovine allergic diagnosis* was music to Little Danny's ears.

My older brother, who died of cancer at age fifty-three, cursed me all the way to his grave: "You didn't have to milk those damn cows, did'ja boy! I milked the damn cows all my life. You got to lay up and sleep in the cold winter time, didn't you boy!"

I sensed anger from older brother each and every time he brought up milking those "damn cows."

To this day, I think of my beloved brother every time I observe some slow-moving milk cow moseying out across a pasture.

Chapter Forty
Time to Cut Hogs

As a farm boy, I enjoyed going to Hammock's Hardware in downtown Canalou.

The Hammocks were what we country folks called *classy* and *cultured*. Besides that, they came to the Bootheel from Burdette, Arkansas, same as my maw and paw, and they didn't seem to mind that I always brought my farm dog named *Hitler* into their well-stocked hardware store.

Most often, we'd journey to Canalou from our farm to replace a broken bolt or get a "shoe-repair kit" at the hardware store.

A shoe-repair kit at Hammocks Hardware? It's okay for nonfarm folk to ask that.

Actually, you can't begin to imagine my boyish surprise when those metal clamps Daddy Whittle called shoe-repair kits were actually rings that were placed in young pig's snouts to keep the hogs from learning how to root themselves out from under our barnyard fences.

We called them shoe-repair kits for obvious reasons. When our one and only pair of leather, store-bought shoes had the soles separate, Daddy would get out his special pair of wire-pliers with an extended metal snout on them and clamp the leather sole back to the main body of the shoe, thus those hog rings were our family's shoe-repair kit, Bootheel farm country style.

"There's at least another a hundred miles left in those shoes," Daddy would proudly proclaim with satisfaction at the end of a shoe repair. The "hundred miles" was the mileage we'd have going up and down those endless rows of cotton in our repaired shoes.

But picking cotton wasn't the job I dreaded most on the farm. No, it wasn't until I learned the meaning of *CASTRATION*.

My older brother explained the end result of castration: "We're going to make girls out of those young boy hogs."

Whew-wee, although I was young and didn't understand about a swine's reproductive system, that sounded painful to me!

Uncle R. T. Reed was in charge because he was an expert with a knife, and I overheard him describe castration as what the Japanese did to some of our soldiers during World War II.

To this day, hearing the word echoes and jars around in my soul.

My job that first day on hog-cutting detail out in one of our barn's stalls was to hold and spread the two hind legs of the young male hogs. Which meant I was up close and personal to what Uncle R. T. was about to do with his special razor-sharp knife.

Uncle R. T. explained why we only did the young pigs. "We cut 'em young because it hurts them less, and there's less chance of them bleeding to death."

With that explanation of hurting less, I was unprepared for the *screams* let out by those young pigs when Uncle R. T. began slicing and dicing with his knife. Hog screams sound eerily like human screams.

And that's when I jumped up and declared "This ain't right! Ya'll can take a two-by-four and beat me, but I ain't doing this to those hogs."

I may have been our farm road's first pacifist before we knew what that word meant.

I may have been able to handle it if I had not heard castration was what Uncle R. T. said the Japanese did to some of our soldiers during WWII. As a child, I could not imagine one human doing that to another human. As an adult, I still can't get a handle on that kind of inhumane conduct.

I was judged a sissy by my older brother and sister later that night when some "mountain oysters" showed up fried on my supper plate. When that happened, I did manage to ask permission to leave the table before I bolted out the back door to, as Daddy Whittle phrase it, "blow chunks."

For uneducated college folks who don't know a lot about farm life, a "mountain oyster" is farm dinner table code for a male pig's extracted testicles.

To this day, I've never thrown a mountain oyster past Whittle lips.

Chapter Forty-One
Wandering Livestock

During my Bootheel growing up years, livestock was often the root of feuds and squabbles between farm families.

The condition and security of a farmer's fence and barn was often the way farm families judged one another.

The weaker a fence, the greater that a lazy farmer's livestock was going to get out in another farmer's valuable fields of crops.

If a man didn't keep a good strong fence, that generally meant the farmer was slovenly in his attention to other farming details. He was probably also self-centered and didn't properly care for his own family and business or concern himself with his neighboring farmers' crops and financial well-being.

Hog pen fences were the most troublesome and required constant upkeep because a rooting hog can quickly root its way through a weak spot in the fence. Generally, cows and horses were less troublesome to keep penned than a bunch of bothersome rootin' and gruntin' hogs.

With their strong snouts, pigs appear born to root, judging from the satisfied-sounding grunts they emit when rooting with their noses buried in gumbo mud.

By putting a ring in a young pig's snout and causing them pain would sometimes stop them from rooting under the fence.

However, let's stop right here to pay respect to one smart, socially-sophisticated swine.

A legendary family story goes back to Momma Whittle's days as a young farm girl growing up in Calhoun City, Mississippi, farming country.

"I had this pet pig named Tommy," Mother shared. "Anywhere that I went, Tommy was sure to go."

Their friendship was born one cold winter night in a sharecropper's barn on a large farm the family worked on during the Depression. The Whittles were sharecroppers chasing the American dream of one day owning their own farm. They would finally achieve this dream at Canalou where former swamp ground could be bought cheap in the 1930s.

"It was hard, starving times in the Great Depression with every kernel of corn, every ounce of cotton, every butter bean in the garden crucial to a family's existence," Momma traced back to another century. "And so it was with little pigs."

Sharing her story from her death bed, Mother described what normally happened to the runt pigs of the litter.

"Since it was the Great Depression, when food for humans and grain for the animals was so hard to get, your Grandfather Stockton would often take the runts and do away with them by slamming their heads up against the side of the barn," Momma described.

"Ouch!" I wished I hadn't asked for details.

"That was because a runt, normally, would not survive anyway, because he'd be rooted out eventually by his bigger brothers and sisters from getting nourishment from the sow momma's teats," Momma added. "It was generally wasted grain and resources to try to get a runt to survive.

"But that night, this little porker, the runt of the bunch, looked up at me, and seemed to smile, right at me, and lo and behold, to my surprise, Poppa let me keep the little pig," Momma declared with a smile despite the fact she was suffering from ravages of advancing pancreatic cancer.

"Being that there was a cute little farm boy named Tommy I had noticed at the country store in Calhoun City, where we did credit business until cash crop harvesting times, I named my pig 'Tommy' too," Momma declared with a satisfied smile on her face.

I asked at this juncture: "Momma, are pigs stupid?"

"Oh no, at least my Tommy wasn't dumb, not by a long shot," Momma declared. "He was so smart, that he went to the outdoor two-holer [sometimes called the toilet, shack out back, and/or the Moon Room] just like the rest of the family."

Say what?

"That's right. Tommy pooped over in the corner of the outhouse, in a special little box I had fixed for him," Momma described. "I knew neighboring farm kids that didn't have enough sense to always get to the outhouse before taking care of their business.

"And every time I'd go to the outhouse, Tommy was sure to go too," Momma added. "And more often than not, he'd take care of his business while I took care of my business, in private."

We're talking a *refined swine* here, but that's enough said about that end of the pig business.

Pig business can be serious on a working farm.

Probably the most serious dispute Daddy Whittle had with a neighbor farmer was over pigs, pigs that repeatedly got out of a neighbor's barn lot.

I recall multiple times Daddy had to leave our farm during the crucially-busy time of crop growing and eventual fall harvest seasons to go make repairs on this neighbor's constantly sagging and weak barnyard fences. And that was usually during the crucially-busy time of crop growing and eventual fall harvest seasons.

And time after time, those neighbor's hogs kept getting out, to the point Daddy plain ran out of pig patience.

He lost his cool one particularly hot day when the corn had started tassling. Of course, the corn patch, with its tasty soft morsels of rich yellow and tender ears of corn, was where that bunch of hogs headed in their fastest pig-trots.

"I've had it," Daddy declared firmly upon entering the back porch of our farm house. "Those damn hogs are back in our corn field." With that declaration, Daddy got out his .22-caliber rifle.

"No, Danny boy, you can't go with me this time, but I'll take old *Hitler* [Daddy's loyal fierce-fighting farm dog] with me," Daddy directed firmly.

But instead of walking directly down to the corn patch, where those hogs were having a feast, Daddy cranked up our old "A" model John Deere that you cranked by the large spinning wheel on the side of the tractor. Then he hooked it to a trailer.

"Why did Daddy hook to a trailer?" I asked sister June as *Hitler* and Daddy headed hurriedly down to the corn patch.

It was a mere matter of minutes before we had our answer, when gun shots rang out clearly, "bang, bang, bang, and bang!"

Four accurate shots meant four hogs had gone to real hog heaven.

Daddy made each expensive bullet count as each slug hit squarely between their squinty little swine eyes.

However, Daddy, being a good neighbor, loaded up those dead hog carcasses and hauled them down and dumped them in the neighbor's front yard.

Not one hog got in our fields through that particular neighbor's brand new, barbed-wire fence, complete with new sturdy fence posts.

Amen, it was like a miracle how fast that new fence went up.

Chapter Forty-Two

Hog-Killing Day

Hog-killing day was something special on the farm.

Not only was it a long day of hard work, it was also great for country-style socializing when area farm families came together to share the toil, meat, and fellowship.

The warm fellowship took some of the sting out of the freezing cold weather, a pre-requisite for killing hogs so that the newly-butchered pork would not spoil in the prerefrigeration.

We had artist-quality talented people who specialized at various jobs, such as Uncle R. T. Reed, a wizard at wielding a knife to stick the hogs' throats in order to bleed them thoroughly.

To a small farm boy, the first time the family judged me old enough to witness the actual slaughtering process was exciting. I remember being amazed at witnessing the hog's blood spurt high out over several yards after Uncle R. T. had done the throat sticking job.

Since Daddy Whittle was recognized on our farm road as a crack shot with his trusty .22-caliber single-shot rifle, his job was to shoot the hogs squarely between the eyes. It was a matter of barnyard pride to not take more than one shot to kill the hog.

Neighbor farmer A. J. Neel was recognized not only for his butchering prowess but also for taking the time to tell stories to curious farm children.

"I remember back in 1937, when we had hog-killing day on a day that was so cold that the mighty Mississippi River nearby froze over," A. J. reported as he sharpened his ax, knife, and meat cleaver in preparation for butchering.

"I also remember when this family moved in here from some big city, and they brought a hog to be killed and butchered on a hog-killing day of my youth," A. J. continued. "They didn't know anything about killing hogs since they were city-fied folks."

"How city-fied were they?" asked cousin Robert Terry Reed, who like his father, was good at handling knives.

"So city-fied that they asked that their hog be cut up in all pork chops," A. J. reported to a round of guffaws by the adults.

Even as little children, we knew a hog couldn't be cut up in "all pork chops."

A. J. had a small Ford tractor that was ideal for hog-killing day. Because it was smaller than the bigger and more powerful John Deere tractors, A. J.'s little tractor was used to hoist the hog's carcass into the air shortly after the initial killing and hog-sticking process out in the pasture.

Daddy Whittle and other farmers prepared for this part of the chore by throwing a heavy cable over a strong limb on one of our yard's towering hickory trees. The carcass was attached by its hindlegs to a singletree in order to hoist the carcass in the air for the butchering process to begin.

Did you know that the tendons on the back side of a hog's hindlegs are strong enough to bear the hog's entire weight? Ideally, the hogs weighed anywhere from 250 to 450 pounds when it came time to butcher them.

Due to Uncle R. T.'s expertise with a knife, he was the one normally chosen to cut the hog open from top to bottom of the carcass and extract the hog's innards.

How good was he with a knife? So good that he would not

puncture the hog's bladder and would reward to one of the smaller children who would somehow find a way to seal the bladder and make a balloon out of it. The small-fry would sometimes bat that farm-style balloon bladder up and around in the air for hours, which gave them something to do and stay out of the way of hardworking adults.

Since our family did not eat hog innards, called chitterlings, we'd put them in a number three galvanized wash tub and transport them to neighboring families who did eat "chitlins."

Whew-wee, you could smell those chitlins cooking for miles as the putrid smell floated out across the country side. What did it smell like? Just like what you'd think it smelled like, what comes out the back end of a hog.

There were also humorous things that occurred during the otherwise serious hog-killing experience. I was the "butt" victim of this next caper, but I had trouble seeing the humor.

"Danny boy, come here, and I'll show you how to measure a pig's tail," Uncle R. T. ordered.

Not being a particularly bright child, I did as instructed and stepped to the backside of that newly-dead hog's carcass.

"Here, stretch your finger and thumb out like a measuring rod," Uncle R. T. instructed.

I did as I was told. And at precisely the right moment, Uncle R. T. firmly nudged my elbow, thus ramming my measuring finger up that stinking old hog's back end where the sun never shines.

I remembered being red-faced and stunned as I heard all the neighbor farmers laughing at my expense. It took a few years before I found the humor in learning how to measure a pig's tail.

Finally, being old enough to witness the actual slaughtering of hogs also meant that I was mature enough to do some of the work on hog-killing day.

The lowliest, dirtiest job of hog killing was the scalding and subsequent scraping of the course hog's hair from the outer skin. This meant that you not only got covered with that filthy hog hair, but the dirty scalding-hot water would slosh out of the big barrel and cover you from head to toe. Within five minutes, one smelled just like the old dead hog you were working on.

So it was no small thing when I was promoted from hog scraping to stirring the cracklings in our huge, old backyard black iron kettle that doubled as Momma Whittle's clothes wash pot on non hog-killing days. A big fire was set beneath the big kettle in preparation for what we called the rendering process.

To nonfarm folks who may not know what a "crackling" is, let me explain.

A crackling is a chunk of butchered hog skin with a glob of fat and particle of meat attached. The goal is to cook the fat and skin down into lard, which would be poured out of the big pot after the hot fire had cooked the lard (grease) out of the fat and skin. The hot lard was then put into five gallon lard cans to cool and was used year-round in Momma Whittle's kitchen.

A side benefit to being the crackling cooker was that folks acted like they liked you because they wanted to eat a sample of those tasty, piping hot cracklings. However, too many rich and greasy cracklings could make you really sick.

Cooking cracklings was one of the more responsible jobs for a child; you had to be alert to not scorch the cracklings while constantly stirring with a huge wooden paddle. Our family's crackling paddle was a converted old paddle that Daddy formerly used in his fishing boat back in Little River.

This process brought on another story by farm neighbor A. J. Neel.

"Everyone knows our neighbor Truler Trutt," A. J. began his tale. "Everyone thinks she is so religious, but truth is she loves to eat grease. Everyone thinks Truler is saying 'praise the Lord' as she walks to and fro in her front yard prior to church revival meetings; when actually, what she's saying over and over is 'praise the lard.' Truler can't get enough lard in the food she cooks for her husband, Herbert, and little daughter named Truly Pure Trutt."

Always the inquisitive child, I asked why the Trutt family named their daughter "Truly Pure."

"The family thinks they're without sin," A. J. instructed.

Momma Whittle had her hog-killing day specialty too, called blocking out the meat.

Since she was physically strong for a woman, particularly in her hands, arms, and shoulders, she was great at butchering and cutting the hogs into chops, shoulders, and hams. It made for a pretty sight, actually, when she took her fresh-cut parcels of meat and placed them on top of our tin-roofed back porch for cooling. The porch roof kept hungry dogs and cats away from the fresh-killed meat.

Sister June and brother Van also helped during this phase of hog killing.

"I remember it being very hard and cold work in the below-freezing temperature, that's my memory of hog-killing days," Sister June remarked from her current home in Jefferson City, Missouri.

Another indispensible neighbor farmer and cotton gin manager was L. A. McCann.

"We like for Mr. McCann to do our sausage," testified Daddy Whittle. "He makes it lean and spicy, which smells so good when it's being cooked on a cold winter morning for breakfast."

"I never divulge my recipe for sausage making," Mr. McCann noted.

Mr. McCann was also judged an expert at curing hams and salting down shoulders of the hogs.

From start to finish, hog-killing days tended to be long twelve to fourteen hour affairs with few breaks to rest. But all in all, with all the neighbor families coming together, it was an exciting day for a little farm boy.

Chapter Forty-Three

June Carter Cash's Bonnet

The Whittles were first on our muddy farm road to have a radio.

Momma Whittle recalled multiple other farm families gathering in front of our new-fangled, cabinet-style, battery-powered Philco radio on Saturday nights to listen to the Grand Ole Opry out of Nashville.

"They came on mules or in mule-pulled wagons, for mud on our road was too deep for cars and trucks in the wet winter time," Momma described.

The year the Whittle family got a radio was 1945. This link to the outside world indirectly triggered a "crime wave" in our family.

The crime scene began at old "Yeller Dawg" (Yellow Dog) School located near East Prairie, but it was in New Madrid County not far from the Mississippi River.

The caper happened at a special appearance by Grand Ole Opry stars Mother Maybelle and the Singing Carter Family, featuring Little June Carter who later married legendary country music star Johnny Cash.

"Our family was big fans of the Grand Ole Opry out of

Nashville after your Daddy and I managed to save our pennies and nickels to buy a huge cabinet, battery-powered radio," Momma Whittle shared. "Since that was pre-electricity days, before the REA [Rural Electric Association] headquartered in Sikeston] brought electric poles and power lines down our farm road, the radio operated on a big old battery that fit in the back of the radio."

I recall, as a little boy, I would take those gigantic old batteries when the power juice had been used up and play with them for days as part of imaginary airplane flights.

"And on Saturday, other families, such as the Neels, Bishops, Harrisons, Abernathys, and Bramletts, would gather at our house to listen to the Opry, and we were all fans of Mother Maybelle and her daughters," Mother continued. "Your Daddy also loved Uncle Dave Macon on the banjo, and he loved Opry stars who played the harmonica, which we called a mouth French harp."

Thus, the crime scene was set.

"So when it was announced over KSIM Radio up in Sikeston that the Carter Family was coming, a group of us got together and made the long trip [twenty miles] from Canalou to Yeller Dawg School," Momma noted. "And it was worth the trouble, even braving the slick, icy roads, for the winter was severe. And the Carter Family gave one of the best performances of their lives for the little crowd that packed out that old rural school house. The performance was worth the quarter charged for admittance."

Being that it was about twenty miles from the Whittle farm to Yellow Dog School, Mother reported it was after midnight before the family got back home.

"We got in so late, we slept in a little late, you know, until about 6 a.m., before we got up to go out and break ice on the ponds for the livestock to have water and to milk the cows and slop the hogs," Momma traced back to a fading way of rural Americana life. "Finally, after we got back in the house, we warmed up by the kitchen stove where I cooked hog brains and eggs that morning, one of your Daddy's favorite breakfasts."

It was shortly after breakfast that Mother knew a family

member had committed a crime.

"After breakfast it was time to listen to *In Memoriam*– you know–the obituary program done by radio announcer Dick Watkins up in Sikeston," Mother shared. "So that's why I was initially surprised, but pleased, to suddenly be listening that Mother Maybelle was about to come on the radio to do a live broadcast instead of hearing the death notices from around the Bootheel.

"But to my complete surprise, Mother Maybelle sounded upset about something that happened the night before back at Yeller Dawg School," Mother related. "Mother Maybelle said something to the effect that it takes a lot of money for a family to go perform out on the road, and it was still hard times on the heels of the Great Depression [of the 1930s]."

Mother said that she nearly fainted when Mother Maybelle shared that there had been a crime committed at the school house.

"So, I'm asking that whoever it was who stole little June Carter's new red bonnet from one of the school benches to please return it, and there'd be no questions asked," Mother said in restructuring the appeal by Mrs. Carter over KSIM Radio. "I remember thinking how could anyone be sorry enough to steal a little girl's bonnet?"

After the special break for this Opry celebrity in radio programming, Mother said she returned to normal household chores, such as heating the irons on the old "Warm Morning" cold stove in anticipation of ironing some clothes for our family.

"It was wash day. When I took your Daddy's britches down to wash, you can imagine my shock, my embarrassment, and astonishment when out of his pocket fell a little girl's bright red bonnet," Momma shared. "Well, since your Daddy was always full of his mischief, it didn't take a genius to figure he'd been the one to snatch that bonnet belonging to Little June Carter.

"But since he was all the way back working at clearing stumps out of our farm's New Ground, which was more than a mile from the house, I immediately took it upon myself to pack little June Carter's bonnet in an empty big match box and wrap it in plain grocery sack paper. Fortunately, I knew the address of the Grand Ole Opry by heart, since we all listened to that program faithfully each Saturday night."

Mother had another factor to contend with, a newborn baby named Danny who was less than six months old, as she prepared to walk the one-and-a-half mile distance from our farm house to the post office in Canalou.

"It was frigid cold, rain mixed with sleet, so I bundled you up really good and put on my knee boots and got up on the railroad in order to not walk in the deep mud out on our farm road which became impassable each winter," Mother accounted. "But after a half-mile, I got so tired toting you that I had to stop and ask neighbors Mommie and Poppie Gowen if they'd take care of you while I walked to town on business.

"I didn't dare share what kind of business," Mother added sheepishly, "for I was deeply ashamed that a member of our family would take someone else's clothing that did not belong to them. Good clothes were hard to come by in that era. And I didn't let Post Master Don Kochel see me when I dropped the little parcel in the mail box."

Mother said she never brought the red bonnet up to Daddy Whittle.

"It would have just started a row and with three small children and the hard survival of winter upon us. I didn't bring it up about the bonnet, and your Daddy didn't either," Momma said.

Then, about a month later over the WSM Radio channel station out of Nashville that carried the Grand Ole Opry all the way from Canada down to Mexico, Mother said she was again astonished to hear Mother Maybelle thank whoever mailed June Carter's bright red bonnet back to Nashville.

"It made the three mile round trip walk, toting a baby in cold weather, all worthwhile for I knew I'd done the right thing for myself and my family," Mother recalled. "Although it was still cold wintertime, I felt warm and snug for having returned little June Carter's bonnet."

How ashamed of Daddy's misdeed was Momma Whittle? So ashamed she didn't share it until one afternoon in 2003 as she lay on her death bed with pancreatic cancer.

"Thieves were not highly thought of, especially by God-fearing country folks who regularly heard a hell fire and brim stone brand of preaching from the pulpits in that era," Mother shared. "In Canalou at that time, we had three churches, Baptist, Assembly of God, and Church of Christ. All three had good preachers. Sin and thieving was not something we took lightly."

She must have thought it was a good day for a thorough cleansing of her soul, for that was the fateful afternoon she also chose to tell about when our family again "went a fowl" of the law.

She rolled the calendar back to the early 1930s, when most of America, including the Bootheel region of Southeast Missouri, was gripped in hunger in wake of the Depression that started with multiple banks failing and closing in 1929. The Bank of Canalou was among those that closed its doors permanently when the banker left in the dark of the night.

"As far as I know, this next thing I'm about to share is the one thing you definitely cannot write about until after I'm dead and long gone," Momma decreed before journeying back along our family's memory lane through some severely-harsh economic times. "I mean it. I've never shared this with anyone.

"Your Daddy and I were sharecropping on some rich relatives' farm near Lilbourn," Momma noted. "Oh, they weren't rich by today's standards, but they had money enough to go out and party every Saturday night at a night club between New Madrid and Marston.

"Well, at the time, your Daddy or anyone else couldn't find public work, so cash and food was hard to come by," Momma journeyed back in time. "Your Daddy and me were so hungry that when everyone had left to get drunk at some party over in New Madrid, we slipped out to their chicken house and stole a big fat chicken.

"Yep, I confess that we wrung that chicken's head off faster than you say 'Sears-Roebuck' and plucked the white feathers and had that chicken in the frying pan all within five minutes after having snatched it off its roost in the chicken house,"

Momma detailed. "But as soon as we had consumed all the evidence, we went back out in the yard where we'd wrung that chicken's neck and plucked the feathers, you know, to gather up all the feathers and remove all evidence. That chicken was never mentioned as missing either. But you know, I've been embarrassed and repented often when I recall the night your Daddy and I stole a chicken that didn't belong to us.

"But I remember also how good that stolen chicken tasted too," Momma noted with a look of satisfaction.

Although Momma Whittle lived another few weeks, we never mentioned Little June Carter's red bonnet or the stolen chicken again.

We buried Mother at age eighty-three on Christmas Eve, 2003. Being the tough farm lady that she was, she lived more than seven years after being diagnosed with pancreatic cancer. Normally, physician sources tell me, people with pancreatic cancer don't live longer than six months to a year.

Writer's Note: This wasn't my family's last dealing with June Carter Cash. In the mid-1980s, I was contracted as a professional publicist in Nashville to help set up old timey "Tent Revivals" for June Carter Cash and actor Robert Duvall to study in preparation for the making of a movie about a Southern Pentacostal evangelist.

Duvall portrayed the evangelist in the movie entitled "The Apostle," and June Carter Cash portrayed his elderly mother. It's a movie worth seeing if you have not viewed it.

Chapter Forty-Four
Frances Bishop

Frances Bishop was born a farmer's daughter, and she married a farming man.

As a farm girl, she knew hard work and the difficult times that accompanied growing up in the former swamp village of Canalou.

She's never left the region. When asked why she's never left, she responded: "Once you get Bootheel gumbo between your toes and the roots of farming in your soul, it's hard to leave."

When I spoke with Mrs. Abernathy, she told me about one of her scariest nights along Little River.

"I recall, while crossing Little River on our way home, a big black panther let out this terrifying scream that sounded like a woman's death scream," confirmed Mrs. Abernathy "We almost fell in the river, that's how terrifying that panther's scream was. It made the hair on our head and arms stand straight up."

The Whittle, Bishop, and Abernathy families go back as farm neighbors to the 1930s.

"My husband helped your daddy, Hubert Whittle, blow stumps and clear your family's 'new ground' located behind Little

River that flooded so often," Mrs. Abernathy noted while crossing back through the decades of time. "Blowing stumps with dynamite was very dangerous work. Your family moved here in 1938. We had arrived a year earlier."

She described tough living conditions when her farm family lived behind Little River.

She had to cross the river to get to and from town, which could be extremely dangerous during high water periods and during slick, icy winter conditions.

"We grew up behind Little River, but before that we farmed the farm adjacent to your family's farm there at Tram Switch, located about two miles north of downtown Canalou," Mrs. Abernathy noted. "But in 1941, my parents Elmer and Mae Bishop moved us across Little River on the farm belonging to wealthy land-owner H. G. Cathy.

"We had to not only walk through the woods, we had to find a way to cross Little River, which could be treacherous when it flooded which it often did in that era," she added. "One of my girlhood favorite activities was walking beside the river in the woods with my sister, Evelyn, as we gathered hickory nuts and pretty wild flowers. Hulling those nuts was hard on your fingers, but it was worth it that winter when Mother would use them to make candy, cakes, and pies."

Hickory nuts that they gathered in empty tin cans helped raise hard-to-come-by cash in a tough post-Depression economic era.

"Sometimes H. G. Cathy, who also owned one of two of Canalou's cotton gins, would take our shelled hickory nuts and sell them for us, which made us a little spending money," Mrs. Abernathy accounted. "This was in the years 1943-44."

A foot log was initially the family's only entrance and exit across Little River to Canalou.

"It was a good thing when a tree fell, making a foot log for us to cross the river before Daddy and our three brothers Mutt, Odell, and J. E., strung some wire and laid planks across the wire for us to use," Mrs. Abernathy noted. "I recall it was three miles to church and three miles to school, which was before we had school buses. When it rained big, we could not get to school and church. Floods also meant we couldn't get to town to do our trading. Vittles got mighty slim at times."

How important was church to families of that era?

"We walked three miles, rain, sleet or snow to get to church to thank our Lord," Mrs. Abernathy accounted. "Then we walked three miles, rain, sleet, or snow to get back home. Does that tell you how important church was to us?"

Bartering often took the place of cash money.

"We often bartered eggs and farm products for grocery staple items, such as salt, flour, and sugar," she recalled. "Store man Jim Poe was glad to barter with us. Him and his wife Stella were good to everyone, fine upstanding people."

Hog-killing days brought excitement to farm life.

"Dad would kill five to seven hogs at a time in order for us to have meat to eat during the winter months," Mrs. Abernathy noted. "It was hard work, a very busy time, but we enjoyed it.

"I recall we'd cook down the cracklings and have four and five twenty-five pound stands of lard," she added. "Dad was good at butchering hogs. I recall we'd fill a number three wash tub with sausage. Dad liked his sausage hot and spicy. Men mostly did the outside hog killing and butchering work, and women did the inside kitchen duties that go along with hog-killing days.

"One of the women's duties was to cook and can the sausage," Mrs. Abernathy described. "We'd fry the sausage patties and put them in fruit jars, then pour melted lard over them and seal the jars, which we stored upside down. That sausage would keep year-round."

When the pork would run out, they lived off the land.

"Little River was full of fish in that era, so we often fished and would have family fish fries," she detailed. "And the boys would often go hunting, bringing in raccoons, big swamp rabbits, and squirrels for us to eat. We ate a lot of wild game in that period."

But there was one job on the farm that Mrs. Abernathy "hated."

"We had to work hard in order to survive," she confirmed. "But picking cotton was not one of my favorite duties. I was not a natural cotton picker, for I had to work hard in order to get one hundred pounds of cotton picked per day. I'd rather chop cotton in the spring than pick cotton in the fall. Picking was back-breaking hard work."

But entertaining Saturday nights in Canalou helped refresh the family from hard farm labor during the week.

"It was a big day of the week when we'd get on board our farm wagon after the boys had hitched up the mules," she traced back across time. "Merchants Stella and Jim Poe had our favorite grocery store. If we had an extra coin or two, we'd get to go to Greenlee's Skating Rink until that family loaded up and moved the entire rink to Lilbourn. It was a sad day when we lost our skating rink.

"Farm wagons would be lined up solid all along Canalou's Main Street in the 1940s," she accounted. "But we had to be careful and be on the lookout for fights would often break out at the saloons that lined Main Street in that era."

"They didn't just have skirmishes. Seems like when a code of honor was violated, they fought to kill in that era," Mrs. Abernathy explained.

She recalls hitting the floor of a grocery store in order to avoid bullets from Canalou's last Main Street shoot-out in 1953.

"We had our own brand of special fireworks that Fourth of July. Grocery man Jim Poe made us lay down on the floor when bullets started flying on the Fourth of July that year," Mrs. Abernathy recalled. "That was when merchant Tootie Ralph and a black itinerant worker got in an argument over which farmer had the first cottom bloom, neither combatant owned farm land."

Mrs. Abernathy was born one of six children to Elmer and Mae Bishop, who moved to the Canalou farming region in 1937.

She married R. L. Abernathy on December 11, 1945. From that union came two children, Caroline, who resides in St. Louis, and Harvey, who still resides in Canalou.

"It was tough times to raise a family but good times, too, for we were all in the same boat," she concluded. "I had three brothers, Odell, Mutt and J. E., and two sisters, Opal and Evelyn. We were all taught a strong work ethic."

Such was a way of life that has faded forever from America's landscape.

Chapter Forty-Five
No Ordinary Cotton-Pickin' Day

A boisterous rooster would loudly proclaim the rising sun in the east.

And before a typical work day was over, many farm workers would get religion. We'd pray for the sun to mercifully set in the west.

Ordinarily, another sultry-hot, cotton-picking day, which could last from ten to twelve hours, was nothing to look forward too.

Usually, we dreaded another drudgery-filled day in the fall, a task accompanied by chapped and bleeding fingers pricked open by endless repeated contact with sharp, ripened cotton bole spurs, plus sore backs from sustained bending over to snatch thousands of snow-white tufts of cotton.

When backs gave out, we resorted to crawling on our knees, which eventually became painful when cracking open and bleeding.

Did I mention that picking cotton was painful, in addition to be being grueling hard work?

But one day proved different when a resourceful farm neighbor man came up with a plan.

A. J. Neel was beloved by children up and down our farm

road, especially after he came up with a project that generated excitement and pride to our cotton harvest when it was picked by hand labor three times each fall.

A. J. had read in *The Daily Standard* newspaper in nearby Sikeston that time was approaching for the annual National Cotton Picking Contest in Blytheville, Arkansas, located about seventy miles to the south of our location in the Bootheel of southeast Missouri.

That set A. J. on a search to find one of the best cotton pickers our farm region had to offer.

He initially sought out the premier female picker.

I felt big and important when A. J. Neel asked me to accompany him on scouting trips to seek out the region's best male and female cotton pickers. We made inquiries at cotton gins in Parma, Matthews, Wayside, Kewanee, and at the Allen-Davis Gin in hometown Canalou.

Plus, accompanying A. J. allowed me to escape an hour or two during the hottest part of cotton-picking days when the temperature sometimes soared to 100 degrees and above.

An added bonus often resulted when A. J. and I would stop to get a cold Nehi orange soda pop at Jim Poe's Store in the middle section of Canalou's mile-long Main Street. Sometimes a big Baby Ruth candy bar was a bonus for helping A. J. scout out the best cotton pickers.

"Don't tell the other cotton pickers we stopped for a cold soda pop," A. J. instructed me to secrecy. I never told our secret until now.

Finally, A. J. and I came up with the best female contender our cotton-picking community had to offer.

"It's Helen Landers," A. J. chronicled that long ago early-1950s Saturday morning in announcing the end of our week-long search.

He made his announcement in front of the W. M. Moore Mercantile and Grocery, Canalou's largest store.

Telling his choice to Moore's Store clerks John Smith and

Biddy Moore was just as good taking out an advertisement in the Sikeston newspaper.

This resulted in some extreme drama and conversations throughout the community, including G. D. Drake and Larry Drake, brothers who often ran the cotton suck operation at Canalou's last operational gin.

Most folks with Bootheel farm roots will know how a "cotton suck" works to draw the cotton up out of the cotton trailers into the mechanized cotton-ginning equipment.

"You'll find no woman who can out-pick Helen Landers," G. D. Drake confirmed as he unloaded a trailer of cotton from the farms of Jay Hopper and Harry Chaney, whose acreage was located between Canalou, Big Ridge, and Kewanee.

"Helen Landers is the best in these parts," echoed brother Larry Drake as more cotton trailers arrived from the farms of Melton Bixler, Nelson Lumsden, Dale Geske, Roy Johnson, and the Croom Brothers to be weighed and ginned.

The Drake brothers had to shout their opinion over the loud whir of the gin, noise of which could be heard throughout Canalou's corporate limits.

A. J.'s next step was to ask Helen Landers if she'd consent to *go into training* in order to compete in that famous cotton picking contest held in a big city named Blytheville down below the Arkansas/Missouri state line.

So, it was with unusual glee that long ago day that my sister Mary June, my brother Van, and I jumped out of bed to quickly wash the sleep out of our eyes out at the pump house, located next to our farm's hog-wallowing hole.

After a hearty breakfast of fried chicken eggs, salt-laced fatback bacon, thickening milk gravy and biscuits, it was off to A. J.'s field of cotton located a quarter mile from our farm house. We, along with cousins Robert Terry and Sandra Kay Reed, got to pick cotton that day with A. J. since our cotton harvest had been completed.

To take a shortcut, we cut through Roy Bixler's cotton field, where the Bixler girls, Shirley, Annette, and Sue Baby asked where we were going in such a hurry.

"We're going to pick today in A. J. Neel's cotton field," older brother Van bragged.

"So we can watch Helen Landers, you know, watch her go into training for that big cotton picking contest held each year down in Arkansas," added sister June.

"There's money to be won if she wins the National Cotton Picking Contest," accounted my older brother.

There was a lot of excitement, as evidenced by the likes of town boys Earl "Bubby" Davidson, Donald Sexton and Jerry Taul showing up to watch the "drama" taking place in A. J. Neel's cotton patch.

"Danny boy, having Helen Landers come here for training brought us some extra cotton pickers," A. J. judged with pride.

Fast forward to 2009 when I was able to locate and interview the legendary cotton picker named Helen Landers at her quiet retirement home in Morehouse.

Although Ms. Landers didn't win the National Cotton Picking Contest, she recalled the excitement and drama from that long ago era.

"I could routinely pick three hundred pounds of cotton, sometimes three hundred and fifty on really good days when all the elements were right for a good day of snatching and grabbing those cotton bolls," Mrs. Landers confirmed. "That is, if you could say there was ever a good day for picking cotton. It was awfully brutal tough work."

"Do you remember women folks wearing those long-billed homemade bonnets, to keep the sun off their faces?" I asked during our journey back in time.

"Yes, I recall the bonnets, and most women wore long sleeves on our shirts to keep the hot sun from blistering our skin," she answered. "There was an art to sewing and making those bonnets. And picking cotton was hard, but we took pride in what we did," Ms. Landers confirmed.

"And I recall A. J. Neel, and others encouraging me to go enter that cotton picking contest down in Blytheville, Arkansas," she recalled. "I didn't win. But I made a respectable showing."

In my present-day Tennessee hometown, I was privileged to attend church with the late Charley Garner, a legendary cotton picker in his own youthful days growing up at Burdette, Arkansas, which is near Blytheville.

On his best days, Charley could pick 400 pounds and up, verified his brother, Ed Garner, a former Smyrna town councilman.

The Garners and Whittles had worked on the same large farm as sharecroppers at Burdette before the Whittles moved to the Bootheel region of southeast Missouri in the 1930s.

Chapter Forty-Six

Cotton Bloom Debate

Canalou had a unique brand of Fourth of July fireworks!

It was 1953 when grocery merchants W. M. Moore, S. R. Tootie Ralph, and Jim Poe opted to stay open for business on Independence Day.

Two nine-year-old boys witnessed Canalou's special brand of July fourth fireworks that exploded into a knife and gun fight, thus being one of Canalou's last old Wild West-style showdowns on the tiny farm village's mile-long Main Street.

"We were there when two men became argumentative over which farmer had the first cotton bloom that year," confirmed "Crawdad" Bixler at age sixty-nine and a retired Frisco railroad worker. "Larry D. and I were there selling soft drink bottles back to merchant S. R. 'Tootie' Ralph for one cent to have money to buy more fire crackers.

"We had sold Mr. Ralph several bottles, and then we'd go to the back of the grocery next to the railroad tracks, get the bottles back out of the back of Tootie's store, and sell them again to Tootie," Crawdad accounted. "We just happened to be at the place of the shooting at the right time, or wrong time, depending on your perspective.

"We saw shots fired, and the knife brandished that did damage to the combatants," Crawdad confirmed.

Irony of this story: Neither combatant, merchant Ralph or the black itinerant farm worker who called himself Nigger Willie, owned farm land on which to grow cotton.

"We witnessed the entire knife and gun fight. Although Tootie had the pistol, he got the worst of the battle that broke out over which farmer had the first cotton bloom," Crawdad accounted. "The conversation was taking place on the spit and whittle bench in front of Tootie's grocery, and it started with Willie telling everyone sitting there that the farmer had cotton blooms where he'd been performing cotton-chopping duties that week.

"Tootie disagreed, stood up, and announced he would be right back," Crawdad recalled back across the decades. "In the meantime, Willie got up and began walking south on the sidewalk toward Moore's Mercantile when Tootie came back from inside his store, armed with a pistol.

"He ran to catch up with Willie, when he struck the farm laborer with his gun," Crawdad remembers. "At that time, Willie took out his pocketknife and started slicing and dicing Tootie. Tootie took this as a sign that he should start shooting Willie in the lower half of his body.

"I recall neighbor Jim Brumley pulling up about that time, and placing Tootie in his vehicle to transport him to Dr. Sam Sarno's offices in nearby Morehouse to have his multiple wounds stitched up," Crawdad remembered. "Meanwhile, Willie took off running before town Marshal Harvey Campbell ran him down in his pickup to take him to the hospital in Sikeston for gun wounds.

"In summing it up, I'd say Willie got the best of Tootie, although the store merchant had the pistol," Crawdad concluded. "Tootie had stitches all over his head, neck, and shoulders."

Longtime Canalou resident Lee Joe Campbell, brother to the town marshal, recalls Willie running by his house.

"My brother chased Willie after he ran hollering past our house, which was three or four houses off of Main Street, finally catching him and taking him to the hospital in

Sikeston," noted Lee Joe, now deceased. "I didn't see the Main Street show-down, but I witnessed Willie running by our house, hollering he'd been shot in the butt by the store merchant. He was bleeding from his backside as he ran by our house. We'd heard the nearby gunfire."

Present-day Overland, Missouri, resident Alice Jean Harrison VanNoy also recalls the fateful Canalou-style of Fourth of July fireworks.

"I was working as a clerk in Jim Poe's Grocery, which was next door to Ralph's Grocery. I was walking to the front door, to retrieve a gentleman who had forgotten his change for a pack of cigarettes," Canalou native Alice Jean remembers. "That's when Mr. Poe rushed in, grabbed me by the arm, and hurriedly took me to the back of the store, warning that there was about to be a shooting out on Main Street. Once we were safely in back of the store, which sat next to Ralph's Grocery, we heard multiple gunshots."

Life-long Canalou-area resident Frances Abernathy was a customer in Poe's Grocery when the shooting broke out.

"We were told by merchant Jim Poe to lie on the floor to get out of harm's way," confirmed Mrs. Abernathy, who is living her retirement years in assisted living housing in nearby Matthews.

Miraculously, both combatants survived the altercation on Main Street that began over which Canalou-area farmer had the first cotton bloom the spring crop-growing season of 1953.

The itinerant farm worker was never seen again in or around Canalou, and we never heard of any law enforcement prosecution over the altercation.

As the Whittles were going to get some "Jesus" at the Baptist Church the next morning after the fight, I recall seeing merchant Ralph holding court on the spit and whittle bench in front of his store. His upper torso, including head, shoulders, neck, and arms, were covered in snow white gauze you could see from one end of Main Street to the other.

The itinerant farm laborer was a legendary field worker, but no one seemed to know where he came from or where he disappeared to after the Fourth of July altercation.

To Willie's credit, when he worked for the Whittles, he could chop a field of cotton faster than it would normally take five efficient field workers.

Mr. and Mrs. Ralph, who were especially good to children, ran one of the cleanest little groceries in our farm village.

But if you thought life in our little farming community was without fanfare, drama, and excitement, you thought wrong.

Pride often triggered farming competition such as mule pulls and later, tractor pulls.

Sums of money were often wagered between farmers who liked to boast that their mules or their tractors could haul the most weight. Competition was how the on-going rural Americana tradition of mule and tractor pulls was born.

To say that Canalou had a competitive wild and woolly past, as once described in Lilbourn's *Southeast Missouri News* newspaper, is not over-stating the little town's rough-and-tumble social mores.

In her memoirs on file at the New Madrid Memorial Library, Canalou educator Agatha Sissy Weaks Parks, described one of the town's earliest Main Street brawls that resulted in a man's death.

"In that swamp and timber harvesting era, some folks would journey by train to Parma and Morehouse for a supply of liquor," the late Mrs. Parks chronicled. "Ned Nashley returned on the train with a supply of whiskey and became intoxicated. He quarreled with a Mr. Myer, which resulted in a gun fight in which Ned Nashley was killed."

This reportedly happened around 1915 on the front porch of Moore's Store, which at that time faced west toward the railroad tracks that have since been taken up.

So, yes, life in former swamp town Canalou could be a dangerous and tumultuous experience when many men routinely toted pistols and razor-sharp knives.

Chapter Forty-Seven

Canalou Cash Registers

The year was 1996.

It was the first time I had taken wife Pat through my little farming home town of youth.

As we motored along Canalou's original Corduroy Road in front of where the old Kasinger's Grocery and Junk Yard operated, I looked over and grew concerned because Pat had turned pale.

"Is there something wrong?" I inquired as we now passed the precise point where the old Allen-Davis Cotton Gin operated on Main Street.

"You had to be strong to get out of here," Pat whispered as she witnessed for the first time the now ghostly-appearing Main Street.

"It's a ghost town," Pat observed.

What she saw in the present and what I remember as a Canalou-area farm boy are entirely different views.

After being birthed out of the swamps beginning in 1902, Canalou evolved into a vibrant little economic agrarian community, especially after multiple canals were dug to drain the swampy marshes partially created when the Mississippi

River ran backwards during the New Madrid Earthquakes of 1811-12.

Canalou wasn't officially incorporated into a town until 1909, according to records provided from Aurora, Kentucky resident, Les Landers, whose ancestors moved into Nigger Wool Swamp around 1910.

When the swamp waters were drained, some of the most fertile land in world history was open for farming, especially in the 1930s. Affordable farm land triggered further economic development.

Among those were Arkansas sharecroppers Hubert Alexander Whittle and his wife, Ruby Stockton Whittle, who first rolled into town in 1938 riding on a wagon pulled by a team of mules.

"We moved to Canalou from Lilbourn, where we'd had an apartment over the *Southeast Missouri News* newspaper," chronicled Momma Whittle as she lay on her death bed in 2003. "It was a cold, rainy winter night as we slowly rolled into town behind our team of mules pulling our wagon loaded with what meager pieces of furniture and clothing we had."

Mother braved the rough cold weather despite having birthed my older brother, Hubert Van Whittle, only days before.

"Your brother, Hubert Van, was two weeks old, and sister June was only four years old, and it was so cold that we stopped in the Assembly of God Church more to get out of the cold elements than to praise God," Momma Whittle described.

"At least, I thought that was why we were stopping at the church where they were having Saturday night services," Momma recalled. "But during service, I noticed your Daddy taking out his last nickel, the last cent to our name, and placing it in the collection plate. I remember wondering about the wisdom of placing our last coin into the church offering plate.

"But then, a miracle happened there in the former swamp village," Momma accounted.

"Low and behold, it was less than a week before a man showed up in Canalou, which was located way out in the middle of no where back in that era, and paid your Daddy the hundred dollars he had owed us for more than a year," Momma noted with emotion. "It was the miracle that we needed to put down the earnest money down payment needed to buy the hundred acres that your Daddy had his eye on one and a half miles north of Canalou at a place called Tram Switch between Morehouse and Canalou.

"Although your Daddy wasn't a religious man, he was a Christian and gave God credit for that miracle that resulted in our being able to buy those hundred acres of farmland," Momma added. "That money owed us came at a critical time, and we had given up the man ever paying us."

Lifelong Canalou resident Frances Abernathy recalls her late husband, R. L. Abernathy, working with Daddy Whittle in the clearing of timber and the blowing of stumps on what we called New Ground as part of the original Whittle farm acreage.

"It was hard and dangerous work in that era too," Mrs. Abernathy recalls at age seventy-five. "I remember the day that Little Danny Whittle was born and the birth of my nephew, Kenneth, at about the same time in 1944 on our little farm road. My parents farmed the farm right next to your family's farm. I recall numerous small grocery stores had opened up on Main Street by the 1940s."

Commerce in Canalou may have hit its peak in the 1940s with businesses such as Fatty Ford's Jewelry Store and Greenlee's Skating Rink, two of my favorite names for businesses in Canalou that were before my time.

People moving in from surrounding states, such as the Blankenships from Arkansas and the Landers, Engrams, Newmans, Westerfields, and Lawsons from Kentucky and Illinois, birthed the need for multiple small grocery stores in Canalou, remotely located in New Madrid County's northwest corner on a dead-end road that ends at the Floodway Channel.

A small candy store across from Canalou School grounds was a legendary enterprise on Main Street in the 1940s and early 1950s.

Former Canalou-area farm girl, eighty-seven-year-old Maxine Harrison Sittner Berkbigler remembers the little Adams Store that mainly merchandised candy to school kids.

"Mr. Adams, and his daughter, I believe named Hazel, operated the little store in sort of a shot-gun, unpainted building from the school," present-day Texas resident Mrs. Berkbigler recalls. "Many are the days, I'd go and look in the front store glass window where you could see the candy. Many of my lunches were a nickel-bag stuffed to the brim with chocolate-covered peanuts."

Mrs. Berkbigler's parents, Charley and Mary Harrison, were farmers in the Canalou area during the 1930s before moving to the Parma-area of New Madrid County.

Chaffee, Missouri, resident John Sonny Poe, nephew to Cape Girardeau's 112-year-old Florence Robinson Poe, recalls his dad and mom's Canalou store operation.

"The Poes moved from Cape Girardeau to Canalou in 1914," Sonny added. "Aunt Florence married Dad's brother, James Nelson "Butch" Poe, and he stayed in the lumber business throughout their lives, running stave mills in Virginia, Illinois and Charleston, Missouri, before retirement.

"Dad and Mother [Stella Reeves Poe] opened Jim Poe's Grocery in Canalou in 1941," Sonny, age eighty-two in 2009, recalled at his retirement home in Chaffee after a railroading career. "I never took to the store as a career. Dad gave it to me to run more than once, and I'd always give it back.

"They had a good little business in Canalou, but by 1959, after the high school was closed in 1958, business began to fall off sharply, so he and Mother bought the Wayside Gin Co. Grocery up in Morehouse, ending eighteen years in the store business down in Canalou," Sonny recalls. "But I remember all the little stores up and down Canalou's Main Street."

Fire destroyed the Poe's first store at Morehouse.

"I recall that Wayside cotton gin manager Jack Jackson's brother was seriously injured when a gas line exploded in the store, and blew a heavy filing cabinet over on him, which hurt him. But the cabinet likely saved the man's life, since the filing cabinet is credited with keeping a lot of the flames off of him. But he was so severely burned, that it was thought the severe burns later caused his death at a relatively young age," Sonny Pow shared. "That's when Dad and Mom opened up their little grocery in downtown Morehouse. I recall Canalou folks with being loyal, for some of them drove five miles north to Morehouse specifically to do business with my parents."

Alice Jean Harrison VanNoy recalls working in Jim Poe's Grocery in downtown Canalou from May 1951 to August 1953.

"Every Saturday morning, we bagged Great Northern beans in five-and ten-pound bags and would peck potatoes for the afternoon and evening rush," Alice Jean shared. "Stores didn't have regular times to close. We closed when people went home, especially on busy Saturday nights. Potatoes arrived in 100-pound sacks, and beans were in large quantities. I remember Sonny Poe, because of him being left-handed, had a hard time learning to tie the string that hung from the ceiling around the parcels that left the store."

In the 1920s, the Bank of Canalou served as the hub of commerce for the community, along with cotton gins owned by H. G. Cathy, E. H. Percy and Josh Davis. Like thousands of small town banks in the 1920s, the Bank of Canalou closed its doors leading into the Great Depression that gripped America.

However, one Canalou family got their money out of the bank. "My Dad got his money out of the bank before it went belly up," recalled retired farmer Harry Chaney at age ninety-five in 2009. "The banker, after initially telling Dad that the bank was as solid as its brick walls, ended up pleading with him not to take out his cash accrued when he'd sold a bunch of fattening hogs. A few weeks later, the banker left town in the dark of the night."

The brick building that housed the bank still stands, and later became the site for V. E. Hammock's Hardware. The Hammocks lived in quarters on the second floor. Prior to moving to Canalou, the Hammocks lived at Burdette, Arkansas, where Momma Whittle attended school with their sons, Donald and Doug Hammock.

During the 1930s, 1940s, and 1950s, there were the Church of Christ, Baptist and Assembly of God congregations, but they were out-numbered by five to seven saloons/cafes, such as the ones operated by Marvin Drake, Zanie Westerfield and Opal and Ray Merriman.

Early town Canalou had a three-story hotel located beside Louis Houck's railroad spur line that ran from Cape Girardeau down through the Bootheel.

"I lived in the old town hotel as a little girl before Mother passed away," accounted lifelong Canalou resident Gladys Johns Drake. "We didn't have a lot of money, but then no one else did either, so we didn't realize our own poverty."

Sonny Poe recalls the Lampher Hotel building had multiple uses down through the decades of the early 1900s.

"We'd go see a movie there and look over at the great big selection of caskets that were on shelves on the west side of the big buildings west wall, nearest to the railroad," Sonny said. "I don't remember who marketed and managed the caskets, but we had them. That old three-story, white-frame building also served as a post office, with rooms being rented on the top floor.

"There were people who would come to small towns such as Canalou during the late 1930s and bring movies and projectors they'd set up in the Lampher building," Sonny recalled. "It was a huge treat to get to see a movie, which was before J. B. "Boots" Conn built our town's first [and only] theater in 1944."

W. M. Moore's Grocery and Mercantile Store was the biggest retail business on the town's Main Street. But there was also Tootie Ralph's Grocery and Liquor Store, Jim Poe's Grocery, Maw Mathenia's Grocery, Grant Adams' Store, Hammock Brothers Grocery, Nathaniel Hewitt's Whiskey Store, and Barber Shop, Bixler's Service Station, West Smith's Garage, Grover Drake's Blacksmith, and Kasinger Grocery Junk Yard in operation during the 1940s-1950s.

In the 1910s-1920s eras, most businesses faced westward toward the railroad tracks, before there was a Main Street. Some of the earliest businesses, including the first post office, were up on stilts above snake and rat infested swamp waters.

With regional drainage of the swamp, which allowed the paving of Main Street, merchants adapted and made their front store entrances accessible to the east, facing the new and improved Main Street.

As a child, I didn't know how special the people were who ran these little businesses. For example, out of respect for my family in the loss of my father in a 1950 car crash, the merchants never complained about me bringing my farm dog named *Hitler* into their establishments.

Only in a small farm town. . . .

The town had three blacksmiths, including Louis Dean, Leslie Allen, and Shade East. Men talented enough to keep farm equipment operational in the busy surrounding farming community.

Gladys Johns Drake provided a number of billings from her late father-in-law Grover Drake's Garage for services rendered to farmers such as Bert Latham, Melton Bixler, Phillip Newman, Roy Johnson, Bill Newman, Dick Bryant, Phil Coppage, Phillip Newman, Abe Landers, A. J. Neel, Norval Harrison, Elmer Evans, Nelson Lumsden, Elmer Gruen, Lyman Whitten, and Dale Geske.

The bills were for services such as plow-point sharpening and welding of broken cultivators.

Gene Drake, Grover Drake's son, had his own mechanic and repair shop to serve the farmers.

Gladys was married to Grover Drake's youngest son, Larry, who died of a heart attack in the 1990s. Larry and his older brother, G. D. Drake, helped keep the town's last cotton gin in operation through the late 1950s and early 1960s.

Saturday nights in the 1940s and early 1950s were something special, as adult women of the community often sat in their family's truck, car, or mule-pulled wagon while gathering gossip along Main Street and in and around the train depot operated by B. P. Melton.

"We were always amazed that V. E. Haywood and Mrs. Haywood always had their pickup truck sitting in the same parking spot each and every Saturday night," chronicled lifelong Canalou resident deceased Floy Mae Arbuckle Jones Gruen. "As we got older, we realized Mr. Haywood would drive his vehicle up town early in the afternoon to get that certain parking spot and the Haywoods would then walk back up town after the sun went down. This was a way of a lot of the socializing was done in that era."

St. Louis-area resident Alice Jean Harrison VanNoy, seventy-five, recalls skating at Greenlee's Skating Rink before it closed and moved to Lilbourn in the 1940s.

"They only had one pair of skates my size, so I'd get there early to make certain I got the skates," Alice Jean, a grandchild to the Haywoods, recalls from her days of growing up in Canalou.

Much of the recreation in the 1940s and 1950s centered around the town theater initially owned by former Canalou Mayor J. B. "Boots" Conn, who sold to L. A. McCann. John and Jean Summers were the last owners of Canalou Theater that had some of the best first-run movies and all of the popular Western "shoot-em up" cowboy movies during the 1950s.

Mr. Conn's first movie shown in 1944 was *The Life of Jack London*. Charley Conn and his brother "Boots" left Canalou to become lumber business successes in Sikeston and Kentucky, respectively.

Early Canalou entrepreneur Boots Conn sold his service station on Canalou's Main Street to Roy Bixler upon moving to Kentucky in 1952.

A number of Canalou men followed the Conn brothers out of Canalou for the lumber work.

"Boots initially owned the East Prairie Lumber Company, and my father, Willie Landers, and Uncle Bill Landers plus Uncle Bob Lowery and a couple more men from Canalou worked for Boots and Charley Conn as carpenters," noted Aurora, Kentucky, resident Les Landers. "We moved away from Canalou in 1952 as soon as school let out for Dad to start work in Calvert City, Kentucky. Boots' daughters, Jerilyn and Jean, and their much younger brother, James, still own the Calvert City Lumber Co. as of 2008."

The theater brought outside dollars into the community on Thursday nights, Saturday nights, and Sunday afternoons.

Canalou native girl Sue Baby Bixler recalls something special sometimes went on in the dark of the theater.

"I'd hold hands with all three of my boyfriends, starting with Little Danny Whittle, Gale Johnson, and then Willard Robinson, sometimes courting all three on the same night," she described with a giggle. "That theater brought in people to see movies from many surrounding little towns, such as Matthews, that didn't have a theater, which helped generate business for Dad's service station across the street from the two-story theater and café building."

Canalou's population, which never officially numbered more than 500 residents in any official census, would double and triple on Saturday nights when farm families from miles around would come to view the movies at the theater, get a haircut at Nathaniel Hewitt's Barber Shop, and get grocery mercantile staples from the lineup of small stores.

"You couldn't walk down the sidewalks on Saturday nights, that's how many people crowded into our little farm town," described Gladys Johns Drake.

Ernest "Granny" Taul's Pool Hall and Saloon was another popular scene of Saturday night recreation. For example, my pool-playing father, Hubert A. Whittle, and three of his best friends, A. J. Neel, Les Durbin, and L. A. Pete McCann were regulars at the pool hall.

"Your Dad was not the best pool player, but he was a lucky pool player," accounted the late Granny Taul in an interview he did with me when I was a fledgling young reporter for *The Daily Standard* newspaper in Sikeston. "He was a better gambler at poker than he was a pool player. He often won big when gambling in places such as the back room at Hewitt's Barber Shop and the side room in Moore's Store.

"He'd also go gamble in big time gambling places, such as the river boats and Club 18 over at Cairo, Illinois, and a tough place aptly named the Bloody Bucket on the Mississippi River outside of Wykliffe, Kentucky."

Although Canalou was reputed to have its own share of rough and ready saloons in the 1930s, 40s, and 50s, there were one or two places in the Bootheel that even so-called rough and ready Canalou males steered clear of.

"That was Hollywood Courts located between Lilbourn, New

Madrid, and Marston," accounted Alva Jones, born in 1933 in Canalou.

"I was only in the Hollywood Courts once or twice," Jones described. "The last time I went there, someone threw me out the screen door without even opening it and then followed me outside and dragged me all over the rough gravel parking lot. I never went back."

Hollywood Courts made such a deep impression on Jones that he penned a song entitled "Hollywood Courts Baddest Place Between Memphis and St. Louis."

The first stanza has these words: "A lot of the regulars were very bad, you sure didn't want to make them mad, one night they did harm to this lad, as I flew through that door, I was mighty sad."

Sue Baby Bixler described more of the social life of the 1950s-era in what is now an economic ghost town.

"My dad, Roy Bixler, and brother, James Roy, ran Bixler's Service Station across the street from the John Summers Café that was attached to the theater in the same building," Sue Baby recalled. "I'd go get a nickel out of Daddy's cash register and put it in the café's jukebox, so I could dance with some of the older boys that my older and prettier sisters attracted in the back dance room. We'd dance until way past midnight on most Saturday nights. Daddy would have got me if he knew I was putting his money in that jukebox. He thought I was getting it for a hamburger and cherry Coke."

Oliver's Café, which operated only in the 1950s, was famous for introducing footlong hotdogs and chili to our farming community.

Sue Baby, Gladys, Frances Abernathy, Liz Vandiver, and retired Bootheel sports writer Alva Jones were asked for their opinions of what caused the eventual economic death of our once vibrant small town.

"It was the loss and closing of our schools, when we consolidated with Matthews in 1958," noted Gladys. "I remember strong emotions, even tears flowing that first day we boarded the bus to go to Matthews. I remember some folks in Matthews lining the streets and laughing at us as we were hauled to their school. It was not a funny thing to us. Closing our schools closed the town."

"Years later, my aunt Iris Blankenship Drake returned to Matthews when that town finally lost their high school due to consolidation with New Madrid," Gladys recalled. "Iris went back to Matthews, went into each business establishment, and reminded them of the hurt we felt when we lost our schools. Loss of our schools caused the eventual closing of all the little businesses up and down Canalou's Main Street."

"It was the progress of farm equipment, such as the automated cotton picking machines, that replaced us farm laborers in the cotton fields," Jones described. "As a boy, if I needed extra money, I'd go pick cotton. When those new cotton picking machines came along, it started the economic end of our once proud little farm town."

"The closing of the schools, when we were forced to consolidate with Matthews in 1959-60, spelled the end of Canalou as a vibrant town with several thriving businesses ranging from Hammock's Hardware to West Smith's Service Station," detailed lifelong Canalou resident Liz Vandiver.

"I ache when I view the depressed conditions that now exist in Canalou," Sue Baby noted. "I always wanted something better than life in Canalou, and I'm still striving for that. But I want to return some day and clean up our town and remove the blighted old abandoned cars and run down buildings. I was proud to have grown up there and remember so many good and kind people who molded us into good citizens."

Bootheel native John Vest credited that era's farm work with helping him prepare for a successful career in business.

"We hired out as field hands, just like the adults," Vest recalls. "It was hard work, but it prepared us to be efficient, hard-working adults who believed in doing an honest-day's work, for an honest-day's pay. . . . "

Sue Baby recently retired as a heavy equipment dealer, and now serves as realtor, a travel agent, an entrepreneurial restaurant developer plus being a founder of a mortgage company and bank in Enid, Oklahoma.

Former Canalou resident Renda Chaney Buck, who now resides near Poplar Bluff with her husband John purchased a quilt in the 1990s that had been quilted by some ladies from Canalou. The quilt lists the names of all businesses that reportedly ever operated in the former swamp sawmill village:

Church of Christ, Gene Drake's Garage, Marvin Drake's Tavern, West Smith's Service Station, H. G. Cathy Cotton Gin, Hammock Brothers Grocery, Canalou City Hall, Jail, and Library, Oliver's Restaurant, Charles Tootie Ralph's Grocery and Liquor, Bixler Service Station, Assembly of God Church, Lee Allen Black Smith, Taul Pool Hall, Canalou School, Hewitt Barber Shop, Grover Drake Garage, Josh Davis Cotton Gin, W. M. Moore Mercantile and Grocery, Bond Beauty Shop, Bert McWaters' Grocery, Hubert Bond Ice & Coal, Canalou Post Office, Bank of Canalou, John Summers' Theater, E. H. Percy Cotton Gin, Grant Adams Store, Shade East Blacksmith, Louis Dean Blacksmith, Hammock Hardware, Pete McLaurin Grocery, Canalou Baptist Church, Baker Shoe Repair, Zanie Westerfield Tavern, Ray & Opal Merriman's Café/Saloon, and the Lampher Hotel.

Chapter Forty-Eight

Crow cussin'

If farm-style cursing didn't come naturally, it came early.

"Cussin," as it was called on the farm, was a way of life when Daddy Whittle and neighbors would organize, get out their trusty shotguns, and go crow hunting.

But, farmers didn't hunt crows for sport. Killing crows was part of survival on the farm.

Crows loved nothing better than to swarm down on a field of new-sprouted, tender, corn blades. They'd pull and tug on that blade until the newly-germinated, still tender seedling, would pop up out of the ground for crow consumption.

Thus, crow cussin' was how I first learned to cuss by mimicking our community's adult farmers.

And I must have been quite good at it because I won a cussin' contest when I got to second grade at Canalou Elementary School, a chest-swelling status symbol I toted all through young school years.

I knew all the bad words. I didn't know what they all meant, but I knew the words.

Daddy Whittle wasn't the only farmer that those pesky crows drove to cussin'. Farm neighbors John Ling and A. J. Neel would also cuss when crows would swarm down on their corn fields.

Generally, it took a few destroyed fields before Daddy and other farmers would build up a full head of crow-cussin' steam.

One particular crow-hunt was the first time I heard the phrase: "Pesky crows can makes you cuss a blue streak."

"That's the last time those #$!$%# crows will get in our fields," Daddy cursed as he unloaded a load of bird shot from his fancy triple-barreled German-made Sauer shotgun.

Mr. Ling, judged one of the best farmers in our neck of farm country, could cuss a blue streak when going after crows.

And being designated Daddy's official crow-toter would cause my overall galluses to swell with pride.

My scrawny little chest nearly burst with prideful joy the memorable day Daddy and his crow-hunting buddies judged Little Danny Whittle to be the best crow-toting boy on our farm road.

Crows were such a problem in that era that they named a brand of whiskey after the pesky black feathered fiends, Daddy once told me as he purchased a bottle of bonded whiskey at Tootie Ralph's Grocery and Whiskey Store.

Old Crow was also a spiritual brand of whiskey that my family's preaching grand-pappy, Brother Rhodes, would consume before he would step up and preach, "Hell fire" and "damnation" from the pulpit.

Family members will not soon forget the Sunday night that Brother Rhodes preached a scorching sermon that ended with him forecasting the world was about to come to an end.

The next morning, Preacher Rhodes went berserk as he looked out to see dozens of crows falling and bouncing graveyard-dead in my Uncle Corbett Stockton's front yard.

Literally, hundreds of dead birds were plummeting out of the sky, which caused Brother Rhodes to rapidly retreat back inside the house to loudly proclaim to his wife, Granny Grunt Rhodes, "It's true. The world is coming to an end!"

"Shut up, you old fool," Granny instructed sharply. "You need to cut down on your whiskey and quit preaching the world is coming to an end. It scares the little kids in the congregation."

What Brother Rhodes didn't know was that area farmers had baited the corn fields with poison to protect the farm crops from crows that spring.

For when a flock of crows would swoop down and destroy a newly-planted and plowed field of corn, it was more than enough to drive a farmer into a strong tirade of *crow cussin'*.

Author's Note: Thanks to my sister, June Cox of Jefferson City, Missouri, I have possession of a pencil-written check for $1.67 that Daddy Whittle wrote for a pint of 'Old Crow' whiskey at Ralph's Grocery & Whiskey Store in our tiny farm town.

Chapter Forty-Nine

Uncle Harlan

This sixty-five year courtship began in a cow pasture, and that's no bull.

Aunt Doris Burris Whittle, widow of Rombauer Road-farmer Uncle Harlan Whittle, explained the "no bull" connection.

"As a young girl, I had been to a neighbor's farm house but was unable to get the gate open on my return, so I cut through a field to stay clear of the nearby bulls and cows," Aunt Doris recalled. "I was always afraid of big ol' bulls and livestock.

"Well, while I was cutting through the field, I met your Uncle Harlan, who had been sitting under a shade tree in the pasture, taking a break from picking cotton," Aunt Doris stepped back through time. "He later told me I didn't speak, but I thought I did. I was kind of shy, so maybe I didn't. But anyway, that's how we first met. He helped me get the gate open, and I went on my way back home through the pasture and field where there were no big bulls."

At age eighty-six (in 2008) and bravely battling a brain tumor, Uncle Harlan described his version of how he and Aunt Doris first met.

"I was married earlier and had gone to the neighbor Burris' home to borrow a breast pump after the birth of my first son,

Glen," Uncle Harlan noted. "I knew about Doris for the first time then, although we didn't meet. We later spoke for the first time there by the cow pasture.

"I helped protect her from the mean ol' bulls," Uncle Harlan added with an impish grin.

Their first official date was at the old Jewel Theater in Poplarbluff.

Aunt Doris doesn't remember what was playing on the screen, but she clearly recalls her first impression of her "new feller."

Uncle Harlan and Aunt Doris

"We went on our first date with Uncle George Burris, a brother to my daddy, and Iris, a sister to Harlan, and saw a movie at the old Jewel Theater in Poplar Bluff," Aunt Doris noted. "I don't remember what was showing at the movie, but I noted that your Uncle Harlan was a good-looking, smooth-talking feller."

Uncle Harlan apparently didn't watch the movie on the silver screen either.

"Whittle boys always had an eye for pretty gals, and your Aunt Doris was one of the prettiest gals in our neck of the woods," Uncle Harlan judged. "Best days' work I ever did was getting hitched with Doris."

After courtship, they tied the knot and began life together as sharecroppers at what was called the big Trailback Plantation located on the Stoddard County side of the Floodway Channel between Morehouse, Grayridge, Charter Oak, and Canalou. Aunt Doris and Uncle Harlan have three sons, Lonnie, Glen and Dowell.

"Times were tough. Cash and food were hard to come by," assessed Uncle Harlan.

Unlike most Bootheel farmers of that era, Uncle Harlan was not a cotton farmer.

When he was asked about growing cotton, Uncle Harlan firmly replied, "Cotton, which required chopping three times and picking three times, was back-breaking hard work. There were other crops that were easier to make a living with."

However, his refusal to plant cotton caused them to leave Trailback after two crop-growing seasons.

"We didn't live long at Trailback because Harlan refused to plant cotton, which displeased Mrs. Cathy, the lady land owner," Aunt Doris confirmed. "So when Harlan refused to grow cotton, we moved back to the Rombauer area, which was near my parents, [the late Mr. and Mrs. Bill Burris] and Harlan's mom and dad, Tom and Mallie Whittle."

One of the Whittle family's worst tragedies happened at Trailback when we lost Benny Blankenship [in the mid-1940s], a first cousin of mine and nephew to Uncle Harlan and Aunt Doris.

"Benny was driving a John Deere tractor on our farm up on the levy road near Floodway, and when he apparently looked back, the tractor went down off the levy and overturned, killing Benny at age twelve," Aunt Doris noted sadly. "I'll never forget the frantic, sad faces as Harlan and Benny's dad, Herman, worked feverishly for two hours or more in getting the tractor off of young Benny. It was one of the saddest days of all of our lives."

Uncle Harlan's son, Dowell "Pow Pow" Whittle, recalled the tragedy.

"I was very little but recall going in the house and seeing Benny laid out on the bed," Dowell described. "It was quite a shock."

I was so young, the family didn't permit me to go see the body on the bed.

Over the years, we had lost many friends and family, but faith and perseverance often helps farm families get through tough times.

A sense of humor can help too.

To say that Uncle Harlan, and the whole Whittle clan for that matter, have unusual senses of humor would be understating it.

The following is a legendary tale in Whittle family annals.

"I've always loved to read," Aunt Doris recalls. "We'd been moved back to Rombauer from Trailback Plantation when I was in our farm shanty here along Rombauer Road. But your Uncle Harlan didn't like for me to read.

"Well, this time, I happened to be bathing in our new shiny No. three galvanized wash tub and in through the window came this red stick with what looked like a lit fuse on the end of it." Aunt Doris remembered.

In that era of Bootheel farming, dynamite was frequently used by farmers to blow stumps and clear timber.

"So, when I saw that red stick with a fuse, I ran out of the house," Aunt Doris confirmed.

Yes, she had no clothes on.

"It wasn't a real stick of dynamite," Uncle Harlan defended. "I just wrapped some red paper around a corn cob, and she mistook it for a stick of dynamite."

Legend has it that Uncle Harlan tossed the fake dynamite through a window as he drove by their little farm shanty on his new John Deere B model tractor.

"It was several days before I got another home-cooked meal," admitted Uncle Harlan with an impish grin.

In another ruse to discourage Aunt Doris from reading books, Uncle Harlan is credited with pulling his tractor up to one of the shanty's windows, and piping the loud noise into their house, to amplify the poppin' sound that two-piston John Deere models of that era were known for.

"Yes, that also happened," Aunt Doris confirmed at a Whittle-family reunion held at Rombauer in the fall of 2008.

Whittle farmers have always been loyal to John Deere tractors.

Their loyalty is so strong that Dowell, their youngest son, is nicknamed "Pow Pow" because of the noise he verbalized while playing with his little model tractors in the dirt as a young child.

"That's the sound Dowell made," confirmed first cousin Tommy Burris of Dexter. "He'd push those little John Deere play tractors in the dirt and go 'pow pow pow'."

During my youth, our families oftentimes "swapped labor" when my older brother H. Van Whittle and sister June would go to Uncle Harlan's farm to help in fall harvests.

Lonnie, Dowell, and Glen would come to our farm in New Madrid County to pick and chop cotton in turn.

There were no farmers on Aunt Doris' side of the family because her father, William "Bill" Burris, was a construction foreman.

"After I was born at Charleston, we lived at various places in the Bootheel due to Dad moving to the construction sites," Aunt Doris accounted. "Dad worked in the construction, for example, of Highway 25 that runs from Bloomfield down through Dexter to Malden and points south."

Prior to his death Christmas Eve of 2008, Uncle Harlan was the last surviving sibling of my father, the late Hubert Alexander Whittle, a farmer in the Canalou-area. They were born the sons of Tom and Mallie Whittle, along with daughters Etoyle, Iris, and Sudie, who all hailed from Mississippi where the family had farming roots.

Uncle Harlan parlayed his earliest sharecropping days into owning and farming more than 400 acres of prime farm land in Butler County, not far from Poplar Bluff and the Mingo Swamp Refuge, a hold-over from the days when swamp water covered most of the six-county Bootheel region.

Chapter Fifty
Center of Commerce

Most economic life in the Bootheel, flat-land region of southeast Missouri in the 1930s, 1940s, and 1950s revolved around farming, grain elevators, and cotton gins.

For certain, cotton gins reigned with economic supremacy in Canalou, Missouri, my hometown where the population peaked in the 1930s with about 450 humans and forty-one lazy coon dogs that mostly slept and yawned on the town's short Main Street.

The anything-but-lazy farm economy had surfaced after the region of former swamps had been drained with a series of canals.

After the timber was harvested by the 1930s, it was the cotton gin man who held most farmers' future, credit, and crop payments locked in the Allen-Davis Gin office safe.

Fortunately for my family, L. A. McCann was our town's main cotton gin man and a smart fair man with whom to do business.

Oh, it was a thrilling, adventuresome journey for a little farm boy to be asked by Daddy or Momma Whittle to take time away from picking cotton to accompany the next trailer load of freshly picked cotton to the gin.

This meant you got out of the backache inducing hot, drudgery work of picking cotton for a couple of hours.

Oftentimes, on trips to the gin, you got to swig an ice cold Nehi orange belly washer from Maw Mathenia's Grocery. It was even enjoyably cool to retrieve the soft drink by reaching down and pulling it out of the ice cold water in the ice box. I still recall today that delicious, cool chill running up my arm in the hot summer time.

To a little boy, it was high adventure riding high atop that big trailer load of cotton as we zipped down the road creating our own air conditioning. Daddy, who enjoyed a reputation as a good farming man who paid his bills, had a relationship built on trust with the cotton gin man in those lean economic years as the nation recovered from the Great Depression.

When Daddy would get his own crops laid in the spring or harvested in the fall, he'd often work for the needed extra cash at the gin office, weighing in wagon loads of other farmers' cotton or their grain.

Soybeans, wheat, and corn were also brought in by the farmers to the gin's grain elevators that straddled the town's single set of railroad tracks.

As evidenced the day that an itinerate Mexican worker lost two fingers to the cotton gin, being around a cotton gin in operation could be a dangerous business. Other gin workers quickly bandaged the man's hand that was dripping with blood and loaded him into a truck for transport to Dr. Samuel Sarno's office in Morehouse, Missouri, five miles to the north of Canalou.

It sickened me to sit and stare at those two bloody fingers lying in the dirt before, finally, one of the town's dogs came by, took a lick or two, and quietly toted the fingers away in his clenched teeth.

I suppose the adults were too stunned to retrieve the man's detached fingers. It was nothing to see up to thirty wagons lined alongside the town's mile-long Main Street as farmers waited for G. D. Drake, the gin's maintenance foreman, to finish running the gin 'suck' that literally sucked the cotton up out of the trailer for ginning.

After being sucked into the gin, the finished de-seeded lint would come out the other end of the gin bound in big bales of tightly-bound cotton, thus awaiting transport out of our farming region on the nearby railroad tracks. In the cotton gin's peak period of operation during the fall, the gin operation employed between twenty and thirty men as the largest single employer in the little farm town's heyday of rural commerce.

It was a tough life, but I remember we had very good neighbors back then, and we boasted that our "cotton gin man" was one of the best.

Chapter Fifty-One

Ginned Legend

Matthew (not his real name) was a cotton-ginning legend. He was so accommodating to farmers that he became a valued part of the farm culture in the 1950s.

When machinery at the gin or grainery broke down, word spread throughout the community, and everyone looked to Matthew.

One of Momma's favorite stories regarding Matthew is from the day she broke the steel cables that hoisted the front end of trucks and farm wagons loaded with soybeans or wheat. Gravity caused the grain to rush out of the back of the vehicle as the cables lifted the vehicle's front end in the air.

"The look on Matthew's face was crest-fallen when we heard those cables go 'bang!' as they broke, which meant the entire grainery operation for the community came to a standstill with lots of anxious farmers waiting to unload behind me," Momma described. "When the gin or grain elevator was not operational, that meant the loss of crucial harvest time for farmers between periods of rainfall and impending cold weather.

"I don't know who felt the sorriest for one another, me or Matthew, for it also meant a lot of pressure and tension on him, not to mention back-breaking hard work to repair the broken cables," Momma recalled. "The longer Matthew took to fix that elevator, the longer farmers had to sit idle in their fields and trucks. A few hours and days missed during fall harvest could mean the difference of having a profit or loss for a year's hard work.

"But, thankfully, most of the time, Matthew was able to quickly repair the malfunctioned equipment, and the fall harvest of all farmers would continue," Momma noted.

But there were humorous times in that hard-working era too.

For example, former Canalou School classmate Gladys Johns Drake recalls a particularly interesting day of drama that unfurled when the main frame malfunctioned when her late husband, Larry Drake, worked at the cotton gin.

Being that Matthew was a small-framed man, he was the only gin employee thin enough to slide under the gin's big main frame to make repairs.

"Larry told me they made it easier to slide Matthew under the gin's main frame by greasing him down, almost completely naked, with grease normally used to lubricate the ginning equipment and farm tractors," Gladys shared

"In this particular incident, Matthew was already under the gin's main frame when it was determined that [gin operator] L. A. McCann would have to go all the way [155 miles] to Memphis to get the broken gin part," said Gladys. "Being that it was so difficult to get Matthew in and out of the narrow crawl space, Mr. McCann asked if he wanted them to pull him out while he made the five-hour trip back and forth to Memphis. But Matthew agreed that he would just stay under the gin's main frame as Mr. McCann made that long journey."

With that settled Mr. McCann jumped in his sleek new 1955 Plymouth Savoy and disappeared in a cloud of road dust as he sped south toward Memphis.

Well, being that this was a particularly hot time of year, town folks got worried that Matthew, who remained pinned under the gin's main frame, would dehydrate due to the intense heat.

"What town people didn't know was that my husband, Larry, and a few of his buddies were also supplying special liquid to Matthew as he was still pinned under the gin," Gladys shared. "They were quite ingenious in how they did that when someone fashioned a hose out of some small rubber tubing to pipe liquids to Matthew. Well, after a while, someone got the idea to mosey on down to Tooty Ralph's Liquor Store where someone purchased a jug of wine," Gladys added. "You can imagine the look on Mr. McCann's face when he returned five hours later and found Matthew still under the gin but now all liquored up from the wine that my husband and his buddies had piped to their little buddy.

"My husband recalled Mr. McCann's question to Matthew this way: 'Matthew, how the hell did you manage to get soused while laying here under the gin's main frame?'"

As far as towns folks knew, Mr. McCann never did figure out how Matthew managed to get inebriated while stuck under the cotton gin.

Chapter Fifty-Two

Bill Newman

Canalou produced more than just school teachers and farmers.

Native Bill Newman recalls being a merchant and a truck driver. "I had Newman Feed Store there on Canalou's little Main Street in the early 1950s," Canalou High School graduate Newman accounted. "I sold Wayne-brand feed and seed, a brand that's still going, and Corno, a brand that went out of existence."

Like farming, trucking could be a dangerous occupation.

Mr. Newman's life was nearly snuffed out in 1951 when the eighteen-wheeler he was driving from St. Louis to Natchez, Mississippi was hit head-on by another large truck.

Although I was a small tyke, I recall hearing about the tragic wreck that nearly cost Mr. Newman his life. The accident happened in the hot summer months before that new-fangled air conditioning phenomena had snaked its way down into our former swamp bottom land gumbo section of remote northwestern New Madrid County.

His recovery was tortuous. "For seventeen weeks, I was laid up in a full-body cast with holes cut for my arms. And you talk about heat and discomfort, for it got some kind of hot down there around Little River and that low-lying swamp land," present-day St. Louis area resident Newman recalled in 2009. "And the traction, they had me upside down. It was tortuous, a very rough period."

I recall the first time I met Mr. Newman as we students marveled at his huge black back brace, which resembled my grandmother's old corset with bone staves. He required that brace to serve as our new school bus driver.

For little kids, Mr. Newman's "newness" and our little school's bright new school bus were big events in the social order of Canalou.

"I drove the school bus for a period of time before being able to go back to full-time employment," recalled Mr. Newman. "I was glad to get the part-time job."

Born the son of Audrey McWaters Newman and Aymon Newman, he knew early in life that farming was not for him.

Mr. Newman cited pride at having attended fabled old Canalou High School that had a brief thirty-year history before being lost to consolidation in 1958.

"I went all twelve grades at Canalou School and believe America made a bad mistake when going away from small community schools," Mr. Newman noted. "I literally loved my first grade teacher, Mrs. Davis, the wife of [New Madrid] county school superintendent Milas R. Davis. And if you listened, you could learn a lot from mathematics teacher Lenora McCullom, another favorite."

He recalls one particularly tough appointment with the board of education. "The hardest paddling I got was from Principal Todd," Mr. Newman traced back through time. "But I deserved it. The short and fat Mr. Todd was tough but fair. I know I didn't get a lot of paddlings that I deserved.

"And I believe this current creed of no child left behind is a lot of political baloney," he added in a 2008 interview. "If a child doesn't want to learn, you can't make him. And it was nothing unusual for our teachers, some of the best in the world, to have more than thirty-five and forty students in the classrooms."

Was he aware that little Canalou School produced more than forty professional educators during its brief history from 1928 to 1958?

"Doesn't surprise me though," Mr. Newman confirmed. "You had to be tough and smart to make a good life for your family in that former swamp region. We had good teachers, who not only taught you book-learning, but good common sense and practical stuff. . . it was one big family."

He recalls women folks of the community holding quiltings to make bed covering for poor people who could not keep their children warm and snug during the cold winter months.

"Women would gather for a quilting at one of the churches, especially during the winter months when crops were out of the fields," Mr. Newman recalled. "They could really make some pretty quilts, some of which were sold to raise money to help the needy."

His ancestral roots go back to earliest Canalou history when his aunt, 112-year-old Florence Robinson Poe (as of August 27, 2009), and family floated into Canalou in a Jon boat in 1905. The Poes first settled south of Morehouse in 1903 and then in Big Ridge.

"Aunt Flo was more like a grandmother than an aunt, for she literally raised my mother," Mr. Newman shared. "She's one of the most remarkable women in Missouri history, and certainly little Canalou's history.

"When Aunt Flo's parents, Wid and Granny Robinson, first floated into Canalou in 1905, they built their first house by digging holes in the gumbo in order to construct their first home on poles up out of the swamp water that could be anywhere from a few feet deep to ten feet in depth. It was a tough time carving a living out of that wilderness and swamp. But that tough and smart stock of people knew how to survive tough times."

Mr. Newman recalls some of Canalou's rowdiest days, socially speaking.

"We're not talking scuffling here," Mr. Newman recalled. "Particularly during the 1920s, 1930s, and 1940s, you didn't have to go far if you were looking for a fight, a real fight."

"We're not talking mere fisticuffs. We're talking gun and

knife fights where they meant to kill one another," he noted. "I remember witnessing, as a young boy, two men who drew a circle in the ground, and they had a knife fight. That circle ended up being filled with their blood, but fortunately they both lived to fight in another time and place.

"Saloons and pool halls outnumbered churches throughout Canalou's history," Mr. Newman accounted. "It seemed like life-and-death fights broke out every Saturday night when the town was brimming over with farmers' families and sharecroppers' families."

Lifelong Canalou-area resident Frances Abernathy agrees about "life and death" skirmishes on Main Street.

"There were no mere fist fights," Mrs. Abernathy confirmed. "Those men doing the fighting, they meant to kill one another. It was cultural pride thing when a man thought his honor was called into question."

"And there was typical Halloween mischief among young country boys of that era," Mr. Newman described.

"One year me and school buddies, Junior Blankenship and Kenneth Johnson, constructed a corral in the middle of Main Street," Mr. Newman added with a smile. "We put blacksmithy Grover Drake's old cow in the corral. During another Halloween, we disassembled an old wagon and reconstructed it up on the roof of W. M. Moore's Store. Folks wondered for years how and who got that wagon up on that roof. This is the first time I've confessed to these Halloween deeds."

Although in his late seventies, Mr. Newman still works daily, operating a small trucking and pallet business in Crestwood, Missouri, a suburb of St. Louis.

"Many folks from Canalou came north to St. Louis to get good-paying jobs, especially after the town's heyday in the 1940s and early 1950s," Mr. Newman described. "There were no jobs to be had at Canalou, especially after the school closed and all the stores closed. We were taught good work ethics in our little farming community."

He recalls one little store as very special. "Grant Adams and his daughters Hazel and Maude and son Chick had this great little grocery, which sold mostly candy and school supplies, just across the street from our school," Mr. Newman described. "They were good to us children. Teachers didn't mind at recess when we'd run as fast as we could to get our pennies out for that delicious-tasting candy at Adams Store."

Chapter Fifty-Three
Granny Missed the Pot

As a little boy, I thought there was a connection between Sweet Garrett snuff and heaven.

"Lordy knows that snuff tastes heavenly," my grandmother on Momma Whittle's side of the family ledger would proclaim after a fresh dip of finely-ground tobacco.

It was an honor to be the child chosen to walk the three miles round trip back and forth to Canalou from our farm to get "Granny Grunt" a new supply of Sweet Garrett that was made in some distant place on the other side of the Mighty Mississippi River.

"Being from the other side of the Mississippi, that means it's imported snuff all the way from Nashville, Tennessee" older brother H. Van explained to his less-knowledgeable little brother.

To be chosen to fetch Granny's snuff usually meant an extra nickel for some jaw-breaker candy or a Nehi orange belly washer at Kasingers little country store at the north end of Canalou's Main Street.

Grandmother Beatrice Orr Stockton Rhodes was something special, unique, and different—all wrapped up in one—and, she was a snuff-dipping nemesis!!

Her unusual nickname —Granny Grunt—hints of that.

"We named her *Granny Grunt*, because she's always gruntin,' whining, and complaining 'bout things," explained older brother. Brother Van gave anyone who was anyone on our farm road a nickname. Why he designated Mother's momma as Granny Grunt was obvious, for she was a lady, who—I don't know any other way to put this—was always moaning and groaning, except when she'd get a new batch of imported Sweet Garrett snuff.

Plus, with a full handle like Beatrice Orr Stockton Rhodes, "Granny Grunt" was easier for everyone to say.

Granny Grunt could be charmingly sweet, as long she got her Sweet Garrett.

But there was a serious down side to her snuff-dipping.

There were two types of snuff dippers on our farm road in the 1940s. Granny Grunt, may the good Lord rest her sweet foot-washing Baptist soul, was the kind who made the biggest mess you ever saw with her snuff dipping and splattering spittle.

At the other extreme, farm neighbor Myrtle Delemma "Mommie" Gowen, may the good Lord rest her sweet gracious neat non-foot-washing-Baptist-to-the-bone soul, was what would be called "a closet snuff dipper" in today's vernacular.

You never knew that Mommie had a pinch of snuff between her gum and lip and goodness gracious, heaven forbid, if you ever saw her spit.

Granny Grunt, on the other hand, would splatter her snuff-laden spittle on anything or anyone.

One day she even got it all over her face, as she seemed to forget that a strong north wind was blowing down from Dick Bryant's Woods to the north of our farm. Judging from the brown spittle on Granny Grunt's face, I guess that was the day I learned to not spit into the wind.

It should have been a huge celebration the day that Momma Whittle drove to Sikeston to pick up our new Plymouth farm car from Goza-Harper Motor Company. I wasn't along for this ride, but my older sister June, recalls the journey.

"We'd just bought our new car, and when we took it by to take Granny Grunt for a ride, well, she emptied her snuff can out the car window filled with spit as we were traveling about thirty miles per hour," June shared. "It got all over the side and trunk of Momma's new car.

"That's why Momma Whittle got so mad that day. It's one of the few times I ever Momma 'back talk' her own mother," sister June confirmed.

And Granny Grunt would use any receptacle as a spittoon, as Daddy Whittle discovered one night when he came in late from drinking and gambling in the side room at Moore's Mercantile/Grocery Store in downtown Canalou. Daddy woke me up as he was "blowing chunks" off our back porch, having unknowingly picked up and drank out of a glass that Granny Grunt had used as her latest spittoon. Daddy didn't call it "heaving" but had his own description of vomiting.

Beatrice Rhodes

"It's like blowing tree stumps, coming up all at once," Daddy explained. "That's why I call it blowing chunks."

It was one of the sickest, maddest spells I ever saw Daddy have.

It seemed that Granny Grunt preferred used, old, tin peach cans as her spittoon of choice. But when that old brown-colored, snuff-laden residue would start coloring up the bright yellow peaches pictured on the side of the can, well, it wasn't a pretty sight.

Granny Grunt admitted to being only four feet, and 11 inches in height. But she was a huge lady who, for some reason, loved wearing short dresses, another thing that sometimes distressed folks in the family. . . and some female foot-washing church members.

The family called it *the view*.

"We're ashamed to take her to church, for she'll sit there in her short dresses with her fat legs crossed, and you can see 'old glory,'" was the way my sister June described *the view*.

As a little school boy, I initially was taught "Old Glory" had something to do with the U. S. Flag and not Granny Grunt's underwear.

It was a tremendously cold winter night in 1949 when Granny Grunt and her husband Mr. Rhodes, a preacher we were not allowed to call "Brother" after he passed out from whiskey while preaching in the pulpit, came to spend the night at our farm located at Tram Switch.

Beatrice Rhodes, First on the right

How cold were the winters back then? So cold that we children turned blue between the farm house while on the l-o-n-g path to our "shack out back." We made certain to take care of business quickly before getting undressed and slipping in beneath the warm covers to sleep on Momma's newest snugly-warm chicken feather bed mattress.

But in cold weather emergencies, Daddy allowed our family to have one designated "pot," otherwise known as the "honey bucket," inside our farm house.

And the last person to use the pot had the early morning responsibility of immediately taking and emptying the contents over the fence into the hog wallow, as decreed by Daddy, a stern man who had strict "honey bucket" rules.

But something happened that night to forever change the routine and rules of how we dealt with the chamber pot. It was the night we children later decreed as "Granny Grunt's Great Shit Storm on the Farm."

It seemed in her haste to take care of business on that freezing cold winter night, Granny Grunt misjudged, and, well, she missed the pot, which judging from the size of her huge backside, that was no easy thing to do.

Granny Grunt not only missed the bucket, she knocked it over and you-know-what spilled out. . . all over the cold bedroom floor.

Granny Grunt, a huge lady with short legs and arms, couldn't get enough traction to get herself righted, each time she'd try to stand up, she'd slip and back down she'd go. Whew-wee, this was not a pretty sight!

Finally, out of desperation, she pleaded for help, which scared me, a little feller at the time, and sent me scurrying under a bed in the next room.

"Help me, Van," she pleaded to my brother.

"Help me, June," she hollered for my sister.

Finally, Daddy Whittle instructed Granny to crawl on her hands and knees out of the mess on out to the front porch, where "we can clean you up."

That was when we kids were ordered to retrieve several buckets of water to pour over our now very cold, shivering, and naked-as-a-jaybird Granny Grunt.

How cold was she? So cold with all her shivering and shaking, you'd thought she was about to have a Pentecostal church pew-running experience.

It would be a few years before the family finally saw the humor about the night that Granny Grunt missed the honey bucket.

This was one of those incidents we children were never allowed to bring up and talk about, especially while Granny Grunt was still alive.

"And for sure don't go telling the neighbors about it," Daddy Whittle instructed firmly.

And we didn't. . . until now.

Whew-wee!!

Chapter Fifty-Four

Feelin' Froggy

It was spring 1955, a memorable milestone night of drama on Little River.

It was my first official frog hunt, a sort of rural-country-boy, coming-of-age event in our neck of the woods.

I had grown excited when older, favorite first cousin Robert Terry Reed declared it was time for Little Danny Whittle to grow up a notch or two, to wit, go on our first official sanctioned bonafide for-real frog-gigging expedition.

Always before, an adult had declared: "You're too little to go froggin."

So when Cousin Robert Terry made the invite, I'm here to confirm that the galluses of my old faded pair of Liberty overalls swelled with new-found pride.

Cousin Robert Terry, who was two years my senior and smarter than me, achieved hero status in the eyes of this then eleven-year-old tyke when he declared I was old enough to accompany him on a for-real frog hunt.

The source for our frogs was Little River, which was called Little River because it was, when not flooded, not even much of a stream.

Although a pitiful little stream compared to the nearby majestic and mighty Mississippi made famous by Huckleberry Finn and Mark Twain, it was our source not only for frogging but fishing, and sometimes swimming and bathing too. In younger years, we also faced pirates on that little mystical stream.

Since Robert Terry Reed was more mechanically minded than me, it was he who fashioned our homemade frog gigs out of two old, worn-out pitch forks from the barn.

Terry and Sandra Reed

"You gotta have them razor sharp to penetrate the tough old hides of those big, old croaking bull frogs," Robert Terry confirmed as he filed and filed to put a razor sharp edge on those gig prongs.

Since I was a good four inches shorter than my cousin, Robert Terry designated the frog gig with the shortest handle for me.

One last preliminary frog hunting expedition detail consisted of fastening our frog-hunting lights to our cherished St. Louis Cardinal baseball caps.

Although I was a scrawny little boy who stood less than five feet in height and weighed less than eighty pounds, I felt ten feet tall when I strapped on one of those lights. . . an instrument we called a carbide light.

Truth is, those old lights and its chemical called carbide stunk up the night more than they put out a light, but they were all we had to work with in 1955.

Finally, it was time to walk the half mile from our farm house back to Little River that snaked its way through our little corner of New Madrid County.

Since the river was shallow, we went froggin' in knee-high rubber boots.

We hadn't waded more than fifty yards downstream when Robert Terry bagged his first frog.

Being more experienced at froggin', Cousin Robert Terry patiently showed me how to stalk quietly and walk up to a bull frog while blinding the critter with the beam of light.

Low and behold, "SWOOSH," it worked. My homemade gig found its mark. I bagged my first frog on that now long ago foggy night.

A few more steps down the stream, a life-changing event occurred. High drama and terrors are what I'm talking about.

I was out in the middle of the stream after bagging four or five big, ole bull frogs when I felt something *tap, tap,* tapping near the top of my boots.

I looked down, and my heart raced upon seeing five small, but highly-poisonous, cotton mouth snakes all butting their venomous-looking heads up against my boots. Upon seeing my situation, Cousin Robert Terry instructed: "Don't move."

To which, I replied succinctly and firmly: "Don't worry. I can't move," as I stood petrified, scared stiff there in the middle of the stream.

He took on even more special stature when he made his next suggestion.

"Let's shine our lights in one spot, about five feet away from your boots and see if those old snakes will follow the light," Cousin Robert Terry instructed.

Sure enough, when we did, those snakes mercifully followed away from my boots.

Did I mention that Cousin Robert Terry was my hero?

After we breathed huge sighs of relief, my cousin asked about that big, dark, damp spot on the front of my britches.

"It ain't river water," I confessed meekly.

Chapter Fifty-Five
Farm Talk

Saturdays and Sundays, for the most part in rural farm communities, were days not to work. Oh, the more industrious farmers and their farm hands would work maybe half a day.

But mostly, we didn't do much field work, that is, if the crop growing season was under control, which meant that we'd had ample rain and the weed growth had been effectively dealt with. We worked on weekends only if the Biblical "Ox was in the ditch."

"Ox is in the ditch," was a phrase often used by Momma Whittle and other farmers when justifying having to work on Sundays.

"Sodie pops," "cold drinks," and "soft drinks" were words we farm children used to describe Coca-Colas, and Dr. Peppers, not to mention Nehi orange belly washers.

Those were big treats, for example, on Saturday nights when we didn't merely attend a movie.

Saturday nights were when mothers ordered us to wash behind our ears if we were going to attend John Summers' ten-cent Saturday night moving picture show.

And us real youngins had it figured out that the "Midnight

Show" was when older teenagers would smooch in the dark of the theater, out from under the sight of prying eyes of brothers and sisters deemed too little to stay up that late.

Holding hands was the equivalent of courting for us little guys and gals in that old dark theater.

"I saw Little Danny holding hands with Brenda Harlan tonight," older brother Van tattled to Momma Whittle after one Saturday night at the moving picture show. How folks used words to communicate in our little neck of southeast Missouri's "Bootheel" region has always fascinated this former farm boy. This chronology is no way disrespectful to my farm ancestral roots and neighbors, most of whom were the smartest, hardest-working people I've met on this journey through life.

The word "Bootheel" itself is unique as it relates to location, appearing like it could be a part of Arkansas, as opposed to "Boot Hill" where deceased folks reside.

The bootheel region to this day is sometimes referred to as Swampeast Missouri, a phrase dating back before the Little River Drainage District was formed to drain Nigger Wool Swamp that formerly covered six counties that form today's Bootheel agrarian region.

The former swamp bottom land became some of the most fertile farm land in the world when a series of drainage canals were dug after railroads had entered the region.

Trails in the woods preceded plank, corduroy and gravel roads paved roads connected the Bootheel to the outside world.

Which brings us to the word "chat."

We're not talking about flapping those lips in the breeze, to just hear one's self talk.

Chat to many native Bootheel folks meant a very fine form of gravel, slightly courser and heavier than sand.

Chat was a fill substance to give our farm roads a more firm base over which to drive our cars, farm trucks, and tractors over, especially during cold, wet, rainy winter seasons when our mostly-gumbo heavy loam soil became deep clinging mud.

Why we pronounced it "chat" I don't know when most of the rest of America, including Webster's Dictionary, uses the word "chirt" to describe this form of gravel.

The word chat caused me embarrassment when I went to work for a big city newspaper.

"Whittle, we don't use 'chat' to describe gravel in Tennessee," instructed the late Weldon Grimsley, an editor who also grew up in the Bootheel. But editor Grimsley understood where I was coming from.

"I know we called it 'chat' back in Missouri, but in Tennessee, we use the right actual word, 'chirt,' as defined and described by Mr. Webster in his dictionary," Weldon noted one day as he edited one of my first news stories at the *Nashville Banner*.

"Fixin' to" was another phrase from Bootheel lingo.

This phrase also brought critical corrective instruction from my first great newspaper editor, the late Paul Bumbarger, who had the heaviest editing pencil I encountered in my forty-plus years of news writing.

"Whittle, the vehicle accident on Kings Highway route to Cape Girardeau did not happen as the driver was 'fixing to' turn left," editor Bumbarger instructed sternly. "Don't use the language that you may have used out in the cotton patch at Canalou. We're not going to allow fixing to to describe any upcoming circumstance, accident, or event."

The tough editor ultimately became my friend and mentoring force during my fledgling professional writing career that started at the former "Daily Standard" newspaper in Sikeston, Missouri.

Wife Pat also finds Bootheel language patterns intriguing.

"You don't use any unnecessary words, for example, in naming things and places in and around Canalou," Pat observed on her first trip to my former little farming hamlet community located about twelve miles from Sikeston, which was the nearest "big city" with whopping population of maybe 6,000 people in the early 1950s.

"Such as?" I asked.

"Here on your town's old school building, for instance," Pat noted. "Instead of spelling out that it was the Canalou Elementary School, it merely reads 'School' on the front of the building," Pat instructed.

I asked for more examples.

"Over in that town called Essex, instead of having the full name of the community's one and only financial business, the front of the building used one word - 'Bank' - instead of saying First National Bank or the Bank of Essex," Pat said while appearing on a roll now.

The Bootheel is noted for having few curves in roads, which prompted an Arkansas author to pen a book entitled "Where The Roads Never Curve."

"We're not flashy, just functional," I attempted to defend. "For sure, we try not to appear to be getting above our 'raisen'."

"Well, you've succeeded in that," wife fired back.

I recall a memorable visitor back in childhood days when military man Leo Harkey visited our farm on leave from overseas duty in the late 1940s.

Being a native of Boston, Massachusetts, visitor Leo tried to figure out just where "over yonder" was located in our beloved Bootheel farming region.

"Leo would laugh when he'd hear me describe some destination as over yonder," accounted my mother, Ruby Lee Stockton Whittle. "When the visiting soldier wanted to know exactly where Trailback Plantation was located, I responded: 'Over yonder'."

When contacted in the 1990s for research purposes of this forum, Mr. Harkey laughingly recalled: "I never did figure out where 'over yonder' was exactly, but that it was close in proximity to some place called the Trailback Plantation."

Pat made more interesting observations regarding speech and communication patterns that maybe are uniquely heard, written, and spoke in the area of Missouri we natives call "The Bootheel."

"Boot Hill in most other parts of America means something entirely different that it's used here where you grew up," Pat accounted. "Why do you and your folks spell it 'Bootheel' when everyone in else in America spells it Boot Hill?"

"Two different things," I responded.

If I'd been asked such a question back when I was a farm boy, my overall galluses would likely have swollen with pride. For now, I informed this inquiring city gal about the origin of our farming region known as "Bootheel."

"The term Bootheel was coined by local folks to describe the part of Missouri that sticks down like it could be a part of Arkansas," I instructed proudly and slowly, so the city-fied gal could get a handle on Bootheel's origin. "The region, when you look on road maps, looks the shape of an actual heel of a boot."

Since we happened to be in our automobile, Pat reached back and got a road map.

"I see the shape of the Bootheel, but I don't see the town of Canalou listed on this map," Pat noted.

To which I replied, sharply and defensively: "Canalou is so unique it's only found on your better road maps."

Canalou native Marguerite Harrison, who spent her retirement years living up in St. Louis, said there's a standing joke about the Bootheel by folks living north of the Mason Dixon Line that allegedly runs along the railroad tracks that run through Chaffee, Missouri, just outside of Cape Girardeau that overlooks the mighty Mississippi.

"Folks in St. Louis tell the joke, that if you gave the Bootheel to Arkansas, it would raise the IQ of both states," Mrs. Harrison quipped.

No proud Bootheel natives I know ever recognized the attempt at *humor* by those folks up north of the Mason Dixon Line.

Like folks in other regions, we had Bootheel natives that were especially colorful in their language, such as farmer Virgil Knuckles whose farm was located near ours behind Little River.

Virgil didn't just give folks a cussing, for when he was thoroughly upset, he would "give them a good chunk of a cussing."

Which proves that there's mere cussings and then there's deeper, more intense versions of a cussing as in "a good chunk of a cussing."

One of the best farmers on our farm road was the late John Ling, who had his own description of weather conditions.

"What's the weather look like?" I'd hear Daddy Whittle ask neighbor farmer Ling.

"It looks slick cloudy to me," farmer Ling would reply.

We never knew exactly what slick cloudy meant, but farmer Ling seemed to know.

As a boy, we Whittles pronounced onion with a 'g' in the word, as in "ongyen."

However, we spelled "o-n-i-on" correctly during spelling tests at Canalou's "School" of advanced matriculation.

Chapter Fifty-Six

Daddy's Whippings

We never back-talked or sassed any adult.

It was a capitol offense to slam a door or not answer "Yes, sir" and "No, sir" to anyone older.

It was also a family rule not to snatch the last piece of fried chicken when the Reverend. A. C. Sullivant and his wife Alice came from their home in Morehouse to break bread and share fellowship after one of his sermons.

This brings me to corporal punishment dealt out by our hard-working parents.

The second worst whipping I got involved a prayer at the dinner table on a Sunday the preacher and his wife were visiting.

Momma Whittle, being the good God-fearing woman that she was, was proud of Little Danny for learning to say a new prayer. And there was pride evident on her face come Sunday morning when she told me before going to Canalou Baptist Church that I was to say the prayer at the dinner table when the preacher was to share in some of Momma's larruping good fried chicken and thickening gravy.

What was unbeknownst to Momma was that my older brother,

H. Van, and his best farm road buddy, Edwin Ling, would teach me a "new and better prayer" between Sunday school and preaching service.

Finally, the dinner table scene was set. Brother Sullivant had his fork at the ready, when Momma instructed: "Little Danny is going to say the prayer for us today, Reverend Sullivant."

With all heads bowed, eyes reverently closed, and without further fanfare, I proceeded to pray with great enthusiasm: "Praise the Lord, the Holy Ghost, the biggest hog gets the most! Amen!"

No sooner were those words out of my mouth, than Momma Whittle's right hand was slamming up side my noggin.

She knocked me for a winding.

She hit with such force that I ended up on the floor by our new kerosene-powered icebox (refrigerator) that preceded REA electricity on our farm road.

As soon as Mother collected herself, I couldn't tell whether she was more embarrassed by my new prayer or that she had knocked me "for a winding" in front of a holy man.

And as soon as the preacher man left, it was time for the real switching. Where was the American Civil Liberties Union when this clear case of double jeopardy was resulting in me getting another dose of corporal punishment?

Which brings me to another corporal punishment point: I deserved most of the whippings that I received, but to this day, I don't think I deserved to have to go get the switches that were destined to blister my behind.

I compare it to making a condemned man get up and throw the switch to his own electric chair.

Make no mistake; Momma could swing a mean willow tree switch. But Daddy Whittle's floggings were double-tough on back torsos.

Daddy's word was *law*.

And he could tear that backside up when he was really mad or disappointed in one of his youngins.

The worst flogging I ever got from Daddy came at the end of an exceedingly hot day in the cotton field, and I deserved it.

Being too young to chop weeds out of cotton, I was the designated water boy.

My job was to lug a heavy gallon jug, filled with fresh cool water, to the field of hot and thirsty cotton choppers two times in the morning and two times in the afternoon.

It was a swelteringly hot day on my fourth and final trip with the critically-needed water that I fell down on the job.

Actually, I laid down on some newly-tilled gumbo soil in the cool shade of some soybeans that were almost waist-high on a grown man. It must have been about four o'clock when I laid down on the job and meant to take a short nap.

The next thing I knew, it was sun down and Little Danny Whittle's butt was in a heap of trouble.

"We've been looking all over for you, and our throats are parched," my older brother warned as he found me still snoozing in the bean field. "Daddy's mad, and you're going to get a thrashing."

Brother always smiled his mean impish grin when I had an impending punishment coming.

As I said, I deserved most of my childhood whippings, but I believe this was the most severe one I ever got from Daddy. Instead of waiting until we got to the house, Daddy just took off his belt there in the soybean patch and gave me a thrashing in front of the entire crew of thirsty cotton choppers.

Needless to say, I never laid down on my water-toting job again. Looking back on it, I don't think I even sat down for a day or two either.

But Daddy later complimented me on another day of water totin'.

He had hired two dragline operators to dredge another drainage ditch on the back of the new ground leading into nearby Little

River. This was to help take the water away from our crops and fields during flood years.

After four or five attempts at getting cool water the half mile distance from our farm house to the new ground, I realized I couldn't please those dragline operators.

"We were promised fresh, cool water while we're out here in this hot sunshine on this job," one of the operators continued to whine.

I never said a word, but instead of going all the way back to our house for fresh hand-pumped water, I stopped at the barn and dipped the bucket into the cow trough.

So I high-tailed it back to the new ground where one of the thirsty and griping dragline operators seemed to finally be satisfied.

"Man, oh, man. Whew-wee, that's the best tasting water I've ever had," he proclaimed while taking another satisfied gulp of cow-trough water.

I never told him that our cows always seemed satisfied with that water too.

Later that evening, upon hearing my explanation about not being able to please those dragline operators, Daddy said: "That's my boy. That's using your noggin. That cow trough water was plenty good enough for them griping and complaining dragline men."

Although Daddy was not a church-going man, he was faithful in his way. During World War II years, when the preacher came to our house, Daddy would automatically fill the preacher's car with gasoline from our farm's big gasoline tank. Being a farmer, Daddy could get all the gasoline he needed on the farm. Gasoline was rationed to most people, including preachers, during the war.

Chapter Fifty-Seven
Mule Suicide

For certain, it was a day of some stubborn Missouri mule high drama behind Maw Mathenia's little grocery store.

In 1945, Canalou was served twice daily by mail trains, running north and south in the Missouri Bootheel.

On this particular day, a stubborn mule named Jack drew a crowd of people as its owner attempted to get it off the railroad tracks.

Much anticipation began building as town folk began hearing a train approaching before they could see the train. And the mule refused to budge, despite the train engineer was now jarring down hard on his big train's whistle.

Legend has it that a collective groan went up among town's people as they witnessed Jack the mule being ran over by the train.

"That was the day poor ol' Jack, who belonged to Grandfather Abe Landers Junior, unwisely chose to go to the glue factory," noted Les Landers, who has the distinction being born in Canalou in 1940. "Ol' Jack, according to some spectators, just stood there and stared at the big ol' train as it ran over him."

Locals unofficially ruled it the only "mule suicide" in

Canalou's history.

"Well, it's possible that it was Canalou's only known suicide by a mule, for just a few days earlier, Jack's longtime plow-pulling mate named Murt, had died of old age," Les recalled. "It wasn't long after that that ol' Jack, who was also getting up in years, got out of the barn and walked toward downtown Canalou where he gathered an audience by refusing to get off the railroad tracks. Canalou law, at that time, ruled Jack's death was a suicide by a train."

Les Landers recalls his Grandfather Landers using mules on the E. H. Percy Farm the Landers' family tilled out near Little River, about two miles west of downtown Canalou in the 1940s.

"One time, we went to the school house where we watched a Donkey Basketball Game," Les recalled. "The only thing more stubborn than a Missouri mule is a donkey, not to be confused with the few lazy human jackasses known to live in and around Canalou from time-to-time.

"Sometimes, I'd go with my dad [Willie Landers] to be what help I could be on Granddad Landers' farm," Les added. "We'd pick corn and so forth. When we were through, they would unhitch the mules and let me take them back to the barn."

"Good strong and sturdy Missouri mules tend to have minds of their own," Les accounted. "Especially at quitting time.

When it came time to go to the barn, those mules didn't need anyone to drive them as they knew the way," Les added. "You couldn't have stopped them, for they would not stop until they got to the barn. One day, me and the mules came to a gigantic mud hole," Les traced back through time when mules still reigned supreme on Missouri farms. "I tried to rein them to the left. No luck. I tried reining them to the right. I could not change their direction.

Those mules kept right on going lickety-split and busted that mud hole wide open. Trouble was, I lost both shoes in that sticky old gumbo mud that the Bootheel is famous for. After having to follow those hard-headed lop-eared mules barefooted all the way to the barn, Dad came up behind us, laughing, while holding my mud-covered pair of shoes."

I got in on the tail-end of mule farming in the Missouri Bootheel.

The only time I drove a team of mules was when Daddy Whittle gathered and shocked corn on our farm.

For unlearned city-fied types, a corn shock had nothing to do with REA electricity, which we didn't have on our farm until 1951.

A corn shock was created after we'd pulled and shucked the ears of corn, then we'd bunch the stalks in a tight circle and tie them off with baling wire, later to be used as winter feed for our livestock.

In later years, numerous photographers have made pictures of a corn field with corn shocks standing out there. It makes for a pretty picture.

By 1950, the mules' reign on Canalou-area farms was mostly over with the advent of tractors and other mechanized equipment.

But the legend of ol' Jack, the only known mule suicide in the history annals of Canalou, lives on.

Chapter Fifty-Eight
Loss of Floodway Bridge

When the bridge went down over the Floodway Channel during floods of 1944, it disconnected Canalou from the east-west corridor of state Route 80 and was never rebuilt.

It's been said that was the "real beginning of the end" for the once thriving former swamp sawmill village that transformed itself into a vibrant agrarian economy after multiple drainage canals were dredged (started in 1914) by the Little River Drainage District.

Former Canalou resident Arcile Haywood Boyes recalls losing the bridge over Floodway Channel during the floods of 1944-45 and a reason it was not rebuilt.

"Losing the bridge that crossed Floodway was the next biggest thing that adversely affected the economy of Canalou after the stave mill was shut down and our school was lost," Arcile concludes. "The east-west corridor was closed, thus closing down any chance of commerce and growth in that direction and virtually making Canalou a 'dead-end' destination.

"My father, Herman *Fat* Haywood, always credited a rich and politically-powerful land owner over in Stoddard County at the Trailback Plantation with opposing the bridge being rebuilt," she added.

Canalou's town mayor agrees.

"You could say after that bridge over Floodway was lost, Canalou was at the end of the road," describes Mayor James Donald Taul, whose family was one of the earliest immigrant families to be attracted into the original swamp/sawmill village that began in 1902. "Canalou remains a dead-end destination in that you cannot go further west since the Floodway Bridge was never rebuilt.

"One reason the Trailback Plantation landowner didn't want the bridge rebuilt was that he didn't want his farm workers to go to Canalou on Saturday nights," the mayor diagnosed. "Usually, it meant he or one of his farm foremen would have to go to Canalou on Sunday and Monday and bail their laborers out of the calaboose after a Saturday night in Canalou, which had five or more saloons and multiple gambling rooms at any given time during the 1940s."

"You've got to have a reason to want to come here now," added former Canalou Mayor Charles Joyce.

That bridge ended up being rebuilt down near Charter Oak, an unincorporated Stoddard County community about five miles to the south of Canalou.

So what was the original attraction that drew people to Canalou from surrounding states?

"For some, it was being on the run from law," confirms former Canalou resident Les Landers. "My grandfather was on the run from the law in Kentucky when he came to the swamp in the early 1900s. He was later cleared of shooting that deputy sheriff back in Kentucky. He then became town marshal of Canalou."

Retired New Madrid Policeman David Blankenship, born and reared on a farm near Canalou, credits farm machinery with triggering the economic demise of the town.

"Cotton and corn pickers replaced the sharecropping families to a large extent," David noted. "When that mechanization happened, that ended jobs that sharecroppers could do, which ended up taking trade away from the little grocery stores in Canalou. My family came here up from Arkansas for the farming originally."

"For my family, it was land, wanting to elevate themselves above sharecropper status," describes Canalou native Bonnie Blankenship Boutz, daughter of former Arkansas farmers Conliff and Ruby Lucy Blankenship and David's sister. "The Blankenships were attracted to Canalou in 1925 by the affordable, rich farm land that followed the draining of the swamps and clearing of the timber."

"We initially settled near the River Ridge community that once had a little school one mile south west of Canalou, between Charter Oak and Little River," noted the former school girl who graduated from Canalou High School in 1954.

"The farming economy was good in the 1940s, so good that it attracted friends and family to follow us here from Arkansas, especially during the fall cotton harvest season," Bonnie accounted.

Cotton was still "king" in that era, having replaced the timber industry as the primary economic trigger.

"We had relatives and friends who came and lived in tents in our front yard during the cotton picking season," Bonnie traced back in time. "They would cook their meals in our smokehouse, but at night they slept in tents.

"Some were gifted cotton pickers, such as Arkan-sawyer Ernest Weiland, who could pick up to four hundred pounds in a day," Bonnie recalled. "He and his family were one of those families who lived in a tent in our front yard. You gotta remember, this was not long after the Great Depression, and cash was hard to come by, so cotton picking was one way for a family to earn cash money in that era.

"As for me, I could barely get one hundred and seventy pounds a day, and that was on my better days," Bonnie said. "Ernest Weiland was gifted, if you call cotton picking a gift."

"I was in seventh grade [in 1947] before we got electricity," Bonnie confirmed. "Heck, it was after I graduated from high school that we had indoor toilets. We had the little building everyone used behind the house. Indoor plumbing and electricity were big advancements on the Blankenship farm."

David recalled a cholera outbreak in the early 1950s that nearly wiped out his father's hog operation.

"It was serious business losing those hogs," David described. "Dad lost seventy-eight hogs, a huge loss both in terms of cash and meat for our family."

"The hogs would be walking around in the barn lot and drop to the ground, kick a few times, and they were dead," added David. "We couldn't bury the infected hogs because cholera stays in the ground, so we had to burn the carcasses.

"I recall stacking the hogs on top of brush piles and burning them that way," he noted. "It was a serious outbreak that hurt a lot of farmers in the pocket book and in their winter supply of meat."

David also recalls picking cotton and shucking and shelling corn.

"I remember shelling corn by hand during the cold winter months when we couldn't work in the fields," he added. "Your hands become very tender and sore."

After graduating from Bloomfield High School, David became a law enforcement officer and served in New Madrid for twenty-two years before retirement and moving to Jackson, Missouri.

"Canalou produced a number of law violators," the former police officer confirmed.

"I recall having to arrest a few friends and neighbors from Canalou, including several of the Drake boys, especially Jimmy Drake," David noted. "We arrested Jimmy several times.

"I recall Canalou always being a rough and woolly little town," David added. "You had to be alert to not put yourself in harm's way. I remember that a man named Bad Bill cut a man's abdomen from one side of his torso to the other side of his torso in a barroom knife fight around 1950."

Former Canalou farm girl Patsy Hopper Bixler recalls one particular *mean* town marshal in Canalou.

"One thing you could usually see on Saturday nights was the local marshal, Charley Asa, arresting someone for drunkenness," Patsy recalls. "He would hit them in the head and put them in a pickup truck and drive them to the jail with blood dripping down their white shirts.

"He was real handy with his black jack and most often arrested some of the Waters' boys, a large family in our farming community during the 1940s," Patsy added. "Those boys would come to town with their hair all slicked down with Rose Hair Oil and their white shirts. Charles Asa was a mean, tough marshal."

Chapter Fifty-Nine

Norman Harrison

Canalou's first (and only) theater was built in 1944 and premiered "The Life of Jack London" on the big screen.

Later, it was the Lone Ranger, Lash Larue, Roy Rogers, and Gene Autry chasing desperadoes across theater owner John Summers' new silver screen.

Prior to 1944, there were traveling projectionists, including those from Morehouse's Dillon Theater who would set up a movie screen and charge Canalou area residents a small admittance fee.

Sometimes these traveling movie projectionists showed their movies in Canalou's old three-story Lampher Hotel that also served as a place for folks to buy caskets. Other times, they'd set up on the empty lot formerly occupied by Greenlee's Skating Rink that had moved to Lilbourn.

By the 1950s, it was two teenaged boys, Norman Harrison and Johnny Summers, who had the huge responsibility of our town's Thursday night, Saturday night and Sunday matinee movies in their hands. This was during Canalou's heyday economic era of mostly agrarian-related commerce. Norman, in his early seventies as of 2010, recreates this Americana small farm-town scene.

"It was nothing unusual for me to look out of the second floor projection room window that faced Main Street and see cars, trucks, tractors, mules, and farm wagons lined up and parked from in front of John Summers' Theater all the way back out of the town's city limits out by Kasinger's Grocery to the north," recalls Norman Ernest Harrison, son of the late Norval and Marguerite Haywood Harrison.

"Most of the time Johnny, theater owners John and Jean Summers' only son, would run the projector during the week, and I'd run the projector on the weekends. And when I'd look to the south, vehicles and farm wagons would be lined up that direction all the way past West Smith's Service Station down to the school at the other end of Main Street."

Parking space was a premium.

"It was nothing unusual for the downstairs auditorium and upstairs balcony to be filled with several hundred people on Saturday nights when the sidewalks were brimming over with people coming in off the farms," Norman Ernest explained.

"I remember my grandparents would take their International pickup and park on Main Street by mid-afternoon, so they would have a parking space from which to socialize on Saturday nights. When the sun went down, Dado [grandfather Haywood] and Momo [grandmother] would walk up town, and sit in their truck Dado had parked earlier and visit with other folks meandering up and down Main Street. And then, they'd drive their truck back home late that night. You had to get to town early just to get a parking space on Saturdays."

Saturday nights were a social happening, rural Bootheel style.

So what was the pay to operate the town's movie projector?

"I got all the cheeseburgers I wanted, and John Summers' Café had the best cheeseburgers in town," Norman Ernest revealed. "Sometimes, I'd just drink a cherry Coke. We all loved Jo Ann Summers' cherry Cokes and fresh hot popcorn. I recall the smell of that popcorn and cheeseburgers would permeate the whole theater, and out on Main Street for that matter. Of course, I got to see the shows free too."

His toughest theater task was keeping the film of that era from breaking.

"That was most often the cause of the movie screen going dark. Film in that era was brittle and broke easily," Norman recalled. "And then, sometimes the arc would fail when the two heat rods would not automatically come together. That was the source of light that lit up the big screen."

As a little boy, I recall the night theater owner John Summers proudly displayed his new expensive big movie screen. To celebrate the new screen, John put a fire-eating Native American man up on stage for entertainment.

The fire-eater not only ate fire that night, but stumbled and ran his elbow through Mr. Summers' expensive new screen.

Exit drunken Indian pronto, stage right!!

Former Canalou farm girl Patsy Hopper Bixler remembers viewing movies before J. B. Boots Conn put in the first theater.

"We didn't have a movie theater until 1944," Patsy recalls. "Prior to that, every Saturday night a projectionist from Morehouse's Dillon Theater would come down to Canalou and show movies in the old Lampher Hotel. There were not many seats, just benches and plenty of seats on the floor. A pot-bellied stove was the heat-source.

"We were proud when we got a theater," Patsy added. "Grade school kids all marched down to the theater during school hours to see movies such as *Snow White*, *The Yearling*, and *Bambi*. It cost us ten cents. And when we finally got our own theater, when it rained the movie's floor would fill up with rain water and could not be used until the water went down. Because Canalou sat so low, and the water level was so high, you could drive a pump just about any where and get water. Remember, it'd only been a few years since the swamp had been drained."

"Before the theater was built, we'd often go to Morehouse to the Dillon Theater," Patsy added. "We'd see those wonderful musicals of the 1940s with Ginger Rogers and Fred Astaire, Gene Kelly, Betty Grable, and Rita Hayworth. Then there were the crime dramas starring Edward G. Robinson, Charles Boyer, James Cagney, and Humphrey Bogart. Before each movie they'd show a newsreel about World War II. That news feature segment was entitled *The Eyes and Ears Of The World.* "If a service man was going to be shown in a newsreel from a specific area, that family would be notified of it, and a circle appeared on the screen around that local serviceman."

I personally recall the way John Summers' kept law and order in his theater. He would thump our noggins with such force with his thumb. We didn't misbehave that much.

In first and second grades, school buddies Harold David Bryant, Kirky Durbin, and myself competed for the affections of pretty little lasses Rosemary Hopper, Sandra Hill, Sue Baby Bixler, Gladys Johns, Ellen Campbell, and Brenda Harlan. It was heart-pumping excitement to sit and hold hands with any of those pretty little fillies.

But it was farm neighbor girl Sue Baby Bixler who blew my mind one night when we were in junior high school. We were smooching in the back of the theater, when Sue *Baby* ran her tongue in my mouth.

"That's what we call French kissing, Danny boy," Sue Baby instructed as I sat stunned and red-faced in the dark after being tongued. Although it had been more than forty years since the last movie was shown at the little cinema, the pretty yellow brick building stood until a fire of mysterious origin occurred in 2009. Fallen theater bricks help give present-day Main Street a ghostly appearance.

Chapter Sixty

The Buck Doesn't Stop Here

The influential Missourian, Harry Truman, made famous the phrase: "The Buck Stops Here."

Another not-so-famous Missourian made medical history when he proclaimed: "The Buck *doesn't* stop here."

Medical experts gave Bootheel native John Buck Junior the prognosis he would *never walk again* after a catastrophic four-wheeler accident snapped his neck during a fateful family outing in 2004.

As a newspaper columnist, I originally wrote about his tragedy.

A hush swept through my Tennessee newspaper office in 2005 when young Buck, the son of former Canalou, Missouri, residents Renda Chaney Buck and her husband, John Buck Senior, *walked* up the front door steps and into the newsroom.

"Well, I'm from Canalou, Missouri, and I'm here to tell you, this Buck does not stop here," Buck said. "I took my first steps back in November and have been making progress ever since."

When John stepped unannounced into my newspaper office, I fell into my seat. It had been only a few months since I had written the story about him. During that time and through our news interviews and his positive approach to life, young Buck had become a friend and a person I admire very much!

His wife, Pat, described her husband's breakthrough first steps.

"John and our daughter Kelly, who always believed her dad would walk again, were in the back of the house one afternoon when I came in all frazzled from work." Pat accounted. "I heard John yell out: 'Pat, come back here.' And then Kelly yelled: 'Momma, come quick!' Finally, when I got to them, there stood John. And he took his first step. Kelly burst out in joyful tears, and I did too, and we all celebrated and gave thanks to God," Pat described. "Tears were gushing down all our faces."

Nashville Vanderbilt Medical Center neurosurgeon Paul Boone, who was on duty when Buck was brought to the hospital after his almost fatal accident near Bowling Green, Kentucky, described his patient's prognosis.

"He was presented to us on July 18th, 2004, unable to move his lower limbs," the doctor recalled. "Based on extensive examinations and X-rays, we determined Mr. Buck would be paraplegic, a permanent condition where the legs would not work again."

But subsequent surgery and faith improved the prognosis.

"And Mr. Buck recovered quite well from that surgery," Dr. Boone assessed, "but the prospect was still dim that he'd ever walk again.

Through the months, he's made remarkable recovery, a big part of which was his positive attitude. Plus, his intense motivation to seek therapy, working his muscles in his lower extremities began to pay off."

Dr. Boone quickly added, "This is by no means a common occurrence. For the vast majority of patients, there's no recovery. Mr. Buck and his determination are clearly the exception."

Because Buck Junior wouldn't give up, worked hard, and had faith, he made it successfully down the road of recovery.

"Yes, prayers went throughout Tennessee and back in Canalou, Missouri, where John grew up," credits Pat Buck.

"I never gave up hope," Buck added. "I knew I would walk again. And I never let depression set in. My family and our way of life back in Canalou do not let you get down or feel sorry for yourself."

Today young Buck regularly drives himself from his home in Tennessee to visit his parents, Renda and John Buck Senior, at their home near Poplar Bluff.

"We're very thankful and proud of young John," noted his mother.

"There's no quit in our son," added young John's proud father. "No doubt his faith and his don't-quit-attitude learned back in the Bootheel helped in this miracle."

Their son is now used by the medical profession as an inspiration to others: "They've had me come twice to meet with patients at the Shepherd Center in Atlanta, plus I've often spoken to patients here in Tennessee.

"There's one man I've met with after he'd been diagnosed as paraplegic, and he's up walking again," young John Buck noted. "In fact, he's out-doing me, and he's inspiring me now to get up off my butt and work harder.

"My wife, daughter, my parents—you can't write it down on paper how important they have been to me," he added as he stood unaided without crutches or cane. "Of course, we credit God for helping give us the courage to have the faith, and I want to credit my Canalou upbringing where folks know about tough times. It took a tough and smart stock of people to endure the swamps and carve out the farms that came later."

If there is anything I know about Canalou, it is that Canalou has produced some courageous people.

Chapter Sixty-One
Whiskey Flowed

In Chicago, to the north, it was the Daley political machine.

In Kansas City, to the west, it was the Pendergast political dynasty.

In Memphis, to the south, it was the Boss Crump political empire.

In New Madrid County, in the heart of Swampeast Missouri, politics was ruled by (the late) J.V. Conran.

What did the above have in common in the 1930s, 1940s, and 1950s eras? They were all Democrat-controlled political machines.

How do I know this?

At a young age, I became, albeit a tiny, part of the Conran political operation in New Madrid County.

I didn't know what was about to happen, but I knew something special was taking place when we (children) were told not to open a mysterious big cardboard box that arrived the day before election on our remote farm house front porch.

Upon arrival, it was the natural thing to do to want to open that box, for it was seldom we got a parcel that size delivered to our remote farm house.

However, the next morning, election day in New Madrid County, neighbor farmers Norval Harrison and A. J. Neel not only opened the box, they told us what to do with the contents.

"You take these [whiskey bottles] and give them to the black cotton choppers in the fields," A. J. instructed his young team of election workers. Being the youngest child in the small group, I ran out in those cotton fields swelled up like a cocky, little rooster.

Multiple half-pint bottles of bonded bourbon were placed in every pocket I had in my newest pair of overalls, including two in my top bib overall pocket.

It was high drama for a nine-year-old farm boy to be asked to help on Election Day.

The scenario went like this after I walked out in the middle of a cotton patch on (the late) Ott Barnett's farm in the Big Ridge-area filled mostly with black folks with their cotton hoes.

"Do you wanna go vote?" I asked this elderly black gentleman.

"Naw, sir," he replied.

With that, I partially revealed one of the half pints of whiskey.

And I repeated the question: "Do you wanna go vote?"

"Yessss, sir," was the reply after the elderly gentleman saw that I was armed with some store-bought bourbon.

And although I was not old enough to go with the big truck loaded with potential voters to the polling places, I was driven on to the next field of farm workers where another big farm truck was waiting to load cotton choppers.

In looking back, the New Madrid-brand of politics was highly synchronized. Even the farmers didn't seem to mind that their field workers were taken away from their toils on Election Day, New Madrid County-style.

Legend has it that those big trucks would take the voters not only to Canalou, but also to Morehouse, Matthews, Portageville, Catron, Parma, Risco, Gideon, Marston, and

Lilbourn voting precincts as part of the powerful J. V. Conran political machine.

A Lilbourn, Missouri, native son recalls his family's Bootheel political heritage.

"I was born in Lilbourn, and my aunt was one of the Democrat Committee workers," described Bootheel native Garry Lewis, now a successful (retired) lawyer and investment person in Baton Rouge, Louisiana "However, my father [Dub Lewis] described himself as one of only two Republicans in New Madrid County during my youth, and he jokingly said he couldn't locate the other Republican."

How potent was the Bootheel Democrat political machine in that era?

If you think the Veterans Administration hospital in Poplar Bluff is there by accident, you'd be wrong.

The late A. J. Neel, our farm road's recognized foremost authoritative political analyst when it came to Democrat politics, explained how the VA hospital came to be built at Butler County.

"It happened as political pay-back when Harry S. Truman was first running out of Kansas City for the U.S. Senate in 1936, before he became vice president, and then later, he became one of the best presidents in U.S. history," A. J. shared his political/history lesson.

"The deal was that if J.V. Conran would influence the Bootheel in favor of Truman, the newly-elected Senator from Missouri would one day deliver a VA hospital in southeast Missouri," A. J. noted. "Truman delivered on his promise with construction of the John J. Pershing VA Hospital in Poplar Bluff."

I was always proud that Momma Whittle and beloved neighbor A. J. Neel were chosen each year to work the election polling place at Canalou School. They were designated Democrat poll watchers. Among Canalou Republican poll workers were former Canalou Mayor L. L. Arbuckle and family friend L. A. Pete McCann.

"Although we poll workers were friends, on election day, the voting and recording of votes was very serious business,"

Momma Whittle explained. "Canalou was one of the few polling places in that era that had a number of Republicans, so we made certain each and every vote got counted."

"As youngsters in the Bootheel, we were certainly aware of the Democrat machine," noted native Canalou resident Alva Jones, who resides today in Freeburg, Illinois. "Grandfather L. L. Arbuckle, as our little town mayor, was a staunch Republican. On election days, close attention was paid to counting each and every vote in Canalou."

It must have been frustrating for GOP supporters in that era, for, as I recall from earliest childhood political recollections, no Republican ever got elected to office in New Madrid County.

And after I got old enough to leave the farm to work at the newspaper in Sikeston, no Republican ever got elected to office in New Madrid County because J. V. Conran's political machine was still potent leading into the 1960s.

Momma, from her death bed in 2003, explained our family's motivation about getting involved in politics.

"In the 1940s, it hadn't been long since the swamps were drained, and it was still pretty rough country to travel, so we needed help with our roads real bad," Momma noted. "Your daddy and A. J. Neel went to New Madrid, and were told by J. V. Conran if they'd help deliver a strong turnout for Democrat candidates, we'd get help with our roads that got impassable because of the deep heavy gumbo mud during rainy winter months.

"And we needed help in getting electricity out to our homes and farms. Besides, the twelve dollars we made for a day's work at the polling place was good spending money, for cash was still scarce in those lean post-Great Depression years," Mother added.

We were told firmly by Momma Whittle: "Never ever tell it that you youngens gave out election-day whiskey."

And we didn't, until now.

Lilbourn native John Buck, age sixty-eight in 2012, also remembers 1950s era politics in New Madrid County.

"My Dad was a farm boss for Barton Farms in Catron," recalls Buck, who formerly resided in Canalou after marrying Harry and Faye Chaney's daughter, Renda. "Dad didn't work in elections, but I remember that in Lilbourn, where they voted at City Hall, there would be people in cars, who would slip you a half-pint of whiskey.

"I had a cousin named Jack who liked whiskey, and Jack would tell us he got multiple bottles of liquor by voting multiple times. It was black and white folks who got whiskey for voting in that era, and I don't remember one Republican ever being elected."

"I remember seeing them haul voters from the huge farms where they had hundreds of black and white farm workers in the Catron area," Buck recalls. "And my wife tells me they did the same on election days in the Canalou area."

John and Renda Buck presently reside near Poplar Bluff.

In looking back, our parents took Bootheel-style politics very serious in the 1940s-50s.

Chapter Sixty-Two

The Blue Woods
By Ronnie Carl Launius

Author's Note: Morehouse, Missouri, brothers John and Ronnie Carl Launius provided huge encouragement and details for this book. The following is a "guest chapter" penned by Ronnie Carl, entitled "The Blue Woods." It captures the essence of the era's boyhood years in the Bootheel.

There are only a handful of men alive today who could possibly remember The Blue Woods. And those men are spread so far and wide, the likelihood of more than one or two of them ever reading this is very remote.

Back in Morehouse, Missouri, where we spent our youth, The Blue Woods were an important part of our daily thoughts and conversations. Many a summer day was spent in speculations over what could lie out there in The Blue Woods. What mysteries could be hidden within that hazy horizon? What adventures? What danger lurked there?

I lived on the last street on the southern edge of Morehouse. My back yard opened into a cotton field. Beyond the cotton field was Little River. And beyond Little River, there lay The Blue Woods.

My pals and I played in the cotton fields. We had our army

games there. We scouted and fought Indians there amongst the ridge rows. And, if an occasional cotton bole got picked and tossed like a hand grenade, well, it only lent realism to our fun.

We waded out into the water moccasin infested waters of Little River to gather cattails. You could soak the cattails in kerosene and make a dandy torch or a flaming arrow to shoot at the covered wagons just like the Indians in the movies at old Dillon Theater. Had our mothers known, they would have had heart attacks.

Pipe bombs on the Internet? Hog wash. You take a glass marble, a giant firecracker, and a piece of lead pipe. You crimp the pipe on one end so just the firecracker wick can get out. Light it and you've got yourself one heck of a little cannon. It will embed the marble in the side of a wood shed, or better yet, an outdoor privy.

When we teamed up for BB gun fights, we all put on sunglasses for eye protection. No one had to tell us, we just did it. Have you ever taken a BB shot in the forehead? Stings like the dickens.

On a warm summer day, we would venture down into the bayous and swamps of Little River. We worked for a week one time building a log cabin down in the swamps. It was a swell little cabin. It had a doorway and a window. It was *Our Place*. We fought rival hordes of cross-town kids over that cabin. And we held the day. Then we burned it to the ground to prevent anyone else from happening upon it and using it. It was OUR cabin!

But the call of The Blue Woods was strong.

You could just barely see them when you looked south across the fields, across Little River. Way off in the far distance, there laid The Blue Woods. We speculated that maybe they were as far south as Canalou. Perhaps Charter Oak? We knew they were a long way off. Too far to walk and no roads or paths to get there any other way. The Blue Woods would remain a mystery.

Sometime in the mid-1950s, progress came to Morehouse. They began building a new highway. It was to pass just to the south of Morehouse. Everyone in town speculated as to what effects this would have for the town.

We knew! My pals and I knew!! They were destroying The Blue Woods. Road graders and men with surveyor's tools were invading The Blue Woods.

My friends and I rode our bikes out to the construction area one day to take a look at the giant earth movers and see what was happening to The Blue Woods. But, where were they? Where were The Blue Woods? All we saw were wheat fields and cotton blooms. There were no "Blue Woods." There never had been. The Blue Woods were a mirage.

Yes, if you look off into the distance, off toward the horizon, you can see a purple haze. A diffusion of the air where it meets the heavens. Thus were our "Blue Woods," only in the imagination of a group of small Bootheel boys.

But, The Blue Woods will live forever. The unreachable place. The place of dreams. The place of wonders to behold.

Yes, I still remember The Blue Woods, and I bet if you tracked down any of those other pals of mine, they too would tell you about *The Blue Woods*.

Chapter Sixty-Three

River Drama

There's "The Big River" and then, there's "Little River". By "The Big River," we're talking about the mighty Mississippi, America's premier stream that's been eulogized, romanticized, and called many names, including Old Man River and Big Muddy.

And historically that legendary big river is known for running backwards during the New Madrid Earthquakes of 1811-12, which helped feed the swamp waters where Canalou, Missouri, was eventually spawned starting around 1902 as a sawmill town built initially up on stilts.

One mile west of Canalou and about twenty miles away from the "Big Muddy" was the "Little River," reportedly named by earliest French explorers.

Although puny in size compared to the Big Muddy, Little River had its treacherous moments, too, but provided multiple pleasurable moments to little farm boys.

Little River was an adventure source for farm children when we played pirate games on mystical moon-lit nights or when we went gigging or froggin' for bull frogs. However, Little River was a BIG source of food, especially critical for survival of earliest white settlers who floated into the swamp in the early 1900s to harvest the timber.

But like the Big Muddy, Little River could be dangerous during life-threatening floods, which frequently happened before Nigger Wool Swamp was dredged and drained by the Little River Drainage District headquartered today in Cape Girardeau, Missouri.

The late Uncle Harry Robinson, who trapped fur-bearing animals up and down Little River, once compared the stream to a woman: "She either loves you up with good vittles or treats you like a dog during dangerous flooding season."

Uncle Harry became a beloved part of Little River's legend and lore with his lifetime of trapping, and hunting, and story-telling.

Like myself, Canalou native Alva Jones grew up on the river.

"My family and I lived alongside Little River about two miles south of Canalou city limits," Alva traced his Bootheel roots. "My grandparents, Mr. and Mrs. L. L. Arbuckle, lived right on the river about one hundred yards from a wooden bridge where the stream made a sharp turn west again near Nelson Lumsden's big farm. The water at that time was fast-flowing and maybe fifteen to twenty feet wide as it passed under our nearby wooden bridge."

He recalls neighbors named Harwood, Streets, and Harris, in addition to numerous relatives named Greer and Newman.

The Whittles had neighbors along our stretch of the river, north of Canalou, named Bixler, Abernathy, Nickles, Lathem, Evans, Bishop, Scott, Bramlett, Land, Knuckles, Wilson, Wilkerson, Breedlove, Hood, Ling, Reed, Neel, Bridwell, Bryant, and Scott.

Present-day Freeburg, Illinois, resident Alva Jones said some of his fondest boyhood recollections go back to the flowing waters of Little River.

"The Little River was a place for great childhood memories," Alva recalls. "In the summer when not hoeing cotton or corn, I was always fishing with Grandmother Arbuckle behind her house, and still have a cherished snapshot of her fishing in the river, complete with her arms being covered in long sleeves and her face being protected from the sun by her big bonnet.

Grandmother Arbuckle didn't step out in the sun without that sun bonnet.

"We probably had the best fishing hole anywhere up and down the stream at that time," Alva added. "The Brannum Hole, about two miles further north, was the only other good fishing spot.

"One thing about the river in those days, it had many varieties and sizes of fish, including catfish, perch, goggle-eye, bass, carp, buffalo, and another that was such bad eatin' I won't even mention the name," Alva floated back in time. "Sometimes, some buddies and me gathered crawdads to sell to adult fishermen for a few coins that we'd take to Jim Poe's Grocery Store to buy some candy."

"But don't think fishing was a mere sport to families of that era," Alva instructed.

An ample meal of fish was called a mess in our neck of the woods there by the river.

"Fishing wasn't a sport," Alva accounted. "If we had a good morning of fishing, we had a good meal for supper, along with cornbread and green onions. Yummy, it was a meal fit for kings. At that time, we mostly ate pork, as did most rural folks in our region, so a good MESS of fresh fish was a real treat, and Grandmother Arbuckle could fix it so good."

To some early settlers in the former swamp, Little River was a primary source of drinking water.

"I remember Great Uncle Elmer Greer lived south of my grandparents in a log cabin, and the only water he had was what he took from the river" Alva recalled. "I didn't like to drink it, but I did on occasion. There was another remote cabin out there in the swamp by Uncle Elmer's cabin, reputed to have served as a hide-out for the Jesse James Gang back in the 1800s."

Watching grown-ups take fish out of the river was very dramatic Alva had mentioned. "I always enjoyed the time of year that men folks would get to hankering for a big mess of fish," Alva began. "They would put a net across the narrowest part of the river, and walk in chest-deep water. And when the big ones hit the net they would reach down and pluck the *biggest* fish out of the net, and throw them up on the bank for us youngsters to bag.

"Unlike fishing, froggin' might be considered a sport," Alva noted. "It was a popular thing to do along the river, although I couldn't bring myself to eat a frog if someone cooked it for me. But froggin' was an important part of growing up there in our beloved back-water country."

Snakes were nothing to take lightly.

"But you could always hear one of the grown-ups warn: 'Look out for the moccasins.' Truth be told, there were a lot of snakes along that river.

"One night, when one of our men folks took me and older brother Arley on our first frog hunt, we were eager to learn everything," Alva added. "That is while we were still moving slow in our little Jon boat and close to the bank, when our adult host took his big gig and ran it up my leg and yelled 'snake in the boat!'

"I jumped out of the boat, into the water, waded out, and went home!" Alva accounted. "I never forgave that man, and I never went froggin' again either."

"There was believed to be a legendary snake that hung around our nearby wooden bridge" Alva noted. "I had heard that a huge, biggo snake lived and slithered around the old bridge over Little River.

"Grandmother Arbuckle had seen it, and several others along the river did too," Alva shared. "Personally, I never saw the big snake.

"But one day when I was in first grade, I stayed late at Great Uncle Emmitt Greer's house in downtown Canalou. With no bus service in Canalou, I had to walk home. Upon arriving at the bridge at about dusk, with no large snake in sight, I bolted and ran as fast and hard as I could across the old bridge. I ran so fast I probably jarred the old bridge's beams that held it up."

It wasn't unusual for men of that era [1920s, 1930s, 1940s, 1950s] to trap mink, muskrats, and raccoons along Little River, before it became only a trickle of its former self.

"One thing I'd never seen before was that little porcupine I saw in second grade at school," Alva shared. "Someone had trapped it on the river and brought it to town for all the curious folks to eyeball. It was a strange-prickly-looking little animal, and how it ever got to our part of the country, no one knew, for porcupines were not natural in the habitat along Little River."

Current Canalou Mayor James Donald Taul talked about commerce along Little River. "In the 1930s and 1940s, prominent cotton gin man H. G. Cathy had a sawmill operation along the river at the Brannum Hole," Taul noted. "My family regularly forded the river in a wagon to haul back kindling wood to build fires at our house in downtown Canalou. That was before they built the bridge leading from Canalou out to cross over Little River."

My innocence was lost Little River. One day Momma Whittle ordered my older brother and me to go take a serious bath at the river.

"Wash under your arms and behind your ears," Mother instructed firmly.

So there I was, minding my business while lathering up with some of Momma's fresh, homemade soap stark naked, when this car full of giggling teenage girls pulled on the bridge and stopped. The girls looked up and down the river! It wasn't a problem, since I had hid out of their view behind a big willow tree. That is until my older brother, H. Van, with his warped sense of humor, shoved me in all my natural glory out from behind the bushes out into the middle of the stream.

As if I didn't appear stupid enough standing there stripped naked with no clothes, brother was emitting "ooohh, ooohh, ooohh" monkey sounds behind bushes beside the river unseen. I must have looked like a hairless baboon that had escaped from the little zoo to those touring girls. Upon seeing me, they gunned their car to disappear pronto in a cloud of dust on our unpaved farm lane.

Chapter Sixty-Four

Farm vs. Town

I was doing this radio talk show in Nashville back in the early 1980s when WNAH-Radio hostess Gladys Bane asked: "Were there any minorities in Canalou, Missouri, where you were reared?"

"Heck, we were the minority but didn't know it," I replied instantly.

But first, before we got on the air, I had to teach the lady radio personality how to properly pronounce C-a-n-a-l-o-u. Like most unlearned city-fied folks, she wanted to pronounce it starting with "Canna" as in "Canna-lou."

Natives always knew an "outsider was amongst us" if they pronounced "Canna" instead of the proper enunciation of "Canal"-ou.

Nashville radio personality had tried to do some home work, advising she couldn't find Canalou on her road map. . .

"Canalou is only on your better roadmaps," I quipped defensively.

But that interview got me to thinking back to childhood days in and around Canalou.

Until that media interview about my boyhood life back on

the farm, it had never actually dawned on me how uniquely historic our culture was. And how actual few of us there are who can claim tiny Canalou, Missouri, as an ancestral base of origin.

Putting it plainly, I didn't realize how unique the culture I grew up in was until I got away from the Bootheel. Sometime, you can't see the forest when amongst the trees.

At any one time in the community's brief and unique history, there were never more than 500 folks who actually resided in Canalou corporate limits, according to any official census after first white settler, Dan Kreps, came out of the East to open his original sawmill camp in 1902.

The village is now an economic ghost town.

"Canalou now has about three hundred and ten people, but no businesses," shared Canalou Mayor James Donald Taul. "I remember only one census when the town had more than four hundred and nine residents."

I remember sadly back in the 1990s, upon returning to Canalou for a school reunion, that the only commerce going on along the town's mile-long Main Street was a solitary pay telephone. It looked ghostly, for the town's last pay phone was hanging exposed to the elements without a booth on a bare utility pole.

The telephone company didn't think enough of it to provide a protective phone booth. Main Street really appears ghostly now, for that last pay phone has disappeared as the very last vestige of non-government commerce.

The last actual business, other than the government-operated U. S. Post Office that operated on Main Street, was Larry and Gladys Johns Drake's Grocery that closed in the early 1990s. It was located where Nath Hewitt had a thriving liquor store back in the 1940s.

Gone forever, except in our memories, are thriving businesses such as Moore's Store, Tootie Ralph's Grocery, Jim Poe's Mercantile/Grocery, Hammock's Hardware, Grover Drakes Garage, Granny Taul's Saloon/Pool Room, Ray and Opal Merriman's Saloon, Kasinger's Grocery, Percy Cotton Gin, Allen-Davis Cotton Gin, Bixler's Service Station, Summer's

Theater and Café, Maw Mathenia's Grocery, West Smith's Garage, Lampher Hotel, and the Bank of Canalou.

And by the time my generation came along in the late 1930s and early 1940s, Canalou's first cast of frontier settlers was either dead or getting old. Some of those settlers, such as Elisha Allen and Harry Robinson, were legendary swamp camp town characters, the type of which Hollywood couldn't conjure up.

Elisha, for example, came to Canalou on the run from the law and ended up as one of the swamp village's first law men.

Harry, on the other hand, floated into town in 1905 in a Jon boat and made his way through his legendary life mostly by hunting, trapping, and fishing. I can't recall him ever having what would be considered a regular job.

Few children actually lived within Canalou city limits during the 1940s, school records confirm.

"I was born in 1940," describes Canalou native Les Landers, now a resident of Aurora, Kentucky. "By the 1950s, there were less than twenty town boys my age to chum around with. So few that we could all gather in under the Canalou Church of Christ, for games. . . you know. . . games that boys like to play when girls come around.

"Counting the girls our age, there were only thirty to forty total town kids in the 1940s, out of a population between three hundred and four hundred people," accounted Landers, at age sixty-eight in 2010. "As I was growing up, many of the residents of Canalou were some of the earliest settlers in Canalou, who had grown old and had no where else to go. Some had literally floated into what became Canalou. Some old timers shared they walked long distances. . . just walked in and took up residence in the swamp town."

"The vast majority of children in Canalou School during the 1940s and 1950s were not from Canalou proper," verified Alice Jean Harrison VanNoy, one of three children born to farmers Norval and Marguerite Haywood Harrison. "Most of the children were from out-lying farms, either belonging to the farm owners or those families who worked on the farms."

Elizabeth Vandiver Scott Tidwell initially lived outside

Canalou city limits.

"My aunt Patsy Stoker reminded me that my father, Ocie Vandiver, and grandfather, Carl Stoker, rented farm land from Nesselrodt & Campbell [of Lilbourn] in the Charter Oak area, about five miles south of Canalou," Elizabeth shared in 2008. "Farmer Dude Wrather later rented it."

The acreage included a uniquely-named parcel: "Honey Island."

"I don't know why the land was called 'Honey Island,' but there was a cemetery there in the middle of our field," Elizabeth recalled. "Thus, it looked like an island."

Remember times were still tough, economically speaking, in this era immediately on the heels of the Great Depression.

"The cemetery had no headstones," she remembers. "The graves were marked with fruit jars and scraps of paper with names of deceased folks. The names had long since faded away when we lived there. Times were tough back then."

"We often found arrowheads and Indian marbles [made of clay] in the fields, especially after the land had been tilled," Elizabeth added. "Although we didn't have fancy clothes or nice new cars, we were happy. Tractors, if you were fortunate enough to have one, didn't have air-conditioned cabs in that era."

One could say that a form of racial integration came to the farm long before it happened in the rest of America.

"Migrant workers, both black and Mexican, came through and worked with us in the fields during fall harvests," Elizabeth noted. "We all worked in the fields in order to eat and to buy our school clothes and shoes. There were no racial problems in the fields while we worked."

There was something special about Canalou Saturday nights, especially for children.

"Saturday nights were special because we went into Canalou to buy our groceries and dry goods," Elizabeth accounted. "Menfolk often sat on benches in front of the seven small groceries that lined Canalou's Main Street. They'd discuss the latest news and gossip. Cars, trucks, and wagons could be viewed all along Main Street.

"Moore's Store today would be considered small, but to a farm child, it seemed like a big deal—a big place to shop. I remember merchant Biddy Moore always spoiled us by sneaking us candy out of eye-sight of his father, W. M. Moore. That was special, giving us candy and peanuts when we left the store."

Elizabeth's family, and the family of Alice Jean Harrison VanNoy, lived both in and out of Canalou corporate limits.

Alva "Alvie" Jones was also a hybrid farm kid and town lad.

"I remember sharecropper was a bad word, but that was what the vast majority of our ancestral farm families were in the early days of Canalou's farming existence," credited Alva Jones, age seventy-seven in 2010. "And there were not that many 'town' kids roaming the streets of Canalou when we lived there. We didn't realize it then, but Canalou's demise had started in the 1940s, early 1950s because the young folks were having to move away in order to have good-paying jobs."

"I grew up north of Canalou on the family farm," recalls Jerry Neel, at age seventy-five, the son of farmer A. J. Neel and his wife, Nell. "I remember it was a busy little town, especially on Saturdays and Saturday nights, when all the little stores [seven] and Nath Hewitt's Barber Shop would be filled with people."

Farm boy Neel was recruited straight out of Cape Girardeau's Southeast Missouri State College by the Ralston-Purina Co. in St. Louis, a firm he stayed with until retirement.

Dunklin County, Missouri, resident Jackie Marion Gunter Adkerson, a niece of A. J. Neel, recalls spending the summers at Canalou and the Neel farm.

"Canalou was a busy little town in that era, even had it's own theater, which was kind of unusual for a little town that size," recalled Jackie Marion who grew up south of Hornersville, Missouri's southern-most incorporated town in the very tip of southeast Missouri's Bootheel region. "As a little girl, I recall being amazed at the number of stores Canalou had."

Canalou native Les Landers, whose parents followed lumber-related jobs to Kentucky in 1952, laughed when sharing Canalou's "recreation" and "social" scenes of the 1940-1950 era.

"During the summertime, all those children you saw at school, you could see every one of them in town on a Saturday night," Landers accounted. "There were horses and mule-pulled wagons in my earliest days there. I recall there were hitching posts for the horses and mules still in the early 1950s in front of Moore's Mercantile and Grocery.

"I have concluded growing up in Canalou was totally different than if you lived on a farm," Landers added. "More children lived on the farm than lived in town. For example, my town buddies included just a few other boys, such as brothers James Donald, Jerry, and Larry D. Taul, Johnny Summers, Ronnie Hewitt, Harley Bixler, brothers Larry and Lonnie Lawson, Kenny Lasters, Harold Dean Mathenia, and Norman Ernest Harrison. Those were the other town boys.

"Female friends my age included Shirley Ann Bixler and her sister, Annette, Berta Jean McWaters, Jo Ann Summers, Linda Lawson, Betty Smith. . . these few kids out of a population of three hundred to four hundred people," Landers added

Only jobs available to town kids were farm jobs.

"Goodness, how I hated working in those cotton fields," Landers continued. "In the fall, there would be a truck come into town from some farm. A couple of aunts and a few cousins, my sisters and I would all get on that truck, and at daylight we would be standing in the middle of a cotton field, and those rows looked so long I doubted if I would ever get to the other end. I seldom got more than a hundred pounds in one day's picking, so since the farmer was paying three cents a pound, I made three dollars. Our lunches were wrapped in newspapers and were usually a baloney sandwich with a warm Pepsi to drink. We were really lucky if there was a tree close by where we could sit in the shade while we ate. This was all the work that was available for the young people."

His Aunt Helen Landers was a legendary cotton picker, able to snatch more than 300 pounds of cotton on her best days.

Canalou's Main Street was the hub of commerce and social

life.

"I remember older folks would sit in their cars and trucks on Main Street on Saturday nights, and families would go back and forth up and down the street socializing with one another," chronicled the late Floy Mae Arbuckle Jones, a graduate of Canalou High who went on to become a professional educator after getting her degree at the college in Cape Girardeau.

"And there were tractors pulling wagons parked everywhere, for very few of us had automobiles in the early 1940s," her son, Alva Jones, recalled. "In earlier times, mule-pulled wagons lined Main Street, especially during fall harvest times and on Saturday nights."

"Although there were never lined-off parking spaces, parking space was hard to find, especially on Saturday nights," Les Landers noted. "It was necessary to come to town on Saturday, for the people had worked all week and needed supplies. So coming to Canalou was a Saturday and Saturday night ritual."

All of the above agreed that the Canalou's economic death was sounded with the last ringing of the school bell in 1958. That old bell, which always had a big crack, now sits silent forever on the lawn of Canalou Baptist Church, located across from where the railroad tracks once ran through the heart of town. Now the tracks have disappeared.

An inscription on the bell shows it was presented to the church by family members in the names of Don and Vera Kochel, bedrock members of Canalou Baptist Church throughout the 1940s and 1950s.

The Kochels were important to the entire community as longtime U. S. Postal Service workers at the Canalou Post Office.

The post office had to be moved to the former Canalou Elementary School building in 2008 due to stench of death of the latest owner of the former theater building. The body went unnoticed for a number of weeks before anyone found the owner, who resided alone in the old theater's second floor apartment where last theater owners, John and Jean Summers, resided in the 1950s.

The theater building, constructed in 1944 by former Canalou businessman Boots Conn, was destroyed by a fire of mysterious origin in early 2009. Fallen bricks from that landmark two-story building still remained scattered on the town's ghostly-appearing Main Street as of 2010.

Chapter Sixty-FIVE

Watermelon Country

Flash back!

My head swirled in July of 2009 when Aunt Doris Whittle directed me to pull off the road to get some fresh-harvested Bootheel-grown watermelons at a produce stand located on old Highway 60 between Fisk and Poplar Bluff in Butler County, Missouri.

As we were moseying through the stand's wide selection of various-sized melons, I commented to Aunt Doris: "Seems I've been here before. Either that or I've dreamt of being here before."

With that declaration, Aunt Doris, who remains a sharp, lovely, and dignified farm lady in her eighties, smiled and recalled: "I brought you to this vegetable stand when you were a little boy back in the 1940s."

Upon hearing our conversation, present-day produce proprietor Mike Crafford joined in the conversation: "That's very possible, for our family has operated this produce market here in this spot now continuously since 1935. And, yes, we still grow most of our own produce. I can understand your flash back for we haven't changed the roof line and original posts of our stand during that past seventy years. I'm the third generation, and my daughter will be the fourth generation."

Thus, I understood my flash back.

After thumping a few melons, someone asked how I could tell if a melon is ripe by that method.

Since my sister June was with me and Aunt Doris, I replied: "If the 'thumped' melon sounds like the 'thump' when I 'thump' my sister's noggin, I know it's good and ripe."

Sister June didn't seem to appreciate my formula for watermelon-thumping.

After paying a mere $5 for a particularly huge melon, I asked "Watermelon Man" Mike where they were grown.

"Right here in the Bootheel, down around Hornersville and Kennett in Dunklin County," Watermelon Man directed. "That light loam dirt down in the lowest Bootheel region grows some of the best melons to be found."

"I can tell you know your melons," he added, "by the way you walked past the ones more high-priced that have the popular, trendy names. There are no finer melons than the ones grown in that dirt around Hornersville and across the state line at nearby Manila, Paragould, and Leachville, Arkansas."

That triggered another personal "flash back!" down boyhood Memory Lane from having grown up in the Bootheel.

At age thirteen, I was privileged to spend the summer visiting former Canalou farm neighbors; (the late) A. J. Neel, his wife, Nell and his mother Myrtle Delemma "Mommie" Gowen; after they'd opened their little state line grocery that straddled the Missouri and Arkansas line about five miles south of Hornersville.

After growing restless from fishing in nearby Little River that summer, I quickly made friends with Jim Rawls, the son of well-known, successful farmer, the late Jeff Rawls, who grew hundreds of acres of some of the biggest watermelons of which I'd ever laid eyes upon.

And this was in the 1950s before extensive fertilizing enhancements and breeding of melon varieties.

Since my family back in New Madrid County didn't grow

melons in our heavy gumbo dirt, it was tasty high adventure to be asked by Jim Rawls to walk out in his father's field, and select the biggest and prettiest melon we could find, crack it open, eat "the heart" out of it, and not get in trouble!

How tasty were they? So tasty, I recall Whittle lips flapping at the mere thought of getting to the melon patch.

My overall galluses nearly burst with pride the day Jeff Rawls and his two grown sons, Bud and Joe, came to the store and asked A. J. Neel if it would be okay to ask me to help in the melon harvest.

With A. J.'s approval, I accepted the job and was really excited, especially when I learned I'd be making fifty-cents an hour if I was strong enough to help load the heavy melons.

Although I weighed only ninety-eight pounds, I was strong for my size, especially in my shoulders and arms from previous farm work. I was excited at the prospect of working alongside grown "professional melon men."

Since some of those melons weighed in excess of sixty pounds, I was assigned as "a catcher" up in the trailer. I would catch those melons tossed up by the more mature and stronger male melon farm workers.

Although it was a strenuous job catching those big melons, I thrived at the challenge, and it beat the heck out of the back-breaking never-ending dull drudgery of chopping and picking cotton back in Canalou.

It felt like I was being paid for having fun.

I remember it pleased me to no end when farmer Rawls and his sons complimented me at the end of the harvest for being a good, steady watermelon worker.

Another highlight of that summer was making friends with a river boy named Pee Wee, who later went on to become a highway patrolman. I also got to spend time with special childhood friend Jackie Marion Gunter, a niece to A. J. Neel and beautiful daughter to Jack and Monte Gunter. The late A. J. Neel and Jack Gunter remain etched forever in my soul as two of the top five most compassionate men I've known in my walk through life.

Jackie Marion and her current husband run a successful trucking company out of Kennett.

Those few weeks of loading melons passed quickly, and as it turned out, this was THE SUMMER I made huge strides from childhood toward maturity.

Author's Note: You don't have to take my word about how good those Bootheel watermelons taste. Upon sharing one in July 2008 back in Nashville with country music stars Marty Stuart and his wife Connie Smith and Marty's parents, John and Hilda Stuart, I was instructed: "Don't come back from Missouri without another load of Bootheel-grown melons."

Song bird Connie Smith went so far as to send a personally-autographed picture to "Watermelon Man" Crafford in appreciation for his tasty melons harvested and transported out of Hornersville.

Chapter Sixty-Six

Tractor Accidents

Most farmers in our region took great pride, first in their mules, but then later in their farm tractors.

For one thing, money was hard to come by to purchase tractors in the 1930s and 1940s when most farmers were beginning to replace their lop-eared stubborn Missouri Mules with mechanized tractors.

Although mules could hurt you, especially with their flying hooves when angered, farm tractors were equally dangerous.

I know because our family lost two young cousins in farm tractor accidents.

Other farm families were hit just as hard.

Canalou, as a community, was emotionally rocked in the early 1960s when well-liked John Mitchell, a farm boy one school grade ahead of me, got killed while working with his father on their farm between Canalou and Charter Oak.

The hand-clutch on the old two-piston-era John Deeres was dangerous, for if you left the tractor's power-drive on, even while the tractor was not in motion, a touch or minor bump of that clutch would power whatever farm equipment was attached to the tractor at the time.

Our understanding was that John's death came as he was working under a bush-hog (pasture/weed cutting attachment ordinarily pulled behind the tractor) to clear debris out, when a relative bumped the hand-clutch up on the tractor. That caused the large cutting blade under the bush-hog to swirl, therefore, tragically ending John's life while still in his early twenties.

John was married to another friend of youth, Aimee Hammock. The Hammocks and Mitchells were two of the most respected families in our farming community.

It was in 1952 when little JoAnn Scott, a classmate of mine in second grade, perished when falling off a tractor driven by her father, Lawson Scott.

"JoAnn took her father some water, and asked for a ride," a relative to the young girl described. "Initially, Mr. Scott didn't want her to ride, but she pleaded, 'Daddy, I brought you some water, now you give me a ride on the tractor.'

"JoAnn was riding on the fender, and the plow struck a root, and came to a sudden stop, and she fell in front of the tractor, and it broke loose," JoAnn's cousin Martin Scott confirmed. "The tractor ran over her head. Her father picked her up and ran all the way to the hard [paved] road near the Blankenship's farm house a quarter-mile away."

One thing I admired about the Canalou culture of my youth when one family hurt, we all suffered because that's the way farm neighbors did things back in the small farm era.

A tractor tragedy had hit the Whittle family hard in 1947, when a cousin, Benny Pritchard, was driving a tractor on Uncle Harlan Whittle's farm over in the Trailback community, located in Stoddard County just across the big Floodway Channel from Canalou.

This farm, by way the crows fly, was only two miles from our farm over in New Madrid County on the east side of Floodway, which had no bridge crossing since a flood washed it away back in 1944. However, it was almost fifteen miles away from our farm house when you had to drive between Canalou and Trailback on the dirt roads that oftentimes were impassable because of rain and mud.

Uncle Harlan and Aunt Doris went on to have very successful lives as farmers over in the Rombauer community near Poplar Bluff, where they still resided in 2008.

Another cousin on Momma Whittle's Stockton side of the family perished in the early 1950s when Uncle Corbett Stockton still had his farm down between Dale and Burdette, Arkansas, not far from the big Blytheville Air Force Base.

Cousin Leroy Stockton was a little boy when he died on the back of big earth-moving machine.

He had climbed on back of the machine, unbeknownst to Uncle Corbett, who was driving the tractor pulling the big machine to help put his land to grade to better drain excessive rain water from his fields.

It appeared that little Leroy had jumped on the back of the earth-mover for a ride, and when Uncle Corbett triggered the lever to release the dirt contained in the big machine, that tripped a big iron bar on back of the machine. It was our understanding Leroy died instantly when that big bar hit him squarely on his chest. Uncle Corbett didn't know the boy was riding on the back of the machine.

It wasn't but a few years after that that we lost Uncle Corbett, who died at an early age, we felt because he had lost his youngest son. He and his family had moved to the Lavalle community between Parma and Charter Oak when we lost Uncle Corbett, the only brother to Momma Whittle and my Aunt Durette Reed from Burdette.

Momma Whittle also nearly died on a tractor, not from an accident, but from heat-stroke.

It was 1954, a wet year, and the temperature was hovering up around 100 degrees as Mother was cultivating soybeans that were nearly overrun with weed and vines due to the rains. Her stroke happened as she kept getting on and off the tractor to clear the plow points of clinging vines.

It was terribly hot muggy day.

I remember being terrified when Momma came stumbling on the back porch, her face all blotched with white, blue and red spots. Fortunately, older sister June was there and knew to get cool cloths on Momma's forehead and placed her feet in a pail of cool fresh hand-pumped water.

As a young farm boy, I had a near tragedy and then, a real tragedy as a result of tractor accidents.

My first near-tragedy happened in the mid-1950s when I was disking in the new ground that Daddy Whittle had cleared of timber and stumps back in the late 1930s.

I remember being sleepy that hot afternoon shortly after the noon meal, called dinner in that era, as I drove our new 60-model John Deere, which was a lot more powerful than our older A model John Deere that you cranked with a huge spinning wheel on the side of the tractor.

And I made a near-fatal mistake, after being repeatedly warned by Momma Whittle and older brother, H. Van, to never drive the tractor with my arm and elbow resting between the spokes of the tractor's steering wheel.

I was disking among some tall careless weeds, head-high to a grown man, there by Little River, when the tricycle-style front wheels of the tractor hit a stump I failed to see in the weeds.

When that happened, the steering wheel spun, and because my right arm was carelessly resting inside the spokes of the steering wheel, the force of the spinning steering wheel threw me over on the big left tractor tire.

What saved me from major injury, or possible death, was the fact the stump's impact caused the tractor to stall, and the engine to quit on its own. Otherwise, I could have been thrown behind the tractor and run over by the big disk I was pulling behind the tractor.

I was fortunate that day and still shudder when remembering my life could have been snuffed out so early.

It was in the spring of 1957 that my life changed dramatically, for the worst physically, in another tractor accident.

I had been fishing when neighbor farm boy Vernon Shorter offered me a ride home on the back of his tractor. Being that it was more than a two-mile walk from this fishing hole on Little River to our farm house, I took Vernon up on his offer.

We were about a mile west of Canalou on the newly-rocked road between town and Little River, when Vernon, for some reason, suddenly jerked the steering wheel of the tractor.

I was not without fault, for I was holding two fishing poles in one hand, as I was standing on the tractor's back drawbar, when the sudden jerk of that steering wheel threw me off balance.

Upon seeing that I was headed in the direction of the tractors big back right tire as that big Super M model Farmall, which would do about thirty miles per hour in road gear when moving at full speed

I recall thinking I would be better off if I pushed back away from that big wheel, which could have thrown me high in the air and possibly in front of the tractor. When I used my legs to push myself backward off the tractor, I came down on my tailbone there on that rock-hard gravel road.

And as I lay there, stunned in the middle of the road, I knew my life had changed, for at the moment my two legs instantly went numb. Subsequent X-rays at St. Francis Hospital in downtown Cape Girardeau, the nearest big city to tiny Canalou, showed I had crushed the sacrum between my hips and spine.

Therefore, since age fifteen, I have walked with a limp and I've had a lifetime of pain. But I've had a very blessed fulfilled life. I had both hips replaced surgically in the 1990s decade. Due to modern medical miracles, I'm still walking.

If there is a moral to this, it's to follow all safety rules when operating or merely being around big powerful farm machinery.

Chapter Sixty-Seven

Handshake Stockton

Nicknames seem to run in our farm family.

For example, my brother Hubert was nicknamed "Bibber." But his earliest nickname of life was "King Fish," given to him by farm neighbor John Ling.

Sister June Whittle Cox had a childhood nickname of "Snow Princess." It was I, the little brother, who crowned her with the royalty-sounding nickname.

We'd been told Grandfather Harve Stockton had died of a stroke.

Cousin Robert Terry Reed, a son of mother's sister Durette Stockton Reed, confirmed he, too, had always been told Grandfather Stockton had died of natural causes, but he'd heard whispers as a little boy that someone may have ambushed Grandfather Stockton. So you can imagine my shock in December 2003, moments before Mother passed, when she shared: "Your granddad was actually murdered out in the stall of our barn. The murder was never solved."

Grandpa Stockton was killed while pitching hay.

I never got another chance to get my mother to elaborate

about how Grandpa Stockton died. He's buried at the Burdette [Arkansas] Cemetery not far from Blytheville.

Mother's shocking disclosure came during an interview I was doing about various names and nicknames people in our family have gone by.

"Your grandfather had a nickname," Momma shared. "He was known as Harve 'Handshake' Stockton, because of his good reputation in business. If my father ever shuck hands on a deal, our neighbors knew they could take the deal to their bank"

I'm sad to have never met Grandfather "Handshake" Stockton.

Mother's names, however, are the most interesting.

"I had multiple nicknames," Mother shared from her sickbed. "The first nickname I know of was 'Jane'."

In the mid-1970s, Mother needed a birth certificate from her birth state of Mississippi. This seemed like a simple request.

"No big problem, I thought," Momma Whittle recalled in restructuring her trail of multiple names. "Come to find out, I not only had multiple nicknames but multiple real names given to me that I never knew about," she shared with obvious agitation. "When I wrote to officials in Mississippi asking about my birth date down around Calhoun City, Mississippi, they wrote back they had no records of anyone named Ruby Lee Stockton being born on my birth date."

"However, they did share they had a birth record of an infant female named 'Zada' Stockton at that time and date at Calhoun City," Mother shared. "That was where I was born, and the date jived at my birth date."

For years after that, Mother saw red when reminded of the fact that she wasn't named what her parents had told her she was named.

"After checking with my own mother, I found out the family didn't give me my name [Ruby Lee] for my first two years of life," Momma shared emotionally. "I guess they called me like they'd call a puppy or a trained pig: 'Hey you come over here.' Can you imagine having a child, and not naming her?"

"I had a pet pig named 'Tommy' that I thought enough of to give a name as soon as Daddy told me the pig was mine," Momma recalled. "I didn't let that pig run around without a name."

This brought Mother to another source of concern. Not only did she have multiple names down through life, she had multiple nicknames too.

"For the first two years, the name they called me most often was Jane," Mother noted. "And that wasn't thought up by my parents, who were slow to ever name me. It was an aunt, who

Stockton Family Wagon

was crazy about me as a little girl, who tried to get them to name me Jane. So they did off and on, if it came in handy." So, how did she end up being called "Ruby Lee?"

"How the hell do I know where 'Ruby Lee' came from?" Mother would respond with obvious anger. "I asked my own mother, and you know what, she didn't even know where they came up with the name Ruby Lee. Which as I found out, wasn't my real name anyway. And for sure she didn't have a clue who put 'Zada' on my official birth certificate."

Mother went through more than five decades of life before she found out "Ruby Lee" was officially an alias.

"There is no record of a Ruby Lee Stockton ever being born any where in Mississippi, so I was in my fifties when I finally learned my real name is Zada, as listed on official State of Mississippi records," Momma decreed. "To this day, I don't know who put 'Zada' on the birth certificate.

"I guess every name I ever had was a nickname," Momma noted. "Jane, which according to my older sister, Durette, was quickly adapted to 'Liza Jane.' And as I got older my sister told me someone adapted that into 'Little Liza Jane.' I guess I'd answer to anything as a little girl."

So when Momma Whittle prepared to die back in 2003, I asked her what she wanted on her tombstone: "Heck, just put any ol' name over my grave. I'll answer to any of them."

Her tombstone in hometown Smyrna, Tennessee, reads: "Ruby Lee Whittle, Farm Lady, Great Mother."

Harve Stockton and Wife
Beatrice Rhodes

Chapter Sixty-Eight
REA

Before the Rural Electric Administration turned on the power down our farm road, there were only kerosene lamps. Prior to kerosene lamps, Momma would try to read to us from even dimmer burning candles.

Those expensive kerosene lamps and fragile globes were off limits to children.

"You've got to use warm soapy water," Momma instructed as she gently removed the suet and smoke build-up on the globes from our two cherished kerosene lamps. "And handle them gently, for they're very fragile and very expensive."

Lamps, due to fuel and flame, were off limits to little children.

I remember Momma went ecstatic the day Daddy Whittle brought home a super-duper, highly-advanced Aladdin kerosene Lamp with its sophisticated, but delicate, wick that glowed so much brighter than the old kerosene lamps that required wide cloth wicks.

The brightest glowing lamp was used by Mother to read her Bible at night. Although electricity had been in nearby Canalou for a number of years, neighboring farms on Tram Road were left in the dark until the 1950s.

"We didn't have electricity until 1949," verified Canalou-area farm girl Patsy Hopper Bixler, who's living her retirement years in Cape Girardeau. "That's when REA finally got lines to our farm."

"We had electricity down in Dunklin County and in the Stateline community that straddled the Missouri and Arkansas line all my life," noted sixty-five-year-old Jackie Marion Gunter Adkerson, who now resides in Kennett. "I remember visiting Uncle A. J. Neel's farm at Canalou in the 1950s, and there was no electricity and no indoor toilet. I thought that odd."

"I was in the seventh grade at Canalou School before we got electricity," confirms Bonnie Blankenship Boutz, now a resident of Jefferson City, Missouri. "It was a big day when we finally got electricity. But I was out of high school by the time we finally got indoor plumbing, ending the era of the outdoor toilets in our family."

It was about 1948 that Daddy Whittle and farm neighbor A. J. Neel got their heads together and came up with the idea to make the long, twenty-five mile trip all the way across the county to visit Bootheel political kingpin J. V. Conran in New Madrid regarding electricity.

That was also about the time that Daddy and Momma began cultivating what turned out to be lifelong friendships with Herbert Bailey and Fay Thomason, two executives with the Southeast Missouri Regional REA office in Sikeston.

As a boy, I didn't put it together that friendships were born out of politicking, based on the desire for us to get electricity up and down our farm lane.

Electric lights were important in more ways than one, for in our eyes, electric lights would make us equal to those city-fied folks up in Canalou, Sikeston, and Morehouse.

It required politicking country style.

Never shall I forget the first big outside breakfast feast Momma and Daddy prepared over the open fire to cook fried chicken, hot pork sausage, thickening gravy, fried potatoes, and homemade biscuits especially for those two REA families from the big city of Sikeston, located about twelve miles away from our rural home place.

I took an immediate liking to the strangers from the city of Sikeston, and they seemed to like me and the rest of the Whittles and Neels.

The Bailey's son, Larry Bailey, immediately became like a big brother to Little Danny Whittle, and everywhere that Larry would go, I'd go too. Although he was the same age as my older brother, Van, he didn't mind a little kid tagging along on their adventures. I frequently spent weeks at a time visiting Larry and his family up in Sikeston.

Plus, I had never met any male adult like Fay Thomason. His wife, Pistol, was, from first glance, one beautiful, cultured-certified sophisticated city-fied lady.

Fay, with his ethnic German background, taught Momma that first breakfast feast to start putting onions in her fried potatoes, a recipe that I still love to this day.

As part of our parents' friendship, Fay Thomason also gave Daddy a highly-prized German-made, Sauer three-barreled gun, with two .12-guage shotgun barrels, with an accompanying 30.6 rifle barrel beneath the two shotgun barrels. Today, such a gun, I'm advised by collectors, would be worth thousands of dollars. The gun was ideal for bird hunting and deer hunting. It was a beautiful piece of German craftsmanship, complete with hand-engraved silver etchings of birds and deer.

So you can tell that the friendships initially born with a desire to get electricity up and down our farm road, advanced well beyond the politicking stage. It wasn't long before each family's children would take turns spending the nights, even weeks and vacations, with the other families.

In fact, on the night of Daddy's fatal car wreck in 1950, it was at the Bailey's house on Murray Lane up in Sikeston where Mother left us while she went to the Missouri Delta Community Hospital to check on Daddy.

After we learned of Daddy's death early the next morning, I went to a big Sikeston city school with Larry, an intense adventure for a pre-school farm boy.

Daddy had lived long enough to see the light poles go up on our farm lane before his death. He just didn't live long enough to see the electric lights turned on in the spring of 1951.

The day was so important that farm neighbors journeyed up and down the road to see each farm family's light bulbs glow. And this was in broad daylight! Getting kerosene lamps had been big, but nothing compared to getting electric lights.

At our neighbor Harold David Bryant's house, we just sat and stared, as if hypnotized, at that glowing light bulb dangling from the ceiling in the center of the room.

It was like magic when Harold David and I would pull that string, and, mystically, the light bulb would start glowing.

So big, we all gathered at A. J. Neel's house and got on our knees, kneeling in prayer, giving heavenly "thanks to God, President Truman, J. V. Conran, the Baileys, the Thomasons and THE REA!"

We were all so excited, most families left their light bulbs on continuously, night and day, for the first few days.

Electricity revolutionized our lives on the farm, from ice boxes to refrigerators, heavy old-fashioned irons that had to be heated on the coal stove before our mothers could iron our clothes to go to school and church. The list of improvements is endless.

Momma also had a white gas fueled iron, that was so cantankerous to use she simply tossed it in the trash heap when she got an electric iron.

Electricity also brought electric fans, a huge step toward battling the intense heat of the summer and fall.

That was good living.

Chapter Sixty-Nine

Momma's Sharp Tongue

Daddy Whittle had a temper, which he often lost after Momma would verbally slice and dice him.

Married when Mother claimed to be fourteen, she and Daddy were like two hard-headed, ill-matched Missouri mules, one wanting to go one way and the other headed in another direction. How they got together to have three children remains mystical.

After the Whittle children grew up, they came up with a tally that Momma Whittle was really only thirteen when they jumped over the broom stick down on a big plantation they share-cropped at Burdette, Arkansas, where a legendary cotton picker named Charley Garner routinely sacked 400 pounds of cotton per day.

For young, unlearned city-fied folks of today, that meant they "tied the knot" as in "gettin' hitched" share-cropper farmer-style.

For their honeymoon, they journeyed to Hayti, Missouri, to visit a café known for its hamburgers. . . the first time Momma had a store-bought sandwich.

"That was the first and finest hamburger I ever tasted," Mother shared with us children.

But oil and water, they don't mix.

So it was with Momma and Daddy Whittle, who fought like cats and dogs, especially when Momma would get on his case real hard. It seemed Momma made her most vicious verbal assaults on Daddy when he was especially tired and she was at her "row's end" from toiling long days and nights in the fields.

A lot of their fist fights started at the end of long hard work days. When the shouting started, that's when I headed for the barn to hide up in the hay loft, muffling my ears so I wouldn't hear the screaming and hollering back at our farm house.

"Whew, your Momma can sure slur your Poppa to a slouch," observed a hired field worker one day as our parents were cursing one another.

Since money was scarce in the post-Depression era of the early 1940s, I never understood how our parents could justify throwing and breaking dishes they'd worked so hard and long to acquire.

If Daddy hurled a saucer, Momma would toss a cup. If Daddy threw the milk bucket, Momma would toss the water bucket and dipper—each one trying to top the other.

Daddy wasn't your typical overall-wearing farmer with tobacco juice running down his chin. He was a "dude" who liked nice expensive-looking suits, ties, and dress shoes, especially when he'd go to town to do some serious gambling and whiskey consumption.

One of my childhood remembrances was accompanying Daddy to Sikeston to Norton's Shoe Store across from the Bank of Sikeston and White's Drug Store, where Daddy let me drink my first-ever, store-bought Cherry Coke as he bought a new pair of Buster Brown dress shoes across the street.

Momma, however, out-did herself the next day Daddy was working back in the new ground across Little River at the back of our farm.

I don't know what triggered her, but one couldn't help but note her anger as she took an axe to Daddy's new pair of Buster Brown shoes, chopping them into little bitty pieces before depositing the remnants over into the hogs' wallowing hole.

In my youngest years, I never knew Daddy to drink. But as their constant nagging and badgering grew, Daddy began disappearing for days and days in non-crop tending season. Oftentimes, I learned later, he was going all the way to Cairo, Illinois where he liked to drink whiskey and gamble at Club 18 or on riverboat casinos that paddle-wheeled up and down the Mississippi River.

I learned a little of this history about my father as recent as 1997 when wife Pat and I were motoring to Poplar Bluff from our home in Tennessee to transport my ailing Mother back with us.

Take note that what happened along the river on this date in river port town Wickliffe, Kentucky was 47 long years after my father had perished in a 1950 car crash.

As Pat and I pulled our car down by the Mighty Mississippi at Wickliffe—to let our dog, Precious, do its business, I noted three elderly gents whittling away and sitting under a cotton wood shade tree about ten feet from the water's edge.

"Gentlemen, my name is Whittle, and I can't whittle a lick," I proclaimed as I eased over in their direction.

I often use my somewhat unusual last name to break the ice with strangers.

With that, one of the aged gents, after spewing out a wad of tobacco-laden spittle in the direction of an old hound dog there on the river bank, made the following proclamation: "I knew a Whittle once. . . a farmer over in the Bootheel of Missouri, across the river. Can't recall his first name though."

"Could it have been Hubert, Hubert Whittle who farmed over at Canalou in New Madrid County?" I asked, by now totally enthralled by what this whittlin' man may know about my father.

"Yes, sir. Yes, siree, that's his name, Hubert Whittle, a good gambling man," the whittling man continued taking his memory back across the decades as smoothly as he slid his razor-sharp knife over his cedar stick.

"My mind's kind of fuzzy now since a lot of water has gone down this ol' river since 1950 when I last saw him down at the Bloody Bucket, which still is in operation not far out of Wickliffe," said the man who knew my Daddy in a different context than I knew him as a little boy and son.

"He was very good at poker and would win money just about every session, as long as he didn't drink too much," the gentleman beside the river floated back through time. "But sometimes he'd drink too much and lose. But Hubert Whittle, yes, he was a good gambling man."

One night I recall my sister, brother, and I hiding out behind the chicken house when Mother locked the house, refusing to let Daddy come inside. It was about midnight when Daddy rammed his foot through the front door to enter his own home. The ensuing fight lasted several hours before our parents quit fighting, probably out of sheer exhaustion.

But don't get the idea Daddy was irresponsible when it came to farming and taking care of business. He was a stickler for paying his bills in full and on time. That was the good part of his reputation. Plus, he was recognized as a good farmer.

Momma, on the other hand, could be a tough task master who was prone to fuss at Daddy, especially behind his back to blood-kin on her side of the family. But like Daddy, she was totally honest in her business dealings.

When word of some of that back-biting got back to Daddy, we children knew there was going to be hell to pay.

Never shall I forget the night that Daddy, after thrashing soybeans from dawn to when the dew fell that evening, got off the tractor to drive our big farm truck the ninety-mile distance between our home in the Bootheel and Burdette, Arkansas, where Mother's mother, Beatrice *"Granny Grunt"* Stockton Orr Rhodes and her new preaching husband lived on Uncle Corbett Stockton's place.

I remember the next morning, after he had travelled all night to help his mother-in-law move; he climbed right back up on the tractor to resume the field work without sleep.

Although I was only four years old at the time, I clearly remember the stinging words coming from Mother and Granny Grunt as they talked about my father in the shack-out-back later that very day.

They spoke words as if Daddy was sorrier than a low-down, egg-sucking, non-hunting-bitch-in-heat dog.

I never really liked my grandmother much after that. They were trashing a man, my Daddy, who had worked around the clock during crucial crop harvest time to help move them to Missouri. Although a small boy, I was old enough to understand they were trash-talking Daddy after he'd tried to help them move from Arkansas to Missouri.

Momma Whittle had her good points in that she kept a clean house, kept her youngin's clean and in church, and believed in paying our debts on time. And she, like Daddy, never seemed to tire when it was crop work time, or time to kill and butcher the hogs for us to eat on through the winter.

Both parents insisted on good manners with "yes, sir" and "no, sir" being automatic responses to adults from us children. Being taught "yes sir" and "no sir" eventually helped get my first newspaper job away from the farm.

When Momma would take that sharp tongue and slur my Daddy to a slouch, well, you could count on there being a hellacious fight on the Whittle farm that night.

Those were the nights we knew to go hang out with the pigs and cows out at the barn.

Chapter Seventy
Musial Homers

My earliest St. Louis Cardinal Baseball memory?

The day the Cardinals traded fabled outfielder Enos Slaughter.

That was the day the Whittle family decreed, took a blood oath, to never, ever listen to another Cardinal game on radio.

And we didn't—that is until spring training began down in some mystical land called Florida.

How much were the Cardinals etched into the fabric of life down in the delta, cotton-growing country known as the Bootheel area of southeast Missouri?

So much so that it was discussion of latest exploits of legendary players such as Stan Musial, "Vinegar" Ben Mizzell, Jabbo Jablonski, and Rip Ripulski that helped us cope with the hot, dull doldrums and torture of picking cotton in the fall and chopping cotton in the spring.

Actually, Jablonski and Ripulski didn't make baseball's Hall of Fame, but I've always thought Jabbo Jablonski and Rip Repulski were awesome baseball-sounding names.

My older brother, H. Van Whittle, could list every player on every National League team and the batting averages, fielding percentages, and earned run averages of every Cardinal who played in the 1940s and 1950s.

How did we keep up with the Cardinals out in the middle of remote cotton patches?

First, we had our trusty Delco radios, although static-filled, that we could tune in to Sikeston, Missouri's KSIM Radio where announcer Dick Watkins would proclaim each Cardinal team as possibly the greatest in history.

We believed it because we wanted to.

Having started picking cotton at sun rise each fall morning, older brother and I would race from the cotton patch for lunch to see who could snatch the *St. Louis Globe-Democrat* sports page first to read the latest chronicles of scribe Jack Herman.

If sports writer Herman proclaimed it, it was Cardinal fact-forever etched into the countless baseball statistic conversations we'd have in the hot dusty cotton fields.

Those spirited conversations, which often evolved into arguments, helped pass the time that seemed to stand still when the temperature would top the 100-degree mark in the shade.

Farm neighbor A. J. Neel was also good at quoting baseball statistics, and it was he who took me to see my first Cardinal game in St. Louis.

Announcer Harry Carey eventually evolved into our most quoted source of Cardinal information when he took over as the chief Cardinal game announcer in the early 1950s.

It was ol' Harry and his creative versions of Cardinal games that took me on one of my first steps of maturity.

For when television came along, I found out, to mixed emotions, that Harry would often lie about a "screaming line drive" that, in reality, was no more than a bloop hit over second base.

But, Harry's creative Cardinal broadcasts became colorful Cardinal lore for us farm children in the Bootheel.

I've often said that radio was better than television for baseball, from a pure fan's perspective.

Radio permitted one's imagination to soar with the Cardinals each spring training, for example.

How come radio was good for baseball legend and lore?

It was listening to the games on KSIM that I conjured up my boyhood's first mind's eye picture of how the old Sportsman's Park stadium in St. Louis must have looked.

Since I only had knowledge of Canalou's tiny baseball diamond that had several large oak trees for shade over the two or three bleachers, in my boyish youth I pictured the stadium in St. Louis with having lots of trees, probably, bigger Major League-sized trees.

See, that's how radio caused you to conjure up your own images, which I think is good not only from a sports perspective but good for a little boy's mental development. It allowed this farm boy to stretch his baseball visions to their fullest glorious dimensions.

How much was Cardinal baseball lore etched into our farm region's life?

My sister Mary June had started dating this guy from Malden, Missouri, who had been all the way to England because he was in the Air Force.

Typically, the family, along with country preacher man A. C. Sullivant, would gather out under the shade of our farm's front yard patch of hickory trees after a Sunday dinner of Momma Whittle's famous fried chicken and neighbor Marguerite Harrison's larruping-good thickening gravy.

It was during one of those lazy, folksy Sunday afternoon sitting under the tree sessions that sister's latest beau, after bragging that he had traveled to England, asked my sister: "Have you ever been out of the country?"

To which sister June confidently replied: "Sure have. We went to two St. Louis Cardinal baseball games last summer."

That settled the issue.

Momma Whittle made one historic trip to a Cardinal game. It was raining cats and dogs that crop year down in the Bootheel, but they managed to get in a double-hitter up in St. Louis, located about 160 miles north of our cotton fields in New Madrid County.

That was the day Stan "the Man" Musial knocked not one, not two, not three, not four, but FIVE homeruns out of the ballpark.

We later asked Momma Whittle why she never returned to witness a Cardinals' game.

"You can't top Stan Musial's five home runs," she decreed. "Why would I want to go back?"

Enough said.

Race, Soldiers, School, Church, and Careers

Mary June Whittle's Eighth Grade Class

Chapter Seventy-One
Canalou Heroes

World War II provided some high drama to a little farm girl, although tiny rural remote Canalou was never declared *strategic* in any military operation.

"Daddy [the late James William Jay Hopper] was exempt from serving because he was a farmer, but he wanted to serve," declared Patsy Hopper Bixler, who was eight-years-old when the Japanese bombed Pearl Harbor. "One summer he wanted to go so bad that after the crops were laid, Dad went to St. Louis and worked in a defense plant."

"But, as a little girl, I thought the Japs might be here any time," Patsy recalls."Once a bomber was on its way to some destination, but it was so low; we thought it was a bombing run. What a joke. They wouldn't think of bombing a rural place so remote. But to a child, anything is possible.

"We lived near a crossroads, and two or three neighbor farmers rushed and got their cars and trucks, with their lights turned on, to make a lighted runway for the bomber to make an emergency landing," Patsy noted. "It was a gravel road and the bomber ran off into a field, where a fence finally stopped it. The military placed a guard on it until they could pull it out of the field."

There was another military accident in that era.

"A pilot, training as a fighter pilot from nearby Malden Air Force Base, was killed when his plane crashed near Charter Oak, unincorporated community located between Canalou and Parma," Patsy shared.

"Every Wednesday at Canalou School, we'd march to the post office to do our part in the war effort by buying savings stamps," Patsy said. "For ten cents, you could buy one stamp. When the book was filled, it was worth five dollars.

"The post office had ominous signs such as 'Loose Lips Sinks Ships' and there were horror pictures showing *Hitler*, Mussolini, and Hirohito," Patsy traced back in time. "And I remember troop trains coming through Canalou. It seemed everyone was in uniform. Our school dropped sports, for all the boys had gone off to war.

"There were prisoner-of-war camps throughout America, including New Madrid County at Marston," Patsy notes. "These were heavily guarded. We had black-out nights where Mom placed blankets over our windows. All the little towns, including Canalou, had an honor roll listing its soldiers in service. Ours was located between Moore's and Ralph's groceries in downtown Canalou. We studied it carefully to see if anyone's status had been changed to 'killed in action.'

"Cars had bumper stickers asking if the trip was necessary. So Jimmy Hickey's Rolling Store was popular because no one could make a wasted trip to town," Patsy added. "He had a panel truck all rigged up with shelves with marvelous things. But the best was a coconut lollipop. Jimmy would park his Rolling Store under our yard's two big shade trees."

Farmer Abe Landers Junior had three sons fighting the Germans and Japanese at the same time.

So what are the odds of two of his sons from tiny Canalou, Missouri, passing each other while on the march, and stopping to chat on a battlefield somewhere in Germany during World War II?

They may be about the same odds that had to fall in place for Willie A. Landers, and Raymond "Gube" Landers, plus a third brother, Leslie "Chuck" Landers, for all to have survived front-line fighting during World War II against the Germans and

Japanese.

Not much is known about Canalou men who fought in World War I.

But during World War II, Korea and Vietnam, numerous soldiers from the tiny village served with courage and valor when asked by their nation to do so.

At least two Canalou area soldiers gave their lives in service to our nation and mankind during WWII.

Private First Class Zolen Newman, born near Canalou in 1921, gave the ultimate for his nation when he was hit by a German artillery shell in the attack on Hattan-Rittershoffen, France.

"He was killed in action on or about January 13, 1945," military records show.

"Private First Class Zolen Newman, called Bill, was the son of Mary Newman, the baby sister of Grandfather Abe Landers Junior," reported Les Landers, who was born in Canalou in 1940. "His sister Judy married Dale Lasters, who live here not far from me in Kentucky. His family received a Purple Heart medal in his honor. He was killed in January, just four short months before WWII ended."

WWII Army Corporal Harold E. Bell of Landers Ridge is also listed as killed in action. No other details were available.

The following is about two other soldiers, one from WWII and one from Vietnam, both of whom received multiple medals for bravery while under enemy fire.

Army Private First Class Willie Alvin Landers, son of Mr. and Mrs. Abe Landers Junior, of Canalou, served with the highly-famous Co. K Unit in the history-making 102nd Ozark Division that fought through Holland and then the hedgerows and house-to-house combat against German soldiers in their last throes of war.

About meeting his brother on a German battlefield, Willie stated: "We stopped and talked a few minutes as our units were moving past one another, with permission of our commanding officers."

Although he fought in multiple battles, including Battles of Immendorf and Apwieler, Willie Landers never talked much about what he saw and suffered, including hunger, extreme cold, and danger.

How hungry did Landers get?

"I'd heard a WWI veteran describe one time he was glad to get a frozen cabbage to eat. I thought that would never happen to me," Landers said in his only newspaper interview in 1991 before he died. "We were glad to get anything, including eating frozen cabbage, as there was no stopping or taking a break as our Army rolled through Germany to get within fifty miles of Berlin."

Few Canalou citizens, past and present, know about his bravery in WWII. And few current Canalou residents know that their mayor, James Donald Taul, is a highly-decorated Vietnam War veteran.

Why is that?

"Canalou folks don't talk much about stuff like that," advised Mayor Taul, who had to be asked multiple times to share his Vietnam War experiences.

It wasn't until 1991 that Willie Landers finally agreed to accept a host of Army medals presented to him near his home in Kentucky on the fifty-seventh wedding anniversary he and his wife celebrated.

"It took a cooperative effort on behalf of all his children for us to not only get the Army to come forth with his medals but to get Dad to receive the honors," reported son Les Landers.

On October 5, 1991, Willie Landers received two Bronze Stars for bravery forty-six years after he'd helped win the war against the German Nazis and their SS troops, along with a European/African Middle Eastern Campaign Medal, WWII Victory Medal, WWII Army of Occupation, and a Combat Infantry Badge.

On that date, he granted his one media interview, by explaining thusly to a reporter from the *Paducah Sun-Democrat*: "Talking about it brings back lots of memories. And there are things I just don't talk about."

He described that toward the war's end, German women and little boys were forced to front-line fighting.

"We faced boys as young as fourteen," Landers recalled. "The kids had the German SS at their backs and the Allies in front of them. Either way they were going to die."

"When the war ended, I wasn't interested in medals," Landers reported. "I just wanted to get back to Canalou and my family."

He didn't like military life.

"I found it hard to take orders that made no sense, so I pulled lots of KP duty," the farm boy from Canalou described.

Mayor Taul finally consented to sharing actual military records listing his bravery under enemy fire. The following Vietnam-era battle took place in April 1970.

"Sargeant Taul, as Heavy Weapons Infantry Advisor, and his team made contact with a numerically superior Viet Cong force," records confirm. "He helped organize and deploy a reaction force of South Vietnam Army Regulars when they became penned down by heavy enemy fire. Sgt. Taul repeatedly exposed himself to enemy fire in order to direct friendly forces and provide illumination from hand flares. After being supplied with a machine gun, he placed a heavy and accurate volume of fire on an enemy machine gun sufficiently to force the enemy to withdraw. He then remained in the area to direct medical evacuations.

"Sgt. Taul's heroic actions were in keeping with the highest traditions of the U. S. Army and reflect great credit on himself."

For this particular battle, Sergeant Taul received the Army's First Oak Leaf Cluster.

Military records show that in a December 1969 battle, Sergeant Taul "received a report that three friendly soldiers were seriously wounded by a booby trap in the midst of extensive and complex minefield. The soldiers were wounded in a heavily wooded area with two deep canals between their location and in face of grave danger, and with no thought to his personal safety, Sergeant Taul took it upon himself to negotiate the minefield and to personally carry one of the seriously wounded soldiers back through the minefield to the medical evacuation pickup point."

Other medals received for bravery and valor by Sergeant Taul include two Bronze Stars, Army Commendation Medal, Defense Service Medal, Air Medal, Combat Infantry Badge, Vietnam Service Medal, Vietnam Campaign Medal, and Meritorious Service Medal.

Former Sgergeant Taul is the son of the late Ernest Granny and Edna Taul, who were among first settlers shortly after the earliest sawmills were opened to harvest the timber in the Nigger Wool Swamp starting in 1902. Numerous other soldiers with farming and timbering roots in Canalou also served with military distinction.

Mayor James Donald Taul

Chapter Seventy-two

Second Grade 'War Zone'

Ever walk into a room and meet someone you knew instantly you didn't like, and you also knew instantly didn't like you?

Such was the start of my second grade school year when by the bad luck of school officials using alphabetical order, I was chosen to go into black-hearted teacher Old Lady Cox's room.

Lucky pupils got to go into the classroom of Delois McWaters, one of the legendary best to ever teach at our great little country school.

Second grade should be mostly innocent and an emotionally-smooth learning experience. I grew and learned but mostly the wrong things and definitely not smoothly. And there was nothing innocent about it.

Our early school days had already been traumatized greatly with the burning of our beautiful old three-story red brick school house during my first grade year under the tutelage of beautiful teacher Mrs. Billie Margaret Greer. That old school, built in 1927, was the anchor and soul of tiny farm town Canalou that sits in the northeast corner of New Madrid

County.

The fire resulted in my first grade class holding classes temporarily in an old abandoned pool hall and then moved to a nice residential house on the town's last active cotton gin property.

So, it was an emotionally-scalding experience for a little boy to meet the adult Mrs. Cox, who flat out didn't like me.

But let it be clearly understood I already knew how to take up for myself and was mischievous and with strong personality traits passed down to me by Daddy Whittle. Plus, I was probably angry because of my beloved father's death. So I was not without blemish or fault in what followed in my traumatic second grade school year.

So let us begin to recreate this emotionally-scalding journey through second grade.

When first entering the room, I looked up and there this strange woman teacher stood. I was shocked and greatly disappointed that Mrs. McWaters wasn't my teacher. The only redeeming factor was that my two favorite little girlfriends, Rosemary Hopper and Brenda Harlan, were also in Mrs. Cox's class with me.

It should have been an enjoyable time for no other reason than we were in a brand new pretty little school building.

Things were bad from the start, for example, Mrs. Caper caught Rosemary, one of the prettiest little fillies matriculating in second grade, passing a note to me. Okay, it was an I-like-you-do-you-like-me kind of note.

Well, it thoroughly embarrassed me, yes, even angered me when the teacher chastised pretty little Rosemary in front of the whole class.

And when I expressed my feelings to Mrs. Cox, she brought her leather strap down several times across my shoulders.

Thus, my first paddling was received in a school setting.

After my flogging, Mrs. Cox calmed her emotional feathers enough to settle back up at her desk.

When she put her head down, focusing on grading some papers at her desk, I began penning a note of my own, not to Rosemary but to the teacher.

Upon completion of one of my earliest, but very memorable literary efforts, I crawled quietly and unseen to the front of the room, right up to Mrs. Cox's desk, where I deposited the note.

Finally, after what seemed an eternity, after I stealthily got back to my little desk, we heard this roar at the front of the room. It was Mrs. Cox bellowing loudly, "Little Danny Whittle, I'll whip you again!"

Mrs. Cox had found the note! I remember the note word by word. It began thusly: "Dear Mrs. Cox." I began it that way because my parents and farm neighbors Mommie Gowen and Nell Neal insisted that we always be mannerly and courteous, especially to elders.

The note went on to read: "Dear Mrs. Cox, I hate your guts very, very much."

Not being a bright child, I signed the note: "Little Danny Whittle."

Thus, my second flogging came across my shoulders from Old Lady Cox's leather strap. This was two whippings within a fifteen minute period.

But in her excitement, the teacher forgot a large book on my desk as she huffed and puffed her way back up to the front of the room. From there, she bellowed loudly: "Little Danny Whittle, get that book up here to me pronto!"

And I did. But she didn't say how to send it.

So I airmailed that book and my aim was accurate as it sailed smoothly through the air and came squarely down on top of Mrs. Cox's pointed, ugly ol' noggin. Being a large book, the force of the airmailed parcel caused her to wobble a step or two before she came roaring back to my desk to administer yet another whipping across my shoulders. Thus, a third flogging, all within a few minutes lapsed time.

From there our relationship got worse. I could do nothing right in the teacher's eyes, and she could do nothing right in my eyes.

I ended up with a total of seven spankings, and I was only in second grade.

I truly earned and deserved my last flogging, however.

Even by second grade, I was already fascinated by words and would read anything I could get my hands on. And I knew and remembered all the cuss words I'd heard all the older men and boys use down at the pool hall or while we were all out hunting crows and other varmints.

I didn't know what all those curse words meant, but I knew the words.

So one day, older third grader Larry D. Taul put me and my favorite schoolyard buddies Kirky Durbin and Harold David Bryant up to the idea of holding a cussin' contest. If recollection serves, I think we concocted this contest in order to attract the attention of you guessed it, the pretty little second grade lasses.

Well, as fate would have it, I was judged the winner of the first official, and as it turned out, our only "Second Grade Cussin' Contest."

But by mid-afternoon, the teacher had heard about our schoolyard cussin' contest. "I understand you're the one using the worst and ugliest old curse words, Little Danny," Mrs. Cox accused accurately.

"Yes, ma'am," I replied guiltily, but note, I didn't forget my manners. Actually, I was proud of my cussin' title.

With that, Mrs. Cox gave me another flogging. So this was my last memorable spanking that I got in second grade. And I think I'm safe in reporting that my record of seven whippings in second grade was never broken.

Mrs. Cox ended up passing me under condition (not ready academically to advance) to third grade. Like I said, I was not a particularly bright child. I think she passed me just to move me on out of her sight, and I can understand her reasoning. Interestingly, I made good grades under the tutelage of other elementary school teachers.

Later in adult life, after I began my professional newspaper writing career, I penned a column about black-hearted memories of my second grade school year, to which, I got a note in the mail that read:

> Little Danny Whittle,
>
> I've admired your writing career from afar all these years. And I'm so sorry you have such black-hearted memories of your second grade school teacher.
>
> Your second grade school teacher.

Chapter Seventy-Three

Bell Ringer

From day one, I used my noggin at our little country school of advanced thinking.

I can modestly claim to being an outstanding pupil from the get-go.

At least, I stood out.

Weeks had seemed like eternity until I finally came of age to officially crawl, due my short legs, on the big yellow school bus driven by George Lefler, who doubled as our school janitor long before the title *custodial engineer* came into vogue.

Mr. Lefler had endeared himself in my pre-school years because he would take the time to stop the school bus to hand over the marbles he'd saved for me when cleaning his bus at the end of each day's bus run.

Further endearment came when he and my favorite farm neighbor of all time, Poppy Gowan, would save their empty tobacco sacks ideal for storing my valuable stash of marbles.

Oh, for sure, it was bigger-than-life excitement that first day I stepped on the bus behind my older brother and sister Hubert

Van and Mary June, the family veterans at this going-to-school business.

As fate would have it, that first day of school turned into a bell ringer, literally and figuratively.

Two things primarily had me excited about starting first grade in teacher Billie Margaret Greer's class. One was getting out of dirty, hot, and mostly boring field work. A close second was all the pretty little girls I saw there on the school ground.

Not just any girls. I'm talking Brenda Harlan and Rosemary Hopper, the "two foxes" of first grade, not to mention Ellen Campbell and Sandra Hill with their blond hair and pretty, big blue eyes.

I noticed that those pretty little girls were showing interest in the school yard's big bell that Superintendent H. H. Harlan, a native of nearby Grayridge in neighboring Stoddard County, rang each day to declare school in session.

And since I coveted those little fillies' attention, I decided to show off before the first school bell officially clanged.

So I bragged to Brenda and Rosemary I could crawl up inside that big bell.

"You can't do that," declared Brenda, School Superintendent Harlan's beautiful little daughter.

"Can too," I boasted.

After successfully getting to the top of the concrete base upon which the big bell sat, I slithered on my tummy until I got mostly inside the big bell, except for one strategic part of my body.

As I started to ascend on up into the bell, I misjudged the bell's close proximity and proceeded to cut a huge gaping gash on the top of my scalp as my head came into contact with the bell's sharp edge.

Although the pain was not that severe, I freaked when blood started running profusely down my forehead and into my eyes. I was bleeding so profusely that I reminded myself of those hogs we'd killed and butchered each winter on our farm.

Unable to get the bleeding stopped, teacher Mrs. Harlan, the superintendent's wife, wrapped my head in towels and floor-boarded her brand new, shiny automobile the seven miles to physician Sam Sarno's office in nearby Morehouse, the nearest neighboring town that had a doctor.

I was very ashamed of the fact that my blood got all over the Harlans' new car. I was even more ashamed later that day when I finally walked into teacher Billie Margaret Greer's first grade classroom with my head heavily-bandaged with snow-white gauze and tape.

See, I was a standout student from day one. And, yes, I used my noggin from day one.

Today that old school bell sits forever quiet in the yard of Canalou Baptist Church as a memorial to former Canalou Post Office officials Don and Vera Kochel. There's a crack in the bell, but contrary to popular town opinion of my youth, my noggin didn't cause it.

Chapter Seventy-Four

Morehouse Tigers

Small school sports in the Bootheel during the 1930s, 1940s, and 1950s consisted mostly of baseball, basketball, and volleyball.

Most of our region's small rural schools couldn't afford to field expensive football teams. Most Bootheel families were poor, but then, no poorer than next farm neighbors. Same held true for our rural schools. But we never called ourselves poor, and for damn sure we never allowed any outsider to call us poor.

In most communities, the collective hearts, souls, and pride soared on the backs of athletic teams, especially the basketball stars of legendary status in the glory years of my youth in the 1950s.

Although Canalou High's Yellow Jackets achieved the improbable by winning the New Madrid County Tournament in 1957, that hardwood/hoops era truly belonged to nearby Morehouse and Puxico Schools and communities.

Canalou's one-year of 1950s glory was a brief spark in the dark compared to the Morehouse Tigers fabled run of winning many consecutive county tournaments, for example.

Books, such as *They Call Me Mr. Ryan* by Bootheel author Matt Chaney, have been written about those dream teams of the

1950s.

Present-day St. Louis-area resident Ronnie Carl Launius and his brother John who still keeps the candle burning in Morehouse, recounts the stars produced out of the Puxico and Morehouse's Bootheel basketball dominance era of the 1950s.

Ronnie and John, both of whom are writers at heart, and gifted writers at that, shared their remembrances. They recalled 1955, for example, the year that Bootheel basketball, more specifically, the Morehouse and Puxico brand of run-and-gun round ball, was show-cased nationally.

"When St. Louis University's Billikens met the Memphis State Tigers in New York's Madison Square Garden in the N. I. T. tournament in 1955, according to our father, four of the ten starting players were from Morehouse, our hometown and the neighboring town of Puxico in Stoddard County," the Launius brothers accounted.

They're talking the likes of Morehouse's Joe Todd on the Billikens and Puxico's Win Wilfong at Memphis State.

Morehouse High graduate Norman Vickers was a rebounding machine with records that still are listed at Jonesboro's Arkansas State University.

"I went on to Arkansas State where I started on the varsity my freshman year," Vickers accounted. "Their latest basketball media guide lists me as the third most in total rebounds, 343, with an average of 13.7 rebounds per game. Both figures are for my freshman year at ASU."

"I graduated [from high school] in 1955, so I was at the end of the era [of great Morehouse teams]," Vickers described at age seventy-five in 2011 from his home in Marion, Arkansas "Chiefly, I was a rebounder and played defense."

But he could score too.

"In a game against Grayridge [high school], I scored thirty-four points," Vickers tallied. "I kept tipping the ball up because they [opposing players] were waiting for me to bring the ball down. This was not a problem because I dominated the boards in all the games I played. If you tip up enough times, it will fall in."

So with that kind of drama and talent, there is no mistaking the importance of game nights in Bootheel basketball of the 1950s.

Other good teams came out of towns like Bloomfield, Marston, Bernie, Malden, Sikeston, Lilbourn, Essex, Oran, Illmo-Fornfelt, Advance, Bell City, Charleston, Grayridge, Matthews, New Madrid, and Bragg City, but Morehouse and Puxico set the Bootheel's basketball banner quite high.

Bootheel basketball fans automatically knew they were at a game of importance when they'd see Sikeston's KSIM Radio news truck roll up in front of our small gymnasiums, or witness Bootheel newspaper sportswriters Bob Gray, Alva Jones, Barney Dubois, and Ray Owens arrive at the gymnasiums. Radio announcer Mike Shain was legend to us rural-farm-sports-enthusiasts.

Retired South Western Bell Telephone employee Ronnie Launius chronicles a typical 1950s-era "Morehouse Tiger Game Night" by taking a stroll back through time when effects of long cold winter nights were neutralized by heated competition on the hardwood.

"Whole towns were caught up in each winter's basketball frenzy," Ronnie Carl, a 1960 graduate of Morehouse High, remembers. "Game nights dripped with drama."

"Well, before the game starts, bleachers are filled to capacity as KSIM Radio announcer Mike Shain sets up his broadcast equipment," John Launius described.

"When sports announcer Mike Shain, a Bootheel broadcasting legend, came to town, you knew it was a big game," echoed Ronnie.

"The Tigers are playing a home game, and revenge is in the air." Ronnie said in recreating the importance of this particular game with nemesis Puxico High's very talented Indians.

They still savor (as of 2009) that revenge from 1955 at the town's present-day, early-morning coffee-swigging Front Street Market restaurant's liars table.

Let's join the Launius boys on their joyful nostalgic journey back in time. "Last year's [1954] season ended when Morehouse lost to Puxico in the state tournament in the semifinals," Ronnie chronicled back across the plowed fields of time. "Tonight a weaker, less-experienced Puxico team comes to Morehouse. Revenge! Sweet, sweet revenge!"

"Mom hurries with the dinner dishes because Cora and Murrell Newton are coming over to listen to the game on the radio and play some competitive Canasta," Ronnie details. "Tearing through the twilight on my bike, I race to the gym to get a seat, along with buddies, in the highest bleachers to get a birds-eye view of action on the court."

The years seem to fade from the brothers' faces as they recreate their youth.

The whole town was caught up in a festive atmosphere, much like that characterized in the legendary great *Hoosiers* sports movie starring Gene Hackman. Morehouse's tiny gym was crammed with spectators, including fans standing shoulder-to-shoulder in the halls.

"By game time, the pretty Morehouse Cheerleaders will have performed their crowd-pleasing favorite yell at least twice: 'Two bits, four bits, six bits, a peso. If you're for Morehouse, stand up and say so!"

"By this time, the vestibules at each end of the court were stacked with nonsports-playing boys of the community," Ronnie accounted. "Referees constantly had to remind them not to stand out on the court. Grade school principal James Coppage patrolled the hallways to keep order, along with custodian Ashley Craig."

It was in the third quarter, when victory was obvious, that Morehouse Cheerleaders echoed a cheer about Doyle Denbow, a fabled Morehouse player who went on to college basketball fame and later returned to coach Bootheel high school basketball. The cheer had the rhythm and flow of a popular song of the mid-1950s about a character named Bimbo who was known for going down the road to "see his girl-e-o."

"Denbow, Denbow, where you going to Go-e-Go? Going down the court to make another Goal-e-O," the cheers would rock the small Morehouse gymnasium rafters.

Morehouse native Donnie Savage was also a player for the

Morehouse Tigers. "Although I weighed only thirty-five pounds in first grade, I could shoot hoops," Savage explained. "My favorites for the mighty Tigers of that era were Larry Chapman, Doyle Denbow, Kenny Morse, and Mike Tyler. When listening to Mike Shain on KSIM Radio, I'd keep the points they scored on a scrap of paper."

In his own high school playing days, Savage averaged twenty points per game as a junior and nineteen his senior year of 1963.

Morehouse Coach Gene Herrod had brought the run-and-gun style of round ball to the Bootheel out of Kentucky in the early 1950s. In addition to a great starting five in this memorable "1955 revenge game" against Puxico, he had talented sixth man Bobby Dickerson to come off the bench.

Alas, after Morehouse drilled Puxico on this particular game night, it was time for celebration. We're practically talking about Morehouse's entire population of 1,500 people.

"Ah, yes, it's Friday night, another memorable evening at the Morehouse gym and another victory for the Morehouse Tigers. Now most of the teenagers hurried to the Tiger Grill to celebrate over milk shakes and hamburgers. Most adults preferred Freda's Café for barbecue sandwiches before calling it a night," recalled Ronnie.

And Morehouse's legendary tough lawman the late Slim Stinnett, was always nearby in his patrol car, overseeing the town's game night celebrations.

How dominant were Morehouse teams of the 1950s?

"Morehouse won the New Madrid County Championship several times during the 1950s decade. One year the county wanted to have a tourney and let the winner play Morehouse. Nothing doing! We sort of liked beating up on those fancy bigger schools with their slick hardwood courts and shiny glass backboards." Ronnie teased.

He also explained how Morehouse produced so many talented players and teams.

"All little boys in town wanted to be star basketball players. They worked at it and practiced tirelessly. For example, we lived next door to Joe Todd, one of the brightest basketball stars in Bootheel basketball history. Missouri basketball fans may recall that name, for Joe Todd helped the St. Louis Billikens gain national prominence during the mid-1950s."

It was an honor for the Launius boys and other boys of the neighborhood in Morehouse to help, now deceased, Joe Todd never miss a daily practice.

"I was never blessed with the talent or skill of Joe Todd. And folks all agreed that Joe had a gift for basketball. Yes, Joe had a gift all right," Ronnie described. "Living next door afforded me the opportunity on many occasions to help Joe scrape the snow and ice from his backyard court so he could get his daily regimen of practice. Joe's gift was his drive and determination to be the best basketball player he could possibly become."

Many boys of the Bootheel, including Grayridge, Canalou, and Morehouse youth, could not afford traditional store-bought hoops and backboards for backyard courts. No problem. We were taught to be resourceful by our parents and forefathers who bravely and determinedly managed to carve out good lives for us in the former tough and rugged swampland timber forest region.

"Kids in our town played basketball year around," Ronnie added. "When one of us boys wanted a basketball goal, it never occurred to us that we could go to the store and buy one. You went out to that pile of old lumber where your dad had torn down a shed, and you picked out the smoothest boards you could find, pulled out the rusty nails, and built a three-foot by four-foot rectangle."

Thus, you had your backboard.

Now that metal hoop required some poor country-boy ingenuity.

"After the wooden backboard was mounted on the side of your shed or a nearby tree, by selling soda bottles to the grocer and taking scrap iron to the town's blacksmith shop, you eventually got enough money [about one dollar] to have a metal basketball hoop. You didn't get a net for that price, but it worked for us."

Daddy Whittle, who had his own blacksmithing tools there on

our farm between Morehouse and Canalou, forged, bent, and hammered our back yard's cast-iron basketball goal for my brother H. Van Whittle to hone his skills as a talented point guard for the Canalou High School Yellow Jackets.

Although a new century is upon us, those of us blessed to have grown up in the 1950s in the rural Bootheel can still hear the cheers for our respective little school basketball teams. They were our identity. Time is proving, to this product of small community schools, that America made a major mistake by going to huge non-personal school campuses.

Special thanks go to Launius brothers John and Ronnie Carl for taking us back to the glory years of the hot Bootheel brand of basketball of the 1950s.

Chapter Seventy-Five
Grayridge School

Robert L. Rasche. Owen J. Taul. What do those two deceased men have in common?

They're two of the greatest educators in Missouri Bootheel history, and that's not just one Dan's opinion.

Although Canalou native Mr. Taul never taught me personally, his reputation is legend in our little home town and in Lilbourn, where he served as superintendent for a long time.

Former Canalou resident John Buck, who grew up in nearby Lilbourn in New Madrid County, echoes Mr. Taul's greatness: "He'd listen, and then support you even if [you were] up against an unfair teacher," John endorsed. "If not for Owen J. Taul, I'd have never graduated."

Mr. Taul must have taught John well because John was smart enough to marry a Canalou girl named Renda Chaney, the pretty daughter of Faye and Harry Chaney. Plus, John left Hart's Bakery in Sikeston to become general manager of the largest bakery in Tennessee before his retirement in the 1990s.

If not for Grayridge High Superintendent Mr. Rasche, I'd not have graduated from high school, much less had a world-traveled newspaper career.

As a student, I could be really smart or really dumb, according to grade cards of my past.

It depended on my motivation, mood, interest, and, to some extent, on the teacher in front of the classroom.

In second grade, for example, I was passed under condition by a teacher who didn't like me, and I certainly didn't like her.

In first grade, I made good grades, complete with excellent deportment reports from teacher Billie Margaret Greer's class at Canalou School of higher ciphering and advanced thinking. She was probably the nicest and prettiest lady teacher I ever had.

I made average grades the following years at Canalou School.

But the smartest move I made as a student didn't have anything to do with class work and grades. It had more to do with critical teenaged-emotional survival.

After we lost Canalou School in 1958 due to consolidation with nearby Matthews High, things did not go well for me at the new school. A few other Canalou students, such as Willard Robinson, had already dropped out of school.

My exodus from Matthews High started at the beginning of tenth grade when a popular Matthews student and I got called to the office by a male teacher.

The reason I was there was for playing hooky. I don't remember the other boy's alleged misconduct, but when the teacher threatened to use the board of education on our behinds, that student said he wasn't going to take a whipping. He further indicated if there was any whipping, it would be done "like a man." So I said I wasn't going to take a paddling either.

At that point, said teacher backed off giving us a paddling. But word got back to me that I was going to be expelled for allegedly threatening a teacher, so I developed an exit plan.

Since fellow former Canalou School students Scotty Scott and Johnny Arbuckle had already transferred to Grayridge High School over in Stoddard County, I thought that would be the smartest move for Little Danny Whittle to make.

Making the move from Matthews High to Grayridge High School involved two things: one, Grayridge was over in Stoddard County, separated from Canalou and New Madrid County by the bordering Little River, and two, I had to convince Momma Whittle I was going to quit school if I had to continue at Matthews. Now don't think Matthews High didn't have some quality educators. Those good teachers included Mr. and Mrs. Hershel Yates and Principal Mr. Conrad.

Actually, I managed to transfer to Grayridge High by tricking Momma Whittle. I caught her on one of her busiest days on the farm and asked: "Is it alright that I ride to school with Scotty Scott today?"

After getting an affirmative nod from my preoccupied parent, I hitched a ride with Scotty and his dad, Ed Scott, back to Little River where Grayridge school bus driver Walter Wyman picked him and Johnny Arbuckle up every day.

I transferred that day and met with Grayridge Superintendent Robert L. Rasche, a man destined to have a huge impact on Little Danny Whittle's life. It was high adventure to meet all those new teachers and boys and girls who seemed so nice.

But I had hell to pay as Mother saw me walking through our soybean fields back to the house that first afternoon after getting off Mr. Wyman's bus.

"Why did you play hooky?!!" Mother asked angrily.

"I didn't," I replied innocently. "I went to Grayridge School where you said this morning that I could ride to school with Scotty Scott."

Mother rolled her eyes a bit with that report but remembered that she had, in fact, given me permission to go ride to school with Scotty Scott.

After telling Mother I would quit school if I had to continue going to Matthews High, she reluctantly agreed to let me switch to Grayridge.

And we got in Mom's six-cylinder, over-sized, and under-powered Plymouth Savoy the next morning, and she drove the twelve miles from our house to Grayridge where she met Superintendent Rasche for the first time.

Although I was now officially a student at Grayridge, I was not about to miss marching with the Matthews School Band, both in Malden (two weeks later) and in that summer's big Bootheel Cotton Carnival Parade in Sikeston. I had practiced long and hard to march in that parade.

But I remember the confused looks on the faces of Grayridge students Stella May Gromer, Lois Frala, Sharon Taylor, Gwendolyn Zuba Sutton and Bernice Bower faces as they saw me marching on the parade route in a Matthews High Band uniform.

I kept my promise to Momma by improving my grades at good ol' Grayridge High.

In my senior year, Mr. Rasche's asked if I knew I lacked a math credit in order to graduate. I think I had failed algebra five consecutive years, which was by no fault of teachers. I'm not gifted in mathematics.

I pleaded honestly: "Yes, sir, I know I don't have a math credit, but I will never be able to pass algebra no matter how hard I try. I just have a mental block when it comes to algebra."

That's when Mr. Rasche's sense of humor surfaced, for I saw a wry grin come over his face when he instructed the following: "Danny boy, tell you what I'll do. If you'll go round up twelve other little idiots, I'll tell the math teacher, Mr. Keller, to offer an idiot math class this year."

Well, being that me and most of my school buddies often qualified at being young idiots, it was no problem rounding up twelve other students. For that, I'm grateful to Mr. Rasche. I think I made solid C's in that special "idiot math" class.

By this time in my life, I was a confused and angry young boy, especially since I had lost a daddy at age six, and then, I broke my back on a farm tractor at age fourteen. Thus ending any chance of playing sports in high school to follow in the footsteps of my locally famous athletic brother, Van, who had been an all-star basketball player back at good ol' Canalou High.

Failure to get a diploma at Grayridge would have kept me from my ultimate newspaper career that took me around the globe on a paid basis over the next forty-five years of this exciting life's journey.

Like I said, if not for Mr. Rasche and English teacher Omar Brooks, and plus school board member Hugh Parks, a lifelong family friend, I'd never have graduated from high school.

It was Grayridge English teacher, the Reverend Omar Brooks, who gave me confidence to have a professional writing career.

There were other great educators from the Bootheel who profoundly touched my life and channeled me in a positive direction. Those educators include Earlyne Barnes, Homer Decker, Billie Margaret Greer, Wayne Cashion, Mrs. H. H. Harlan, and Mrs. E. E. Evans.

Owen J. Taul

I'll put our small school teachers up against teachers from big campus schools anywhere, any time!

Special Grayridge school friends I made included Gwendolyn Zuba Sutton, Sharon Williams, Rueben Jones, Jerry Kelly, Carolyn Barnett, Danny Rice, Rayburn Wilson, Ocia Williams, Faye Mitchell, John Vest, Donald Alexander, Ann Rice, Carroll Duckworth, Sharon Taylor, Bob Steele, Bob Barber, Bob Noyes, Larry Geise, Paul Polley, Kenneth Bratch, Eugene Mitchell, Larry Tubbs, Mary Hann, Carlene Smith, Larry King, Gail Goza, Sandra Hewitt, and Carlos Taylor.

Many of these friendships I renewed at the 2008 Grayridge High Reunion, where I was privileged to be the guest speaker.

But I was sad to learn on New Years Day 2008, that Rayburn Wilson, a boy born to farm, had died of a stroke at age sixty-four. And we earlier lost pretty Sharon Taylor to ravages of cancer. Jerry Kelly had died of a head injury. These were folks who positively befriended me at a critical teenaged period of my life.

Chapter Seventy-Six

Sinking Sand

According to the Good Book, a church should be built on solid rock. But there are no big rocks in the Bootheel, at least, not until you dig down fourteen to fifteen feet because of the centuries of loam and silt build-up from the waters and back-waters of Little River, Castor River, St. Francois River, Mississippi and Ohio Rivers.

Canalou's Church of Christ was originally founded in 1912 as The Christian Church. Not only was the building unique in its "Bootheel" construction and foundation, the Church doctrine split into two-for-one congregations: the Arbuckle faction that believed in funding and supporting orphanages and the Taul faction that differed in that doctrine. Thus, there were separate worship services in separate buildings, one on the west side of Canalou and the other on the east side of the railroad tracks that ran through central Canalou.

Two former Canalou youths recalled early days spent in the congregations.

"My grandfather, L. L. Arbuckle, led that faction that supported orphanages, so, yes, I grew up going to that church," confirmed Alva Jones, now a resident of Illinois.

"I attended there as far back as I can remember, until we moved to Kentucky in 1952," confirmed Kentucky resident Les

Landers. The building Landers attended could be described as unique Canalou-style architecture.

"As for the building itself, the structure was built with the entrance of the church high up off the ground, which then sloped downward toward the pulpit," Les said. "The reason being was so that the persons who were sitting in back could see over the heads of the persons sitting in front of them.

Enter nonchurch related games by children.

"This made for an ideal opportunity for all of the kids in the neighborhood, including Larry Lawson, Johnny Summers, Ronnie Hewitt. Jimmy Hunter, Bobby Goins and others, along with myself to crawl under the front of the building. There it was tall enough that we children could stand up and walk around. That was under the [late] Owen J. Taul's branch of the Church of Christ.

"Girls who played there included my sisters Trudy, Jean, and Sharon Landers," added Les. "Our cousins, Bonnie, Lena, and Mary Tharp played there, too, along with neighbor girls Patsy Hewitt, Rose Marie Grimes, plus sisters Mary, Wanda, and Betty Canoy and Shelby Jean Newton.

"You've heard the old country adage: 'Getting an education out behind the barn,'" Les continued with a smile. "Well, there was a lot to be learned under that church building, too, for curious little boys and girls."

Due to the New Madrid Fault line and the swamp drainage, Les has a theory that his boyhood church was built on shifting soil, as opposed to rock.

"Now here is where the New Madrid Earthquakes and multiple rivers come into play, extending right down to the present time," Les describes. "The so-called New Madrid Fault is a very active geological anomaly in that the fault became exceedingly active on December 16, 1811. And over the next two years, more than 2,500 earthquakes were recorded by a man in Louisville, Kentucky. Amazingly, those earthquakes are still occurring on a continual basis on that fault.

"Because of the geology, the Bootheel largely consists of loam and silt coming down from the north for centuries. Since the last ice age, there is no solid rock base which will support buildings," Les continued his theory.

Earth tremors that have continued to be present have caused a settling of most buildings in the Canalou region.

"Most of these small tremors can only be measured by modern-day detection instruments and not felt by people. But many times, as a small boy living in Canalou, I have laid in bed at night when all was perfectly still and quiet, and I could feel tremors of the bed as the ground would be moved ever so slightly. I remember the last strong tremor I felt was in 1976, when the earth shook so strongly that several people in Sikeston left their buildings in fear."

"Thus, the ultimate demise of the Canalou Church of Christ building was brought about by the lack of a solid rock foundation along with those earth tremors," Les ordained.

"The structure was not built on a solid foundation," Les confirmed. "In other words, the structure, in modern vernacular, had a very small foot print, to wit, a series of small concrete slabs which supported a tremendous amount of weight.

"As a result, when the ground was wet, which was often due to multiple floodings before the region was drained effectively by the Little River Drainage District," Landers prescribed. "With the soil softened by rain, each small quake took its toll, causing the building to sink a fraction of an inch. But over time those fractions added up. The last time I saw the building, just before it was raised, it was sitting flat on the ground with the support pillars being of no support at all as they were completely buried by the weight of building pushing them down into the soil."

One former business building, Hammock Hardware, is the only sentinel remaining of past commerce on Canalou's now vacant Main Street. The old theater building, constructed in 1944, stood until fire of mysterious origin destroyed it in early 2009.

"It's because those buildings were constructed with different and substantial footing, thus they remained strong and standing," Les noted. "If you notice, most homes in the Bootheel are now built on the slab foundation method, thereby giving the structure a much larger foot print to sit on."

Southeast Missouri State University Department of Agriculture Chair, Dr. Michael Aide, details the history of soil types in the primary six-county region that comprises the unique Bootheel farming region that produces thirty percent of Missouri's total agricultural output.

"The Bootheel and its soil very fascinating and so rich in terms of crop-growing capabilities," Dr. Aide described. "The ancestral Mississippi, and the Ohio River for that matter, ran all over the Bootheel, for example, the rock cliffs you see going to Delta on Highway 25 from Cape Girardeau, which was the bed of the ancestral Mississippi that carved out those rock cliffs.

"It also changed course, and ran in the bed of the present-day St. Francois River," Dr. Aide Added. "The ancestral Mississippi and Ohio also ran on the western edge of Dunklin County, where Kennett sits, and through the Malden area and the Lower Morehouse Valley. So with all the rich silt buildup, the Bootheel is second only to the Central Valley of California in terms of crop production and versatility because of soil fertility.

"Due to the water routes of the ancestral rivers, the soil ranges from sand to clay, which is heavy dirt locally called gumbo," Dr. Aide accounted.

As for building foundations, Dr. Aide basically agreed that any type of building not constructed on a solid under-pinning foundation would ultimately slowly sink because of the soil makeup throughout the Bootheel.

Chapter Seventy-Seven

Brother Rhodes

Brother E. L. Rhodes was a preaching man, a hell fire and damnation evangelist, who could get a crowd stirred up.

And sometimes, someone who went by the name of "Holy Ghost," helped him get folks riled up to the point, they'd start running up and down the aisles between church pews, according my older brother and sister.

But as a little tyke, it always amazed me how those church folks, who were running blind and seemingly out of control while filled with that spirit thing, somehow they knew to step over the bodies of the sisters who had "been slain in the spirit."

"It must have been the Holy Ghost that kept them from tripping over those passed-out sisters," older sister June responded when I asked about that factor.

At that point in time, Brother Rhodes was a star in our family and community for that matter.

That is until one fateful night while he was holding a *spirit-filled* revival at a little foot-washing Baptist Church between Dale and Burdette, Arkansas.

Brother E. L. Rhodes was the only preacher in family history. We country folk thought it was kind of good when he married my grandmother, Beatrice Orr Stockton Rhodes, for on the

Whittle side of the moral ledger, we were known to come from a long line of serious "sinners."

So when Brother Rhodes and Grandmother Stockton tied the knot, it was a big righteous deal since he was sure to have a good influence on the Whittles when we tended to "lose our religion" and cuss when working in the hot sun on the never-ending rows of cotton.

"Danny, comb your hair and wash good behind your ears tonight for we're going to hear Brother Rhodes preach at his new church," Momma Whittle instructed.

So after Momma Whittle and my sister June inspected behind my ears, it was time to go to church. Since it rained that day, the church house was filled as farm folks came from miles around in mule-pulled wagons and farm trucks to hear the new preacher man.

I remember thinking that my overall galluses would burst with pride that night as Brother Rhodes, a new-ranking member of our family, was introduced in the pulpit.

He kind of started slow, you know, before that Holy Ghost thing got to moving on the sisters and brothers who, like me, came to church dressed in their very best pair of overalls.

Brother Rhodes seemed to be building up a good head of preaching steam as the Holy Ghost finally began moving him around while the preacher swung his arms wildly up, down, and all around on the preaching platform.

The spirit was really beginning to move it seemed, as a few sisters began *falling* out in the spirit.

I had another burst of pride when my older brother, H. Van, was designated as one of the catchers of the ladies as they were falling backwards on the floor.

My sister June was also one of the chosen ones that night, for she'd been chosen to throw a holy sheet over the legs of the fallen sisters, you know, with something to do with protecting their modesty. I remember not knowing what their modesty looked like, but I knew those sheets were being used to cover those fallen ladies' drawers.

It was about fifteen minutes into the sermon, when something started happening that mystified this little farm boy.

"Momma, I can't understand what Brother Rhodes is saying," I remember saying.

"Shhh. . . you don't understand. . . he's talking in unknown tongues," Momma Whittle said in shushing me to keep me quiet.

All of a sudden, as Brother Rhodes bent over one of the fallen sisters, who had been slain in the spirit, a bottle of bonded Old Crow whiskey popped out of his coat vest pocket.

He was really talking in tongues now because we couldn't understand one word that came babbling out of his mouth.

Suddenly, you could hear nothing but dead silence in that church house because apparently the Holy Ghost had cut out when that bottle of bourbon slid across the church house floor.

When that happened, Momma Whittle turned crimson in color, as she gathered up all three of her young'ins and told us to get in the back of our Ford pickup.

And all of sudden, the slain sisters suddenly knew to wake up too.

"What happened?" I remember asking. "Was Brother Rhodes filled with the holy spirit?"

My older brother responded: "Heck, he wasn't filled with the Holy Ghost. Brother Rhodes was filled okay, soused, crocked, and drunker than old Cooter Brown."

I never did know anyone named Cooter Brown, but as a little boy, it stood to reason he was from the town of Cooter.

We only heard Brother Rhodes preach that first and last time. . . for Momma Whittle never quite forgave him for getting in the pulpit all tanked up on whiskey.

Although I was a little lad who didn't understand a lot of what went on that night, I knew some of the sparkle had left Brother Rhodes when Momma issued the following decree to her children: "He don't deserve to be called *Brother* since he disgraced the Holy Ghost, the church, and this family that night he got soused in the pulpit."

From that day forward, he was demoted in stature to being called Mr. Rhodes.

Amen!

Author's Note: Whether to refer to the preacher as "Mr." or "Brother" became a dispute in our family. My favorite first cousin of youth Robert Terry Reed said his mother (Durette Stockton Reed, a sister to my mother, Ruby Lee Stockton Whittle) insisted her children refer to him with the more reverent "Brother" title.

Uncle R. T. and Aunt Durett Reed holding Robert Terry Reed

Brother Rhodes and Wife

Chapter Seventy-Eight

Brother, A Hero

It happened at 7:30 p.m. October 24, 1950.

A neighbor man knocked on the front door of farm neighbor A. J. Neel's farm house where

Momma Whittle, sister June, brother H. Van, and I were visiting.

Our family's life changed dramatically this fateful cold night.

"Mrs. Whittle, your husband has been in a serious car wreck," bearer of bad news Norval Harrison reported. "Can I drive you to the hospital in Sikeston?"

My older brother, at age eleven, bolted out the front door screaming at the top of his voice.

He took off running wild down the nearby railroad tracks stretching between our farm hamlets, Canalou, and, Morehouse. Brother was so terrified upon hearing of Daddy Whittle's wreck that one of our farm neighbors had to chase him down in a farm truck as brother ran hysterically out across the country side.

Although only age six at the time, this scene remains permanently etched in my psyche and soul.

Brother Van had his first of hundreds of nightmares starting that night when Daddy Whittle perished from injuries received when he and his new Hudson car hit another car head on in front of Sikeston's KSIM Radio Station.

Following Daddy's death, older brother took on the responsibility of doing most of the man-sized jobs, including planting the crops in spring, chopping and picking cotton, and leading the harvest of crops when fall came.

Sister June helped take up the slack, too, not only working in the fields but doubling in household chores. She also assumed some parenting duties over baby brother. I didn't realize it then, but my sister and brother lost a lot of their youth due to the increased responsibility.

It was nothing unusual for Brother to get up at 4 a.m., go to the barn, milk the cows, and then chop weeds out of the fields until our school bus driver Earl "Eagle-eye" Jones motored down our farm lane.

Van and farm neighbor boy, Bruce Gene Bryant, took on more "hero" status on our farm road after Daddy Whittle perished. These two preteenaged boys managed to harvest our wheat and soybeans the next year by miraculously keeping an old cantankerous Minneapolis-Moline two-row thrashing machine operational.

Sister June also took over many chores as Momma Whittle adapted in becoming one of the best farmers in the country. Early mornings during harvesting season were hectic.

Upon hearing Eagle-Eye's sounding of the bus horn coming down our dirt road in a cloud of dust, brother Van would bolt from the soybean patch and put his head under the spout of our outdoor pump. My job, as the little brother, was to hand-pump the water as fast as I could as big brother washed the grime of field work from his face, hands, head, and shoulders. And I, the baby of the family, looked on with envy as brother and sister climbed on the big yellow school bus.

I tell you, older Brother and Sister held a heap a ranking in this little farm boys eyes.

But don't just take a little brother's opinion. The following is the opinion of Charles Rhoden, former classmate of Van's at Canalou High.

"Van was probably the most admired person in our class of 1957," Rhoden confirmed. "I never saw him lose his temper or speak an angry word to anyone. But the air around him and the determined look on his face told everyone, including the bullies, this was not a person to mess with."

Another vivid memory surfaced recently as I was going through the family's scrapbooks that contains newspaper clippings verifying Van was voted on a four-county basketball All-Star team by the Sikeston *Daily Standard* newspaper in 1957. Sister June was one the school's pretty cheerleaders, and it was she who coined Brother's nickname Bibber he took to his grave in 1991.

Those old press clippings contained an account of our small school's "Big Game" when the out-sized, but mighty Canalou High Yellow Jackets were pitted against perennial basketball power Morehouse Tigers in 1957.

Canalou's fighting five consisting of guards Bibber and Norman Ernest Harrison, forwards Harry Joe Chaney and Larry Lawson, and high-scoring center Billy Gene VanNoy stung the mighty Tigers that night with a stunning thirty-nine to thirty-eight upset in the New Madrid County Championship Tournament at Lilbourn's new gymnasium.

Canalou had not won the championship since 1938 and never won it again since our school was closed in a consolidation in 1959.

How good was Bibber?

Lilbourn native John Buck described Van's exploits this way: "He was the biggest thing to ever [go to the bathroom] between two rows of cotton."

Retired Bootheel sportswriter Alva Alvie Jones penned in his Southeast Missouri newspaper column, "Van Whittle is the best guard in New Madrid County."

Although we didn't realize it at the time, the closing of our school sounded the death knell of our farming hamlet's businesses.

Tears were in many town folk's eyes as they gathered on the school grounds, sadly watching as we boarded the bus to go attend nearby Matthews High School to start the 1959 school year.

Bibber went on with life after high school, but for big brother, the remaining decades of his life were painfully difficult after he was diagnosed with Crohn's Disease, a debilitating stomach lining malady that ultimately required multiple stomach surgeries when more than fifteen feet of his festered intestines were removed.

Finally, at age fifty-three, he died with stomach and many bone cancers, which was caused in part due to a weakened immune system triggered by Crohn's, which Pershing VA Hospital doctors in Poplar Bluff diagnosed.

Bibber's heroic status was further magnified at the VA Medical Center as he bravely fought his maladies.

His positive attitude learned early in life at Canalou not only amazed family but also medical staff people as he bravely dealt with excoriating gut-wrenching pain in his abdomen, and later in his bones as the cancer spread.

Although church-going folks, members of the family wondered about the fairness of Bibber's lingering excruciating pain. But a hospital security officer helped put it in perspective for us one day in the hall way.

"Maybe the reason your brother has been left to linger is the fact he has touched all of the staff's hearts with his religious faith, courtesy, and sweet spirit in spite of all the pain he's gone through," the officer confirmed.

After multiple trips back and forth to Missouri from my home in Tennessee, I knew it was my last time to see my brother alive as his condition continued to weaken.

Bibber and I had a tradition of always having a practical joke to pull on or tell one another each time we parted.

As his favorite nurses were hovering over his bed, I shared one of my favorite "big brother" stories.

"You nurses think my Bibber is a saint, but let me tell you

a true story," I began my final farewell to my dying sibling. "When I was a few weeks old, back on our farm in New Madrid County, Momma Whittle missed me out of my crib.

"She said she ran frantically through the house searching for her newborn baby boy when she noticed out a bedroom window that older brother was walking down our farm lane with a dirty, dusty, and filthy soybean sack slung back over his shoulder.

"Spying that, Momma Whittle said she bolted out of the house to catch up with my brother, who was age five at the time. She said whatever was in that dirty old burlap sack was raising cane.

With the stage set there by Bibber's death bed, I then shared that it was me in that dingy old soybean sack, for he had agreed to swap his little new baby brother to a neighbor farmer who had a prized Shetland pony that older brother held in high esteem.

"Yes, my loving brother had swapped me, not for a full-sized horse but for a midget horse," I shared as Bibber and the nurses were racked with laughter.

"It's the best deal that never went through that I ever made in life," Bibber managed to tell his nurses between guffaws and waves of pain.

When he was laughing the hardest at our old farm story, as Bibber forgot his pain for a moment, I spun and walked out of his hospital room choosing the sight of his smiling and laughing face as my final memory of an older brother who was larger than life in a little brother's eyes.

Hubert Van Whittle, named for my late father, died at age fifty-three in 1991.

He grew old before his time.

Author's Note: In a 2010 interview session, Canalou native Larry Davidson shared that someone asked if brother Van had donated his body for medical research. When I verified that it was I who made arrangements for that to happen, at my brother's request, Larry imparted: "That's something that Van Whittle would do."

Chapter Seventy-Nine
Last Day of Sports Glory

Did you see the movie *Hoosier* about a small country high school in Indiana winning the state championship in the early 1950s? This was before they divided up into large, medium, and small divisions.

As residents of a small farming community, we lived a similar experience when the stinging Yellow Jackets from our tiny Canalou High School had a fighting chance of defeating the mighty Morehouse Tigers, the team that dominated regional hardwoods and headlines in the early 1950s.

Morehouse and Puxico produced outstanding teams throughout the early 1950s with such legendary names as Johnny Schott, Doyle Denbow, Grady Arnold, and Winn Wilfong.

But drama began building during the winter of 1957 when Canalou High's fighting five kept ringing up wins despite the fact the school had less than 130 students and a town of never more than 450 people in population. The real build-up in anticipation came as the New Madrid County Tournament championship game approached.

"Finally, after they'd won about fifteen games, newspapers and radio stations, along with fans, began keeping tabs on the Canalou Yellow Jackets," confirmed retired sports writer Alva Jones.

Morehouse, as in keeping in the past few years, was favored to win the tournament although Canalou's fighting five had beat them earlier in the year, but that was on Canalou's home floor," Jones penned.

Although it was a New Madrid County championship, fans from throughout the Bootheel packed the new gymnasium at Lilbourn High.

"This single game, generated more talk and fan interest throughout the region than any other single game in 1957," Jones recalled. "You could not get a seat, as fans stood in the halls any space they could find to get a glimpse of the most competitive basketball ever seen in the Bootheel."

Sikeston and Poplar Bluff CPA Thomas J. Cox, who had been a star player at Malden High earlier in the decade, was among those on hand, along with Lilbourn native John Buck.

"Although we didn't have a team left in the tournament, we came to see Van Whittle, the baddest thing to ever. . . between two rows of cotton," Buck confirmed. "He was not Canalou's highest scorer, but he was the best player in the country."

"I thought Canalou had a chance of finally ending Morehouse's reign over Bootheel basketball," added Cox, who remembered, that he had to stand under the second tier of Lilbourn gym seats to view the game.

Finally, the day of *the game* was at hand.

Meanwhile, cars and farm trucks began lining up behind the big yellow school bus on Canalou school grounds early that cold winter afternoon.

Merchants closed businesses early as the caravan of vehicles paraded on the town's short Main Street, faithfully following and cheering behind the team that had captured their interest and hearts. Oliver's Restaurant and Summers' Café, the town's two favorite gathering points for some of the best chili dogs, cheeseburgers, gossiping, and bragging, even closed down their coffee pots for this game.

The starting lineup that night were forwards Larry Lawson and Harry Joe Chaney, pivot and the team's highest scorer Billy Gene VanNoy, guards Norman Ernest Harrison and Whittle the only senior on the team that had amassed a record of twenty-five wins and five losses leading into the championship final.

Another reason for the peak-level of interest among Canalou residents was that the remote school had not competed successfully for a county championship since 1937. To say the Yellow Jackets were underdogs is understating it.

"There had been a long drought," recalled Donald Sexton, likely the most dedicated sports fan ever to walk the hallowed halls of Canalou High. "But we thought we could beat Morehouse."

"If Canalou had a weakness going into the season, it was lack of height," Sexton added. "Although VanNoy was the team's best rebounder, he was the tallest starting player at only six-foot one." So they had to rely on smart defense and a well-rounded game of ball control to compete with the bigger and faster teams."

"Whittle was the play-making guard who controlled the tempo of the games," confirmed the late fan and farmer A. J. Neel. "You had to control the basketball to have a chance at winning, particularly the teams with the larger rebounding players. No one could steal the ball from Whittle."

How devout was Neel to the team, although he had no child playing on the squad? It was him and player Whittle who devised the team's patented two-three zone defense that helped make up for the team's lack of size. And it was Neel and his wife Nell who kept a scrapbook of newspaper stories from newspapers throughout the Bootheel and presented it to the Whittle family after the season.

Morehouse, which featured several taller players including excellent scoring center Larry Harris, was known for a high-scoring tempo with a record showing several games above ninety and 100 points the previous five seasons.

Although Canalou's fighting five had scratched out a hard-fought victory over the Tigers earlier in the season, Morehouse was still favored to take the championship.

Former Sikeston KSIM Radio sports broadcaster Mike Shain, now retired from KFVS-TV in Cape Girardeau, remembers the rivalry and widespread interest leading up to the game.

"This was the most talked-about game in the region," Shain recalls. "Although Morehouse was favored, Canalou had lots of fan support, not only from their small town but from throughout the region."

Finally, it was time to take the floor as Lilbourn's gym filled to more-than-recommended capacity.

"It was one of the biggest turnouts for a basketball game in Lilbourn," confirmed spectator James Donald Taul. "My uncle, Owen J. Taul, was superintendent of Lilbourn High at that time, and he confirmed the heavy turnout as people came from miles around to view the game."

The tempo started fast with Morehouse controlling the tip-off. Scoring started slow, however, with both teams playing tough defense. First one team would jump out to lead by a few points, and then the other would edge back to lock up the score. Momentum edged back and forth as fans cheered and moaned, depending on the current course of events for their favored team.

Canalou top-scorer VanNoy recalled the game from his home in Little Rock, Arkansas, in 2007.

"Our championship game with Morehouse was the most talked about game of the year," confirmed VanNoy. "We were underdogs, and for good reason. Morehouse had speed and height. We were not fast or tall. Plus, Morehouse had a speedy guard named Sonny Bryant.

"Although I had an average of twenty-four points per game, I knew Morehouse would be after me, especially with their taller center Larry Harris one of the best in the state," VanNoy recalled. "So we played ball control, since Whittle and Harrison were two of the best guards around."

Although lethal with his jump shot from ten to fifteen feet, VanNoy was vulnerable from the six foot three Harris.

So he changed his deadly jump shot.

"I always positioned my body between the basket and the taller players, whether on offense or defense. When I was on offense

I altered my shot under the basket," VanNoy described. "The taller players, particularly Harris, could block my usual jump shot. So instead of that shot, I shot from waist lifting the ball from my mid-section straight up to the basket, using my body to block out the taller players."

With defense and heady playing, the Yellow Jackets edged out Morehouse by the slimmest of margins, thirty-nine to thirty-eight, holding the normally-high-scoring Tigers to fewer than forty points.

"Whittle had a good head and was the best point guard I ever played with, and I played on in the military and in college," credited VanNoy.

Canalou lifelong resident Lonnie Lawson, whose brother (the late Larry) was an integral part of the starting five for Canalou in 1957, credited Whittle with being a leader on the team.

"He could not jump; he couldn't run with speed, but he could score on you or run a play successfully using his head anytime he wanted," farmer Lawson credited. "I don't know how he did it, but he was a great point guard."

Underdog Canalou had its following.

"Most of the crowd not from Canalou wanted Canalou to win because Morehouse had won so many championships in that era," chronicled Lilbourn resident Buck. "That was one night that our new gymnasium literally rocked with cheering as people turned out from several counties to view the competition."

Chapter Eighty
Crawdad, Nicknames

Say Alva, Gary, Jerry, Sue, and Cordell, and most folks with Canalou roots won't know of whom you speak.

Say Bixie, Jaybird, Hollywood, Coon Dawg, Sue-Baby, and Crawdad, however, and they'll likely know you're talking about folks with some of the most colorful nicknames our unique little former swamp town had to offer.

But my favorite of all time is Gary "Bixie" Bixler. At age sixty-four, he is the youngest son of the late Mr. and Mrs. Melton Bixler, a highly-respected Canalou farm family. Gary may be the *only person* in the world with the nickname: "BIXIE."

Repeat it after me, say it real fast. . . "Bixie Bixler!" See, it has a colorful ring, and he's one of the nicest, most well behaved former little boys to have gone through Canalou School before it closed in 1958.

But Bixie's older brother, Cordell, now age sixty-nine, has perhaps the most famous nickname of all time in Canalou annals of history.

We're talking Crawdad here.

Cordell's nickname goes back to Lilbourn, Missouri, where the Bixlers lived in Cordell's youngest years (the mid-1940s). Here they farmed with his uncle, Paul Crouthers.

"How I got my nickname goes back to another uncle, Ted Bixler," Crawdad recalled back across the decades. "While living at Lilbourn, we lived by the railroad tracks. In front of our house was a big water tank where steam engines would take on water. Which made the ditch in front of our house have water in it all the time—year round—which was a good place for crawdads [crawfish] to live," Crawdad noted. "And they flourished, for there were hundreds of them. So Mom would fix me a little pole with a string attached with a piece of bacon hooked on my safety pin fishing hook.

"And I would place it in the water, and when the line started to move, I would gently raise the pole and shake my crawdad off in the bucket," Crawdad added. "And I'd do this over and over. . . but after catching a bucket full; I would then dump the crawdads back in the water to catch them again the next day. So I guess I was the first to come up with what is known today as catch and release.

"My Uncle Ted was the one who attached the 'Crawdad' nickname on me. It has stuck on me through all my life, along the countless millions of miles I journeyed as part of my career with the Frisco Railroad before I retired."

But, there was something else that made "Crawdad" widely known outside of the Bootheel of Southeast Missouri.

That journey began back in the 1990s when Crawdad started a hobby of collecting various brands of hot sauces.

"I love spicy food that is cooked well," Crawdad explains, "So, after a period of time around 1995, we counted up and I had around 1,200 bottles of various hot cooking sauces, which became more of a nuisance than an enjoyable hobby.

"It was in the 1990s, that I came up with the idea of starting my own label of sauce, thus the name *Crawdad's Classics*," Crawdad noted about how his life took on added spice and flavor as he neared retirement age.

"After many trials and errors, I finally got the recipe that makes Crawdad's Classics hot sauce unique, if I do say so myself," Crawdad confirmed. "Since retiring in 1999 from railroading, I've marketed many thousands of bottles and cases. I guess the nearest place to Canalou that stocks Crawdad's Classics, is the

Harvest Café in Matthews where the farmers from Sikeston, Kewanee, Matthews, and Canalou gather each morning for breakfast and some creative exchange of farm tales."

Canalou native Alva Jones, now age seventy-seven and a resident of Freeburg, Illinois, has toted two nicknames on his trek through life.

"Friends and family didn't like pronouncing Alva, so my first nickname became "Alvie," which is the name I went by during my teenage years when me and my older brother Arlen, who went by the nickname 'Arlie,' on our dry cleaning routes through Canalou, Lilbourn, New Madrid, Parma, Charter Oak, Hills Store, Catron and Lavalle. No one from that area knew us by our real given names, Alva and Arlen. . . It was Alvie' and "Arlie."

So, how did Alva "Alvie" Jones acquire his present-day Hollywood nickname that we hear at each year's Canalou Reunion?

"The nickname 'Hollywood' also goes back to my younger years. . . actually to a place I wasn't ever supposed to go, you know, the infamous Hollywood Courts saloon and tavern that sat menacingly on the highway between New Madrid and Marston.

"Well, I went there in search of romance, but instead, upon walking through the front door, someone threw me back out pitched me out on the gravel parking lot and then proceeded to drag me around the parking lot a time or two," Alva Alvie Hollywood Jones confessed. "Thus, my nickname 'Hollywood' was attached to me by a certain writer I know from Canalou."

In his teenage years, Hollywood was best known, however, as Alvie Jones, sportswriter for *The Southeast Missouri News* newspaper based in Lilbourn, Missouri, during the 1950s when Canalou had very talented basketball and volleyball teams.

"My newspaper pen name was Alvie, and that's what most readers knew to call me by," Alvie Hollywood noted.

Jerry "Coon Dawg" Hunter, who made it with me from grades one through eight before we lost Canalou School in 1958, got his nickname from his youthful hunting days.

"It was former Canalou neighbor John Buck who hung *Coon Dawg* on me," Coon Dawg confirmed at the 2008 Labor Day Canalou School Reunion. "Most folks don't know my real name: Jerry. I just answer to Coon Dawg."

Jerry "Jaybird" Wilkerson, who also attended the 2008 reunion, noted his nickname goes back to his earliest days of youth when his family farmed on land owned by prominent Canalou farmer (the late) Melton Bixler.

"I can't remember not being called Jaybird," Jaybird confirmed "It might have had something to do with me always being slender and skinny, you know, without much of a rear end."

Jaybird's large Wilkerson family lived on the farm across the railroad tracks from A. J. Neels' place on our farm road of youth.

Sue "Baby" Bixler is a Canalou legend in her own time, being one of the community's most colorful and financially successful people in town history.

"I was the baby of our family, so it was natural that I got labeled Sue-Baby," Sue-Baby confirmed. "Some folks have stopped in my Enid, Oklahoma, hometown and asked if they knew where to find Sue Bixler. . . they didn't know who I was until the ones asking directions added that I was also known as Sue Baby,"

She had another nickname during her childhood years. Her popularity was amplified by her multiple boyfriends she taught to smooch in the dark of John Summers' Theater when we got together and started calling her "Sweet Lips."

"Yes, I proudly answer to Sweet Lips, too," Sue-Baby concluded.

My first nickname of life was placed on me by a loving black lady named Rosie, who lived in a sharecropper's shanty on our farm in the early 1940s. She and her husband Rueben called me "Little Black Boy," since I've always had a dark complexion.

Chapter Eighty-One
'Egg caper'

We didn't have a lot of crime in our farm community during the early 1950s.

But *mischief*? There was plenty of that at our little country school.

The year was 1955, an otherwise noneventful year as far as the doldrums of working in cotton and soybean fields go.

However, it was the year of the *egg caper* that began in the school cafeteria headed by Opal Evans, Mary Newman, Agnes Evans, and Anna Lasters. *Egg caper* plan hatchers included older brother H. Van Whittle and his high school buddies, Billy Gene VanNoy and Bruce Gene Bryant.

"We need to take an uncooked egg back to study hall and throw it on the tattle-tale girl who informed teacher Homer Decker that we played hooky," observed my older brother.

Whittle and Bryant's initial egg-snatching responsibility involved distracting the cafeteria cooks as VanNoy was designated to snatch an egg off the cafeteria's long counter.

Once outside the cafeteria, VanNoy handed the egg off to Bryant to tote the 200 yards back to the main school building.

Once inside the building, Whittle and VanNoy met Bryant.

"I've still got the egg," Bryant confirmed to them.

"Okay, since you're left-handed, Bryant, you throw the egg once we're outside study hall," VanNoy plotted.

"Being left-handed means who ever throws the egg doesn't have to reveal their face to the study hall full of students," added Whittle. "It's a natural for a lefty."

Finally, it was time for phase three of the *egg caper*.

Once they stepped stealthily outside study hall, it was up to lefty Bryant to hurl the egg at the precise moment the mathematics teacher Homer Decker stepped in the doorway! Thus, the egg exploded on the top door frame, near Mr. Decker's forehead and proceeded to slowly drip and ooze down to the teacher's face and eyes.

Bryant looked around in dismay, red-faced and left-handed, for moral support, but VanNoy and Whittle were nowhere to be found.

Since Bryant felt no allegiance to those who abandoned him, Bryant spilled his guts about the *egg caper* to Canalou High School Superintendent Van Sharp, a fair but firm school disciplinarian.

"Who all was involved in the *egg caper*?" asked the school administrator.

Once Bryant confessed, VanNoy and Whittle were rounded up and brought to the superintendent's office.

That's when Mr. Sharp launched his full *egg caper* interrogation.

"VanNoy, what was your role in the *egg caper*?" Mr. Sharp questioned *sharply*.

"I snatched the egg," VanNoy confessed.

"Okay, Whittle that leaves you," Sharp continued his probe. "What was your role in the *egg caper*?"

"Sir, I was there in the cafeteria as the egg was being snatched, but, sir, I never touched the egg" Whittle began slowly. "And yes, sir, I saw the egg being toted across the school yard. But again, sir, I never touched the egg.

"And, sir, it's true that I was there when the egg was tossed," Whittle added. "But, sir, as you can see, I saw the egg, but I never touched the egg as it was being lifted out of the cafeteria. And, sir, it's true that I witnessed the egg being toted across the baseball diamond. But again, I never touched the egg. And it's true, I saw the egg being tossed, but, sir, again, I never touched the egg."

"Okay Whittle, since you never touched the egg, you may go," Superintendent Sharp instructed, at which time VanNoy started to leave the superintendent's office too.

"No, Mr. VanNoy, you'll have to stay since you were an accessory," the school official judged firmly.

As my allegedly-innocent, older brother Van Whittle left the office he could hear the noise of the firm and hard application of Mr. Sharp's board of education on the behinds of Bryant and VanNoy.

Finally, at the conclusion of the painful paddling, Bryant and VanNoy were allowed to rejoin Whittle out in the hallway.

"Whittle, you didn't do a dab-burn thing did you boy?!" addressed Bryant heatedly as his face was still red from the pain of the hard paddling.

"You're innocent," added VanNoy sharply to Whittle. "You saw the egg, but you never touched the damn egg."

"You see, since I never touched the egg, I was judged innocent," Whittle said in summation of his innocence.

And that was one of the little school's dramas of mischief, a brief but welcome departure from the melancholy of hard farm work and sometimes dull school classes back in 1955.

Chapter Eighty-Two
School Bus Drivers

Country school bus drivers were important in the fabric of Bootheel life of my youth. One of the best drivers was Walter Wyman.

Being that our farm house sat a mile outside of the official Grayridge district, it was good ol' Mr. Wyman who would fudge a little and drive across Little River, the boundary between New Madrid and Stoddard counties, to keep me from freezing or getting soaked to the bone during inclement weather.

Blessed was I a few years ago when encountering Mr. Wyman the night I was privileged to be guest speaker at the Grayridge and Essex and Richland School reunion held in Dexter.

It was obvious Mr. Wyman has a bear-trap quick mind and memory when he asked: "Danny Whittle, do you remember that long ago day when you asked me to take the long, slowest way to the school house because you were in some kind of trouble?"

"Yes, sir," I replied. "I'll never forget that day for I knew that Superintendent Bob Rasche knew that I, Jerry Kelly, Rueben Jones, and Buddy Scowden had played hooky the day before and that we had an appointment that day with Mr. Rasche's infamous board of education."

I never had a bus driver I didn't like, including my first Mr. George Lefler at tiny Canalou School of advanced thinking and higher ciphering. Mr. Lefler endeared himself to this little farm boy even before I was old enough to climb on that biggo bus and attend school.

Once a week he would stop in front of our house and hand me a sack full of marbles. Marbles were hard-to-come-by, *store-bought* treasures to a poor farm boy.

So Mr. Lefler was already a hero in my eyes before I got to ride on his bus as an official school boy.

How much power did drivers of my youth have? So much so we students judged them as "rolling sheriffs" with absolute authority to enforce discipline and school rules.

Which brings me to driver Earl Eagle-Eye Jones. It's with great pride that it was I who came up with the "Eagle-Eye" title in Mr. Jones' name.

It was a real privilege later in life after I became a newspaperman that I got to interview Mr. Earl "Eagle-Eye" Jones about our shared bus experiences.

I couldn't wait to ask this beloved gentleman how it was that he always seemed to have eyes in the back of his head when it came to catching me in mischief.

"It's simple," Eagle-Eye shared. "When Little Danny Whittle got quiet, I knew to keep an eye on you."

And Mr. Earl Eagle-Eye Jones never missed a trick or caper that I tried to pull on his school bus.

Amen!

Chapter Eighty-Three

From Cotton Field

Bob York, Dick Watkins, Paul Bumbarger, Mike Shain, Paul Harvey, Jackie Robinson, C. L. Blanton Junior, and Charles L. Blanton III—what do these men have in common?

They were media personalities who most inspired my leap from the farm fields of New Madrid County to a forty-plus-year journalism career where I was paid to go around the world, not once but twice, to meet and interview notable people.

The late Paul Harvey, an internationally-known celebrity of actual news gathering, was likely the most intelligent man I have ever interviewed. This was evident when he came to speak at a Sikeston, Missouri, Chamber of Commerce banquet.

It was another man invited to speak at a Chamber banquet who challenged and inspired me, but he was not a news-gathering personality. It was the night former Brooklyn Dodger baseball player Jackie Robinson not only spoke but stood up in front of the podium and courageously criticized the local N. A. A. C. P. leader who had picked him up at the Cape Girardeau Airport in an inebriated condition.

"You are not setting the example our future leaders of America need to see," Mr. Robinson spoke in admonishment of his tipsy host driver of the evening.

Mr. Robinson was internationally-known as the first black man to break the "color" barrier of Major League baseball back in 1948.

The night he spoke in the Bootheel region of Southeast Missouri, he stepped to the forefront of my personal list of heroes, not for baseball, but for being bold and honest enough to chastise his inebriated driver in front of the audience that packed Sikeston's National Guard Armory.

But, it was KSIM Radio personality/newsman Dick Watkins who was my very first news hero. Mr. Watkins was *The Voice of All Things* news that happened in our remote rural America locale. Actually, his radio station's "Story Book Lady" was my "very, very first" media star, but I never met her or knew her real name.

Watkins became a living legend in my boyhood eyes the day that Daddy Whittle, in a surprise move, pulled our farm truck off of Highway 60 into the parking lot of KSIM Radio.

"I'll take you in and let you meet Dick Watkins," offered Daddy Whittle. "And maybe the 'Story Book Lady' too." I was about age four at the time. As fate would have it, Daddy perished two years later when he crashed his car in front of KSIM Radio Station.

Fortunately, during our tour, Mr. Watkins was in and took his *valuable radio celebrity time* to actually tour us around the station. Sadly, we missed the "Story Book Lady."

KSIM was in a tiny building on the highway between Sikeston and Morehouse, but in a little boy's eyes and heart, the station was the window to the outside world away from the dull drudgery of farm work.

So you can imagine how often I pinched myself upon rubbing

shoulders with Mr. Watkins after launching my own news-gathering career at Sikeston's five-day-a-week newspaper formerly known as *The Daily Standard.*

How I began my own news-gathering career was unusual.

When honored to be asked to speak now at universities and high schools, one of the favorite stories that students always want to hear is the way I began my "professional journalism career"

Actually, it was two Sikeston businessmen named Earl (both now deceased) who initially helped launch me in the direction of news papering.

First there was Earl Jarvis, owner of Jarvis Motor Company, for whom I was privileged to work for as a seventeen-year-old car salesman. How good at car sales was I? So good that I sold *one* used car in six months' time and lost Mr. Jarvis $300 on the deal. It was at this point that Mr. Jarvis called me into his office and began the conversation thusly: "Danny Whittle, a hard worker you are—you've tried hard—but a car salesman, you are not."

Although he was firing me, he was nice about it so nice that he offered to give me a good reference in future job hunting.

Enter Earl Ferrell, the former manager of a drive-in theater north of Sikeston who liked to deal and view automobiles on Mr. Jarvis' car lot.

"I've heard about this fantastic janitor's job down at the local newspaper office," Mr. Ferrell directed me one morning after hearing I had been terminated. "Maybe you could get the job."

Being that I had on my best starched-and-ironed blue jeans and my one and only black narrow string tie that day, I hot-footed it at noon to the local newspaper office. But upon entering the newspaper, I saw that the usual protective group of secretaries in the outer office were out.

But I heard movement over in a side office.

Upon knocking on that office door, I was greeted by two men named Blanton.

It startled me when the senior Mr. Blanton, who was publisher of the newspaper, asked in his booming gruff voice: "Can I help you sonny?"

I said: "Yes, sir. I'm here for that job."

"Come on in, and we'll talk about it," offered the publisher's son, Charles L. Blanton III.

As I was headed to a chair, one of them asked: "Can you type?"

Which amazed me, for I remember thinking, *Man, that must be a classy janitor's job, having to know a little typing.*

And as I was being seated, I remember replying proudly: "Sir, I'm up to seventeen words a minute." Now I know that is really slow in typing skills, but then, for a teenage farm boy, seventeen words a minute was pretty doggone fast compared to the other hairy-legged farm boys in my little school who had also taken typing.

But it was the next question that totally surprised me, and ultimately changed my course in life. "How long have you wanted to write sports?" the eldest Mr. Blanton asked.

I think I swallowed once, maybe blinked twice, and then lied like a dog.

"All my life," I responded.

Later, after they hired me as an untrained sports writer, one of the Blantons advised, they had hired me because of my audacity and voracity. I thought they might be cursing me, so I had to go look those two big words up.

Enter newspaper editors Paul Bumbarger and Bob York into my life. If not for the patience of these proven seasoned professionals of news gathering, I would not have survived that first tough year breaking into news writing.

How inexperienced was I? The first football game I ever saw I was covering for the newspaper. Since Canalou and Grayridge, Missouri, schools weren't big enough to have football teams, I'd never witnessed a pigskin game. Oh, I knew what a quarterback was because they were the players reputed to get all the pretty girls.

In that era, the mighty Sikeston Bulldogs regularly reigned high in the ranks of Southeast Missouri football schools under the tutelage of coaches Bill Sapp and Norman Lambert. This was before Norman became rich and nationally-known for his throwed rolls at Lambert's Café in Sikeston.

It was Mr. York who took a personal interest in the way I approached newsmakers with this sage bit of advice: "We primarily cover two types of people, crooks and politicians, and sometimes there's no difference in the two."

Mr. York literally stayed in the news-gathering saddle well into his eighties. Even then he could gather more news than anyone I've ever worked shoulder-to-shoulder with.

How long had Mr. York been gathering news? So long *legend* has it that he had covered the Indian wars out west, during which, in one skirmish between Native Americans and the U. S. Army, an errant arrow knocked the hat off his head.

The day in the mid-1960s that Mr. York keeled over at his desk with a stroke remains permanently etched in my soul. Remember, I was just *a young kid reporter* among the older, more mature dozens of employees who worked at *The Daily Standard*. As Mr. York fell across his desk, he instructed the newsroom staff to "go get Danny Whittle. . . he'll know what to do."

I followed the ambulance from the newspaper office to the hospital in Sikeston. After being there in the emergency room for a few moments, Mr. York looked up at me and stated gruffly: "You need to get your butt back to the newspaper, and finish putting the paper to bed." I did as he instructed.

One of my first big, but upsetting, personal honors was to be asked to be one of the pallbearers at Mr. York's subsequent funeral.

Later in life, it was Mr. Bumbarger, with his tough editing pencil, who taught me I could not write in the same vernacular that I had grown up using back in my little farming home town.

"Whittle, the wreck north of New Madrid didn't happen as 'the car was fixing to turn left'," Mr. Bumbarger yelled out across the newsroom. "You have to use words precisely in their true meanings when you write news stories. You can't write news stories like you talked back at Canalou."

Mr. Bumbarger also taught *high* ethics that goes into truly fair and balanced journalism, not to be confused with the type of news reporting, or shouting, that is on American television today. He was the first editor to break down the true meaning of the word ASSUME to me.

It occurred one morning on deadline when Mr. Bumbarger questioned the accuracy of one of my stories. To which I replied that I "assumed" that my information was accurate.

"Whittle, as a reporter, when you ASSUME anything in news gathering, it generally makes an 'ass' out of 'u' and 'me,' the editor," Mr. Bumbarger instructed firmly.

What truly helped get me through the earliest days of news writing, more than anything, was the fact that as a school boy, I had always read anything I could get my hands on, which served me well when I was given my *big break* to get into newspapering. That and a good, strong work ethic taught by Momma and Daddy Whittle and my older brother and sister, H. Van and June.

Plus, I got out old newspaper files and mimicked well-written news and sports stories by former *Daily Standard* sports editor Barney Dubois and *St. Louis Globe-Democrat* sports scribe Jack Herman.

I grew up a lot in those first fledgling years of news gathering. My primary competition coming from former KSIM Radio News Director was Mike Shain, who went on to higher news-gathering fame when he became the now legendary anchoring news director at prestigious KFVS-TV station in Cape Girardeau. He is now retired.

Shain and I, although we worked in a small-town news market, broke some important stories, including the time a Scott County tax collector was put out of office because of irregularities in the way accounting for tax dollars. Our investigative reporting helped expose this problem at the Scott County Courthouse in Benton, Missouri.

Probably our most infamous story was the mid-1960s murder

of Mrs. William Lewis, a prominent Sikeston lady, by a young kid named Tommy Thompson. We regularly dealt with highly professional law enforcement people such as Sikeston Police Chief Arthur Bruce and Scott County Sheriff John Dennis, both now deceased.

Although we were highly-competitive, Mike and I became close friends, along with his wife, Doris, who cooked some of the best tacos I've ever laid lips around.

I also worked briefly on newspapers in Cape Girardeau and Poplar Bluff before leaving the Bootheel in the early 1970s to become a feature writer for *The Nashville Banner,* one of the most prestigious afternoon newspapers in Tennessee.

I wrapped up my newspapering career in June 2006, serving my last twenty years as a columnist and feature writer for the *Daily News Journal* in Murfreesboro, Tennessee.

It was there that I made a bit of history by being the first journalist in state newspaper history to accompany the Tennessee Air National Guard into an active war zone, the ethnic-cleansing genocidal war in Bosnia.

I also helped break the news during the early 1990s about the deplorable plight of state-run orphanages in the former communist bloc country of Romania. In the going and covering of life in foreign countries, I learned to appreciate how blessed we have it in the good, old United States of America.

For only in America could a farm boy walk into a newspaper office applying for a janitor's job and come out as a news writer, thus launching a career that let me interview remarkable people around the globe.

And for certain, having a news-gathering career *beat the hell* out of chopping and picking cotton back in Canalou.

Chapter Eighty-Four

Race Relations

Let's talk black and white here.

Bigotry is a subject folks don't like thinking about, but it was part of the fabric of life in the Bootheel region's culture of southeast Missouri where I grew up in the 1940s and 1950s.

A lot of Americans don't realize Missouri has Deep South Delta-style farming country along the Mississippi River, much like that in Mississippi. And we had social morals similar to the Deep South's culture.

Was I reared a racial bigot?

Yes.

Did I know I was a bigot as a boy?

No, for our elders taught us that was the way things were ordered to be.

Some Southern Baptist preachers used Bible verses telling us the races were not equal and should not mix.

My first paid job off the farm was to take half-pint bottles of bonded bourbon out to cotton fields during elections. I remember my first encounter with an elderly black gentleman cotton chopper.

"You wanna go vote?" I asked.

"Naw, sirrrr," the field worker replied slowly, never ending the rhythm of his cotton hoe as it chopped through careless weeds, cockle burs, and morning glory vines.

With that I pulled up a half-pint of cheap whiskey out of my front overall chest pocket, making it visible to the gentleman with the long-handled cotton hoe.

"Do you wanna go vote?" I asked again.

"Yes, sirrr," he replied as he went to load on the back of a large flat-bed, grain-hauling truck that was used to haul voters in New Madrid County in the 1940s and early 1950s. The trucks didn't just go to one voting precinct; they were hauling black folks to vote repeatedly at places like Canalou, Lilbourn, Parma, and Catron. And I don't recall hearing any farmer complain about their field workers being taken out of the field to go vote during election years.

I didn't realize as a little boy that I was part, albeit a minor part, of a very strong and effective New Madrid County political machine ran by Democrat political boss J. V. Conran in the first half of last century.

Although a mere child, was I wrong to hand out illegal whiskey to poor black field workers?

Yes, but I didn't know I was wrong since I witnessed white neighbor adults whom I respected do the same in previous elections. In fact, it was one of our family's nearest neighbor men who drove me around to cotton fields in the region surrounding Canalou, Charter Oak, Lavalle, and Hill's Store during my first paid job off the farm.

My second memorable boyhood experience with racial matters came at John Summers' Theater during the fall of 1953 when Mexican laborers poured into the Bootheel to make money by picking and harvesting cotton on small farms that dotted the region.

Older brother H. Van Whittle's first non-farming employment came as a ticket taker in the theater's balcony where black folks sat segregated from white folks.

On this one particularly busy night at the theater, brother seemed very nervous when he got into the farm truck for Momma Whittle to drive us home after completion of the singing cowboy western moving picture show on the silver screen.

When asked by Mom what was wrong, Van replied that there had been a knife fight in the balcony that night between some black men and Mexican folks.

"The black folks and Mexicans don't like one another, and they got into a fight," Van answered our mother.

Mother made certain that was the last night brother served as a ticket taker up in the balcony. Shortly thereafter theater management decided it was safer for Mexican laborers to move down into the lower auditorium to view the movies with the white folks. It worked for I recall no fights breaking out in the theater after that move.

Although I never saw a sign posted to this effect, I was told by my community elders that Canalou had an unspoken, but strictly-enforced code in the 1920s, 1930s, and 1940s: No Niggers in Town After Sun Down.

But when the movie theater was built in the early 1940s, that rule must have disappeared for I don't recall black people not being allowed to spend money to attend the movie, although they were segregated in the balcony.

There was only one black resident in the history of Canalou, and she served as a house maid for wealthy merchant W. M. Moore, who had the biggest grocery/mercantile business in Canalou leading into the mid-1950s. The only time I recall seeing this quiet lady was when she'd come to the post office to get mail from postal workers Don Kochel his wife, Vera, and Jean Summers, wife of the theater owner.

There was one other notable racial incident that occurred during my childhood at Canalou, and that was when a grocery merchant got into debate with a black cotton chopper over which farmer had the first cotton bloom.

I remember meeting this black man when he was hired to chop weeds out of our cotton fields. I recall Momma Whittle crediting him with being the fastest cotton chopper she'd ever witnessed. I never met anyone in Canalou who knew the man's last name. He was never seen in our part of the country again after being shot multiple times in his legs and buttocks by merchant Tootie Ralph.

Did maturity change my outlook toward folks of other races? Yes, but not before I made some serious social and moral mistakes having to do with race.

Incidents happened after integration occurred at Grayridge High School, now known as Richland High School after consolidation with Essex High School in the early 1960s.

It was in a third period art class, which I took only because my heart throb, Gwendolyn Zuba, was in the class, that a short, black male student reportedly insulted Phyllis Winstead, little sister to Teddy Winstead and a classmate buddy of mine. Upon hearing that and looking over at the accused, who was sneering at Phyllis, I motioned for him to meet me in the back of the room. He acted more than happy to do so. Thankfully, some girls warned the teacher that there was about to be a fight, and she stopped the confrontation. This teacher and students who warned her about an impending fight may have saved my life, for I learned later the fellow student was brandishing a knife.

But that wasn't the end of it, not by a long shot. After eating lunch at Maggie Pennington's Café, which was a popular eatery located just off Grayridge school grounds, pal Jerry Kelly and I returned to the halls of the high school where this little guy, about my own size and height, and his sister were waiting on me.

There was also a small crowd of other black students gathering in the hall as the other student, his sister, and I moved our differences out to the front school yard there at the foot of the school flag pole. I recall all three of us loudly cursing and threatening one another. His sister was holding a big rock in her hand and this time I saw the switchblade knife come out of her brother's pocket.

Unbeknownst to me, my pal Jerry Kelly (now deceased) was holding the school's front door closed, thus keeping the other black students from joining in on the heated discussion and confrontation going on out in the school yard. Kelly's actions might have saved a full-scale riot from breaking out.

But as we were circling, about to go toe-to-toe, thankfully Superintendent of Schools Robert L. Rasche stepped on the scene and broke up the confrontation. What a relief, for I was really scared but didn't want that to show, you know, the male-pride-being-scared syndrome.

And upon coming back to school the next day, which gave us all time to cool down a bit, Mr. Rasche called me and the other would-be combatant to the office.

Instead of paddling us, Mr. Rasche, being the brilliant educator that he was, used diplomacy, although I didn't know what "diplomacy" meant at that time.

"You will meet here at school and get along," Mr. Rasche instructed.

To which I replied smart-aleck like: "I'll meet them halfway."

To which Mr. Rasche replied emphatically: "You'll meet them all the way!!"

I knew to keep my mouth shut from that point on after Mr. Rasche spoke.

As far as I know, there were no similar confrontations between whites and blacks that first year of our school integration. There were no other words exchanged between me and my would-be combatant, although we'd glare at one another from time-to-time when meeting in the hall.

I can't say that there weren't other dramatic incidents that began my personal heart-felt change in attitudes toward folks of different skin color, but it began happening for real after Mr. Rasche gave us his stern long-lasting talk. I really respected Mr. Rasche.

By the mid-1960s, TV, radio, and newspapers were bringing news reports of race riots happening in places such as Little Rock, Birmingham, and Philadelphia into our Bootheel homes. By the time I got my first sports writing job in the mid-1960s at *The Daily Standard* newspaper in Sikeston, Missouri, restaurants and dime store lunch counters across America were being forced by newly-enforced federal laws to permit black people to dine on the premises.

I recall discussions were held in the newsroom that we might have to cover possible racial confrontations such as at Sikeston's Little Man Lambert's Café when and if it was integrated. Fortunately, there was no incident to cover when first black people entered this legendary landmark business in Sikeston.

Although only a sports writer at the time and not covering what we called hard news, I had a clear understanding of my newspaper management's position regarding racial news.

"We don't put nigger news on our front page," I heard Standard Publisher C. L. Blanton Jr. repeatedly instruct newsroom editors Paul Bumbarger and Bob York during my earliest newspapering days at *The Daily Standard*. "It only promotes their protests."

When I filled in as editor in the absence of my first two mentor editors, I, too, received that direct order from Mr. Blanton.

I personally felt the sting of our society's racial bigotry as a sportswriter while starting my writing career in Sikeston, when I asked in my Whittle Sports' Shavings personal column how Howardville High, an all-black school, could not be a seeded team in the annual New Madrid County basketball tournament being held in Risco, Missouri.

If recollection serves accurately, Howardville had won more than twenty games during that winter's basketball season and had beaten several higher tournament-seeded teams from all-white schools during the season leading up to the tournament. Not being seeded first, second, third, or fourth meant Howardville had to face the best of the best teams early in order to have a chance at winning the tournament championship.

I remember dreading going to Risco to cover the tournament after my column came out. And not surprisingly, I was met at the gymnasium front door by one of the white New Madrid County school superintendents, who told me in no uncertain terms that I had been wrong in questioning the non-seeding of the black high school.

"You don't need to be meddling in our black folks' business down here," I recall the superintendent's words clearly.

Did I do the right thing? I think so.

Do I condemn myself today or other folks of my childhood era for our bigotry? No, for our elders taught us that was the way it was supposed to be. And we were taught to listen to our elders. But today, as a famous song writer once warbled, "Times Are a Changin'," since for the first time in American history, a black man has been elected U. S. President.

While at the *Standard*, I covered two race riots my first and my last over in nearby Cairo, Illinois. Although I knew none of my coverage would make it in the *Standard*'s news columns, the *Associated Press* news bureau out of St. Louis had asked if I would go on a Sunday to Cairo where there had been dangerous rioting, looting, and shots fired throughout the past week. Most of this activity had been taking place at night in protest of a young black man's death while jailed in Cairo for an alleged crime.

I recall being asked by another newspaperman covering the riot whether I was "packing heat." I told him no. We then decided to work together because of personal safety concerns, although I never knew his name or his newspaper.

These riots, in one Dan's opinion, virtually destroyed the downtown economic commerce of Cairo, a former economically-vibrant little riverfront city.

It was there I first met the Reverend Jesse Jackson, who was just coming on the national stage of the 1960s civil rights movement. I recall taking a photograph of Jackson as he led a march through downtown Cairo that now long ago Sunday afternoon.

Three things struck me in wake of covering my first and last race riot. One is that when you get a mass of people, you get a mess, socially speaking. Two in retrospect I've wondered the wisdom of that particular riot because it virtually destroyed the little river city's business district and jobs, both in the present and future. Three it was terrifying being a white guy among all those angry black folks who marched behind Reverend Jackson.

Was Cairo racially divided in that era? Yes. But was it wise to cause the shutdown of businesses, which resulted in a severe loss of jobs in the little river city? Judging from the number of still-closed businesses I see when driving through Cairo today, the city appears to still be economically reeling from those long-ago riots.

A most remarkable incident of racial overtones at *The Daily Standard* newspaper didn't happen until after I left Sikeston to work for a newspaper in nearby Poplar Bluff.

I remember motoring into the parking lot of the Holiday Inn in Poplar Bluff one afternoon when a news bulletin came over the radio that American civil rights leader, the Reverend Martin Luther King, had been assassinated in Memphis, Tennessee. In more ways than one, 1968 was a terribly distraught year in America and the world, especially after Robert F. Kennedy was assassinated later that year.

I recall feeling fear and being personally distraught, for at that time more civil unrest had begun fermenting after approximately 26,000 Americans had already been killed in Vietnam's civil war.

I feared full-scale civil war in America was about to break out at the time. That war, which was eventually escalated by Presidents Richard Nixon and Lyndon Johnson, ended up claiming the lives of more than 56,000 Americans. It reminds me also of America's invasion of Iraq following the September 11, 2001 terrorist attack.

Combined with civil unrest among the races, 1968 was a dangerous time to be a newspaperman.

It was early the next morning after MLK's murder at Memphis' Lorraine Hotel that my newspaper office phone rang in Poplar Bluff. It was a frantic call from Charles L. Blanton III, the son of *Daily Standard* Publisher Charles Blanton Junior.

"Can your paper print our paper in case we're burned out?!!" asked Charles Blanton III excitedly.

"What's going on?" I asked.

"We didn't carry the news of MLK's assassination on the front page, and they're marching in front of our offices as I speak."

Charles Blanton III advised with obvious distress in his voice. "I'm afraid they're going to burn us out."

After assuring my former boss that our paper's press could accommodate his paper in case his office was destroyed by angry protestors, I learned later that the news of MLK's death had been placed in a brief on an inside news page as the *Standard* editor on duty followed management's standing order of "no black news" on the front page. And the black citizens of Sikeston were angry and upset.

As it turned out, the newspaper office in Sikeston was not torched and the newspaper continues today in the same plant but under different ownership.

I will always be grateful for the newspaper-publishing Blantons, including Charles Blanton Junior, Charles Blanton III, and Allen Blanton, for giving this country boy from Canalou with no formal college training in journalism the opportunity to be a professional newspaperman. Special thanks also go to my earliest *Standard* editors, the late Paul Bumbarger and Bob York, for their belief that one day I could measure up to their standards.

Sikeston resident Allen Blanton, who was part of the Blanton newspaper management and son of Charles Blanton Junior, about the newspaper's former racial policy: "Young people today might not understand the way it was back then regarding the races, but, yes, that was our newspaper's policy in that era. It was that way at some other newspapers in that era too."

My forty-plus years of gathering news and meeting wonderful, courageous people of all colors, nationalities, and creeds around the world has been a wonderful, educational journey.

May the good Lord help us all be more civil and courteous to one another as we enter a new era as America has its first black president.

Chapter Eighty-Five

Major Hooper Penuel Pens Memories with Whittle

It was the first time in Tennessee Guard history that media actually accompanied professional citizen soldiers into an active combat zone. We received excellent coverage from everyone, especially from foreign war correspondent Danny Dale Whittle, a columnist with *The Daily News Journal* in Murfreesboro, Tennessee.

Long may these observations live, which I'm calling "Whittleisms."

When asked to take the assignment in Europe, Whittle, being from tiny remote Canalou, Missouri, had to ask: "Where's Bosnia?"

Being from Canulu, uhg, I'm sorry, Canalou, it was hard for him to grasp a location in Europe since he'd only been "out of the country" one time, and that was to attend a St. Louis Cardinal baseball game as a boy.

During the eleven-hour flight over the Atlantic in our fleet of C-130s Hercules, we were instructed to insert small rubber sponges in our ears to protect us from the deafening sounds of the big plane engines. Whittle must not have heard the instruction, for he thought it was bubble gum.

Once on the ground, Whittle never missed an opportunity to boast about being from his little hometown back in Missouri. That was evidenced in Frankfurt, Germany where Whittle was asked about his education by a high-ranking Air Force officer.

"Sir, I went to the College of Canalou Tech Higher Institute of Matriculation," responded Whittle, who subsequently had a tough time explaining details and location of "Canalou Tech."

Whittle's sense of humor was spread across Europe.

During these dangerous flights in and out of Croatia and Bosnia, not to mention touchdowns in Nova Scotia, Germany and Italy, Whittle convinced folks in all five countries that he was a famous TV evangelist from Canalou when not working as a foreign war correspondent. We were glad he left his sermons at home.

During our most dangerous mission, which came in Sarajevo, Bosnia, where our aircraft was hit multiple times by Serbian ground fire, Whittle decided to promote his boyhood hometown by attaching "Canalou" and "Tennessee" T-shirts to food and medicine parcels going out to starving and wounded civil war refugees.

I still wouldn't be surprised to see one of those Canalou T-shirts on CNN.

Before our flights into combat zones in Sarajevo and other areas of Bosnia, we were issued flak jackets and Kevlar helmets for protection against possible enemy fire.

Well, Whittle, the wonder boy from Canalou, knew what to do with his flak jacket. Lo and behold, we found him sitting on not one, but two flak jackets.

When asked for an explanation, Whittle replied thusly: "The Serbs don't have an air force... they're shooting from the ground up at our relief-flying planes. So in case I want to have a family one day, well, I'm sitting on my flak jackets... you know, protecting the family jewels...."

We took that to be some Canalou-inspired, down-to-earth country boy logic Whittle-style.

Aside from all the Whittleisms and his Canalou colloquialisms,

I can say truthfully that I don't know when I have seen our troops bond together with the media as they did on these dangerous flights in and out of Bosnian war zones.

Dan was able to gain the respect and trust of all the soldiers as they joked and carried on our global relief missions. His subsequent eight-article series of stories back in Tennessee reflects his character and ability to get to the heart of wartime stories. And I think Dan gained a lot of respect for our dedicated, highly-trained and brave Air National Guard citizen-soldiers.

As a public information officer, I observed that while Whittle doesn't take himself too seriously, he takes his news-writing responsibilities very serious. . . traits I'd say he learned back in his beloved little hometown of Canulu. . . ugh. . . . Sorry Whittle, C-a-n-a-l-o-u, Missouri.

ABOUT THE AUTHOR: It was 1993 when author Dan Whittle made history as a foreign war correspondent in Bosnia-Herzegovina. This story was written about the author by retired Guard Major Hooper Penuel, who accompanied Canalou, Missouri, native Whittle and other media professionals into Bosnia while the Tennessee Air National Guard's 118th Airlift Wing flew medical and food relief missions to war refugees. Whittle retired as an active newspaperman in 2006.

By Major Hooper Panuel

Chief Tennessee Guard Public Information Officer

Index

A

Abernathy, Frances 87, 90, 222, 223, 224, 234, 238, 245, 265
Abernathy, Kenneth 238
Abernathy, R. L. 141, 225, 238
Adams, Chick 265
Adams, Grant 22, 241, 247, 265
Adams, Hazel 239, 265
Adams, Maude 265
Adkerson, Jackie Marion Gunter 317, 335
Aide, Michael 377
Alexander, Donald 373
Allen, Elisha 52, 53, 54, 315
Allen, Leslie 12, 50, 53, 60, 242
Arbuckle, Coela 34, 74, 136
Arbuckle, Floy Mae. *See* Jones, Floy Mae Arbuckle
Arbuckle, Grandmother 309, 310, 311
Arbuckle, Johnny 76, 370, 371
Arbuckle, L. L. 75, 302, 303, 309, 374
Arbuckle, Norma. *See* Busby, Norma
Arnold, Grady 387
Arnold, Perry 85

Asa, Charles 136, 292
Asa, G. A. 86
Astaire, Fred 295
Autry, Gene 293

B

Badgley, Ed 86
Bailey, Herbert 161, 335
Bailey, Ivarene 161
Bailey, Larry 162, 336
Baker, J. Val 85
Baker, Tom 193
Bane, Gladys 313
Barber, Bob 373
Barnes, Earlyne 373
Barnett, Carolyn 373
Barnett, Ott 301
Barnham, Catherine 35
Bell, Harold E. 350
Berkbigler, Maxine Harrison Sittner 238
Bishop, Elmer 223
Bishop, Evelyn 223, 226
Bishop, J. E. 223, 226
Bishop, Mae 223
Bishop, Mutt 223, 226
Bishop, Odell 223, 226

Bishop, Opal 226
Bixler, Addie 89
Bixler, Annette 138, 229, 318
Bixler, Charles Lee 138
Bixler, Cordell 140, 392
Bixler, Gary 143, 392
Bixler, Grandmother 142
Bixler, Harley 318
Bixler, Melton 36, 141, 142, 229, 242, 392, 395
Bixler, Patsy 124, 125, 126, 127, 129, 130, 131, 133, 291, 292, 295, 335, 348, 349
Bixler, Roy 141, 158, 229, 243, 245
Bixler, Shirley 138, 229, 318
Bixler, Sue 87, 90, 138, 187, 229, 243, 245, 246, 296, 395
Bixler, Ted 393
Blankenship, Benny 253
Blankenship, Conliff 36, 290
Blankenship, David 289, 291
Blankenship, Junior 265
Blankenship, Ruby Lucy 290
Blanton, Allen 416
Blanton, David 171
Blanton III, Charles 415, 416
Blanton Junior, Charles 413, 416
Blanton Senior, Charley 95
Bogart, Humphrey 295
Bolin, J. H. 86
Bond, Hubert 80, 135, 163, 247
Bond, Virginia 133
Boone, Dr. 298
Boutz, Bonnie Blankenship 290, 335
Bowers, Bernice 372
Boyer, Charles 295
Boyes, Arcile Haywood 12, 13, 288
Bramlett, Lavern 161
Bramlett, Mary Jane 169
Bramlett, Waddell 161
Bratch, Kenneth 373
Briney, R. Kip 86
Brooks, Omar 373
Brothers, Croom 36

Brower, Ann 117
Brower, Betty Jo 117
Brown, Cooter 380
Brown, Paul M. 121
Brumley, Jim 233
Bryant, Bob 71
Bryant, Bruce Gene 171, 383, 396, 397
Bryant, Dick 71, 242
Bryant, Harold David 107, 159, 176, 296, 337, 357
Bryant, Jane Hicks 71
Bryant, Yvoin 88
Buck Junior, John 297, 298, 299
Buck, Kelly 298
Buck, Pat 298
Buck, Renda Chaney 111, 151, 297, 299, 304, 369
Buck Senior, John 111, 297, 299, 303, 304, 384, 388, 395
Bumbarger, Paul 277, 401, 404, 405, 406, 416
Burris, Bill 253
Burris, George 252
Burris, Tommy 255
Burris, William "Bill" 255
Busby, Daryl Gene 75
Busby, Norma 74, 75
Butler, Billy 35

C

Cagney, James 295
Campbell, Ellen 109, 110, 296, 360
Campbell, Jeanie 111
Campbell, Lee Joe 110, 233
Canoy, Betty 375
Canoy, Mary 375
Canoy, Wanda 375
Carey, Harry 344
Cashion, Wayne 373
Cash, Johnny 216
Cash, June Carter 216, 218, 221
Cathy, H. G. 223, 240, 247, 312
Chaney, Faye 127, 369
Chaney, Harry 11, 131, 142, 151, 153, 154, 155, 229, 240, 369

Chaney, Harry Joe 151, 384, 388
Chaney, Jewel 140
Chaney, John 151
Chaney, Matt 362
Chapman, Larry 366
Clark, Bennett 96
Cole, George P. 70
Coleman, Dewayne 74
Coleman, Ed 95
Colston, Sally 12
Conn, Charley 243
Conn, J. B. 81, 241, 243
Conrad, Mr. 371
Conran, J. V. 91, 93, 94, 95, 96, 122, 300, 302, 303, 335, 337, 409
Conran, Susan Robbins 93
Cooper, Authur 86
Coppage, James 365
Coppage, Phil 242
Cox, El Freda 68
Cox, Thomas J. 388
Crafford, Mike 321, 322, 324
Craig, Ashley 365
Crouthers, Paul 143, 392

D

David, Harold 88
David, Michael. *See* Parkes, Michael
Davidson, Earl 230
Davidson, Larry 65, 386
Davis, Josh 240
Davis, Milas R. 263
Davis, Mrs. 263
Dean, Louis 242, 247
Decker, Homer 373
Denbow, Doyle 365, 366, 387
Dennis, John 407
Dickerson, Bobby 366
Dorris, E.P. 86
Dowdy, Ray 151
Drake, G. D. 229, 257
Drake, Gene 242, 247
Drake, Gladys Johns 87, 241, 242, 244, 245, 260, 314
Drake, Grover 241, 242, 265

Drake, Helen 89
Drake, Iris Blankenship 246
Drake, Larry 229, 242, 260, 314
Drake, Marvin 240, 247
Dubois, Barney 364
Duckworth, Carroll 373
Durbin, Kirky 107, 296, 357
Durbin, Les 155, 156, 244
Dwight, Bill 22

E

Eagleton, Thomas 96
East, Shade 242
Engram, George Allen 42, 43
Engram, John Anderson 39, 40, 41, 42
Engram, John Coleman 41, 44
Engram, Joseph Allen 43
Engram, Joy. *See* Whitten, Joy
Engram, Mabel. *See* Winters, Mabel Engram
Engram, Minnie 41
Engram, Nat 40
Engram, Ora. *See* Summers, Ora Engram
Ernest, Norman 51
Evans, E. E. 373
Evans, Elmer 242
Evans, Grady 35
Evans, Opal 396

F

Ferrell, Earl 403
Ford, Bob 17
Frala, Lois 372
Frank, Wilson 86
Frizzell, Dan 194
Fuchs, J. R. 92, 96

G

Geise, Larry 373
Gene, Bruce 88
Geske, Dale 229, 242
Gilmore, Durward W. 94
Gilmore, Ernest G. 94
Goins, Bobby 375

Golightly, James 40, 41
Gowen, Marion 180
Gowen, Myrtle Delemma 89, 165, 166, 178, 179, 219, 268, 322, 356
Gowen, Poppy 219, 359
Goza, Gail 373
Grable, Betty 295
Granny Robinson. *See* Robinson, Caroline
Gray, Bob 364
Greenlee, Carles 79, 81
Greenlee, Curtis 78
Greenlee, Homer 81
Greenlee, Kirby 81
Greenlee, Leonard 81
Greenlee, May 81
Greenlee, Sherm 77, 78, 79, 80, 81, 82, 83
Greer, Billie Margaret 107, 114, 354, 360, 361, 370, 373
Greer, Elmer 310
Greer, Emmitt 80, 136, 311
Grimes, Rose Marie 375
Grimsley, Weldon 277
Gromer, Stella May 372
Gruen, Elmer 36, 242
Gruen, Floy Mae Arbuckle Jones 242
Grunt, Granny 250, 267, 269, 270, 271
Gunter, Jack 323
Gunter, Jackie Marion 166, 323, 324
Gunter, Monte 323

H

Hammock, Aimee 63, 326
Hammock, Donald 63, 240
Hammock, Doug 240
Hammock, V. E. 63, 240
Hann, Mary 373
Harkey, Leo 278
Harlan, Brenda 276, 296, 355, 360
Harlan, Ed 72
Harlan, Frank 72
Harlan, H. H. 360, 373
Harlan, Lee 72
Harper, Brenda Gayle 117
Harper, Judge Roy W. 91, 92, 93, 94, 95, 96, 122
Harper, Nancy 122
Harper, Rodney 91
Harris, Fred 36
Harris, Larry 389, 390, 391
Harrison, Charley 239
Harrison, Marguerite 51, 199, 279, 294, 315
Harrison, Mary 239
Harrison, Maxine 81, 161, 199
Harrison, Norman Ernest 293, 294, 295, 318, 384, 388
Harrison, Norval 160, 161, 199, 242, 294, 301, 315, 382
Harry, Chaney 152
Hartly, Lin 69, 70
Harvey, Paul 401
Hawkins, Charles 144, 146, 150
Hayden, W. T. 86
Haywood, Arcile. *See* Boyes, Arcile Haywood
Haywood, Dado 200
Haywood, Herman 12, 288
Haywood, Mr. 242
Haywood, Mrs. 242
Haywood, V. E. 242
Hayworth, Rita 295
Hearnes, Warren E. 96
Henry, Carmen 118
Herman, Jack 344, 406
Herrod, Gene 366
Hewitt, Nathaniel 244, 314, 317
Hewitt, Patsy 375
Hewitt, Ronnie 318, 375
Hewitt, Sandra 373
Hickey, Jimmy 349
Hicks, Dee Wayne 71
Hicks, Jane Bryant 70
Higgins, Walter 24
Hill, Hubert 65
Hill, Sandra 296, 360
Hilton, George Washington 78, 80
Hilton, May 77
Hilton, Virginia Dismuke 78

Hindrum, Sherman 119
Holman, Haskell 96
Hopper, Betty 133
Hopper, Fay 131
Hopper, James William Jay 124, 125, 129, 131, 155, 158, 229, 348
Hopper, Johnny 133
Hopper, Mary 124, 125, 126, 127, 129, 131
Hopper, Patsy 81
Hopper, Rosemary 133, 296, 355, 356, 360
Houck, Louis 7, 11, 21, 68, 84, 141, 241
Hoyt, Levi 86
Hunter, Jerry 394
Hunter, Jimmy 375

J

Jablonski, Jabbo 343
Jackson, Jack 239
James, Frank 17
James, Jesse 17
Jarvis, Earl 403
Joe, Lee 234
Johns, Gladys 296
Johnson, Gale 244
Johnson, Gay 78, 138
Johnson, Jerry 78
Johnson, Kenneth 265
Johnson, Neil M. 94
Johnson, Offie 78, 138
Johnson, Roy 36, 78, 138, 229, 242
Jones, Alva 59, 75, 84, 134, 136, 138, 245, 246, 303, 309, 310, 311, 312, 317, 319, 364, 374, 384, 387, 394
Jones, Arlyn 134, 138, 311
Jones, Earl 383
Jones, Esta Scott 137
Jones, Floy Mae Arbuckle 34, 35, 36, 37, 59, 137, 319
Jones, John Alva 138
Jones, Rueben 373
Joyce, Charles 289

Judge Cavanaugh 78

K

Keller, Mr. 372
Kellum, Mr. 117
Kelly, Gene 295
Kelly, Jerry 373
King, Larry 373
Kirkpatrick, James C. 96
Knuckles, Virgil 279
Kochel, Don 88, 131, 219, 319, 361, 410
Kochel, Vera 89, 170, 319, 361, 410
Kochtitsky, Otto 12
Kreps, Dan 9, 10, 20, 21, 24, 74

L

Lambert, Norman 405
Landers, Abe 137, 154, 242
Landers, Bill 243
Landers, Gube 140
Landers, Helen 228, 230, 318
Landers, Jean 375
Landers, Judy 350
Landers Junior, Abe 55, 285, 349, 350
Landers, Leslie 11, 12, 47, 50, 53, 54, 60, 61, 69, 135, 137, 201, 237, 243, 285, 286, 289, 315, 317, 318, 319, 349, 350, 351, 374, 375, 376
Landers, Louise 89
Landers, Mae 89
Landers, Mary Scott 137
Landers, Raymond 349
Landers Senior, Abraham 12, 54, 60, 61
Landers, Sharon 375
Landers, Trudy 375
Landers, Willie 243, 286, 349, 350, 351, 352
Lasters, Ailene 89
Lasters, Dale 350
Lasters, Kenny 318
Latham, Bert 36, 141, 142, 144,

146, 147, 150, 242
Latham, Irene 150
Latham, Margie 146, 150
Launius, John 305, 363, 364, 368
Launius, Ronnie Carl 43, 305, 363, 364, 365, 367, 368
Lawson, Larry 318, 375, 384, 388
Lawson, Linda 318
Lawson, Lonny 36, 144, 188, 318, 391
Lefler, George 200, 359
L. E. Weaks 98
Lewis, Bertha 121
Lewis, Brenda Gayle Harper 91, 92
Lewis, Dub 302
Lewis, Garry 91, 116, 117, 118, 119, 120, 121, 122, 302
Lewis, Gayle Harper 116
Lewis, George 121
Lewis, Henry Lee 120
Lewis, Melissa Kay 120
Lewis, William 117, 120, 407
Ling, Edwin 282
Linge, Elmer 86
Ling, John 158, 249
London, Jack 243, 293
Long, Linda 117
Lowery, Bob 243
Lumsden, Nelson 36, 141, 142, 229, 242, 309

M

Mathenia, Harold Dean 318
Mathenia, Maw 241, 257
Mays, Joe 22
Mays, Sue 116
McCann, Charles 36
McCann, L. A. 36, 154, 156, 164, 171, 183, 184, 185, 215, 243, 244, 256, 260, 261, 302
McColgan, J. W. 71
McCullom, Lenora 263
McDonald, Olivia 44
McLaurin, Pete 10, 21, 247
McWaters, Bert 144, 163, 247
McWaters, Berta Jean 318

McWaters, Delois 354, 355
Melton, B. P. 242
Melton, Mrs. 89
Merriman, Opal 240, 247
Merriman, Ray 240
Metcalf, Mrs. 89
Midkiff, Heber O. 47
Mitchell, Eugene 373
Mitchell, Faye 373
Mitchell, John 325, 326
Mizzell, Ben 343
Moore, Biddy 100, 317
Moore, W. M. 169, 228, 232, 265, 317
Morgan, Tom 140
Morse, Kenny 366
Muir, Mrs. 82
Musial, Stan 343, 346
Myer, Mr. 235

N

Nance, Berta Jean Latham 142
Nashley, Ned 235
Neel, A. J. 156, 160, 165, 166, 170, 178, 179, 180, 181, 187, 189, 200, 212, 214, 215, 227, 230, 242, 244, 249, 301, 302, 303, 322, 323, 335, 337, 344, 382, 389, 395
Neel, Jerry 317
Neel, Nell 89, 317, 322, 356, 389
Newman, Audrey McWaters 263
Newman, Aymon 263
Newman, Bill 85, 242, 262, 263, 264, 265, 266
Newman, Lois 141
Newman, Mary 350, 396
Newman, Phillip 140, 242
Newman, Zolen 350
Newton, Cora 365
Newton, Murrell 365
Newton, Shelby Jean 375
Nichols, Guy 144, 145, 146, 147, 148, 149
Nichols, Janie Hill 149
Nichols, Vincent 144, 145, 146,

147, 148, 149, 150
Nickell, Frank 114
Noyes, Bob 373

O

Ogle, Zula 99, 101, 102, 110
Owens, Ray 364

P

Parkes, Maria 98, 102, 103, 104, 105, 112, 115
Parkes, Michael 18, 19, 97, 98, 99, 103, 104, 107, 108, 110, 111, 112, 113, 114
Parks, Agatha 14, 15, 17, 97, 108, 114, 187, 235
Parks, Albert 97
Parks, Hugh 373
Parks, Mildred 163, 170
Pendergast, Tom 94
Percy, E. H. 146, 240, 247, 286
Peridore, Albert 146
Peridore, Ruth 145, 146
Poe, Florence Robinson 3, 4, 5, 7, 8, 48, 239, 264
Poe, James Nelson Butch 239
Poe, Jim 109, 163, 200, 224, 225, 232, 234, 240, 241, 310, 314
Poe, John Sonny 239
Poe, Sonny 240, 241
Poe, Stella 224, 225, 239
Polley, Paul 109, 373
Powell, C. A. 86
Pritchard, Benny 326

R

Ralph, S. R. Tootie 225, 232, 233, 234, 235, 411
Randall, Joe 42
Rankin, Walter 86
Rasche, Robert L. 192, 193, 369, 371, 372, 373
Rawls, Jim 322, 323
Reed, Durette Stockton 51, 201, 327, 330, 381
Reed, Robert Terry 146, 201, 205, 206, 211, 212, 213, 229, 272, 273, 274, 330, 381
Reed, Sandra Kay 229
Rembrandt 99
Rhoden, Charles 384
Rhodes, Beatrice Orr Stockton 267, 268, 341, 378
Rhodes, Brother 249, 250
Rhodes, E. L. 378, 379, 380, 381
Rhodes, Mr. 270
Rice, Ann 192, 193, 373
Rice, Danny 373
Rice, Loren Ray 193
Ripulski, Rip 343
Robinson, Caroline 48, 49, 65, 264
Robinson, Edward G. 295
Robinson, Florence. *See* Poe, Florence Robinson
Robinson, Harry 5, 6, 48, 50, 61, 62, 65, 309, 315
Robinson, Wid 61, 64, 152, 264
Robinson, Willard 5, 64, 66, 244, 370
Rogers, Ginger 295
Rogers, Roy 167, 293
Roosevelt, Franklin D. 92
Rosie 395
Roy, James 245
Rueben 395

S

Sapp, Bill 405
Sarno, Dr. Samuel 79, 161, 162, 233, 257, 361
Satterfield, Zurel 81
Savage, Donnie 141, 365
Schott, Johnny 387
Scott, Aileen 138
Scott, Artie Baughn 22
Scott, Ed 136, 138, 371
Scott, JoAnn 326
Scott, Johnny 158, 172
Scott, Lawson 326
Scott, Scotty 370, 371
Sexton, Donald 230, 389
Shain, Doris 407
Shain, Mike 364, 366, 389, 401,

Shorter, Fay 199
Shorter, Vernon 328
Siler, J. B. 86
Slaughter, Enos 343
Smith, Betty 318
Smith, Carlene 373
Smith, Connie 324
Smith, Jerry 118
Smith, John 100
Smith, L. L. 86
Smith, Pink 21
Smith, West 246, 247
Stanley, Henry 125
Steele, Bob 373
Stinnett, Slim 366
Stockton, Corbett 249, 327, 341
Stockton, Durette 333
Stockton, Grandfather 208
Stockton, Harvey 327, 331
Stockton, Ruby Lee 332
Stoker, Carl 316
Stoker, Patsy 316
Stuart, Hilda 324
Stuart, John 324
Stuart, Marty 324
Sullivant, A. C. 156, 163, 170, 281, 282, 345
Sullivant, Alice 281
Summers, Jean 243, 294, 319
Summers, Jo Ann 139, 294, 318
Summers, John 101, 107, 109, 136, 243, 293, 294, 295, 296, 318, 319, 375, 395, 409
Summers, Ora Engram 41, 42
Sutton, Gwendolyn Zuba 372, 373

T

Tarpley, K.W. 86
Taul, Donald 318
Taul, Edna 89, 137, 353
Taul, Ernest Granny 244, 353
Taul, James Donald 10, 49, 76, 114, 289, 312, 314, 390
Taul, Jerry 230, 318
Taul, Larry D. 318, 357
Taul, Owen J. 369, 375, 390

Taylor, Carlos 373
Taylor, John Russell 112
Taylor, Sharon 372, 373
Tharp, Bonnie 375
Tharp, Lena 375
Tharp, Mary 375
Thomason, Ed 75
Thomason, Fay 335, 336
Thompson, Tommy 407
Tidwell, Elizabeth 315, 316, 317
Todd, Joe 363, 367
Todd, Mr. 263
Truman, Harry S. 91, 92, 93, 94, 95, 96, 122, 297
Trutt, Herbert 214
Trutt, Truler 214
Trutt, Truly Pure 214
Tubbs, Larry 373
Turner, Bessie 79
Tyler, Mike 366

V

Vandiver, Liz 245, 246
Vandiver, Ocie 316
Van Gogh 98
VanNoy, Alice Jean Harrison 108, 161, 199, 200, 234, 240, 243, 315, 317
VanNoy, Billy Gene 384, 388, 390, 391, 396, 397
Vest, John 246, 373
Vickers, Norman 363

W

Wagoner, Okie 47
Watkins, Dick 173, 218, 344, 401, 402
Weaks, L. E. 97, 98
Weiland, Ernest 290
Welsch, Charley 126
Welsch, Rose 125
Welsh, Bobby 126
Welsh, James 126
Welsh, Jimmy 126
Welsh, John 126
Welsh, Margarette 126, 127, 128

Westerfield, Ida 86
Westerfield, Isaac Coleman 43, 85, 86
Westerfield, Zanie 240, 247
Whitten, John Lyman 36, 40, 199, 242
Whitten, Joy 39, 45, 46, 84, 85
Whittle, Doris 51, 251, 252, 253, 254, 255, 321, 322
Whittle, Dowell 252, 253, 255
Whittle, Etoyle 255
Whittle, Glen 252, 255
Whittle, Harlan 251, 252, 253, 254, 255
Whittle, Hubert 51, 74, 140, 141, 155, 156, 159, 160, 161, 163, 166, 167, 169, 170, 175, 179, 180, 204, 205, 206, 209, 210, 211, 212, 219, 222, 237, 248, 250, 256, 257, 269, 271, 280, 282, 287, 328, 334, 335, 338, 339, 340, 341, 355, 367, 382, 383, 406
Whittle, H. Van 64, 134, 160, 162, 171, 172, 175, 181, 215, 230, 237, 255, 268, 271, 276, 283, 312, 328, 330, 336, 343, 359, 368, 372, 379, 382, 383, 384, 386, 388, 390, 406, 409
Whittle, Iris 252, 255
Whittle, Lonnie 252, 255
Whittle, Mallie 253, 255
Whittle, Mary June 87, 88, 89, 162, 172, 176, 198, 210, 215, 250, 255, 268, 271, 322, 327, 330, 345, 360, 378, 379, 382, 383, 384, 406
Whittle, Pat 236, 277, 278, 340
Whittle, Ruby Lee 51, 160, 169, 170, 172, 173, 176, 179, 180, 199, 202, 203, 208, 209, 214, 215, 216, 217, 219, 221, 237, 240, 256, 268, 269, 275, 278, 281, 302, 312, 327, 331, 334, 338, 339, 342, 345, 346, 371, 379, 380, 381, 382, 386, 410
Whittle, Sudie 255
Whittle, Tom 253, 255
Wilfong, Winn 363, 387
Wilkening, Jim 36
Wilkerson, Jerry 395
Williams, Ocia 373
Williams, Sharon 373
Wilson, Rayburn 373
Winters, Mabel Engram 41
Wrather, Dude 316
Wright, Wayne 22
Wyman, Walter 371, 399

Y

Yates, Hershel 371
York, Bob 401, 404, 405, 416